American Indian Painting

WAKA, Zia Pueblo. *Dancers Coming from the Hills*. Ca. 1937. Tempera.
Katherine Harvey Collection, Museum of Northern Arizona.

American Indian Painting

OF THE SOUTHWEST AND PLAINS AREAS

By Dorothy Dunn

THE UNIVERSITY OF NEW MEXICO PRESS • 1968

© The University of New Mexico Press, 1968. ALL RIGHTS RESERVED. The publication of this book was assisted by a grant from the Ford Foundation. Composed, printed, and bound in the United States of America by the University of New Mexico Printing Plant. Library of Congress Catalog Card No. 68-19736. *First edition.*

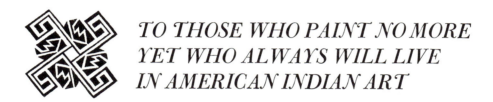 *TO THOSE WHO PAINT NO MORE*
YET WHO ALWAYS WILL LIVE
IN AMERICAN INDIAN ART

Foreword

I count myself most fortunate in having had the rare privilege of following the career of Dorothy Dunn, from the day that she descended upon Santa Fe with her youthful determination to encourage the tribal arts of the Indians of the Southwest.

I could willingly fill another book with incidents revealing her zeal and dedication to her self-appointed task of all these past years, but that would be merely repeating what is so clearly revealed in this all-inclusive story of the arts of the Indians.

It is a great satisfaction to find at last that the monumental work is now presented.

KENNETH M. CHAPMAN
Santa Fe

This study of American Indian Painting has been pursued over a period of more than thirty years. It began in the Art Institute of Chicago and the Field Museum of Natural History, then extended to the Pueblo, Navajo, and Apache reservations, the Museum of New Mexico, the University of New Mexico, and to museums and archaeological sites of the Southwest and Mexico. Findings in the Studio of the Santa Fe Indian School led to related researches on the Sioux Reservation of South Dakota, and in various universities, libraries, and art collections of North America and Europe.

The book seeks to provide a broad introduction to a subject heretofore little known in itself and in its relationship to the history and art of the United States.

Examples and findings, assembled from several fields, offer here a representative view of a specialized art which must be considered in the light of pertinent facts of culture and history. The presentation is necessarily composite. It is not couched exclusively in the terminology of either the non-specialist or the specialist, although it would be correctly informative to the one and held truthful by the other.

In an initial survey where new ideas are explored and certain conclusions must be tentative, it is not only inevitable but desirable that all aspects be considered in order that the record may be fairly presented. Therefore, numerous ideas, frequently in opposition, have been incorporated here. Names of many who have brought their diverse wisdoms to the context have been mentioned, for their works stand to enlighten various facets of a complex and little-pursued study.

There are many people whose assistance has been valuable to this work. Although it is impossible to name here all to whom I am grateful, I wish to make

Preface

appreciative mention of those whose direct help has been most influential in the completion of this book:

Kenneth M. Chapman of the Laboratory of Anthropology and the University of New Mexico for his scholarly and generous professional counsel throughout my Indian art studies, and for criticism of sections of the manuscript; Charles Fabens Kelley of the Art Institute of Chicago for criticisms and for helpful interest in my work since my student days; Olive Rush for thirty years of staunch support and for criticism of sections concerning modern murals; Margretta Stewart Dietrich who projected her indispensable participation even beyond her lifetime; Frederic H. Douglas of the Denver Art Museum for extensive guidance in museum researches; René d'Harnoncourt of the Museum of Modern Art and the United States Indian Arts and Crafts Board, and W. Carson Ryan of the University of North Carolina for recognition and encouragement of the early stages of the work; John Walker of the National Gallery of Art for reading the manuscript and providing invaluable assistance; Edward B. Danson of the Museum of Northern Arizona for invariable helpfulness; Harrison Kerr of the University of Oklahoma for resourceful and generous help; Raymond Jonson of the University of New Mexico for creative criticism of the manuscript; Frank H. H. Roberts, Jr., of the Smithsonian Institution for advice on the first chapter; Robert Elder of the National Museum for repeated assistance with Plains Indian material; Watson Smith of the Peabody Museum of Harvard University for permission to study the Awatovi murals before publication of his report; Bertha Dutton of the Museum of New Mexico for providing early opportunities to study the Kuaua murals; Bella Weitzner of the American Museum of Natural History for guidance in research; May

Carothers Llewellyn and Leslie Van Ness Denman for decades of valuable advice and encouragement; Etta D. Hanson, Elizabeth and Frank S. Cummings, and Suzanne and James R. Dixon for spontaneous and generous cooperation; Ruth and Charles de Young Elkus for sustaining interest; Mary Benjamin Rogers for sponsorship of exhibitions pertinent to the project; my daughter, Etel, who, in her own field, has been an inspiration; and, above all, my husband, Max Kramer, for his continuous wholehearted support of this work in every respect.

I wish also to thank the individuals and institutions named in the plates for permission to reproduce paintings and other arts from their collections. With respect to the University of New Mexico Press, I gratefully salute Winifred Gregory, perceptive and heartening editor, and I give my appreciation to other members of the staff upon whose cooperation this volume depended.

Certainly to the Indian people, particularly the artists with whom I have worked and the families with whom I have lived as a friend and not as an investigator, I wish to acknowledge and to express my gratitude for the uncounted ways in which they have contributed to my own appreciation of their art. I hope they may find this record of their own art of some value to themselves, for this work has been done as much for them as for other people. I should like them to know that the writing of it has been accomplished solely for the honor of having had the privilege of helping them share their art with others as they have shared it with me.

DOROTHY DUNN

xii

Contents

When the name of the artist is known, it is given first, followed by the tribe, the title of the work, and the date. The description, or medium, is followed by the site in the case of ancient works. The name of the collector or museum is followed by the catalog number when it is available.

COLOR PLATES

Illustrations

XV

BLACK-AND-WHITE FIGURES

Plate I. Ma-Pe-Wi, Zia Pueblo. *Ceremonial Corn Grinding*. 1938. Tempera gouache. Margretta S. Dietrich Collection.

Plate II. HA-WE-LA-NA, Zia Pueblo. *After the Deer Hunt.* 1935. Tempera. Collection of Dorothy Dunn.

xix

xxiii

XXV

Introduction

American Indian painting not only is the first painting the continent produced—it is the first American painting in which abstract style and certain other characteristics now commonly associated with contemporary art were developed to an advanced degree. Centuries before Columbus, America had such an art; and she has it now. Yet Indian painting remains comparatively unknown in its own land and among the arts of the world.

Indian painting is New World conceived. It is not an outgrowth of the mature arts of other countries. It contains a rich variety of symbols and forms that are peculiarly expressive of cultures slowly evolved within a vast new land. It reveals the aboriginal concept of man's relationship with the unique American environment—the soil and the gigantic terrain, the powerful natural forces, the indigenous substances and beings.

Within the primeval continent, each major area eventually produced a characteristic response to particular challenges and influences through its own functioning art. Thus, during the long course of time, numerous different arts emerged. They embodied, through peculiar symbols and typical motifs, the philosophies vital to regional peoples within a greatly diversified geographical setting.

In painting, the abbreviated rendering—the significant, concise abstraction—was summoned to convey meanings too immense for detailed statement. Symbols, concentrating and unifying complex ideas, became intelligible to all members within the respective tribes, and a predominantly abstract art finally prevailed throughout Indian America.

Although the original symbols were designed to fulfill particular needs in those earlier times, they frequently were invested with such basic significance as to render them valid for intelligent appreciation far beyond the groups and periods for which they were created. Particularly is this evident in the modern painting of the Southwest and Plains areas of the United States. This art directly inherits ancient native motifs and projects them through acquired media into the present era where they have a surprising appropriateness.

Contemporary painting of the Southwest presents striking patterns conditioned by an arid, brilliantly lighted land. It is mainly an art of contrasts, without half tones; of frank, direct statements composed in pure, flat color. It retains the essence of reality through devices unassociated with the reproduction of superficial aspects of nature, but derived through centuries of selective observance of natural constructions and operations. Thus, earth and sky are represented in elemental forms and spare lines—terrace of mountain and arc of cloud; native plants and creatures are enlivened in graphic suggestion of their essential features; dance and drama are enacted in the conservatively ordered motifs of their performance in life; and symbols of fertility, germination, growth, and renewal are integrated withal. This art, maturely developed in its own traditions, produces an ingenious diversity of capricious and sedate improvisations upon its fundamental designs, and multifarious inventions within the genre.

Modern Plains painting is at once charged with the vitality of authoritative drawing and graced with the whimsical decorativeness of exotic color. Usually more objective than Southwest art, it displays dynamic portrayals of contests, hunts, ceremonials, and mythical emblems of the most spectacular days in Plains history. It perpetuates in new media much of the untamed spirit of Plains hide painting, the traditional art which depicted Plainsmen, horses, and buffalo with originality and conviction never equaled in any other painting inspired by the region. It recreates the wild aloofness of the unbounded western prairies and the proud sportsmanship of the men who rode and fought there, and it recalls obsolete customs in characteristic yet imaginative manner. In its forceful techniques and direct compositions, this painting, while manifestly modern, offers a remarkable interpretation of an American scene that is gone forever.

Since the latter part of the nineteenth century, when the modern developments in Indian art began, painting (and drawing) from both these areas has been making invaluable contributions to recent world art. Far more of it undoubtedly has been lost than has been preserved; yet, such representative examples as are presented here indicate the quality and diversity of that which remains and continues to develop.

In accordance with the depth to which one wishes to appreciate this painting, he should become acquainted not only with the successive forms and styles through which it has evolved, but with American history not yet written in the texts, and American peoples rarely called by name, for it is these which have determined the nature and content of Indian painting.

xxvii

Figure 1.   Early Pueblo. *Terraced and Interlocking Designs*. A.D. 1200-1300. Black paint on woven cotton blanket. Clarkdale, Arizona. Arizona State Museum.

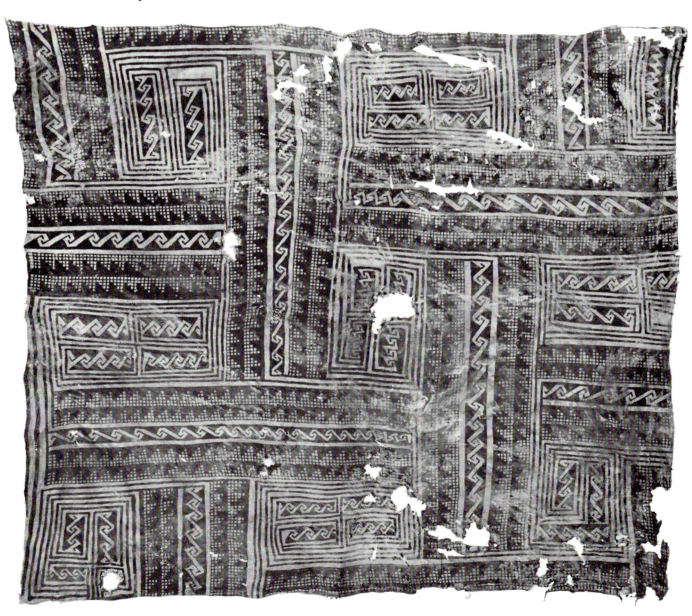

Backgrounds of American Indian Painting

1

American Indian painting, as an art in its own right, is of the twentieth century, although the beginnings of art in America reach back over the thousands of years that passed before the dawn of history in the New World. In the course of obscure millenia, and the comparatively few historic years following, Indian painting slowly developed from an expression within fetishistic, tribal confines to an art which has universal esthetic significance. As in the history of any art, the remains which chart the course of Indian painting's archaic manifestations are intermittent and fragmentary, and their relationship to later arts is little understood.

Some of the earliest men in America were rudimentary artists. Their paints, palettes, engraving tools, and painted and engraved artifacts have been found among archaeological recoveries from lowest levels in various archaic sites. These date from around nine thousand years ago, according to agreement of conservative scientists and exploratory checks by radioactive carbon; perhaps more than twice that long ago, in the light of advancing studies.[*1]

It is considered to have been at the close of the Pleistocene period or near the beginning of the Recent that, as the Wisconsin ice sheet receded, Asiatic hunters found an ice-free corridor for descent from Bering Strait into the interior of North America.[2] Then, the ancient artists fashioned with skill and symmetry their stone weapons and employed the magic of earthen paints in hunting the long-horned bison, the shaggy mammoth, the musk-ox, and other beasts that roamed

*Superscript numerals refer to the notes organized by chapter that appear at the end of the text, beginning on p. 369.

1. The Earliest Art

in their seasonal habitats along the lake terraces, in the springy valleys, or on the bleak, rigorous plains of the vast new country.

The first evidence that the earliest Americans had artistic proclivities came to light only recently. The search for Early Man in the New World had produced results which became credible in 1927, when, near Folsom, New Mexico, a peculiarly fluted projectile point was proved to be embedded in the matrix between two ribs of a great bison of a species long extinct.[3] The early hunter had left no trace of his own person, yet the symmetrical beauty of the fragile, leaf-shaped point attested that Folsom Man made tools of livelihood which were inadvertent works of art. So fine and thin had been the flaking of the nineteen points excavated at this site that only one whole blade remained. This longitudinally concave-faced point seemed unrelated to the Solutrean forms of Europe, but rather to resemble certain Asiatic points. It became the classic Folsom point, the standard by which all such points were thereafter identified throughout a wide range.

Indications of Folsom Man's instruments and engravings appeared seven years later at the Lindenmeier site near Fort Collins in northern Colorado where lithic specimens that had weathered to the surface of ancient deposits led to deeper finds of artifacts of about ten thousand years ago which established the basic Folsom complex.[4] Among the stone tools were flaked gravers, some with "needle-like points" suitable for drawing lines such as appeared on several objects found at the site.[5] The latter included two fragments of polished bone bearing "finely cut lines which appear to have been components of some kind of decoration," also two bone discs with radiating lines incised around the edge, and an engraved soapstone.[6]

Figure 2. Archaic Plains. *Line Engraving on Bone and Stone*. 8000 B.C. Linden-meier Site, near Fort Collins, Colorado. Bureau of American Ethnology, Smithsonian Institution.

4

Frank H. H. Roberts, who made the discovery, also noted "good evidence that the makers of the Folsom points were users of red paint," for he found many fragments of hematite with surfaces smooth and striated from rubbing and several pieces of sandstone stained with red pigment.[7] The latter, he suggests, might have served as palettes and as instruments for working color into skins and other substances.[8] Comparison of this evidence with uses of hematite by recent Indians indicates that Folsom Man also found pigment necessary to his way of life.

Hematite red and other colors decorated weapons found in Gypsum Cave, near Las Vegas, Nevada, a site evidently somewhat more recent than Folsom. Near the bottom of the cave, beneath layers of debris verifying more than eight thousand years of cultural sequences, a rock slide, and a depth of silt and ground-sloth hair and dung, Mark R. Harrington discovered large fragments of two painted atlatl* dart shafts. He identified these and several other similarly painted fragments found in crevices of the cave as belonging to "our earliest culture associated with extinct animals."[10] Bones of the American horse, camel, and dire-wolf also appeared in the cave.

The dart-shaft fragments, made of elder or a vanished species of wood, are painted in several ways. Some are only rubbed with red paint or are crudely marked with smeared bands of red, brown, or black, while others are highly decorated with transverse bands and longitudinal stripes, zigzag lines, fine cross-hatching, dots enclosed in rectangles, mottling, and spirals. Some of the latter seem to have been negatively painted by a stencil-like process in which a portion

*Aztec word for "throwing stick, dark thrower."[9]

Figure 3. Sloth period culture. *Archaic Designs.* Gypsum Cave, Nevada. Ca. 6000 B.C. Painted atlatl dart-shaft fragments. Southwest Museum. Frank S. Cummings photograph.

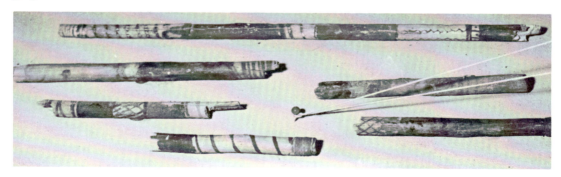

of the shaft was covered with a spirally wound strip, the remaining area painted by applying red or black pigment entirely over the section, then removing the protective strip to reveal a light, unpainted spiral on a solid ground. Another fragment shows a technique whereby zigzag designs were scratched in brown paint, the marks of the instrument remaining lighter in color after the paint had dried. The decoration suggests a more advanced stage of painting than that indicated in the Folsom finds, particularly in the range of colors which include red, brown, gray-green, dark green, blue, and black. Harrington calls it an "extraordinary exhibition of very early American art."[11]

Additional indications of art appeared in other of the earliest sites. In Sandia Cave, near Albuquerque, New Mexico, Frank C. Hibben discovered gravers, similar to those found at the Lindenmeier site, in the Folsom layer of remains along with bones of the mammoth, camel, and other extinct mammals.[12] Gravers were found also to be an integral part of the Borax Lake and Lake Mohave complexes of early Recent times in southern California.[13] Fifty such tools came from below the surface of the latter site.

In the lowest level of the Signal Butte site in extreme western Nebraska, dating from some eight thousand years ago, finds of both rough and ground pieces of hematite and limonite paint occurred, along with twelve incised bone fragments bearing simple geometric designs.* Paints and engraved bone fragments were present also in the two upper levels at the site.[14]

Bone fragments with chevron designs, bone beads decorated with spiral and other incised lines; paints of hematite, diatomite, and white clay; and stones for grinding hematite, still covered with smears of red powder, were discovered in south-central Oregon caves.[15] These were among artifacts from stratified sites, some of which were buried in Pompeiian manner under volcanic ash deposited at least five thousand years ago by erupting Mount Mazama which now forms the rim of Crater Lake.

In the East, where Folsomoid implements have given evidence of Paleo-Indian hunters, only stone gravers[16] have so far appeared to indicate formative art tendencies for that period. However, more distinct finds of embryonic art expressions have come to light in sites defining archaic hunting-gathering cultures that followed. These included bone implements with painted or incised decorations, also pendants and pins of engraved and carved bone, and shell ornaments

*A round-pointed fragment with crossed bars looks like that illustrated in Newcomb[17] as *Mirage Rock*, a Navajo supernatural power, carried in the medicine bag and symbolized in sandpaintings of Beauty Way.

Figure 4. Archaic Plains. *Geometric Designs Engraved on Bone.* Ca. 6000 B.C. Level I, Signal Butte Site, western Nebraska. Bureau of American Ethnology, Smithsonian Institution.

with incised designs.[18] Most of such objects appeared in the Late Archaic Period which ended about 2000 B.C., according to present tentative datings.[19]

Returning to a consideration of Folsom finds, it should be noted that against the validity of claims for Paleolithic manifestations of art in America, some respectable statements have been made. A word might be said about them in passing. Arguments have been given that the extinct animals may have had a later survival in America than elsewhere, making it possible for incoming man to have been associated with them relatively late.[20] For instance, N. C. Nelson cites the missing representative art features of Early Man such as have been found in Europe and Africa: the "pictorial representation of the contemporary animals on which his existence largely depended . . . either in incising or painting on limestone cave walls or by engraving and sculpturing on pieces of bone, antler, and ivory . . ." and suggests that something apparently is wrong "when we are asked to believe that the American Indian, who more or less faithfully pictured the animal life about him much as did his hunting kin in the Old World, was little if at all impressed by his most unique and gigantic contemporaries."*[21] However, it might be recalled that the really great finds of Paleolithic art in Europe were made comparatively recently and that exploration, even appreciation, of the New World's cultural history has barely begun.

Much mystery still surrounds the early inhabitants themselves—Folsom Man and Sandia Man, Abilene, Pinto Basin, Cochise, Lewisville Man, and all the others who once lived in the long-deserted caves and valleys, on the leveling

---

*A petroglyph of mastodon-like appearance, from near Moab, Utah, is illustrated by Julian Steward, and by M. R. Harrington who expands the problem.[24]

7

slopes of the Rockies, and along the eastern shores.[22] Aside from a very few discovered remains, such as those of Midland Man in Texas,[23] almost nothing is known of the physical characteristics of America's most ancient inhabitants. From these examples it has been deduced only that America's Early Man was an essentially modern type of Indian whom most authorities regard as Mongoloid.

It is generally agreed, on the basis of long-established lithic and linguistic evidences which trace their movements along the northern entrance route, that the first American inhabitants came from Asia in successive waves of migrations.[25] But, among various theories as to Indian affiliations, recorded for more than three centuries, there are those which suggest that trans-Pacific movements at an early day may have resulted in infiltrations from Australia, Melanesia, and other areas in the South Seas.[26] Perhaps early men, if not Early Man, came into the New World by more than one route, for varied origins certainly are indicated in the arts.

8

CULTURAL RELATIONSHIPS

The breach is great between the first American cultures and the early agricultural horizons in which painting began rapid progress. During the long formative interval, there passed a hazily known procession of hunting-fishing-gathering peoples whose arts appear to have been largely fetishistic.

In the advancing stages of the New World's cultural growth, through regional developments and intermingling influences, these peoples eventually produced tribes whose arts, languages, and other cultural features acquired group distinctiveness according to localities. Thus, different culture areas, each with characteristic elements and traits, became defined to greater or less extent. There were major areas and minor ones within these, according to A. L. Kroeber.[1]

The major areas of reference here are the Northwest and Northeast, the Southwest and the Southeast of the North American continent above the Mexican border; and Middle America, denoting southern Mexico and Central America.

The Northwest, with its bold and massive examples of carved and painted wood, seems to stand most alone. Its basically fishing and hunting cultures lacks the resemblance to the agricultural, ceramic, and ceremonial patterns of Middle America that are present in the Southwest and the Southeast. Yet it is the Northwest which was the original American base of certain peoples later drifting into the Plains and the Southwest. The Northeast, although only recently within the range of major studies, is worth noting because of indications that Asiatic traits were carried through the northern forests into it, developed there, and later diffused southward and westward.[2]

10

2. Basic Considerations

The areas most influential in the art under consideration are the Southwest, for many centuries the home of Pueblo culture and the more recent Pueblo-influenced Navajo and Apache cultures; and the Southeast, which gives evidence of being the source of certain Plains culture traits.

The Southwest has been the area of more stable and continuous developments than has the Southeast. Cultures within it can be traced back to very early horizons, if not approximate beginnings. Moreover, various sites and phases of cultures have been actually dated by tree-ring analyses[3] and are coming under further scrutiny through radioactive carbon tests. It is in the Southwest that the environmentalists and the diffusionists of culture controversy can meet amicably, for here both indigenous and intrusive influences have been at work in somewhat even proportion on the cultural evolvements of the area.

In contrast, the growth and relationships of the Southeast have been much more obscure. The archaeological clues there have been more vulnerable because of heavier settlement and more destructive climate; yet, enough remain that primary threads of recent cultures, such as Plains and Woodland, pertinent here, can be traced in them. Steadily, more facts are coming to light[4] and are changing the balance of known cultural interactions and influences.

The Southwest and the Southeast, unlike in many respects, had certain fundamentals in common. A number of their principal culture traits emerged from what seems to have been a common agricultural base supposedly originating in Middle America. Dr. Kroeber states that these areas belong to the "great block of truly American culture culminating in the Middle or sub-Isthmian region," representing limbs from the same trunk.[5]

Figure 5. RAYMOND NAHA, Hopi. *Palulukonti Ceremony*. 1962. Tempera. Collection of Mr. and Mrs. James R. Dixon.

The Southwest, because of its geographical position, its relative degree of general cultural advancement, and certain specific similarities with Mexico, such as masonry, painted pottery, cloth weaving, rain ceremonies, and priesthood, has been customarily regarded as the "gateway through which passed or filtered most of the cultural flow from the higher centers of Middle America to the remoter portions of the continent."[6]

In agreement, various manifestations point to Middle American influence upon and through the Southwest: a single family, the Uto-Aztecan, ranges from

12

Idaho into Mexico and on into Guatemala. Its members are a highland people preferring an arid terrain, who are mainly agriculturists, varying in intellect from the Maya and Aztec to the "Digger" Indians of Nevada.[7] The sky-father, earth-mother complex, a universal feature of Southwest religion, was typically developed in Middle America.[8]

Pueblo characters and symbolic designs, as depicted in painting, compared with such figures appearing in Aztecan and Mayan codices,[9] show similarities in both content and style, from ceremonial forms and personages to small details.[*] Even certain aspects of the great mural paintings of Bonampak and Chichén Itzá's Temple of the Warriors are expansively reminiscent of some features of prehistoric Pueblo mural art.

Likenesses of symbolism and ritual are evident in drama, particularly between the Pueblos' plumed serpent, called by various names, and the mythical serpent of the Aztecs, Quetzalcoatl, who corresponds to Kukulcan, feathered serpent of the Maya. In ceremonials of Soyaluna and Palulukonti, in which effigies of the Hopi's plumed serpent, Palulukon, play title roles, there is close resemblance to Nahuatl rites of Mexico.[10] The serpent was important in mythologies of Chiapas, Yucatán, and Mitla where it was carved and painted on façades and elsewhere. It was sculptured on the Temple of Quetzalcoatl in Teotihuacán where its features appear related to those of Palulukon. The Hopi Corn Mist Maid, Shalako Mana, bears likeness not only in name to Xalaquia of Aztec ceremonies.[11] Shalako Mana, a powerful figure in Hopi art and religion, may well have come northward with other symbols of the maize culture which is said to have arisen in Middle America and to have become the dominant factor in the evolution of native American culture.

The Southeast shows comparable indications of associations with Middle America. Art remains, especially those of "Southern Cult" influence, offer ostensible evidence of links between the two areas. Southeast ceramics, although a characteristic regional development from the Early Woodland period, shows in some later pottery puzzling likeness in general style and certain details to Middle American wares. For example, tetrapodal vessels and effigy jars, in the shapes of bulbous birds, human beings, and animals, and bowls with effigy handles are

---

*Instances include figures striped in the manner of Pueblo clowns; eagle dancer, owl, serpent, and Nataka-Coyutl personages; dance staff with vertical flag and macaw feathers; bordered mantas and kilts, hair styles, ceremonial ornaments; stripped-tree ceremonial pole topped with symbolic articles; representation of anatomical attitudes and features, plant forms (corn, tree), water, feathers; numerous abstract design unit details.

13

Figure 6. RAYMOND POSEYESVA, Hopi. *The Shalako Mana.* Ca. 1930. Tempera. William and Leslie Van Ness Denman Collection.

common to both areas. Particularly is this so in the southern Missouri, Arkansas, and northern Louisiana district as compared with southern Vera Cruz and Zacatenco sites. Vessels and figurines from Copilco, Las Colinas, and from the interior of Teotihuacán's Pyramid of the Sun in the Valley of Mexico are remarkable for their resemblance to some of those from the interior of temple mounds[12] of Arkansas and environs. In fact, the temple mounds proper had features in common with Middle American pyramids.

Metalwork, removed by more than millenia from the Old Copper industry of the Great Lakes, appears in the Southeast in ornamental copper pieces. Beaten flat, with designs engraved, cut out, or repoussé, these items are suggestive of influences from craftsmen of the higher cultures to the south.

Engravings on clay and shell, distributed rather widely among artifacts of the Southeast, suggest intriguing affinity in general style with Middle American art. In motif and execution they frequently resemble certain Mexican designs employing line pattern, although specific details are different. Also, in such figures of

14

decoration on mound objects as the winged serpent and eagle warrior, likenesses to the Mexican and Mayan counterparts are striking. Especially is this true of line designs on shell gorgets in which the human figure in godlike form and dress appears in the same attitude and conception as in Aztec codices. Eye-in-hand and wide-jawed skull symbols from Moundville, Alabama, also have Aztec connotations, for such motifs are found in association with Mitlantecutli, the Death God, in the codices.

Such resemblances of style and motif as are evident in these objects present one of the most baffling mysteries in Southeast art. They have been commented upon throughout Southeastern studies by various authorities and students since the days of W. H. Holmes who, beginning in 1880, went to some length to illustrate and describe similarities.[13] Recent inquiries have resulted in tentative attribution of the likenesses to a "Southern Cult," which appeared fairly late in the mound-building stage of the Southeast,[14] to earlier influences from Middle America that may have led to fairly independent Southeastern developments,[15] and to connections that "may be demonstrated as basic and early as well as relatively superficial and late."[16] Excavations on the northwest coast of Mexico substantiate the possibilities of long migrations from the interior of Mexico northward,[17] and suggest that similar expansions of Middle American peoples may have extended to both the Southeast and Southwest areas (of the United States) as well. Other studies favor trade rather than mass migrations as means of transmission of cultural elements.[18]

Mounting evidences appear prominently in the arts to verify connections between various basic culture areas. Possibilities of two-way avenues of New World migrations are receiving increasing attention.[19] Such findings, barely begun to be made, are question marks as well as clues in the absorbing mystery of aboriginal American cultural relationships. They merit consideration in the study of recent native arts in which vestiges of ancient motifs persist.

BEGINNINGS OF PAINTING

COLOR, LINE, AND SYMBOLISM

Painting in America evidently followed the universal course of formative art which led through the initial use of color and elementary drawings to an eventual development of regional forms, techniques, and styles.

15

Color was employed upon weapons of the hunt and probably upon the bodies of ancient hunters and dancers because color, if only in shapeless daubs and smears, seems universally to have been endowed with precious attributes of its own. Red was most often used because of its prevalence in accessible clays, and also because of its association with the red of blood which itself sometimes served as fetishistic paint.[20] Blood and breath were the most plainly representative of vital requirements of both man and beast, and therefore were demonstrated in painting. Survivals of such symbolic use of red pigment were told by the Spanish chroniclers[21] and are seen in Indian paintings of the present day.

Drawing, beyond the crude markings of hunting scores and other rudimentary scratchings, found its first form in pictographs. These schematic figures were engraved or pecked in rock as petroglyphs, or were drawn and painted on a variety of surfaces. Thousands of such drawings remain today in protected or unsettled areas, including whole canyons of imposing galleries of "regal and unearthly beings of heroic size which may be gods or may be men."[22]

Pioneering students were impressed by the extent and variety of pictographs. George Catlin, early artist-explorer, writes, "Of these kinds of symbolic writings and totems . . . recorded on rocks and trees, in the country, a volume might be filled . . . ."[23] And Henry R. Schoolcraft did so in his early North American studies which illustrate Indian ideas of enchantment and magic in all kinds of figures of animals and natural phenomena symbolically drawn or painted in color on bark, bone, skin, rocks, music boards, and grave posts. He notes a widespread use of the breath-of-life line extending from heart to mouth of man and beast.[24]

Pictographs have particular meaning in a study of Indian paintings, for certain connections between pictography and its obvious parent art, the dance, can be fairly well traced in present Indian practice. The living relationship between the ceremonial dance and drawing is still evident in the two arts.

Through the dance-drama, the participant becomes the animal, hunter, warrior, growing plant, water-bearer, or whatever his needs demand. He draws the rain from heaven by representing the lightning, clouds, water serpent, or other being, and he becomes a god by impersonation in pantomime that reveals the substance of his prayer to the supernatural powers. In certain dances, salient features are concentrated through more finely specialized movements into motion symbols, or gestures, commonly understood by the group.

The elementary pictograph appears clearly to be the graphic capture of the motion-symbol. For example, the horizontally undulant motion of the hand, covered with paint or holding a piece of ochre, produces the simple meander representing flowing water; the air tracing of zigzag lightning becomes the angular lightning symbol; lines described by downcurving palms, moving upward and outward in semicircles, become the arcs of cumulus clouds, and so on.

Observers of both gesture and pictographs in Indian America have remarked upon the relationship. In perhaps the most extensive studies of pictographs that have been made, Garrick Mallery observes that pictographs give permanent record for ideas to which gesture gives transient expression, and notes that, "It was but one more and an easy step to fasten upon bark, skins, or rocks the evanescent air patterns that still in pigments or carvings preserve their ideography or conventionalism in their original outlines." [25] Maximilian, Prince of Wied, notes in his early Plains travels that the reproduction of gesture lines in pictographs was most frequent in the attempt to convey subjective ideas.[26] And Jesse Walter Fewkes, that analytic observer of both ceremonial and painted symbol, states that primitive man probably first identified with motion his belief that everything was possessed of a magic power for good or evil, and that later he adopted symbols such as those for breath-of-life.[27]

Even today one may see gesture symbols, or pictographs-in-action, in the Green Corn Dance of the Keres Pueblos of the Southwest, where the Koshare* make signs with their hands and arms for growing plants, and the men of the chorus trace clouds and rain in the air above their heads in rhythm with the chant and drumbeat. These gestures combine with exact symbols of rattle sound and costume motif to make the audio-visual prayer more fully articulate:

> *And they made a cloud and they made it break*
> *And they made it rain for the children's sake.*
>
> . . . . .
>
> *This was a god that you could see,*
> *Rain, rain, in Cochiti!* [28]

Pictography in some instances was approaching writing and was used to a certain extent in communication. Characters frequently repeated became conventional, and in their later form ceased to be objectively recognizable. This was so in birchbark drawings, and in attempts at narrative representation in pictographs of the Southwest. But the main purpose of the art apparently remained one of magic symbolism, of totemic meaning, or of religious significance.

*Religious officers known also as Kossa, Paiakyamu, and by other names in various Pueblo groups.

Whatever the pictographs were to the individuals and tribes who made them, it is clear that such graphic beginnings helped lay the foundation for paintings in earth colors, tempera, and oils that were to follow for centuries and into the present day. Many of the symbols and conventions thus established persist and become elaborated in later stages of painting. A modern Sioux artist erects a fairly naturalistic horse upon the old hoof-track symbols which, to the casual observer, may appear to be only hooks instead of horses' hooves. The Pueblo painter banks pictographic clouds above a semirealistic cornfield because, to him, not only are they filled more heavily with rain, but with ancient meaning.

FORMS, TECHNIQUES, AND STYLES

Various forms, techniques, and styles of foundational painting emerged in relation to the widening variety of ceremonial accoutrements, dwellings, tools, utensils, and many objects made in the evolution of Indian cultures.

Environment exerted a heavy influence in this connection, for the climate of highland or lowland, seacoast or inland prairie; the regional fauna and flora; and the accessibility of neighboring influences were of tremendous importance in shaping the arts of early tribes. In regions where food was adequate in natural production, art emphasized needs other than rainfall. It may have appeared as warrior fetishes, healing charms, or the like. In areas of scant rainfall, the arts were mainly employed in supplication for rain. In places where fish or game animals were the principal source of livelihood, art was dominated by a fetishism used in the enticement and further abundance of game. It was a propitiatory art, a magic where the occult influence was based upon a likeness between things, and often employed prey-god fetishes to implement the medicine power of great prey animals in the hunt through sympathetic magic. As the contest for game or other natural advantages between groups increased, painted battle charms and warrior symbols became important.

Elementary art forms were thereby mainly determined, and, insofar as painting was concerned, whether a work was to be portable or fixed—a totem on a buffalo-hide shield, a mural altar on an adobe wall, a fetish on a fishing boat, or a motif on a clay jar—depended first upon requirements of the area.

Even though a variety of choices are possible within a locale, art forms are strongly influenced by the materials at hand which are most suited to their construction. Clay, sandstone, buckskin, willow, or shell, for instance, almost tell in their names the limitations upon functional forms which could be made of them, or what sort of painting, if any, might be associated with them.

Techniques, in turn, are largely determined by both the form required and the materials available, for there are inherent in the media limitations upon ways in which they can be successfully worked. Considering a certain form that must be made and the material that must be used, the possible techniques narrow down to a few choices if the finished product is to serve its particular purpose.

Styles arise first from the meshing of all the influences and demands of form and technique. Some styles are firmly governed by technique. For instance, the painted decoration of a ceramic jar, through its fluidity, might have illimitable possibilities of style, whereas the incised decoration, more confined by technique, would offer far less variety. And, regardless of other factors, styles in certain areas must keep within the bounds approved by the group, as in the employment of certain symbolism.

Beyond such confinements as technique and custom, it is the artist alone who determines style. Style is a fine term. It has a freedom beyond the prohibitions of form, technique, and group custom; it results from these, plus the human factors of emotion and creativeness. In the final analysis, style is an intangible quality, but it is the element that, above all others, distinguishes the art of one people from that of another and the work of one artist from that of another. Styles are the genes of culture which carry the differentiating elements of its myriad traits near and far, intermingling them in endless variety.

The most direct influences upon forms, techniques, and styles of the earlier Indian painting considered in this study were those exerted mainly through the textiles and basketry, ceramics, and various ceremonial equipment.

Textiles and basketry produced much of the geometric design which carried over into painting on pottery and less confining surfaces. Geometric rendering is a natural result of weaving techniques because the manipulation of warp and woof, of core and reed, imposed restriction on line.

To illustrate such influence upon painting, one might consider the gradual evolution of a basket into a painted bowl as the process has left its trace in the Southwest: The rudimentary unadorned basket adopts a form similar to that of a gourd receptacle. In time, a more advanced type of basket acquires decorative terraces and stepped meanders produced by the weaving technique. A later innovation introduces a clay lining in the basket, producing a crude, unfired pottery form like that of a flaring basket. The first decorative feature of such a container results from the basket impression, but eventually it imitates the basket's coils.

Advancing through the actual buildup of clay coils, the corrugated texture and the form of the basket suggestively continue in much of the first fired pottery. **19**

Figure 7. Pueblo. *Meander Patterns.* Ca. A.D. 1200. Western New Mexico. Tularosa Black-on-White pottery olla. Field Museum of Natural History. Cat. No. 263,591.

At last, experimental smoothing frees the pottery surface from its rough basket-like texture, and it is ready for painted decoration. Yet, going back to the parent art, the painted design at first follows the terraced style of basketry decoration, although it could abandon geometric requirements. This is not surprising, however, when one recalls that throughout the history of invention, even to the fast-paced technological developments of today, older forms and styles stubbornly persist before being replaced by the new.

Among people whose art consisted mainly of weaving, rudimentary life drawings tend to show the angular character imposed upon design by the craft. Human figures appear with squarish heads and shoulders, and animals, with

20

Figure 8. Hopi. *Geometric Design.* Ca. A.D. 1350. Awatovi Pueblo, Arizona. Mural painting in earth color on adobe plaster. (Reproduction.) Peabody Museum, Harvard University.

angular horns and bodies. Kenneth M. Chapman, foremost authority on Pueblo pottery decoration, observes that: "This geometric idea must have had a strong hold upon the imagination of the ancient potters for even their drawing of animal forms had all but merged into it."[29] And, comparing a great many life forms as used in design in various cultures, he observes that realism seldom survives the conventional treatment required of such figures when employed as decoration in textiles and ceramics.[30]

Geometric influence upon art styles often continues long after the original use which produced them has waned or even died out, and frequently it extends to new adaptations by groups unacquainted with the origin of the styles. Later artists develop imitatively many typical decorations which have ceased to possess the special symbolic meanings they once had. In an advanced and sometimes decadent stage of design, natural forms are often deliberately geometricized, in a manner not at all required by technique, for the express purpose of producing a conventionalized style for its own sake.

21

Figure 9. Pueblo. *Terraced Cloud Design*. Ca. A.D. 1100. Kiva B, Lowry Ruin, Colorado. Mural in earth tempera on adobe plaster. Field Museum of Natural History photograph.

22 Figure 10. Basketmaker. *Terraced Design*. Ca. A.D. 200-700. Utah. Red and black paint on woven yucca-fibre carrying band. Field Museum of Natural History. Cat. No. 165,170.

Ceramics have had other noteworthy influences upon painting aside from that of design carried through from textiles. The ingenuity of the potters created and adapted countless styles of motifs which have been handed down to the modern painter. In addition to the field of design, the painting of pottery has had a determinant effect on composition and on painting techniques. The restricted areas of ceramic forms have tended to develop ingenious systems in the arrangement of spaces, masses, and lines, and the exacting muscular control demanded by painting on abruptly curving surfaces has for generations required specialized training in meticulous brushwork. Fine standards and practices have thereby been bequeathed to modern painters in pottery-making groups.

Other painting styles and techniques arose from application of symbols to ceremonial objects. This encouraged experiments with new media and tools, and invention of specialized techniques for painting wood, hide, cloth, stone, plaster, and other surfaces.

Various other arts and crafts in the course of cultural development also exerted influences upon painting. Quillwork and beadwork had much the same simplifying, geometricizing effects that textiles had upon styles of design. Engravings on bone and shell ornaments required the refinement in drawing and arrangement necessary to clearly defined patterns in certain styles of painting. Building of dwellings and ceremonial structures, encouraged development of the mural form which had begun to emerge in the later days of pictography. Mural painting developed enlargement of scale, extension of color range, and innovation of techniques for applying paint to broad, flat surfaces.

Thus, in the several arts, artists experimented and consolidated their knowledge through generations until generally feasible techniques were established. Evolution in symbolism, with tendencies toward emphasizing certain motifs, also occurred in the progressive experimentation; and recognizable styles, with infrequent mutations, influenced the successive generations of painters until a certain amount of style fixation resulted in each group and each area.

As the culture grew in variety of manifestations in a certain area, art drew upon its own precedents to create new forms for new uses as they arose, and adapted to its own needs alien forms, techniques, and styles that from time to time infiltrated from other cultures through barter, wars, or peaceful migrations.

The complex pattern made by the diffusion of Indian art traits from tribe to tribe and from area to area shows that a culture could seldom evolve purely in one area, but painting forms, techniques, and styles arose in the several areas, composite yet distinctive.

23

Figure 11.   Pueblo. *Interlocking Geometric Design*. Ca. A.D. 1000-1200. Chaco Canyon, New Mexico. Earth tempera on wood slab. American Museum of Natural History.

OBSERVATIONS ON PRIMITIVE ART

Indian painting is the first art in history to have sprung, full-fledged, from the primitive into the contemporary world at a time when it was peculiarly compatible with both. Although it has won recognition as modern art, a consideration of some facts and assumptions in regard to primitive art may elucidate certain qualities of modern Indian painting which place it in a position of being both old and new, primitive and contemporary.

The term "primitive art" calls for qualification in this respect, even though primitive art itself has been receiving long overdue appreciation and status in the art world in recent years.

Anthropologists question certain implications of the expression. For example, Ralph Linton denounces the erroneously accepted connotations of the term which would assign all primitives to the "childhood of art,"[31] while Herbert W. Krieger pointedly berates the fact that primitive art is usually understood to mean the product of geographic areas and peoples who have for some reason not shared in the technical development centering about metallurgy in Europe.[32] Such a notion disregards the fact that the very lack of technical and material advancement might allow major emphasis upon esthetic and spiritual values.

Franz Boas considers differences of experience as determinant in appreciation:

> It is somewhat difficult for us to recognize that the value which we attach to our own civilization is due to the fact that we participate in this civilization, and that it has been controlling all our actions since the time of our birth; but it is certainly conceivable that there may be other civilizations, based perhaps on different traditions and on a different equilibrium of emotion and reason, which are of no less value than ours, although it may be impossible for us to appreciate their values without having grown up under their influence. The general theory of valuation of human activities, as taught by anthropological research, teaches us a higher tolerance than the one which we now profess.[33]

Perhaps as the world's distances continue to diminish, so will the occasions for the condescension of tolerance in the matter of "other civilizations" and "our own." Primitive art is a good case in point, for "primitive" is a relative term, conditioned by time and place, yet maintaining constant universal elements pertaining to frontiers.

In the broadest view, it can be noted that every age and society has its primitives—its own interpreters and seers in the lead. Whether these appear crude, outmoded, or advanced to the outsider depends upon his point of view in light of his own knowledge, as Boas observes.

Giotto, for instance, while acclaimed a master of form at the last outposts of medieval Italy, was a primitive at the edge of the whole Renaissance; a leader in things to come. The Fauves, unleashing color, became the "Wild Beasts" of their day. Paul Klee, concerned with sap rising in trees, and with forces and directions, freely admitted, "I want to be as though newborn . . . to be almost primitive."[34] And, today, Mark Tobey, exploring from the mines to the heavens, while marking

25

even the flight of the thistledown, paints on the rim of an expanding universe of forms and ideas, revealing a philosophy of interrelationships akin to the Pueblo Indian's own. He may one day be known as a great primitive.

For all their differences, the true precursors and the "genuine primitives" surely must be kindred in the vast "Shape of Time."[35] The muralists of Altamira and Awatovi, of Bonampak and Tarquinia, the pottery painters of Knossos and Sikyatki, and the buffalo-hide painters of the Great Plains, among such forerunners, seem members of a long, long line.

Loosely lumped together with crude efforts of novices, and the admirable folk arts, primitive art loses its identity. Actually, it is virtually impossible to group and generalize about primitive art in its own right. Beyond its constant core of precocity, a few traits seem more or less common, though not exclusive. One of these is naturalness; another pertains to necessity.

Painting of primitive character, wherever it occurs, seems more instinctive than calculated, although a most exquisite calculation is often there. It shows little or no consideration for "isms," even though it might be individually classifiable as certain of a number of "isms," or it might launch new ones. Most frequently it appears to have been done spontaneously, without preoccupation with technical rules. Its evident sincerity and dynamic directness result in authority of statement.

Such expression apparently arises from a fundamental need on the part of the artist or the group—need of a tribe for the primary requisites of existence, need of a cult for instruments of religious manifestation, or of an individual in a restricted and conventional society for personal utterance of compelling ideas. Therefore, paintings of game animals could be sorcery in the hunt to Paleolithic men, symbols of clouds and rain could mean meteorological magic to desert tribes, inspiring representations of the deities could effect a tangible concord between God and man in the early Christian era, and individualistic paintings, tutored or not, could be personal discoveries in regard to some facet of the complex world, real or imagined, for primitive artists in modern societies.

To artists of primitive societies in particular, painting is more often an art of expression than of impression.[36] That is, painting does not seek primarily to portray a subject in a given place and time in a more or less representational manner, but rather to stress the fundamental qualities of the object or power. It is concerned with the inner functions and meanings rather than the superficial appearance of nature, and it sets forth the essential aspects of a subject.

26

Figure 12.   Unknown artist, Zuñi Pueblo. *Shalako*. Ca. 1925. Watercolor. Millicent A. Rogers Foundation.

27

In such painting, outward appearances are often distorted or obscured by the symbolism of the greater meaning of the thing painted. Thus, there is a general lack of extraneous detail because the artists emphasize facts directly. For example, because birds are so often important to primitive peoples as religious emissaries or as a source of food, primitive drawings of them frequently show the egg or become essentially eggs with negligible bird features attached. Or again, birds may have beaks, claws, or feathers abnormally emphasized according to the significance of the creature in a particular society. Similarly, because the heart is considered the life center of a game animal, it is drawn boldly upon the outside of the body. Because two eyes are considered more necessary than one, both eyes are often fully shown even though a head may be drawn in profile. In some instances features considered to be vitally important are repeated more often than they occur in nature and are depicted in entirely unnatural arrangement, such as eyes in a wing or tail.

This primitive artist thus draws his thought-image—the significant features which effect the charm or embody the spirit. He sees the real object completely but sets down only the essence of it, and often his drawing has more of life than that of the artist who tries to include every outer aspect in his portrayal. As a child draws first the body and then the clothing over it, with primary lines showing through, the primitive artist gives right-of-way to basic elements in his interpretations. In picturing the flesh, he does not fail to draw the bone, or even the spirit of a creature.

While the technically accurate representationalist may strive in some degree for modeling and perspective, for the complexities of color as found in nature, for a more or less photographic effect, the primitive expressionist may, as in representing a summer storm, draw a few sweeping curves for clouds, some swift-thrusting barbs of lightning, a plunging descent of clean vertical lines of rain and produce even more pungent realism. The representationalist with technical skill may paint in consecutive stages a series of leaves with all their intricate veinings and shades of color through the changing lights of each day and the metamorphoses of various seasons, while the primitive expressionist may paint a single, eternal leaf which is so symbolically suggestive as to be all leaves in all seasons. Or he may paint scores of variations of his single leaf, basically alike and yet varied in design, and not one like the natural leaf in superficial appearance.*

In primitive society, symbolism is a special system through which ideas as

*See examples in Chapman (91) plates 48-51 and 69-70.

images can be conveyed understandably to an individual or group. A particular symbolism, while completely clear to members within the group which knows the code, may be entirely unintelligible to those outside unless they find the key through acquainting themselves with the conventions upon which the symbols are based. The ultra-abstract eye, claw, and fin symbolism of the Northwest Coast has little meaning to one uninformed of the importance of the bear and killer-whale motifs in Northwest culture. And, in modern society, the now commonly recognized symbol for atomic energy—a dot within ellipses—was meaningless to all but a few scientists only a short time ago. Many examples of modern art contain symbolism that is richly significant but that is understood by only the painters themselves who work in a highly individual manner, and by the limited group that follows their work.

Identical symbols may have different meanings in different instances. A nomadic hunting people develops a symbol system which has very little in common with that of a sedentary agricultural people because the two systems have arisen from particular needs in particular environments. A triangle to an Arapaho may mean a tipi or an arrowhead, while to a Hopi it may be a fertility symbol such as a butterfly, a cloud, or a phallus. A claw, horn, or hoof track may represent an entire creature which is immediately recognizable within certain ethnic bounds. Some art symbols are universal, however, and have been found in slight variation in widely scattered places.

Although it is virtually impossible to consider Indian art as an entity, Indian painting, with an emphasis on that most relevant here, might be viewed in line with the foregoing observations.

Considering all its aspects, Indian painting is not only a natural art, it is mainly of nature, and, in a large measure, for nature. Especially in the Southwest, painting is so much a part of all the arts through which the Indian identifies himself with the universe that to consider it apart from the whole is like examining a single thread drawn from a tightly twisted cord. One art intertwines with and supplements the others;[37] they all unite to join the Indian and his earth and sky and his unseen gods. Art is a way of life. It has a bearing upon every aspect and detail of the Indian's existence—birth, nourishment, rest, growth, learning, work, play, reproduction, healing, even death. In certain tribes, prayer is inherent in all the activities through the oneness of Indian art.

There are no artists, as commonly known, in Indian society. Anyone may be a painter, a craftsman, a singer, a dancer, or a creative participator in some capacity. To be an artist is taken for granted. One's art is for his family, his clan, his

29

tribe. It is an art "possessed in common . . . in which everyone shares, with greater or less degree of ability, but with no limit on participation or on potential skill,"[38] says Alice Corbin Henderson, who was among the first in perceptive understanding of the Indian as artist. To paint a symbol in a bowl, or to work a design on a moccasin, to sing or create a song, or to dance is as ordinary and natural an occurrence for an Indian as to plant a hill of corn or to grind a basket of kernels. Some individuals by descent inherit, or by intensive study assume, certain duties or privileges in the art of the group, but other than this there are no distinctions for the artist in Indian society. One glance at the artist relegated to his island in the general Western society will suffice, by contrast, to emphasize the meaning of a natural artist and a natural art as the expressions are used here.

The Indians of North America were in a late Neolithic stage of culture when the Europeans arrived. In certain basic respects, and despite the imposed acceleration of culture change, some tribes are just emerging from the original stage in which they were found by the Spanish explorers. To Indians who have had any fair chance to remain Indians at all, their fundamental expressions of art remain essentially the same as they were before the white man came.

The needs of late Neolithic men are those which fostered Indian art. The hunters needed game, the seed gatherers needed weather conditions favorable to good harvests, and all needed peace between tribes and fortification against illness. Fulfillment of these needs was sought through multifarious repetition of symbolic game animals, weather and harvest symbols, and fetishes of tribal well-being in the various art forms that pertained to Indian religions. Through painting, the Indian demonstrated that "the surest way . . . to make a prayer effective is to symbolize the matter prayed for."[39]

A symbolic, abstract painting, expressive of essentials, is the only one which could have grown immediately out of such elemental needs. There was neither time nor place for painting that was only decorative. Nor is it likely that there was yet a place for complete nonobjectivity, although some early designs appear meaningless. Indian artists painted in a manner which often implied to them life or death for themselves and their people. Whether a painting looked *like* a subject did not matter at all; whether it could be made to contain the spirit, the life and power of a thing was the whole point of painting. The germ of the corn plant or the life of the entire field might be concentrated in a dot within a rectangular enclosure. The increase of the herd might be ensured by clearly drawing the breath-of-life line on a schematic form indicating the body of the deer.

All the intelligence of observation and skill of draftsmanship so undeniably possessed by the Indian painter could have been used to produce paintings in a

Figure 13. Po-Tsunu, San Juan Pueblo. *Welcoming Dawn*. 1960. Contemporary improvisation on primitive forms. Casein tempera. Collection of Mrs. Keith Wofford.

naturalistic manner had not interests more vital than that of objectively portraying nature been at stake. Boas says of primitive symbolic paintings that "they are not by any means proof of an inability to see and draw perspectively,"[40] and Chapman agrees that "in the representation of certain supernatural attributes of man or of animals the use of symbolic devices . . . was of greater importance than the lifelike portrayal of the subject."[41] This direction of painting to the thought-image rather than to the visual image is also commented on by Linton. He observes that the insistence upon accurate naturalistic representation seems childish to the primitive who, although he admires technical skill, feels that it is being expended for trivial ends in an amplification of the obvious.[42]

Not only symbolic line and form, but color, too, had magic according to its uses in Indian painting. There were colors for the four cardinal points, for the zenith and the nadir, varying with clans, tribes, and specific uses. Colors were designated for good and evil, for time of day and seasons of the year. The corn on the east was usually painted white in a Navajo sandpainting because white is the predominant color for the east in Navajo art. The shield of a certain Kiowa warrior was striped with yellow in keeping with the man's totemic emblem or his designation of band and rank. A certain cloud on a Hopi altar was painted malachite green because of its ritual significance among symbolic clouds of other colors in the altar design.

Thus, each aspect which characterizes Indian painting as primitive art has its own reason for being. Likewise, certain of these same features qualify Indian painting as modern. This seeming paradox may well lie in the fact that international painting, for reasons of its own, increasingly evolves forms and styles, even concepts, not unlike those long and deeply developed by Indian artists.

31

Figure 14.   Mimbres. *Man with "Mobile."* Ca. A.D. 1090. Detail drawn from Classic Mimbres Black-on-White pottery bowl. Cosgrove Collections, Peabody Museum, Harvard University.

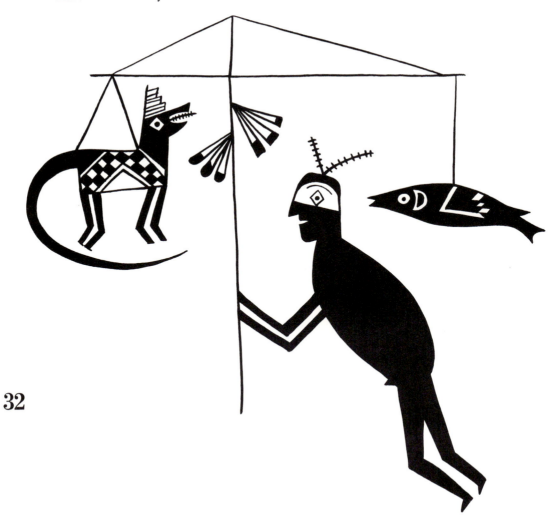

32

Painting Before the Modern School

THE AREA AND ITS PEOPLES

The Indian Southwest centers in a region containing New Mexico, Arizona, southwestern Colorado, and southeastern Utah. Most of the area consists of a mile-high arid plateau which lowers off toward the eastern high plains and the southern desert. Far apart upon its fairly level terrain, sudden mountains rise—the Sangre de Cristo Range, southernmost of the high Rockies, extends from south-central Colorado to Santa Fe. Westward of that lie the rugged San Juan Mountains which give rise to the San Juan River and the Rio Grande. Lesser ranges appear south of these—the Jemez, Sandia, and Sacramento, the Mogollon, Black, and San Francisco. Between the mountains stretch vast open areas accented by mesas, the rock-topped remnants of ancient higher terrain. And approaching the highlands, these tablelands, such as the Mesa Verde and the Pajarito Plateau, become continuous save for deep, interlying canyons which offer secluded shelter among their cave-recessed precipices of stone and tufa.

Below the Gila River there is low-lying desert where only cacti thrive, and, all along the southern border, mainly the thorny mesquite, creosote, and grease-wood grow in semi-desert wastes. But the plateau is more propitious; it is dry yet far from barren. Wide acreages of it are covered with gray-green sagebrush, white-flowered yucca, and clumps of wiry grasses. Along the arroyos rise the pigment-rich, tall, golden chamiso and the purple guaco. Cottonwoods, tamarisks, and willows stand green above streams and washes and in the river floodplains.

On the slopes rising toward the foothills and into the mountains, the coral earth is dotted with piñon, juniper, and golden-flowered rabbit brush. In the lower

3. The Southwest

reaches of the mountains, scrub oak, dye-bearing Apache plume, aromatic sumac, and mountain mahogany grow, while aspens and evergreens climb the high slopes, sheltering the deer, the big-horned sheep, and the large beasts of prey. Rabbits in abundance live in the open ranges, natural habitat of the antelope, while the wild turkey nests in forested canyons. Buffalo once roamed the plains beyond the Pecos River.

The river valleys bear life through the high, dry land. Near the eastern border the Pecos flows southward along the flats. Coursing westward into the mighty Colorado are the San Juan, the Little Colorado, and the Gila, while the "brave river," the Rio Grande, literally carries the destiny of New Mexico down through its heartland. The Salt and San Francisco swell the Gila; the Chama joins the Rio Grande. The little Mimbres flows lustily from the Black Range, then loses itself in a game of hide-and-seek in the sands of southern New Mexico.

Leading into the rivers are countless washes and arroyos made by the violently rushing waters from the short-seasonal rains. In the summer the glistening white cumulus clouds build higher and higher into the blue morning sky, then, past noon, they pelt down their quick deluge upon the dry earth. The water immediately runs off the unsheltered surface, carrying with it portions of the precious soil.

There is scarcely a river without its arroyo-cut wastelands and its deep, rock-walled canyons. These, with the contrast of sharply defined mesas and sand-rounded, red-rock buttes, the jagged volcanic peaks, and the changing-colored mountains, make for spectacular beauty of environment which has left its impress upon the art of the pioneering inhabitants.

Figure 15. Ma-Pe-Wi, Zia Pueblo. *Antelope*. Ca. 1930. Tempera. The Newark Museum.

It is an impression that derives from the terror as well as the beauty of this capricious land. It pertains to a philosophy of existence where harvests of wild-growing foods have always been small; where agriculture became a demanding requirement from early times, and irrigation a necessity; where game animals needed ceremonial protection from indiscriminate slaughter; and where raindrops and seeds became the ultimate symbols of the life of all creatures. For this land,

Figure 16.   AVELINO ARQUERO, Cochiti Pueblo. *Arroyo*. 1937. Tempera. Collection
of Dorothy Dunn.   **37**

from ancient days, imposed a terrific challenge upon the people who lived here. In return for every handful of food they were able to wrest from the water-starved soil, they had to give a dear amount of toil and ingenuity and earnest demonstration of the urgence of their needs.

This is the area into which came various peoples whose distinctive cultures, each peculiarly influenced by the environment, contributed in some respect to the painting of modern times. These, of our study, were the Anasazi, the Hohokam, the Mogollon peoples, the Navajo, and the Apache.

THE PREHISTORIC PEOPLES*

The Anasazi. The Anasazi and their descendants have extended over a long period from around the beginning of the Christian era to the present. They include two consecutive groups: the Basketmakers† and the Pueblos.‡ Their name, Anasazi which fades into the background, was given them by the Navajo. It means "the ancient people" or "ancient enemies.[1]

The Basketmakers[2] were among the earliest people known to have succeeded the builders of the remote cultures of the Southwest. Their home centered in the Four Corners region of the San Juan River drainage and eventually extended well into Utah. Recently, questions have arisen concerning their possible connection with peoples of other areas where similar or perhaps antecedent cultural features have been found, such as those discovered in caves of southern Oregon, the Texas Big Bend region, in Coahuila and Chihuahua in northern Mexico.[3]

At first the Basketmakers were nomads who took shelter in open, natural caves and lived by hunting with the atlatl and boomerang-like club, and by gathering seeds, bulbs, and fruits of wild plants. Later, when corn was acquired, they began to lead the more sedentary life of semiagriculturalists, learning to cultivate a single variety, of a small, red-yellow, tropical flint, in the flood areas of the canyon bottoms below their cave dwellings. As the yield increased, slab-lined storage cists were built in the cave floors and roofed over with brush and mud plaster.

These earlier Basketmakers were weavers of yucca-fibre sandals, carrying

---

* Referring here to those of the period ending circa A.D. 1700. See footnote p. 45.

† So called because weaving of baskets was emphasized in early stages of culture. The name, variously spelled, appears since 1894. Amsden prefers *Basketmakers* as the "simplest version of an awkward and essentially meaningless term."[4]

‡ Spanish for villages. The village-dwelling Indians in the Southwest are called the Pueblo Tribe, or the *Pueblos.*

bands which they wore about their heads to support burden baskets, many sizes of color-banded pouches of twined apocynum, and varied forms of finely coiled baskets with plain or angular motifs. Eventually they began making rudimentary, unfired pottery by pressing wet clay into flaring baskets. They also modeled figurines of raw clay, and they pecked and painted pictographs on canyon walls.

By the time agriculture dominated the economy, the Basketmakers' life presented many new aspects, so many, indeed, that the ensuing phase of culture is sometimes referred to as Modified Basketmaker. Pit-house dwellings, supplementing cave homes, evolved from the storage cists, and settlements increased in population and extent. Beans grew in addition to squash and new varieties of corn. The bow and arrow began to replace the atlatl.

From the unfired pottery, and perhaps from imported suggestion, true coiled pottery developed to the stage where simple painted motifs were applied. Weaving continued and in some respects became elaborated, particularly in sandals which were finely fabricated in intricate patterns and sometimes painted with red and black designs. Turquoise mosaic, set in wood and shell, and polished, drilled bone and stone, contributed to the making of various ornaments. Pictographs in several colors, illustrating animals, human and supernatural beings, and many features of the culture, augmented earliest records in rock galleries of ancient art.

Late in this phase of Basketmaker culture, the earliest or Developmental Pueblo people began to appear. Distinguished by their rounder heads, these initial members of the rising culture had been generally accepted by anthropologists as belonging to an intruding stock distinct from that of the longheaded Basketmakers. However, later analyses indicate that cranial deformation alone may account for the brachycephalic exaggeration of the early Pueblo people.[5] At any rate, it appears that Pueblo cultural features were gaining prominence in the Basketmaker region toward the close of the seventh century.[6]

The Developmental Pueblo Period (Pueblo I and II) encompassed a time of instability and transition. The single-roomed pit houses gradually were superceded by larger, several-roomed dwellings in which masonry was eventually developed. Food was procured in much the same manner as had prevailed during late Basketmaker times, with an increase in variety of crops and advancement in use of stone tools. Pottery was improved to the extent that it became readily distinguishable by the technology and decoration developed during the period. Cotton was cultivated and loom weaving of vegetable-dyed fabrics advanced remarkably. Baskets, although largely replaced by pottery, were still woven as were sandals and geometrically patterned carrying bands. Village life was intensified until there prevailed a widespread distribution of small, differentiated settlements.

39

Religious life within them became more ritualized and centralized with the development of the kiva, a subterranean structure which probably had its inception in the pit-house dwelling.

Certain settlements, ranging outward from the San Juan center of original Anasazi activities, had become so large and so individually specialized by about the middle of the eleventh century that the era of highest attainment had opened for the Pueblo peoples. This is known as the Great Pueblo Period (Pueblo III).[7] It was the epoch of great architectural achievement and ceramic specialization, of community organization and religious intensification. The towered, cliff-set cities of Mesa Verde and the canyon-sheltered towns of Kayenta, the multiroomed communal dwellings of Pueblo Bonito and Aztec, the great kivas of Chetro Ketl and the Zuni district, and many other examples of impressive construction were of this period. Certain buildings show remarkable engineering skill in handling the huge bulk of stone and mortar required in multiple-storied structures of several hundred rooms. The firm rock walls of Mesa Verde's Cliff Palace and the variedly ingenious masonry types of Chaco Canyon's amazing compounds attest to the integrity of the builders of the period.

Art was in ascendancy throughout the region. Excellence was attained in the weaving and lapidary arts. Designs rich in color and intricate in composition were woven into finely textured cotton fabrics, and turquoise mosaics were wrought with fine skill. Pottery of distinctive forms and black-on-white regional decorations dominated the ceramic arts and provided a strong vehicle for the development of painting. True mural painting was practiced through decoration of plastered interiors of some of the buildings.

The people of this period, like their forebears, were agriculturalists whose dependence upon propitious seasons of the rain-drought cycles caused a basic instability in their existence. Tree-ring studies of such specialists as A. E. Douglass and Florence M. Hawley show the recurrence of dry years. A twenty-three-year period of drought began in the plateau area around A.D. 1276.[8] Such disasters, with their resultant evils of deforestation, erosion, and seepage, together with possible local strife and the increasing menace of incoming predatory tribes, undoubtedly contributed to still undetermined reasons for the decline and final abandonment of the great northern centers by the close of the thirteenth century.

Whatever the denouement, the Regressive Pueblo Period (Pueblo IV) began with the mysterious dispersal of the gifted predecessors. Populations rearranged themselves through group and intermittent small migrations, augmenting smaller settlements in outlying districts. New centers began to rise, particularly in the regions of the Little Colorado and the Rio Grande. In the western area, such settlements as Homolobi and Chevlon became important, as did the later towns of the Hopi province of Tusayan, especially Sikyatki and Awatovi. Hawikuh of the Cibolan province became a strategic community. In the eastern region, the Tanoan villages in the Galisteo Basin, the Pajarito Plateau centers of Puyé and Tyuonyi, the Pecos pueblo of Cicuye, the Tiguex towns of Kuaua and Puarai, and the Piro villages loomed into prominence among numerous minor settlements.[9]

In many of these villages, Pueblo culture again became reinforced during a season of apparently favorable economic factors,[10] and artistic activities acquired new impetus. Here the inhabitants, whose culture had been only temporarily and in certain respects regressive, made some of their most significant contributions to American art. Painting, through the mural and ceramic forms, attained to many of its highest achievements during the latter part of the period, often appropriately called the Renaissance Pueblo Phase. The textile arts and several developments in ceremonial design and symbolism also greatly enriched the content of Indian art. In fact, Pueblo art, through its unique unity of forms, was advancing toward full realization when the course of international events swept it forever from its natural channels.

These villages experienced the last normal growth of Pueblo culture. After the arrival of the Spaniards in 1540, native life began to alter progressively in the various pueblos as alien influences thrust forward. There were between seventy and eighty pueblos when the Conquistadores came, but in a century and a half this number had decreased to few more than a score.[11] By 1700, through a succession of wars and rebellions, intrusions and indoctrinations, Pueblo culture, although bravely defended, had declined so greatly, even in remote quarters, that the Prehistoric Period in the Southwest was at an end.

The Hohokam. Returning to the early times of the Anasazi for chronological orientation, one finds other somewhat contemporaneous prehistoric groups whose arts contributed influences to the later developments of painting in the Southwest. One of these is the Hohokam.[12]

The Hohokam were desert dwellers whose homeland was in the Gila Basin of south-central Arizona. They received their name from the term by which their possible descendants, the Pima, designated "those who have gone."[13] They were persevering agriculturists who built remarkable systems of irrigation canals to nourish their crops in a barren land. Their homes were simple one-story houses of wattle-and-daub construction, yet these people amassed earth mounds for unknown purposes, and excavated immense areas for the making of game courts which incorporated the main features of ball courts in Middle America. Unlike the Anasazi, the Hohokam cremated their dead, and with the remains they often

41

placed rectangular stone palettes of classic type which show by their retention of paint particles that they were used in mixing pigments. Modeled figurines, small bells of regional copper, apparently cast by the *cire perdue* (lost wax) process, and pyrites mirrors and sculptured stone vessels found among Hohokam remains seem further to associate these people with Middle America.[14]

Turquoise mosaic and carved or painted bone and etched shell were distinctive among the arts, but it is through ceramic decoration that the Hohokam added much to the enrichment of painting. Through all phases in the four major periods of Hohokam culture—Pioneer, Colonial, Sedentary, Classic—pottery was an outstanding feature.[15] It shows, in the thorough analyses of Emil W. Haury, progression from plain ware to distinctive decorated forms employing some of the most spontaneous and delightful brushwork to be found in Southwest art. The periods most creatively productive of such painting were the Colonial and the early part of the Sedentary when red-on-buff decorations became prevalent. These periods extended between approximately A.D. 800 and 1000, although the Hohokam culture continued to about 1400.[16] In the fourteenth century, the Hohokam had combined with an incoming group from the Tonto Basin, the Salado people, to produce a new cultural achievement, although of less determinant art aspect insofar as painting is concerned.

The Mogollon Peoples. In somewhat the same time range as the Hohokam, another influential culture, the Mogollon, was developing nearby.[17] Mogollon is a regional name for certain tentatively identified groups who lived in southeastern Arizona and southwestern New Mexico, mainly in the valleys of the San Francisco and Mimbres rivers. The Mogollon peoples were art affiliates of both the Hohokam and the Pueblos becoming, in the Classic or Mimbres phase, similar to the latter in certain major art characteristics; so much so, in fact, that it has been customary to consider the Mimbreños as Puebloan.

The earlier Mogollon people,[18] who may have been descendants of the ancient Cochise gatherers of the area, were pit-house builders whose livelihood depended upon simple agriculture and hunting. Their pottery was chiefly plain brown or red, almost entirely without painted decoration, although sometimes bearing textural markings in the clay.

In a later phase, the Three Circle, changes became marked notably in the Mimbres area. Between the years A.D. 900 and 1000, house types altered from pit construction to multiple-roomed, quasi-Pueblo structures of one-story masonry, and ceramic influences from the Hohokam and Anasazi appeared in pottery

42

decoration and other features.[19] While retaining some adherence to plain colors, pottery decoration passed during this period from rectilinear motifs on a brownish background to more facile black-on-white patterns somewhat similar to the predominant ceramic patterns of the Pueblos. Thus, painting styles of certain basic Pueblo characteristics, which also incorporated features derived from the Hohokam, were initiated by the Mimbreños.

When all these changes had been fully effected, the Classic phase of the Mogollon culture, or, as this development has been most frequently designated, the Mimbres culture, was in force.[20] This horizon was approximately concurrent with the forepart of the Great Pueblo Period, and it contributed most from the known arts of the Hohokam-Mogollon area to American Indian painting. After about A.D. 1150, little is known of the inimitable artists of the Mimbres Valley.

The Navajo. The Navajo are not well known archaeologically, but they are generally considered recent comers to the Southwest, supposedly having arrived but a few centuries before the Spaniards.[21] Among the earliest tree-ring datings thus far discovered for Navajo sites in Dinetah,* the Navajo's own traditional homeland in northern New Mexico, are from approximately 1490 to 1540,[22] and 1575.[23] A Navajo Period for a part of this region has recently been dated 1550-1775[24] through archaeological investigations.

If their own legendary history is based at all on fact, one portion of it may furnish a clue to the time of the Navajo's first encounter with the Anasazi. Their origin legend relates that on one of their journeys to explore the Fourth World (which could have originated many miles away) they found "a race of strange men who cut their hair square in front, who lived in houses in the ground and cultivated fields."[25] The houses referred to might have been the semisubterranean pit houses of the early Anasazi whom the Navajo legends mentioned as the Kisani.

The Navajo, or Diné (The People), as they call themselves, are members of the Athapaskan† linguistic stock. Several divisions split off in fairly recent times from the main body of Athapaskans who remained in the far northern area comprising the Alaskan interior, northern British Columbia, and the Mackenzie Basin. One course of migration extended along the Pacific coast, with settlements of small tribes in southern British Columbia, Oregon, Washington, and northern Califor-

---

* Variously known as Dinetqa', Tinetxah, etc., which refer to the same area.[26]
† J. P. Harrington prefers Athapaskawan, which he says derives from the name for the delta region in northern Alberta.[29]

nia, while another, including the ancestral tribes of those now known as the Navajo and the Apache, moved down through the interior into the Southwest.[27] Investigation has not yet determined whether the southern Athapaskans traveled through the High Plains, the Great Basin, the Rocky Mountains, or by a combination of routes, but it is fairly certain that the migrations took generations of time and that traditions of hunting were followed upon the way. "Buffalo singing" still persists as an important part of the Navajo Flint Chant.[28]

In their early Southwest homeland, the Navajo supplemented their hunting ways with those of the agrarians they found living in the region. Spanish chroniclers refer to the Navajo as farmers. In fact, the popular name, Navajo, apparently derives from the tribe's adopted occupation in New Mexico. Fray Alonso de Benavides, witness to part of the history-launching era, records in his *Memorial* of 1630: "But these of Navajo are very great farmers, for that [is what] 'Navajo' signifies—'great planted fields.' "[30] The Tewa Indians say that Návahúu, means "large arroyo with cultivated fields."[31] They use the name in referring to a mound, in the second valley south of Puyé, which they say was once a Navajo settlement.

The main homeland, however, seems to have approximated the legendary Dinetah. The first historic reference to it is contained in Father Zárate-Salmerón's account of Indian-Spanish relations in 1538-1626: " . . . they [the Jemez] replied that [one might] go out by the way of the river Zama [Chama] and that past the nation of the Apache Indians of Nabajú there is a very great river [the San Juan, which] suffices for a guide. And that all was plain with good grasses and fields between the north and northwest; that it was fertile land, good and level . . . ."[32] Therefore, the first verified home of the Navajo lay between the Chama and the San Juan rivers, a region well suited to farming. This is the location shown by the Dominguez y Escalante map of 1776 as Provincia de Nabajoo.[33]

Here, slightly east of their present reservation, the Navajo became integrated in the life of the Southwest. At first they were a small tribe, but their numbers grew by absorption from the Yuman, Ute, the Pueblos, and wandering tribes,[34] for they settled in a marginal territory where they were in association with the peoples of three cultural regions—the Great Basin, the Plains, and the Pueblo.

According to their legendary accounts, the Navajo were poorly clad and poorly fed in the old days, and they had few arts, but they improved both their economy and their arts through association with and adoption of members of other tribes, particularly the Pueblos, many of whom sought refuge with the Navajo after the rebellion of 1680. Not only do the legends tell of very early

44 assistance received from the Pueblos[35] through gifts of corn and other items, but sites in the Dinetah region[36] and statements in old documents[37] also disclose that acculturation had been going on for a considerable time prior to fairly early dates (circa 1706) in the historic era.*

Pueblo, and some Spanish, elements evidently had been adopted into Navajo life in these formative times. In addition to corn, the Navajo cultivated beans, cotton, pumpkins, melons, and chili, using wooden implements. They had sheep and goats, although horses were few and cattle scarce. They built some of their houses of mud, timber, and stone on mesatops which apparently led soon afterward to fortifications incorporating masonry in circular walled hogans and watchtowers. The men still dressed in buckskins, but the women wore Pueblo-style black woolen mantas with red embroidered borders. Weaving became important and was a principal trade item along with baskets and buckskins.

That the Navajo, as they moved farther south and west, took much by raid and plunder from their Pueblo neighbors has been surmised through studies of prehistoric fortified sites,[39] and substantiated through known occurrences in later times, yet there are many present indications of peaceful relationships in depth, particularly in the arts and ceremonials, the finer aspects of which could never have been acquired by force.

Thus, as the Navajo gradually ended the prehistoric period, they were bearers of an amalgam culture best analyzed by Edward Sapir, who finds four strata revealed in their cultural experience from Far North to the Southwest: a basic northern layer representing tribes of the Mackenzie Basin and symbolized in such Navajo word equivalents as "horn spoon" for gourd ladle, "canoe travel" for travel, and "alien food" for corn; an incorporation of Plains culture components as represented in traits more archaic than recent; an initial Southwest adjustment preceding Pueblo influence; a subsequent, definitely Pueblo influence.[40] Surmounting such conditioning foundation is, of course, the Navajo's own distinctive pattern of creative assimilation and invention.

The Apache. Although the Apache are even less known historically than their linguistic kinsmen, the Navajo, certain facts which throw light upon their prehistoric condition stand out in the earliest historical records. That the Apache contingents of Southern Athapaskans came down from the Far North via the High Plains seems fairly certain because the nomadic hunting life of some bands, now considered Apache, was still in full swing upon the Plains when the Spanish

---

* Activation of the Historic Period in the Indian Southwest is variable according to relative accessibility of groups. Designated as the opening date for the historic Pueblos,[38] A.D. 1700 is a wide, irregular borderline for the Navajo and some others.

explorers went on their journey to Quivira in 1541. There is no consensus of opinion as to when the Apache came; however, there seems to be considerable agreement that the Querechos and Teyas referred to by Castañeda and other early writers were most likely Plains Apache.[41] Harrington calls these people Lipanans after the Apache Lipan band of which he says the Teyas (and probably the Querechos) were members.[42] Teya was the name given the Apache by the Pecos-Jemez Pueblos.

The Plains Apache were in frequent association with the Pueblos. They roamed widely, entire bands of men, women, and children going with dogs, travois, tents, and trappings from the scenes of the buffalo hunts to the pueblos of Pecos, Taos, and Picuris, or to places farther south to barter meat, hides, suet, and salt for corn, pottery, and cotton blankets.[43]

A borderline Apache division was mentioned later by the Spaniards as the Jicarilla.[44] One Jicarilla band, the Ollero, "mountaineer," Apache, lived, and continues to do so, in the high country west of Taos, and the other, the Ollanero, "Plainsman," lived in southwestern Colorado and northeastern New Mexico. The two were actually one, with intermarriage recognized; they differed only in geographical location.[45] With headquarters midway between the Pueblos and the Plains, they took advantage of both. Like the early Navajo, they adopted Pueblo agriculture, but apparently to a much more limited extent. Their chief dependence remained upon the hunt, and they continued buffalo expeditions to the plains until the end of the old free days.

Apache movements westward are believed to have reached Arizona not before the middle of the sixteenth century,[46] but there is as yet no archaeological evidence to support this idea. The Spaniards at that time found members of the tribe dwelling in "isolated huts" and subsisting "on the chase alone."[47]

It must have been during their westward progression, or at least when their warlike deeds[48] began to stand them in disrepute there, that the Apache received the name, apachu, "enemy," from the Zuñi who used that designation also for the Navajo.[49] The Spanish version Apaches of the Zuñi name was first recorded by Oñate in 1598. The tribe, as the Navajo, called itself Diné.[50]

A succinct description of the Apache in 1626 is given by Benavides:

> They do not dwell in settlements, nor houses, but in tents and huts . . . move from mountain range to mountain range, seeking game, which is their principal sustenance. However . . . they plant corn and other seeds . . . . They have no more idolatry than that of the Sun . . . .[51]

46   From about 1630 on, the Apache were known by their principal group names,[52] Chiricahua, "great mountain"; Mescalero, "gatherer and eater of mezcal"; and Jicarilla, "cup (*jicara*)-shaped-basket" Apache. Bands eventually acquired geographical designations such as Northern Tonto, Southern Tonto, White River, or San Carlos Apache.

THE HISTORIC PEOPLES

The historic pattern of Indian life in the Southwest had fairly well assumed its broad outlines by 1700. The Pueblos, greatly depleted in numbers, had faced the fact that they were under the rule of an alien power, and that the energies

Figure 17. BEN QUINTANA, Cochiti Pueblo. *Koshare with Ceremonial Staff.* 1939. Tempera. Margretta S. Dietrich Collection.

recently devoted to rebellion should be turned upon maintaining the remnants of their traditions and possessions, which continued to be threatened by the encroaching foreign culture and persisting attacks of other tribes. The Navajo and the Apache, still defying complete subjugation, had extended their domains to outlying regions in order to meet the needs of growing populations. In their several localities, all the Southwest tribes had made basic cultural changes through their acquisition of those most influential material elements introduced by the colonists —horses, sheep, and firearms.

The superficial picture of the Pueblos, save for a much smaller scale, still retained many features similar to those drawn in the accounts of Coronado and verified by subsequent investigation. By 1700, many settlements described in that earlier day were located in approximately the same linguistic group arrangements. The Tanoan pueblos lay along the Rio Grande drainage from the Taos Peaks to the broad valley below Albuquerque. The Keresan villages clustered southward below Santa Fe and westward, through the towns on the Rio San Jose, to the high mesa of Acoma. Beyond, at the western border of New Mexico, stood solitary Zuñi, and up toward the Grand Canyon, the Uto-Aztecan Hopi towns with their small addition of Tanoan refugees.

The pueblos, as the Spaniards had found them, were composed of flat-roofed houses of adobe brick or stone of from one to scores of rooms and from one to five or six stories. These and the kivas were usually grouped about a plaza or arranged to face a wide-open space wherein many of the ceremonials were held. In most villages of the 1700's the Catholic church was prominent or even dominated the scene. Lying outward from the houses, or, in the case of the mesa pueblos, in the valley below, were the fields with their systems of irrigation.

The fields, communally shared, yielded the ancient sustaining foods of corn, beans, and squashes together with such later additions as peaches, apricots, apples, and wheat. Seeds selected for their deep-sprouting, quick-growing qualities were placed far into the soil with the planting stick. Cultivation of cotton continued where climate permitted.

A great amount of weaving from native cotton was done by the men, who had also adopted wool for additional use in blankets and in ceremonial and everyday clothing. Other arts and crafts produced were turquoise and shell mosaics, painted shields and various hunting equipment, ceremonial paraphernalia, baskets, knitted cotton leggings, and leatherwork. Pottery was made by the women.

During the first two centuries of the historic period, the Pueblo scene changed but slowly, although populations continued to dwindle with the entire abandon-

48

Figure 18. CHIU-TAH, Taos Pueblo. *Taos Turtle Dance.* Ca. 1937. Tempera. William and Leslie Van Ness Denman Collection.

ment of some towns.[53] Cicuye, the once great pueblo of Pecos, had fallen victim to Comanche raids and the white man's smallpox. Attacks and disease had brought death and desertion to the last of the Tanoan villages of the Galisteo Basin where only petroglyphed monuments remained to commemorate the peoples who once lived there.

49

Yet, in the twentieth century, Pueblo successors carry on in their several linguistic divisions, in approximately the early historic locations, many aspects of the life of their vanished kinsmen. The Tanoans continue in three groups; the Tiwa* of Taos, Picuris, Sandia, and Isleta; the Tewa of San Juan, San Ildefonso, Santa Clara, Tesuque, and Nambé; the Towa of Jemez. The Keresans are represented at Santo Domingo, Cochiti, San Felipe, Santa Ana, Zia, Laguna, and Acoma. Groups of Shoshoneans of the Uto-Aztecan linguistic family,† populate the eleven Hopi villages, although descendants of Tewa migrants live at Hano, usually considered with the Hopi pueblos. The people of Zuñi remain the only bearers of the culture of the Zuñian "Seven Cities of Cibola."

In these villages, even though modern innovations are steadily increasing, the houses, kivas, plazas, and fields, the arts and occupations show a remarkable likeness to those of long ago. Many of the people, especially the oldest ones with their conservative styles of dress, are much the same in appearance. Ceremonial costume has maintained almost rigid conformity to ancient patterns depicted in prehistoric drawings. The square-cut bang and chongo, and the long-braided hair styles have persisted for centuries among various of the Pueblos as have the straight-woven manta and the deerskin moccasin. Style changes, greater in some pueblos than in others, have crept in from time to time for ceremonial use, such as Plains buckskin shirts and leggings, and a few war bonnets. Commercial shawls and blankets replace those once woven at home or traded from the Navajo, and manufactured fabrics appear in garments which are yet distinguished by their traditional design. The younger generation has largely adopted modern dress for general wear.

Although modern equipment gradually replaces the old, Pueblo occupation in many respects retains its native character. The men continue most of their former activities in the care of fields and corrals. They still weave cotton and wool, mainly for ceremonial use, in certain villages. The Hopi supply by trade most traditional fabrics and garments. The men also paint some of the pottery, work the turquoise, make moccasins, musical instruments, and ceremonial equipment, and, in recent years, many of them have turned to silversmithing.

The women exercise their ancient rights of caring for the houses and owning the furnishings, which increasingly include such innovations as television sets, refrigerators, and gas or electric stoves. They build the fireplaces and plaster the

---

*Present-day spellings will be used in references to modern Pueblo groups for which modernized terms prevail.

† Fewkes says only a small part of the Hopi (peaceful people) claim to have come from the north and that there are evidences that they are a mixed people with a "mosaic of tongues."[54]

walls, in and out. They utilize the harvest of corn; some still grind it as needed on stone metates, and prepare from the meal a great variety of breads and dishes. They make the pottery (except for ceremonial use), and weave most of the baskets, although, with the exception of the Hopi products, few baskets have been made in recent years.

In addition to occasions for work, there are seasons for play in games, contests, and burlesques. Some of these, such as shinny, rabbit hunts, and hoop and dart games, have ceremonial significance; others, including chicken pulls, cockfights, horse races, and burlesques, do not. These last mentioned occasions usually provide satirical fun in mimicking the foibles of cultures other than the tribe's own, particularly that of the "Americano" in which there are hilarious commentaries on tourists, public school programs, the prying investigator, and forever the Spanish Conquistador. Pueblo children participate in most of the adult activities, for the family is a close-knit unit. Certain ceremonies occur especially for them.

In the larger family relationships, the Pueblos divide themselves into matrilineal clans which entertain certain restrictions for the common good, but all the people are united in an essentially democratic society. Certain offices are hereditary, more are elective, none embody despotic power. Everyone shares in and every capable member contributes to the general welfare. Adequate and honorable provision is a matter of course for those members who might otherwise be underprivileged.

The strong band of unity within the pueblo exists most of all in religious concept and practice. The major ceremonial activities center about the earth-sky symbolism of corn and rain, and most minor religious practice relates to this core. Corn was and is the mother food, the one symbolic of nourishment, physical and spiritual, to all the Pueblos. Corn is ritually cultivated, harvested, processed, and stored, and nothing in life is more sacred than the meal from its kernels. For corn, songs are chanted by groups and sung by single planters, dances are patterned into complex seasonal ceremonials—the Corn Dances of fertile fields and the Basket Dances of abundant harvests. Fertility symbols are woven and embroidered into fabrics, painted upon pottery vessels, on walls of ceremonial rooms, altars, and upon many ritual objects. Rain for the corn, signifying good for mankind, is the recurrent theme of prayers expressed in every conceivable way, in the daily activities and those timed by the equinoxes "when the sun stands still," season after season, century upon century, proudly persisting alongside the white man's philosophy and his technological method.

Allied with ceremonies of the field are those of the hunt, for hunting also is

51

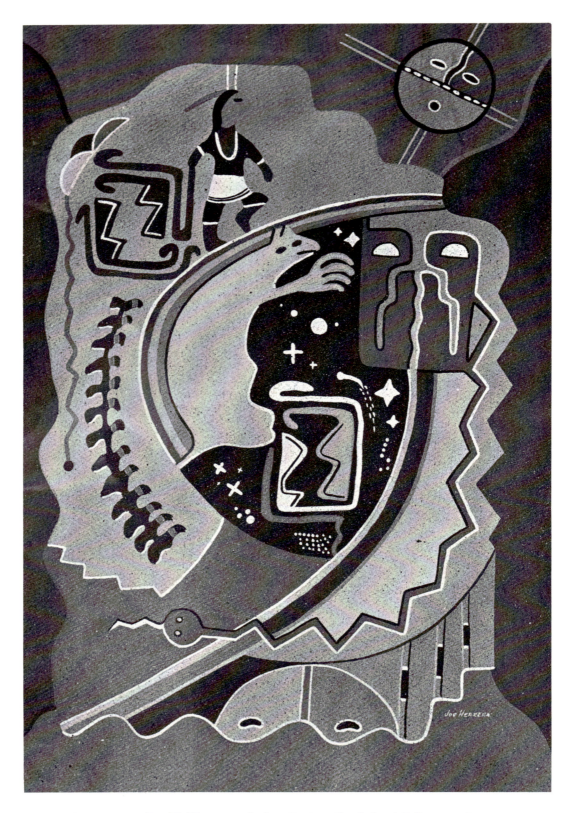

Figure 19. JOE H. HERRERA, Cochiti Pueblo. *Symbols of Fall*. 1956. Casein tempera. Collection of the artist. Tyler Dingee photograph.

communally regulated and practiced; it has never been a sport. For the slain deer, there is ceremonial retribution. Many animals, in fact, are sacred and are dramatized in tribal dances by mortals and by the Kachinas,* the man-impersonated symbolic beings, who also represent natural forces and anthropomorphic personages. There is in such ritual, as in all Pueblo ceremonial practice, an awareness of the value and key participation of each creature and plant and inanimate substance to the whole of life. To the Pueblo Indian, literally everything is possessed of a force for good or evil, and even the evil can be made to serve the good if properly enlisted.

Ceremonies directly concerned with man himself—his birth, illness, human relationships, death—are ordered upon this central theme ultimately stated in symbols of corn and rain. So deeply involved and interrelated are the components of Pueblo ceremonial thought and rite—the religion—that it might be said, in short, to embody man's quest for identification with all nature, his recognition of and his yearning to achieve harmony with the great designs of the universe. In such concept the Pueblo Indian has perhaps advanced to a nobility of abstract thought attained by only the great minds given to religious contemplation.

*Fewkes says Kachinas are breath bodies of clan ancients reincarnated in their traditional form, and that the Kachina cult came from Tanoan villages to become elaborately developed among the Hopi. There are no doubt today, in various pueblos, many Kachinas known only to the Indians themselves.55

Figure 20.   FRED KABOTI, Hopi. *Hopi Kachinas*. Ca. 1918. Watercolor. Collection of Jens Jensen.

In contrast to the Pueblos, the Navajo nation became more populous, and as a result it expanded farther west into Arizona. Early in the historic period it was described as an "extensive province" which reached as far as the Hopi towns, although such an extension of tribal territory at that time has been disputed.[56] Expansion was no doubt due in great measure to the acquisition of horses, which so widened the range of the Navajo that they were able to trade with even the Pawnee in Nebraska.[57]

With the intensification of the roving life, the Navajo appear to have become an increasing menace to the Pueblo villagers, to the Spaniards, and, by 1846, to the American colonists who then took possession of the Southwest Territory. Fort Defiance was established as the first military post in the Navajo country in 1852, and thereafter there were raids and reprisals and mounting wars leading to a calculated military campaign of suppression which culminated in the tragic episode of Bosque Redondo, 1864-1868.[58]

After that disheartening experience of being ruthlessly uprooted by the federal government, the remaining members of the Navajo Tribe were returned to an allotment of semidesert land in their former western range where they valiantly faced a new life ordered in the selfish and unimaginative terms of their conquerors.

In the years since, despite restrictions, violations of guaranteed rights, and coercions, the Navajo nation has increased phenomenally in numbers and has demonstrated a remarkable ability to develop and maintain its unique tribal character. The Navajo have taken on the Spaniard's flocks and have become *Navajo* shepherds, the Pueblo's loom and have become *Navajo* weavers, the European's forge and metal and have become *Navajo* silversmiths. They have acquired horses, wagons, automobiles, ploughs, kegs, and coffee pots and have imparted to each a peculiar Navajo association through mere use. In their adapted apparel—early Pueblo yucca-fibre wraps and later woolen mantas, Ute buckskins, persisting colonial-style garments, blankets of British baize or those from the Pendleton mills, Pueblo cotton trousers and bright headbands, or blue denims and ranchers' sombreros—these people of heterogeneous physical types, have presented a distinctive and often noble appearance unmistakably Navajo.

Names of pueblos have been taken over by Navajo clans.[59] Much Pueblo mythology has been claimed in the retelling through Navajo interpretation, and many Pueblo ceremonial rites and personages have been adapted from their originally more communal uses to the more individualistic purposes of the Navajo. Certain ceremonial features, particularly sandpaintings, have been extended and elaborated until their supposed original Pueblo inspiration has been all but lost

Plate III. KEATS BEGAY, Navajo. *Navajo Sheep*. 1938. Tempera. Collection of Mrs. Keith Wofford.

Plate IV. SYBIL YAZZIE, Navajo. *Yeibichai*. 1937. Tempera. Collection of Mr. and Mrs. Max Kramer.

in their resultant profusion and complexity. (Or were Pueblo sandpaintings Navajo inspired?)

Throughout the historic evolvements, the well-being of this amazingly virile people has been seriously threatened many times—as by the railroad's requirement for land, by encroaching alien interests in range and natural resources, by foreign diseases, by overgrazing, soil erosion, and the necessary reductions of flocks resulting in acute economic distress—yet, the Navajo, through readjustment after readjustment, remain a challenging example of the ability of a people to survive, even to advance, in the face of adversity.

On their reservation, where boundaries have had literally to be pushed outward, the Navajo Tribe in recent years has been undergoing a phenomenal economic change due to the mining of uranium and the development of gas and oil deposits on the reservation. Through comparatively vast wealth suddenly accruing to the tribe, the Navajo Tribal Council is promoting reforms and improvements too numerous and formative to describe here.

Otherwise, the Navajo continue life much in the old ways. They pursue the cultivation of crops and the raising of sheep in the limited amounts the land affords. They hunt but seldom as compared with earlier days. Their weaving of

Figure 21. HA-SO-DE, Navajo. *Antelope Hunt, No. 2.* 1938. Tempera. Margretta S. Dietrich Collection.

blankets has decreased, although silversmithing has advanced in recent years.

The shepherds migrate seasonally to the more favorable ranges, and most of the people are widely scattered in family groups. Many continue to live in their single-roomed, mound-shaped dwellings of earth, rock, and timber, known as hogans, which resemble Far Northern homes much more than they do any Southwest house forms. However, the latter are increasing as are modern community buildings for various purposes.

Chosen members hold councils and admirably discharge and organize tribal affairs, more and more establishing the Navajo as an independent people. The people at large frequently assemble in smaller gatherings to engage in informal sings, or in games and sports—gambling, races, rodeos, and contests. They also unite, often in very great numbers, in attendance upon ceremonials which strengthen and integrate tribal relationships through their dramatic reiteration of the accumulated beliefs and philosophies of the tribe as expressed in song, dance, and the ordered rituals, particularly the Yeibichai,* in which painting plays a major part, and the N'da-a from Enemy Way, originally a war ceremonial.

The Apache, especially the Chiricahua, have had a reputation since the beginning of historic times of being terrible scourges whose depredations resulted in the abandonment of several pueblos and in recurrent battles with the colonists. However, the story has two sides, one of which might give more credit to the Apache than that which now obtains if it were ever told.†

After a series of wars and forays, which engaged them from New Mexico to the Pacific and far into Mexico, the Apache were finally conquered and settled in four reservation areas.[61] The Jicarilla were located near the Chama River on a reservation which encompasses fertile sections of their original Southwest homeland and part of the Navajo's old Dinetah. The Chiricahua were assigned the region of their early historic headquarters in the mountainous country around the Salt and Gila rivers of Arizona. The feared Geronimo was a Chiricahua. Remnants of his band were sent to Fort Sill, Oklahoma, after their capture in 1886 and their

---

*Talking god, "maternal grandfather," or "giant's uncle," principal *Yei* (god) figure who gives the Night Chant one of its names.[60]

†See Abert's journal for one of the rarely recorded instances of Apache honesty and integrity,[62] and Castañeda's account of "faithful friends," "kind people and not cruel."[63]

interludes of imprisonment by the War Department. Some of Geronimo's descendants live in that locality today.

The Lipanans of old have become known mainly as the Kiowa Apache, and, after having been predominantly a Plains tribe associated with the Kiowa in the Black Hills of South Dakota in prehistoric times, they are now settled near the latter in Oklahoma. Some members of the Lipan band, who formerly lived in the Santa Rosa Mountains in the states of Chihuahua and Coahuila, were removed during the Apache relocations by the Mexican and United States governments to the Mescalero Reservation in the timbered region of southeastern New Mexico. There the Lipan dialect is still remembered by a few descendants of that band. The Mescalero also include some members of the Chiricahua band.[*][64]

There are differing arts and customs in the several groups, yet there is a predominant common cultural pattern which, despite its many influences from Far North through Plains to roving Southwest career, sets the Apache Tribe definitely apart from all the others, even the Navajo whom it most resembles in basic mores.

Like the Navajo, some Apache, too, are shepherds, and many also are cattlemen. Others are farmers. The more propitious locations of their government-alloted lands have led to generally better economy among the bands, with the exception of that in Arizona. Strides are now being taken in organizing tribal enterprises for benefiting the people through health and education.

Apache tribal and ceremonial organization is much less elaborate than that of the Navajo. There are rituals of old tribal motive—medicine, war, initiation— with an emphasis on sun symbolism, somewhat overlaid with Pueblo influence. There are still, to some extent, the unstable dwellings, the well-developed basketry, the impermanent forms of the sandpainting and such art forms as are practical to the semi-sedentary herder. In superficial appearance, there is yet among the Apache something of the Plainsman with a suggestion of the colonial settler and an addition from the frontier cowboy.

The Apache pattern is, in many respects, eclectic, yet it is one which somehow retains aloofness and rugged independence. With little more than sense of art relationships as guide, one might trace the core of its ancient motifs back through a long and wandering course to Asia where Tibetan gods of fire and thunder bear resemblance to the Apache Gan.

*The various groups now contain one-time members or descendants of different Apache bands or of other tribes annexed by choice or by government decree.[65]

CONTRIBUTIONS OF THE EARLY ARTS

Certain of the early dwellers created styles and motifs that persisted in the arts which followed, and thus influenced Southwest painting of later years.

CONTRIBUTIONS OF THE BASKETMAKERS

Textile designs of the Basketmakers were influential in the style of motifs adapted in their pottery decorations and pictographic paintings. Triangles, stepped terraces, and zigzag meanders were basic design elements thus carried over.

Hundreds of such pictographs appear near Anasazi sites in the Kayenta district of northern Arizona.[66] Among them are full-view human and anthropomorphic forms, from one to five feet high, with wedge-shaped bodies, square shoulders, elongated arms and legs, and comparatively small triangular heads. Some wear headdresses, and the torsos of a number of figures bear red and yellow zigzag designs, although the most common paint throughout these sites is chalky white. Another group in this locality, painted in red and white, illustrates some aspects of Basketmaker life—basket bearers, deer, the atlatl, and many kinds of artifacts. Pictographs in Desolation Canyon, Utah, include mountain sheep and ceremonial figures. One dancer wears a deer-antler headdress, and two striped Koshare have hair plastered high and stiff in the manner of their modern Pueblo counterparts. Similar painted pictographs appear elsewhere in Utah,[67] and apparent Basketmaker petroglyphs in south-central New Mexico.[68]

Paints such as were used in the pictographs and on textiles have been discovered in Basketmaker sites. In an Arizona site, cakes of red and yellow ochre lay in a cache with a skeleton.[69] Various caves yielded skin pouches containing raw and ground azurite, malachite, and ochre.[70] One collection of such painting equipment includes fragments of copperous and ocherous pigments and lignite black, together with their skin container, grinding stones showing traces of color, and a stubby brush of sinew-entwined stiff vegetal bristles.

Ceramic painting did not advance very far in Basketmaker times. Most of it shows crude attempts to duplicate textile motifs upon the rough, grayish surfaces of the gourd-shaped bowls. Designs in black paint include triangular, line, and dot elements, and a few restricted bird, quadruped, and serpentine forms. Line decorations are frequently dotted or denticulate, or they fence rows of seedlike dots around, across, or quarter-sectioning a bowl interior.

58

CONTRIBUTIONS OF THE HOHOKAM

The Hohokam were such exuberant and original interpreters of Southwest life forms that effects of their pottery painting carried outward to other settlements,[71] encouraging the play impulse in other potters who had not broken the confinement of the more or less rigid patterns of textile-influenced design.

Nowhere in prehistoric Southwest art is there such a profusion of vigorously direct painting as that on the red-on-buff pottery of the Gila Butte, Sacaton, and Santa Cruz phases of the Hohokam culture (about A.D. 800-1000).[72] Most of it conforms to discernible schemes of composition, yet it shows unusual freedom. The general effect is often of a vibrating pattern of all-over units of small forms. Dynamic small figures romp or parade or chain-dance along the stripes and ter-

Figure 22. Hohokam. *Ceremonial Figures.* Ca. A.D. 900. Red-on-Buff pottery bowl. Arizona State Museum. Cat. No. GP 49821.

59

races and scrolls, hardly halted by the strategic masses. Burden bearers stalk in great strides, scarcely leaning upon their tall, crooked staffs—even the old ones, bent with age, seem charged with unusual vitality. The turtles, too, have an animation unheard of in their species. Dogs and goats leap and wag their tails, lively serpents slither with the speed of blue-racers. Birds are in flight, just landing, or about to take off as they stare with bold and saucy eyes. And there are scattered patterns of seeds guaranteed to grow.

In the purely geometric designs, movement of zigzag and diagonal lines is powerful; the turnabout whirl of interlocking scrolls is a balance of opposing motion—centrifugal, centripetal. No sun of Van Gogh ever radiated with more force than some of these, still shining on pottery of the Hohokam. This painting lacks the precision of Sikyatki and the Mimbres, yet it has the bounding rhythm of fast-flowing water, a near-haphazard rendering that seems to represent a full measure of artistic joyousness.

Frederic H. Douglas describes these designs as "almost shimmering patterns."[73] Alfred V. Kidder tells of their hasty, offhand brushwork which appears to have been "scribbled" for textural effect rather than true design, and suggests that they represent the Impressionist School in ancient Southwest art.[74] Charles Avery Amsden says in a meticulous study, "This lively and varied category of decorative figures explains and justifies all Hohokam pottery painting."[75]

CONTRIBUTIONS OF THE MIMBRES ARTISTS

Sometime late in the ninth century, influences began to flow from the Hohokam eastward to the Mimbres Valley, leaving effects upon painting of Mogollon ceramics of the Three Circle phase.[76] Life forms and freer line elements, notably the scroll, came then from the Gila Basin to enliven the more formal styles of earlier ceramic decoration. Mogollon potters incorporated the new elements into painting styles of their own. Although the inspiration apparently came from the outside, the development which followed during the Boldface, then the Classic Black-on-white ceramic phases, was one of such imagination and technical perfection that it bears in every respect the character of a unique artistic phenomenon. Most of the Mimbres paintings are done in interiors of flaring bowls, others on the shoulder areas of water jars. The chalky white slip, which occasionally takes on a grayish or yellowish cast in firing, is the background upon which the designs are painted. Black is by far the most common color, although numerous shades from brown through warm reddish tones to creamy buff appear less frequently. Paintings are of fair size, for most of the bowls are ten or more inches in

60

diameter. Brushwork is sharply and firmly rendered with hairbreadth parallels and unwavering concentrics. Terraced and serrated masses are clean-cut; and curves, interlocking scrolls, and frets, almost mechanically exact. One is inclined to agree with those who have found it difficult to believe that this painting could have been done with the chewed end of a strip of yucca leaf such as is used on Pueblo pottery today.

Painting is both positive and negative; the one as skilled as the other. Weight of masses is differentiated through the use of solid black or varying values of hachure, checks, dots, or waves. White background predominates in more designs than does black ground. Some of the negatively painted examples give the effect of black-slipped bowls decorated with delicate white lines.

The designs fall into two broad classifications: life motifs and geometric patterns. Life motifs are usually combined with geometric borders or units. Fewkes classifies the life forms as conventionalized and realistic;[77] designating the majority as realistic. However, even the conventional life forms possess such strong realism and the more naturalistic ones so great a stylization, that there would seem to be no need for classifying them as to degree of realism. Geometric elements often appear in such form as to suggest conventionalized flower, seed, lightning, and cloud motifs. If indeed these designs represent such subjects, the rain symbolism was conceived by the Mimbreños in even greater degree of abstraction than that of many of the Pueblos.

Compositional schemes of bowl interiors are orderly and usually formal wherein the space is regularly sectioned, segmented, or unit-centered. Other basic arrangements are variously irregular, frequently employing complex asymmetry in an ingenious manner. Many patterns thus formed are static, others involve motion from slight to intense degree; but all force, potential and active, appears completely controlled and confined within the rim of the bowl. Thus, the petals of flower-like forms, or perhaps feathers springing from a sun disc, seem barely to move in rotary motion about the central circle; a swastika framework carries four repeated units in deliberate clockwise movement; or whirling zigzags spin around at incredible speed. Lightning lines counterplay on opposite sides of a quiet motif, or again, a sun-patterned space radiates sharply and evenly into the wide black mass of a border. The plans of asymmetric designs are so varied that each one calls for individual analysis.

Human and animal figures frequently appear as central motifs. These occupy a small circle within almost overpowering geometric surroundings or appear unfettered within a large area encircled by a narrow border close to the rim of the

61

bowl. The figures are usually in silhouette with only the eye indicated by a diamond-, circular-, or almond-shaped space commonly centered with a dot. There is seemingly never-ending variety among the life forms even though they clearly conform to an over-all style of unmistakable distinction.

A consideration for convention in the attitude of different creatures is apparent.[78] Quadrupeds, such as deer, antelope, badgers, rabbits, mountain sheep, mountain lions, and other species, are almost invariably drawn in full profile, although two eyes are sometimes displayed. Flying birds have wings outstretched as they would appear from below, but turkeys and quail are in profile. Turtles, gila monsters, lizards, frogs, and scorpions usually are drawn in flat, top view, with legs outstretched, while fish, serpents, caterpillars, beetles, bees, and grasshoppers seem more characteristically Mimbres in profile. Mythical monsters, humorous gargoyles, and composite creatures, appearing indiscriminately selected as to genus and anatomical features, are as fantastic in attitude as in components. One such product of a fertile Mimbres imagination is a four-legged serpent with a fish tail, a dorsal fin, a deerlike head, and a tasseled horn.

In the paintings of human beings, profile heads predominate, although masked faces commonly appear front view in order to display symbolic features. There is an unpredictable combination of attitudes in the several anatomical parts, so that front-view shoulders may accompany profile legs, or an entire profile may show both arms springing from the base of the throat. Apparently a definite attempt occurs in the depiction of most human figures to render naturalistic attitudes while yet showing most of the essential external features—and, in the case of a well-drawn spinal column for one man, internal parts. Features of dress and accompanying objects are economically but effectively indicated. Chongo and whorled hair styles and feathered headdresses, shields and hunting equipment, rattles, staffs, and ceremonial paraphernalia are all portrayed with convincing realism yet simple stylization. Abstract motifs are usually applied to some area of the life figures as decorative or symbolic elements.

A few of these figures[79] stand in immobile decoration, but it is more usual that they suggest action in the vitality they emanate in natural or fantastic activities. Such are depicted in scenes of a man wrestling with a bear; birds swallowing fishes; a turkey riding bareback on a fox, a badger on a fish, and a man on a deer or a beetle; two tiny dancers with staffs and rattles dancing on the tenuous neck of a crane; a woman in childbirth; two robust hunters leading a reluctant bear; or a precariously balanced man supporting a Calder-like device of fish and a dog.

62 Such episodes frequently forsake confinement within borders or spaced units

Figure 23. Mimbres. *Clown Figure with Antelope Headdress*. Ca. A.D. 1100. Classic Mimbres Black-on-White pottery bowl. New Mexico. Taylor Museum, Colorado Springs Fine Arts Center.

to form expanded scenes of realism such as a hunt, a dance, a gambling game, or a mythical dramatization. In one scene, three tall hunters with hair in chongos, and with bows and arrows in hand, track the deer and leave their own tracks behind.[80] The scene is quite simple—all in solid black except the diamond-shaped eye of each figure. Each hunter's arms connect to one shoulder in an attempt at perspective drawing. Another scene dramatizes the emergence of man through the sipapu from the lower world where beings with tailed appearance climb forth on all fours to venture in creeping advancement around the inner rim. Here is the

63

whole Pueblo story of creation* in a bowl.[81] Again, there is a delightful procession of antelopes moving counterclockwise around a bowl interior, all exquisitely painted in black silhouette with small spottings of white. Variety is in small device; some animals turn their heads, others exchange areas of white on rump, neck, and belly, with no two identically marked.[82]

Such concepts of realism in narrative presentation, first expressed in the petroglyphs, activated on pottery by the Hohokam, and perfected by the Mimbres artists, bore influences into the art of Tusayan, that of other pueblos, and into the modern developments. No less an influence was that of the masterly handling of geometric elements.

During the short time since these remarkable paintings have become known, artists and anthropologists have offered appraisals. Chapman says of them:

> For precision of technique in the handling of fine brush lines and broad spaces in black, the geometric art of these ancient potters is unsurpassed.[83]

And Kidder estimates the work of the Mimbreños thus:

> No ware of the Southwest can approach that of the Mimbres either in technical perfection of brushwork or in the variety, freedom, and sheer boldness of its decorative conception.[84]

Hewett adds:

> They took to life forms of the most striking kind and developed the most marvellous system that I know of among primitive potters of the world. In the use of life motifs, they exhibited a play of fancy that belongs to only master artists.[85]

Indeed, one might say that Mimbres painting attained the undisputable status of fine art in the black-on-white ceramics of the Classic phase. The Classic Mimbres designs are, so to speak, so much ahead of their time that today they can be compared only with the twentieth century's most advanced use of similar elements. Yet these paintings have the ring of truth which authenticates them for their own time and place. It is in this paradox, perhaps, that one is convinced of their fineness and of the enduring universality of their appeal.

64   *This tale, which describes the emergence of man through the sipapu, a small orifice in Mother Earth, is obviously a myth of gestation.

PUEBLO PAINTING

PREHISTORIC POTTERY

The decoration of prehistoric pottery constitutes a complex field in itself. There are unknown stores of pottery art still under the surface of the ground, and many above present riddles of meanings and relationships. At present there are literally thousands of motifs that are classifiable as to pottery type within type, within particular periods and phases of specific cultures in different localities.* They are related yet distinctive. Their immediate kinship is each to a certain family which has been given a name, usually regional or from some outstanding characteristic of form, style, medium, or technology. Thus there are such names as Sankawi Black-on-cream, Kana-a Black-on-white, Sikyatki Polychrome, Cieneguilla Glaze-on-yellow, and the like. Most of the earlier decorated pottery is broadly classifiable as black-on-white, the white varying from chalky purity to pearl gray, depending upon firing and the clay used for slip.

During Developmental Pueblo times, black designs on white-slipped bowls, ollas, and small globular jars became quite prevalent, with a limited use of red paint on backgrounds of light ruddy hue. Motifs were still largely derived from designs of baskets and textiles. Brushwork, although yet comparatively crude, had advanced considerably beyond that of the late Basketmakers. Unit and meander designs were formed from triangles, stepped, plain, or denticle-edged, which were variously combined within arrangements of parallel lines or simple frets and keys. The designs possessed order and vitality; they were balanced but not static and contained rudiments of intricate meander patterns and of involved manipulations of space and form in surface compositions.

These basic paintings advanced to a high degree of specialization in the Great Pueblo Period wherein distinguishing styles became pronounced in the several Pueblo regions. Painting in two of the principal areas might be cited.

In Chaco Canyon—where the cylindrical jar and tall-necked, globular-based pitcher are outstanding forms among bowls, ceramic ladles, and great corrugated storage jars—hached surface patterns and imaginatively treated unit motifs reveal their symbolism. Corn seeds, indicated by dots within little squares dominate many of the designs in bands or terraces; wide groups of parallel lines trace light-

---

*See Hawley (306) for an indication of the complexity of pottery types. See also Roberts (492) for an exhaustive description of pottery from a single district.

Figure 24. Pueblo. *Abstract Design*. Ca. A.D. 1100. Chaco Canyon Black-on-White pottery jar. New Mexico. American Museum of Natural History. Cat. No. H 3227.

ning movements along the edge of a stepped cloud bank. Deep borders within bowls give the impression of repeated units rather than continuous meanders, and most designs are symmetrical. Some curves and scrolls appear in outlined form upon hached ground, or in beaklike extensions on extremely abstract birds. Finely executed hachure occurs to such an extent that it produces a third value often

66

creating the appearance of a gray-on-white pattern rather than the bolder aspect of black-on-white, imparting characteristic lightness to much of Chaco painting.

In contrast, the painting of Mesa Verde is of a sturdier sort. The broader treatment in these more freely flowing, less formal black-on-gray designs imparts to them a quality of assertion and spontaneity. Casual meanders moving around steeply curving bowl exteriors, or encircling squat, in-tapering mugs, or lying within the wide, flat rims of flaring bowls, belie the painstaking calculations which must have governed their proportionate spacing. Life forms—small, silhouetted, abstract birds and quadrupeds are other motifs. A bird takes the form of a triangle or semicircle with beak and tail indicated by single lines. Small, circular eyes animate a terraced cloud, relating it to earth creatures.

Pueblos of the Little Colorado region produced pottery designs of influential character in the period following the Great Pueblos. Life motifs on the pottery of Homolobi, Chevlon, Chaves Pass, and neighboring settlements display features that apparently had found their way north from earlier southern cultures. These, the potters incorporated with designs of their own in reds, grays, black, and white, and eventually passed some of them on to the Hopi towns, particularly Awatovi.[86] Ventral-view birds, reminiscent of those from the Mimbres artists, and quadrupeds of prey-beast appearance were painted together with rain symbols, and with remnants of textile-influenced designs. While these paintings show rather uneven execution, they possess great vigor and often an almost savage quality. Birds appear to be protective fetishes as well as rain bearers, and quadrupeds display teeth and claws of exaggerated prominence as if alerted for battle. Nearly all the creatures have two eyes regardless of head position, and frequently they display breath-of-life lines.

The Hopi province of Tusayan produced what is conceded by experts to be technologically the finest of prehistoric Pueblo pottery. Especially is this true of Sikyatki (Yellow House) which was in ruins when the Spaniards came. The designs of Sikyatki Polychrome ware contain motifs as intricate in organization and almost as adept in execution as those of the Mimbres Valley, yet in most respects are unlike the latter. They are rich in both life and geometric elements; the life forms highly conventionalized and the abstract ones suggestive of symbolism. The deep terra-cotta reds and sepia blacks upon the cream-to-orange backgrounds of Sikyatki Polychrome set it at once apart from all other Southwest ceramics. Emphasis upon elongation of motif is another outstanding characteristic—rectangles and frets drawn out along the outer sides of wide, low ollas, triangles tapered into tall avian forms, groups of parallels stretched like long

67

strings, feathers extended in repeated patterns, and slim serpents describing arcs within the interiors of bowls. Skillful organization appears in the use of the spiral with many intricate designs constructed with it, such as fantastically devised parrots or mythical birds and reptiles moving clockwise, seldom counter, within a bowl. Abstract components of birds—feathers, beaks, or talons—hang upon sky bands stretching from rim to rim, and miniature devices, symbolizing stars or shrines or water creatures, accent open areas with perceptive calculation. The butterfly is a prominent figure, embellished in realistic manner with wing spottings and curling antennae, or reduced to a simple triangle. The fructifying triangle is everywhere in Hopi art, but the curve is seldom apart from the suggestive curve of the bowl. Cloud symbolism is far more present in creatures of water than in its own delineation, and the sun is painted, usually in association with feathers patterned to suggest those of an eagle. Depictions of human beings are relatively few, and those generally of symbolic nature. Shalako, the Corn Maid, and Ahul, Kachina chief of the Powamu festival, are prominent on later Sikyatki wares. The marvel of Sikyatki ceramic art is its advanced concept of composition and abstract design. Many a Sikyatki painting could be placed beside abstract works in a modern gallery and appear completely harmonious with twentieth-century art.

Pottery painting of the Rio Grande area saw outstanding developments on the Pajarito Plateau, the beautiful highland now known for its famous city of Los Alamos. There, where the settlements of Puyé and Tyuonyi flourished, the painting appeared in red or black, some of the latter being a rare glaze paint. The designs show the Avanyu, sacred feathered serpent of the Tewa, and birds distinctively adapted on wide, low pottery forms of grayish white or red. Suns, seed pods, angular clouds, and an occasional Kachina head are also motifs. Life forms, extremely abstract, appear as units placed within bowl interiors or at intervals in bands extending around the sides of vessels. Avanyus usually bear crested-cloud heads and bend their bodies at single acute or right angles, a habit quite different from the multiple-zigzag or reverse-curve movement of most Pueblo serpents. Birds are seldom elaborated beyond triangular or terraced bodies and are often indicated merely by angular lines representing beaks. Much use is made of elongated right triangles and of groups of paralled lines—horizontal, diagonal, or vertical. Some lines are dotted or denticulate as in Developmental Pueblo design. Few seem to have been surely drawn, for the general effect of the painting is rather crude. Nevertheless, the designs are alive and convincingly symbolic.

Typical patterns continued and evolved on the Pajarito Plateau in other pueblos, now long extinct, such as Sankawi and Tsirege, and were carried down

Figure 25.   Hopi. *Ahul Kachina*. Ca. A.D. 1500. Sikyatki Polychrome pottery canteen. Field Museum of Natural History. Cat. No. 21174.

into the Rio Grande Valley to appear on Tewa Polychrome and later wares. Their cloud patterns, Avanyus and bird forms, seed and plant motifs, were forerunners of certain designs used in the ceramics and watercolors of modern Tewa pueblos. In like manner, pottery painting in other Rio Grande settlements of Regressive Pueblo times influenced the art of later potters.

69

PUEBLO PICTOGRAPHS

The oldest known Pueblo pictographs have been found in the original Anasazi homeland where Developmental Pueblo people added their own records to those of the Basketmakers and their predecessors in many sites, and created new galleries nearby. In northeastern Arizona, in the Kayenta region and environs, many petroglyphs and some of the painted pictographs were made by early Pueblo people.[87] These include works from obscure abstractions to rather naturalistic scenes. Human beings, anthropomorphs, and zoomorphs are present in abundance. Most are silhouetted renderings of front-view figures with scantily indicated details of clothing, adornment, hair styles, or headdresses. Some are schematically suggested by lines only; others have bulk and some indication of anatomic proportion. Kokopelli, the flute player and bearer of seeds, appears often as do also huntsmen with snares and lassos for capturing their prey. Mountain sheep, from a half foot to a gigantic six feet in length, most frequently represented among the quadrupeds, appear here in somewhat the same style as they do later upon pottery of Mesa Verde. Serpents in lightning form and antelopes are less prominent, and birds are rare. The corn plant is discernible in a few obscure forms which suggests stalks. Suns, moons, and spiral whirlpools are among sky-earth symbols.

At Betatakin, in the same district, are similar pictographs of mountain sheep and other horned animals, figures representing tailed beings, and serpents, one of which is fifteen feet long. Some are painted with colors of yellow, red, a greenish hue, and white.

Extending far into Utah, other representative early Anasazi sites contain vast numbers of early Pueblo pictographs.[88] In these, the general character of the works just described prevails with a few exceptions.

Among the more unusual yet recognizably Pueblo drawings are scenes depicting a Kachina Dance, buffalo dancers, hunters with bows and arrows shooting deer, a herd of goats with young, a game which looks like shinny, men feeding corn to turkeys, and herding turkeys into a corral. Other figures not common in the Arizona pictographs are cranes, centipedes, frogs, elks, and coyotes. There are many renderings of sheep and serpents, also of sky and weather symbols.

Certain figures notable in this area appear to have been done by members of intruding tribes. The "Great Warrior" group,[89] near Vernal, contains petroglyphs far more advanced in conception and rendering than those of either the Basketmakers or the Pueblos. Another, although much less sophisticated, group[90] has a non-Anasazi look. It depicts creatures like beetles about three feet tall, which seem to indicate warriors behind decorated shields bearing Plains-type motifs.

70

Plate V. Sybil Yazzie, Navajo. *Going to the Yeibichai.* 1937. Tempera. Collection of Dorothy Dunn.

Plate VI. Pueblo. *Mural.* Ca. A.D. 1300. Fresco secco. Pottery Mound, central New Mexico. BPM, Kiva 7, Layer 30. (Tom Bahti reproduction, Dick Dunatchik photograph.) Museum of Anthropology, University of New Mexico.

Petroglyphs of sheep, deer, birds, sun, hands, human figures, and serpents appear among others on the Mesa Verde. Also in southwestern Colorado are typical drawings of human beings, birds, quadrupeds, serpents, tracks, bear claws, cloud symbols, and geometric forms, mostly executed in rough, schematic style.

One notable area of later pictography is the Tusayan region of northern Arizona where, from Regressive Pueblo times through more recent days, some of the Southwest's most interesting symbolic drawings have been made. In 1892, Fewkes described and illustrated many motifs as they appeared in those days.[91] He found drawings numerous on Hopi mesas, usually pecked or scratched, with color applied in a few instances, and noted little difference between more modern drawings and those near abandoned sites. Most of these pictographs are in abstract outline with considerably more detail than those mentioned above for earlier Pueblos. Subjects are masks of various Kachinas, feathered sun symbols, Palulukon, from small to giant size, phallic symbols combined with clouds, corn so abstract that it might be construed as a schematic human figure, shields, rainbows, lightning, clouds, and whirlwinds. These pictographs are unusually well done, with apparent aesthetic consideration for symmetry and proportion as well as concern for symbolic relevance.

The eastern Pueblo area has also produced a wealth of pictographic comment upon the lives of forebears of the present Pueblo peoples and of others who have migrated or perhaps entirely vanished. The Pajarito Plateau contains many hundreds of these. In a study that Dr. Chapman made of more than two hundred cave dwellings in 1915, he drew over one hundred copies of pictographs which he considered most important in the area.[92] These represent human figures and faces, Kachinas, Avanyus, masks, hands, animals, birds, unidentified creatures, bear tracks, feather and other symbols, and geometric designs. Many figures are painted but color is usually fragmentary. Most important among the finds are two representations of hunting scenes which show remarkable realism. In one a wounded stag, accompanied by a doe and fawn, is pursued by seven hunters, some with drawn bows and another hurling a spear. This group is followed by five crouching figures in whom the artist has evoked the stealth of hunters with admirable fidelity. The figures are drawn in line, with freedom and convincing action seldom found in pictographic depictions.

A very large open cave on the Pajarito Plateau, between El Rito de los Frijoles and Cochiti, known as La Cueva Pintada, shelters the drawings of many people from pre-Spanish times on. Some forms are incised, most are painted in red, black, or white. Pueblo designs include simple representations of dancers,

71

Figure 26. Pueblo. *Petroglyphs.*
Prehistoric. Galisteo Basin,
New Mexico. Photograph by
Lowell Miller, 1929.

shields, terraced and semicircular clouds, sun, and animals. Among El Rito de los
Frijoles sites, mainly Tyuonyi, a number of symbols, especially suns, are scratched
and painted on the tufa of the sheer wall above the dwellings.

Aside from the Pajarito area, New Mexico contains many areas of unrecorded vast numbers of pictographs, as yet little explored. Adolph Bandelier referred to some of these, near the now extinct pueblo of Abo.[93] The designs are
painted in red, yellow, green, black, brown, and white on walls of sheltered places
in Cañon de la Pintada. He believed them to have been made by the Piro people
in post-Spanish times because he considered some of the pigments brighter than
earth colors. Among the more common symbols of rain, shields, and headdresses,
are two dance figures—one masked and wearing a painted kilt, the other a black
and white Koshare from whose face a snake descends. Upon inquiry of a San
Juan Indian, Bandelier found that this is a record of the Snake Dance. He was
also informed by a Cochiti man that such pictographic records were made when
a pueblo was to be abandoned.

Some remarkable graphic accounts were left near Santa Fe in the Galisteo
Basin abandoned by Tanoan peoples fully two and a half centuries ago. This
galaxy of petroglyphs includes human and anthropomorphic beings, dancers,

animals of many kinds, stars and planets, corn in all stages of growth and the forces that help it and the pests that hinder its fruition, meanders and other geometric patterns, the Avanyu with characteristic markings, foot tracks and hand prints, Plains-type shields, and totally abstract symbols. Despite the tedious labor required in their making, these pictures have a deceiving look of spontaneity and verve. They seem to live upon the boulders, defying time and the onrush of civilization. They remain to speak for people whose existence in that valley was forcibly terminated, and to give an inkling of the multitudinous American art records yet unrecognized.

PUEBLO MURAL PAINTING

The Pueblo mural form had its inception in the pictographs of Basketmaker times, and perhaps even before, but true mural painting in the Southwest apparently began in late Developmental Pueblo times, circa A.D. 1000. Rudimentary paintings are found on plastered walls of kivas and other rooms in ruins in the Four Corners area. The earliest of these, as now identified, were discovered in the remains of a kiva at Alkali Ridge in southeast Utah. There, fragments gave evidence that a repeated design of diagonal bars, applied in white on the painted plaster surface of the banquette, ran entirely around the circular kiva.[94]

Southward, in the Village of the Great Kivas, with tree-ring dates circa A.D. 1000, wall decorations in a subterranean dirt kiva are illustrated.[95] These appear in the plaster as incised, lightly colored, rectangular and triangular repeated units, plus a checkerboard design and a centipede-like symbol.

Several kivas, circa A.D. 1100, in ruins of Lowry Pueblo, southwestern Colorado, had painted geometric designs.[96] The evenly terraced pattern of one mural, in gypsum white on brown adobe plaster, encircled the banquette.

In the Great Pueblo Period, mural painting continued in the same region. In some of the great structures of that period at Mesa Verde, remnants of simple mural decorations in earth pigments painted upon plastered walls are still visible. In Spruce Tree House, in which walls underwent many plasterings of various colors, a few unit designs and running borders of grouped triangles in contrasting colors are evident. In one room, the lower wall is painted with dark-red iron oxide and white in a pattern of triple peaks extending over the buff plaster of the upper area. In another design, a row of white dots outlines red triangular fertility motifs against black plaster. One comparatively elaborate rectangular line design in red paint on buff plaster remains on an east inside wall near the center of Spruce Tree House. Only about 12 by 14 inches in size, this little motif

73

is a balanced construction of diagonals and triangular forms suggesting a butterfly.

The triangle and dot combination appears in several places on the Mesa Verde, among them Cliff Palace, Painted Kiva, and New Fire House. A textile-type pattern is painted in red on a white wall above a red dado edged with dots and triangles in a third-story room at Cliff Palace.

Figure 27. Pueblo. *Abstract Designs.* A.D. 1150-1300. Mural in earth tempera on painted plaster. Cliff Palace, Mesa Verde National Park, Colorado. National Park Service photograph.

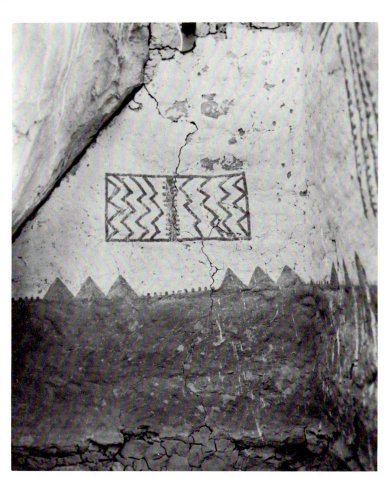

74

Minor murals remain at nearby Aztec Ruin, while bands of meander patterns are executed in red and white paint in a kiva of Canyon de Chelly, Arizona.[97]

In the Renaissance phase of the Regressive Pueblo period, mural painting became an important art, reaching its climax perhaps a century or less before the Spanish invasion. Especially in the Rio Grande central area can the development be followed. On the Pajarito Plateau, fragments of wall paintings remain near sites containing pictographs. Here may be witnessed the transition from pictography to painting, for a semimural stage appears in vestigial decorations on walls of caves carved out of the volcanic tuff. A few of the larger caves which formerly served as kivas show, despite the thick lamp black of subsequent fires, that earth-color designs once formed adornment on repeatedly color-washed walls.

In this same area, the Snake Kiva at El Rito de los Frijoles shows a painted Avanyu undulating above a red dado which encircles the walls to a height of about three feet. Despite the soot, this figure is fairly clear. And, just below the plateau, at the old pueblo of Otowi, a yellow-ochre figure of a mountain lion, outlined in black, is illustrated as having decorated a wall of a large square ceremonial room in East House of the ruin.[98] This now headless beast is pictured as having the elongated body and tail, and the right-angled legs of many such creatures in Pueblo painting.

Down the Rio Grande some forty miles, there occurred the first discovery of full-fledged Pueblo mural art. This and two other groups of Pueblo murals are of such importance as to merit consideration at greater length with a view of the setting of each.

*The Kuaua Murals.** One of the most notable finds of mural painting was that discovered by Edgar L. Hewett and an archaeological group from the University of New Mexico and the School of American Research in February 1935 at Kuaua, a prehistoric Tigua site some twenty miles north of Albuquerque and across the Rio Grande to the west of Bernalillo.[99] There, seventeen painted layers were unearthed and separated from among eighty-five layers of plaster upon the walls of a square, subterranean kiva. Several layers of painted plaster were also found on an altar on the floor of the east side of the kiva.

The Kuaua site, among several ruined villages in the area, had been studied

*This account is based on the initial reports by Dr. Edgar L. Hewett and others of the project, on historical documents and related studies, and on Kuaua murals *in situ* and in scale reproduction. The complete and fully illustrated report, *Sun Father's Way*, by Bertha P. Dutton (The University of New Mexico Press, 1963) is commended to the reader.

many years before by Bandelier who believed it to be that of a pueblo mentioned by the chroniclers of Coronado's expedition who had referred to the group of towns between the Mesa del Cangelon and Albuquerque as Tiguex.[100] Bandelier measured and mapped the ruins opposite Bernalillo and called one Puaray, but was in doubt about Kuaua. Of the latter he writes:

> North of the bridge across the Rio Grande lie the remains of a considerable village. I have not been able to ascertain whether it was one of the historical pueblos of Coronado's time, or whether its abandonment antedated 1540. The name given to me by the Sandia Indians, Kua-ua, seems to designate the site and not the ruin. Still it may also have been the name of the latter.[101]

Coronado is said to have joined Alvarado at these Tiguex towns and to have spent the winters of 1540 and 1541 in one of them, exploring the pueblos north and south on the Rio Grande and scouting into the Plains territory as far as eastern Kansas.[102]

About forty years later, in 1580, Francisco Chamuscado accompanied three Franciscan missionaries up the Rio Grande into New Mexico.[103] The missionaries were thought to have been killed later at Puarai. Reference is made to them by Captain Gaspar Perez de Villagrá, historian of the expedition commanded by Juan de Oñate into the Tiguex territory in 1598.

Writing in the *Historia*, Villagrá says:

> We halted at the pueblo of Puarai, where we were well received. The Indians took the priests to the quarters which had been prepared for them. The walls of their rooms had been recently whitewashed, and the rooms were cleanly swept. The next day, however, when the whitewash had dried, we were able clearly to see, through the whitewash, paintings of scenes which made our blood run cold . . . . There, pictured upon the wall, we saw the details of the martyrdom of those saintly men, Fray Agustin, Fray Juan, and Fray Francisco. The paintings showed us exactly how they had met their death, stoned and beaten by the savage Indians.[104]

Villagrá is known to have been given to exaggeration and this description might well be taken as an example of it. The Indians are unlikely to have made a naturalistic representation as such, much less one recognizable as portraits of certain priests, for to this day Indian artists are seldom intentional portraitists, and it is most doubtful that they would have selected such a subject for mural painting. Murals were done only with symbolic, usually ceremonial, significance.

76
Much more likely of accuracy was Villagrá's description of the murals in

one of the Piro villages, perhaps Trenaquel, to the south where the party had stopped a short time before. Of these murals, he says:

> On the walls of the rooms where we were quartered were many paintings of the demons they worship as gods. Fierce and terrible were their features. It was easy to understand the meaning of these, for the god of the water was near the water, the god of the mountains was near the mountains, and in like manner all those deities they adore, their gods of the hunt, crops, and other things they have.[105]

This description might fairly well be applied to the paintings uncovered at Kuaua. The "fierce and terrible features" undoubtedly refer to the masks worn by the anthropomorphic figures which in their abstract symbolism appeared to be "fiercely" different from naturalistic sixteenth-century paintings to which the Spaniards were accustomed. Water and crop symbolism remarked upon by Villagrá certainly dominated the Kuaua murals, for the paintings were obviously motivated by the necessity for rainfall.

Rain symbolism is revealed in the form of zig-zag serpents, crisscrossed lightning shafts and arching rainbows, fishes, and monstrous fish masks on swimming figures, semicircular rain clouds, angular cloud terraces, and showers of sacred meal or fountains of water droplets profusely spouting forth from ceremonial ollas or from mouths and phalli of anthropomorphic and zoomorphic figures. Mythical Rainbirds with eagle talons and beaks, a parrot with cloud-tipped plumage, and a strangely naturalistic duck with curling tail tuft and a spray issuing from his broad beak are all symbolic water-bearers in various paintings. The turtle is here, and butterflies of extreme abstraction, and something rarely known in Pueblo art before discovery of Layer H-31—the head and torso of a figure in human form united with a cloud bank. This personage appears as Paiyatuma, god of music. In the same panel there is the consummate symbol of fruition, a row of ripening corn plants, tall and slender, with precisely balanced leaves, ears, and classic tassels. The symmetric evergreen tree, another life symbol, is held in the hand of a masked god. A ghostlike unique figure, chalk white with an orange-red frog mask and clownish attitude, is reminiscent of the Koshare in a modern Corn Dance.

Much variation, from seminaturalism to geometric design occurs in the feathers which appear in many relationships. Footprints of different creatures, including man, and hand prints are placed in symbolic reference, usually indicating fertility and abundance. Each sacred olla bears a breath-of-life line; and these lines, hearts, and other vital organs are symbolized in the buffalo, deer, jackrabbit, and in some of the godlike figures.

77

Figure 28. Pueblo. *Paiyatuma, Manifest as God of Music.* A.D. 1450-1550. Kuaua Pueblo, New Mexico. (Reproduction.) Museum of New Mexico.

Certain motifs and the general style of drawing in most of the Kuaua murals furnish conclusive proof that there is a strong relationship between Pueblo and Navajo painting. Here, upon the kiva walls, the all-over effect of the upright tempera patterns is strikingly like that of the sandpaintings lying flat on the ceremonial hogan floor. Suggestive parallels in the two arts can be followed from large forms to small details in many instances. Masked figures of the gods, averaging four and a half feet in height, stand elongated and angular with arms flexed upward at right angles, showing rigid palms and delicate fingers, and with short legs turned sideways as in the Navajo paintings. Flaring and tasseled kilts, fringed sashes, long ear and wrist pendants and neck circlets all seem to be Navajo-related, as do the stiffly held arrows and prayer plumes. The manner of using zigzags, staffs, the looped necklace, and feathers, is very similar in the two arts. Thin outlines against flat color masses are employed throughout as they appear in both sandpaintings and in modern Pueblo painting.

The colors, ranging from white through the natural blues, greens, yellows, reds, and browns to black, used as tempera paint are fairly evenly stroked upon the adobe plaster background, producing a fresco effect, although not true fresco. The technique gives an entirely flat and two-dimensional aspect.

With painstaking archaeological techniques, invented as the work progressed, members of the field group jacketed sections of the walls,[106] removed them to the laboratory, and separated one painted layer of plaster from another, remounted each one, and preserved them all for future use by the Museum of New Mexico, where several reproductions of them may be seen now on walls of the Hall of Ethnology. One set of murals as they appeared at the time of excavation has been reproduced by Ma-Pe-Wi in the restored kiva at Kuaua in what is now Coronado State Monument.

The Awatovi Murals. Soon after discovery of the Kuaua murals an expedition from the Peabody Museum of Harvard University, directed by J. O. Brew, began excavations at Awatovi,* one of the largest of the old Tusayan towns in the Jeddito Valley not far from existing Hopi villages. Here and in the neighboring Kawaika-a, in 1936, another amazing group of murals was found.[107]

Ruined Awatovi, the Place of the Bow People, is still a place of mystery, although it has appeared in records from the time of Pedro de Tovar's visit in 1540 when it was a flourishing town.[108] Castañeda gave an early account of it, and Espejo, who came in 1583, called it Aguato and found kindness and generosity among the natives who gave the Spaniards handwoven "towels with tassels"[110] (probably kilts) and "blue and green ores which they use to color the mantas, and many other things."[111] Frequent explorers, including Oñate, stopped in Awatovi, and gave the name a variety of spellings.[112] Legends of the Hopi tell

---

*Frank H. Cushing, referring to it as Aguatobi, calls it "the leading city of the Province of Tusayan" at the time of the conquest.[109]

that Awatovi's inhabitants were kinsmen of the Badger People who had lived on the Rio Grande.[113]

Early in the seventeenth century, through the zeal of Padre Porras, many Awatovians had been converted to Christianity.[114] The first Franciscan mission in Arizona, San Bernardo de Aguatubi, was established there in 1629.[115] The Navajo called the mission the "Singing-house," and afterward used that name in referring to the ruin.[116]

Dr. Fewkes, in his early explorations of the site, said that the archaeological findings of copper bells and iron hooks and knives showed that the pueblo was under Spanish influence for some time.[117] (The Peabody excavations bear this out with evidence of "at least 160 years of life after Spanish contact.")[118] The Pueblo Rebellion in 1680 severed Indian-Spanish connections for a while, but in 1692, De Vargas came to Tusayan and again brought Awatovi under Spanish influence.[119] Legends of this conquest are well preserved in Tusayan, and other legends of local strife caused by Christian ways versus the native ones have been retold for more than two centuries among the Hopi.[120] Such legends together with early investigations at the turn of the century had presented the following story.

Awatovi had a short life after the reconquest. In the early winter of 1700, it was burned and razed to the ground, and its entire population of "about 800" were the victims of a sudden violence which killed or left them homeless.[121] A large number of men were trapped in the kiva where their remains were found years afterward. There are evidences of massacre and destruction but not of pillage. This encouraged the belief that destruction was accomplished by hostile dwellers of nearby Walpi and Oraibi rather than by an invading tribe. The legends tell that those killed were sorcerers because of alien influences, and that only the children were saved, together with a few adults, mostly women, who knew certain songs, rites, and practices.[122] A priestess, Mamzrau Monwi, who perpetuated the Mamzrauti ceremony, was supposedly one of these. Tapolo, a traitor, is said to have been instrumental in the betrayal of Awatovi.[123]

Fewkes said that the more he studied the situation, the more he believed that the progress Christianity was making after the reconquest "explains the hostility of the other villagers."[124] Contrary to this, Elsie Clews Parsons has suggested that Awatovi may have been destroyed by nomad raiders, possibly Ute, for she believes the reasons for destruction set forth in Hopi folktales are "too frivolous to be credible" and that a Hopi admission of annihilation by the Ute "would have hurt tribal pride."[125]

80 Whatever the cause of its annihilation, Awatovi, together with such neighbor-

ing villages as Sikyatki and Kawaika-a, has furnished a rich source of some of the finest early Pueblo painting. Dr. Fewkes and Walter Hough, those precursors in appreciation of Indian art, recognized this more than a half century ago in their pioneering explorations of the area.[126] Among many notations, Hough recorded a mural painting from Kawaika-a, which he called Kawaiokuh. This is of a semi-human form and a checkered-winged bird figure, with a large meander pattern at the lower border.[127] Related in all respects, this painting offered a clue to the later rich mural discoveries.

Even though Awatovi is still in several respects an enigma, some twelve hundred years of buried history in the old village and close environs have been brought out again through the extensive excavations and thorough reports of the Awatovi Expedition. Now it is revealed that Awatovi alone covers twenty-three acres and contains an estimated five thousand rooms of which only about a fourth have been excavated.[128] Moreover, it is but one of six large sites among hundreds of smaller ones in the vicinity. In addition to murals, the expedition recovered 8,500 pottery specimens and multitudes of sherds and artifacts. Such finds may be but a fraction of treasures yet beneath the surface.

In all, during the five seasons, two hundred and forty murals in the prehistoric and historic kivas of Awatovi and Kawaika-a were recorded and analyzed by Watson Smith in a report[129] that became at once a classic in American Indian studies. In the 1939 season alone, one hundred and seven distinct painted layers of plaster were found in nine kivas, and as many as nineteen painted layers on a single wall. Seventy-three of these paintings, many occupying most of a wall, were well enough preserved to record. As at Kuaua, the murals occurred layer upon layer and presented a similar problem in separation and preservation. Those in sufficiently good condition were peeled off on muslin or rice paper for permanent preservation. Photographs and scale drawings were made of all paintings, and their colors carefully checked with the Maerz and Paul color dictionary.

Colors used[130] are reds (including maroons and vermilion), yellows, blues, greens, browns, blacks, whites, and mixtures of these (pinks, purples, oranges, etc.) derived from various earths, minerals, and carbon.

The paints probably were mixed as in recent Pueblo practice, with vegetable gum, or juices and oils of melon and other seeds as binders, and with water (or saliva to some extent). They apparently were applied in fresco secco manner with a stiff brush upon the natural brown adobe plaster in essentially flat, usually outlined areas.

Drawing, appears in the reproductions to be spirited and direct; organiza-

81

tion of large compositions admirable, especially in abstract designs similar to those which appear on Sikyatki pottery. All representation is unnaturalistic although there is considerable range from seminaturalism in certain human figures to complete abstraction in designs which apparently had their origin in cloud and bird symbolism. One of the earliest murals, appears entirely modern and almost completely nonobjective.[131]

Concern for fruition again seems the principal motive for these paintings. The sky complex is represented in motifs from the full radiating sun to small four-point stars, and from dynamic lightning to placid rainbow arch. Young blossoms and matured corn ears rise together out of the dark rain cloud, or perhaps earth,[132] and corn in full stalk, in checkered ears, or in rectangularly segmented kernels is repeatedly shown in balanced arrangements. The bean sprout, the terraced cloud, and the fertile triangle lie along the hems and borders of ceremonial garments.[133] Creatures associated with water frequently appear. The serpent in imaginative forms with parrot head, or cloud head, or horned crest, his body marked by rainbow stripes or water signs, moves in zigzag or undulation among other motifs. The butterfly, totem of the Poli Clan whose ceremonials were most developed at Awatovi, and the dragonfly, associate of the sprouting corn, are often shown.[134] There are ingenious bird forms—long-tailed parrots, fantastic mythical birds, and a bird with triangular tail and extended wings reminiscent of the northern Shoshone Thunderbird. The eagle is multipresent in his tail feathers and breath feathers[135] which are hung upon shields and pahos, fastened in the hair or held in the hands of Kachinas. Some semiavian creatures are half serpent, half bird; others are more sensed than seen in extreme abstraction where bird merges with cloud.[136]

Fish are uncommon, although there is a noteworthy one, sharply drawn in a manner which resembles a bird—fins like wings, mouth beak-sharp, and tail fanning out in feather fashion.[137] To aid in combating evil forces, the prey animals exercise their power through this painted symbolism.[138] In profile, they display not one aware eye but two, alert ears, full sets of exaggerated claws, and prominent strong teeth, reminiscent of Homolobi and Chaves Pass ceramic figures.

In addition to large, intricately stepped geometric designs suggestive of the finest black-on-white pottery decorations of the area,[139] there are many small abstract units, most of which are circular motifs. Some are annulet style, while others have a central figure such as a dot, a decorated disc, or a four-point star, surrounded by radiating lines or a scalloped or cogged enclosure.[140] Such wheellike units appear scattered through the larger patterns or are aligned in border arrangements. They are ancient motifs, almost hieroglyphics, which appear as petro-glyphs in various places in the Pueblo country, and even in frescos of temples in Chiapas and Yucatán.

The human-like figures representing Kachinas and other anthropomorphic beings are both masked and unmasked. Some are drawn in longheaded profile with square-cut bang and long, descending hair and a single, front-view shoulder and arm. Other beings with circular or wedge-shaped heads are front view except their feet, which appear in a composite top and side view. One symbolic seated figure holds semiflexed arms and legs outward in frog fashion, indicating a fructification rite. Similar figures appeared at Kuaua.

Several full-faced masked creatures are slightly like Navajo sandpainting figures and some of those at Kuaua. These have uplifted, flexed arms, and carry pahos or other ceremonial equipment in their hands. Some wear modern-looking tasseled kilts, ear pendants, fringed rain sashes, and multiple neck bands, the lower strand of which folds over into a figure-eight arrangement. One little "squash woman" of dancing, growing movement, with human face and hair, and leafy vine arms, is in a class by herself for she seems to be neither Kachina nor mortal but a delightful composite of vegetable and human growth—an advocate of the "oneness of nature."[141]

In general, far less in these murals than in those at Kuaua reminds one of Navajo art. Aside from the purely abstract designs, these paintings are less se-verely formal than Navajo sandpaintings. They have a rounder, more casual ap-pearance, although a number of plant and animal designs are vaguely Navajo in appearance, and treatment of certain details, such as in sashes and masks, seems akin to Navajo sandpainting style.

There are some resemblances to Mimbres art in the human figures, and to certain Middle American and Peruvian ceramic and mural motifs such as the jaguar, the wide key, and numerous small units.

Aside from their original ceremonial purpose, and their future importance in the history of Southwest Indian painting, several of these murals might command admiration among recognized paintings as sheer works of art. Such a one is the extremely abstract, asymmetrically organized panorama best described by Watson Smith:

> This is one of the most intricate and meticulously executed of the Sikyatki style of paintings in Layout Group III (2). Little can be said of it beyond the obvious fact that it is made up of an amazingly complex interweaving of highly stylized conventions of feathers, clouds, and birds' tails, in very much the same

83

Figure 29. Hopi. *Abstract Design, Sikyatki Style.* Ca. A.D. 1400. Awatovi Pueblo, Arizona. Mural painting in earth color on adobe plaster. (Reproduction.) Peabody Museum, Harvard University.

manner that similar elements were combined on Sikyatki Polychrome pottery. It is interesting, however, that this design is in reality double, with a focus in the center of each lateral half of the wall area, from which the various details radiate as they would do on the broad upper shoulder of a characteristic squat olla.[142]

This mural, a fairly early one at Awatovi, is painted in red, yellow, blue, and green on a white background.

Among the very earliest and most exceptional murals excavated in this project, is one which extended along three walls of a kiva at Kawaika-a.[143] This is an exquisite work in yellow, white, black and three reds, from maroon to vermilion, painted on a wide band of deep blue. Its selective drawing and skillfully organized symbolic elements are somewhat suggestive of Klee. The painting presents a procession of food bowls, heaped as with flowers, and standing above a

84

panel depicting a most delightful company of birds, frogs, fishes, dragonflies, lightning, corn, and regularly placed, large, trisected rectangles in three tones. Trailing in the upper section is a delicately patterned squash vine somewhat like that in Navajo sandpaintings. Simplification and fundamental design unify the multiple components of this composition. Small patterns seem not to exist here for their own sake, but details such as terraced motifs on food bowls, often associated with clouds, indicate depth of ideas pertaining functionally to the whole. After studying such a painting, perhaps one turns to a thoughtful work of contemporary art with keener appreciation of its relevance in modern society.

Figure 30. Hopi. *Mural.* Ca. A.D. 1350. Awatovi Pueblo, Arizona. Painting in earth color on adobe plaster. (Reproduction.) Peabody Museum, Harvard University.

85

The Murals of Pottery Mound. A further find of murals of the Regressive Pueblo Period occurred at Pottery Mound on the west bank of the Rio Puerco, a tributary of the Rio Grande, some forty miles southwest of Albuquerque. Although this site, which had acquired its name from heaps and deposits of pottery sherds, had been known by archaeologists and others for at least two decades, actual excavation did not begin until the 1954 session of the summer Archaeological Field School of the University of New Mexico with Frank C. Hibben in charge.[144]

Tests revealed three pueblos and possibly a still earlier village. These towns had risen one above the other, through many generations, in the Puerco Valley, which was then traversed by a prehistoric trade route. Pottery fragments mingling in the ruins attested ancient barters and possible intrusions. There were sherds from the distant pueblos of the Jeddito Valley, from Zuñi, the Rio Grande, and other areas—all retaining bits of their identifying designs and technologies. Ceramics further indicated major life of Pottery Mound as circa A.D. 1300-1450 with none beyond the Spanish Conquest.

The first season's digging unearthed a rectangular kiva, approximately 14 by 14 feet, with walls that showed in cross section six painted layers among twenty adobe plasterings. Stripping layer from layer was again a problem as at previous sites. Two painted layers were extricated in the first season.

Subsequent summer sessions brought the number of paintings and groups of paintings to a total of more than two hundred by the 1960 season. All were on subterranean kiva walls, some extending to around forty feet in length. A number apparently had been purposely destroyed, many had eroded along the top, but most were intact enough to admit recording.

The aggregate galleries of Pottery Mound mural art offer characteristics in common with Awatovi and Sikyatki, links to Zuñi and the central Rio Grande, hints of Middle America and even Peru, and more than a few likenesses to twentieth-century abstract art.

In addition to subjects as distant as the heavenly constellations, the murals present a wide range of human, animal, and plant forms, and mythical combinations of these, encompassing styles from almost nonobjective and decidedly abstract to representation in a degree seldom seen in American Indian art.

The painting is in fresco secco, employing a tempera paint of mineral and a few vegetal pigments mixed with water and animal fat, as so far revealed. The palette includes eight shades of red, three of yellow, two of green, two blues, a purple, a maroon, and a bright orange, white, and black. Color range is extensive through mixing and superimposing. Many painted areas are outlined in black, and the general surface effect is flat, although a technical variation appears in the brushwork. Dr. Hibben points out the obviously divergent abilities of the large number of artists who executed the paintings over a long period of time.[145]

The first painted layer to emerge from its centuries of burial revealed, in colors of pink, coral, maroon, yellow, white, black and gray, a procession[146] of creatures as strange as any from medieval Europe. These beings, neither man nor beast, appear to be quasi-insects with humanoid heads, arms, and legs, and large ornate wings. In nice precision, these cicadaesque personages evenly space the wall while airily ascending delicately branching and blossoming stalks that rise from earth to clouds. Indeed, these must be giant beings, for they themselves tower and touch the sky. Surely whimsy as well as religious purpose motivated the artists here, for this painting reveals a play spirit akin to that of the Hohokam and Mimbres painters. It also suggests motifs on Sikyatki pottery. Remarkable too, it appears that earth and three layers of atmosphere are differentiated by color values in the composition.

As this procession meets other walls, it changes to present dancing figures with flexed arms uplifted and feet pointed sideways, in a posture that has persisted through centuries of Southwest art. Intricately woven and embroidered kilts, sashed and tasseled, form part of the costumes, somewhat as in modern cere-monies. Although depicted heads are mostly eroded, some fragments appear to represent masks. One dancer holds a heron as in falconing, and another, wearing a knitted tunic, suspends a small animal on a cord as in Navajo sandpaintings.[147]

The second painted layer shows among other figures bird-derived abstrac-tions incorporating beak and feather designs strongly reminiscent of Sikyatki ceramic decoration.[148] It has a modern appearance as have its Awatovi counter-parts. A later excavated layer presents an extreme abstraction of intriguing as-pect in which a large circular form is vertically crossed by an elongated, vaguely human figure. Its composite, perhaps cosmic, character is further effected by feather-like designs extending bilaterally, and by esoteric motifs on the torso which possibly suggest vital organs of the being. Hibben says that Indian observers have mentioned the vertical figure as "Direction Man" or "World Man."[149]

Equally esoteric is a richly colored composition from the thirtieth layer in the successive plasterings of a kiva wall. In yellow ochre, iron-oxide reds, dove gray, white, and black, the mural depicts variously deeply curved tendril and beaklike patterns surrounding an angular, terraced form some sixty inches high.

87

This is a strikingly contemporary-looking painting despite its pre-Columbian date. Weather charms were very likely intended in its plant- and bird-derived components as in the semicircular forms and the groups of extended parallel lines, all associated with rainmaking.

In stylistic contrast, another mural[150] pictures a relatively naturalistic view of human and bird figures with bowls, baskets, and a display of ceremonial textiles and multiple festoons of shell and coral necklaces. Although primarily elaborately conventionalized, the subjects are fairly realistic in proportion, action, and color. The rather angular attitude of human forms is stylistically exaggerated, but that of a tall, white whooping crane is as lifelike a figure as one is likely to see in Southwest Indian art. He is a beautiful, animated bird with strong wings flapping and long neck and beak reaching over the head of a seated woman in dark Pueblo manta. A quetzal adds a Mexican note, and great headdresses worn by the men are reminiscent of Aztecan and Mayan styles with their tall fanlike arrangements of corn or feathers, attached in this instance to rainbow caps. Embankments of typical Pueblo clouds rise toward the upper edge of the panel, giving a bold black-and-white contrast to the high color appearing below. Comparable naturalism appears in some other panels of the series.

Disregarding the obscurity of much of the subject matter once held vitally important in the murals, these paintings are interesting and admirable in themselves as art that is imaginative, well composed, and spontaneous. Their motif appears primarily decorative to the outsider, who is yet drawn to their vitality and sincerity.

Historic Pueblo Murals. Pueblo mural art has through the years continued much of its earlier symbolism and purpose. Numerous references to it are scattered through anthropological studies of the Southwest. For example, murals in a Hopi ceremonial house were described in 1886 as large figures of prey animals painted in different colors as fetishes. On the west wall was Mountain Lion; on the south, Bear; on the east, Wild Cat, surmounted by a shield enclosing a star; on the north, White Wolf; and on the east side of the wolf, a large sun symbol.[151]

Fetishistic murals were noted in 1900 in the chamber of the Hunters' Society at Zuñi.[152] There, on white gypsum-washed walls, the cougar, grey wolf, and coyote were portrayed in pursuit of elk, deer, mountain sheep, and other game. Birds of prey such as the hawk, eagle, and butcher bird were also symbolically depicted for their power in the hunt. Among other mural paintings at Zuñi were those of serpents and various quadrupeds with breath-of-life lines, sun symbols, four-point stars, and the Knife-feathered Monster, sometimes called the Eagle-winged Messenger.[153]

88

One Hopi mural was remarkable in that it was renewed periodically on the wall of a an alkibva by two women, both maids of the Mamzrauti. It depicted the male antelope, Ta-ka-tcubio, with brownish-yellow coat, traditional white throat, belly and rump markings, a red heart and breath-of-life line.[154] It was a fairly large painting, in which the animal measured thirty-three and a half inches long, eleven and a half inches from back to belly, with legs eighteen and a half inches in length. Aside from internal symbols, the figure was unusually naturalistic; much more so than even the average modern Pueblo painting of an antelope. The original mural was undoubtedly the work of certain women participants in the nine-day Mamzrauti ceremony, although ceremonial painting is understood to be exclusively the work of men.

Fewkes tells of paintings in a ceremonial chamber used by a rain priest who retired alone to a cell to pray for rain at planting time. The priest would live there sixteen days under a roof painted with meteorological symbols—white, yellow, green, and red rain clouds, zigzig lightning symbols and parallel lines of rain.[155]

Other mural examples of sky symbolism are those at Jemez and at Acoma. For Jemez, kiva paintings of the sun, moon, morning and evening stars, rainbow, lightning, rain clouds, and the horned serpent in completely abstract conception have been illustrated;[156] and at Acoma, similar kiva murals of rain symbols, various water serpents, and mask designs have been recorded.[157] In these murals, flat-painted figures, generally outlined, are rendered in a full range of earth colors on white or tan plastered walls. Motifs of stars and planets have stylized human features, and clouds follow the lines of terraces and semicircles.

Various recent observations have included murals and related depictions of animal, cosmic, or Kachina representations in ceremonial rooms at Zuñi, Acoma, Laguna, Jemez, and the Hopi and northern Rio Grande villages. At Tesuque, the tracks of the chaparral cock offered an unusual design subject.[158] At Nambé, a Kossa decorated the central post of a kiva, and a scene depicting the Kachina Mother making way for the Kachina Chief appeared in a ceremonial room.[159] Ritual wall paintings at Isleta represented water beings who rule the weather.[160] An initiation room at Acoma contained simple murals of a Koshare, sky signs, the Eagle, and the Bear.[161]

Indications in many places are that murals were made for special occasions, even were effaced after their purpose had been served,[162] while in other instances sacred murals functioned permanently and were renewed for seasonal ceremonies.[163] The act of mural painting in itself was a ceremonial rite and colors were ritually prepared.[164]

PAINTING ON CEREMONIAL OBJECTS

Paintings upon a variety of ceremonial objects from prehistoric times to the present have afforded a productive source of motif and technique for devel-

89

opment by modern painters. Each accoutrement had its particular symbolic function toward rainmaking, fertility, hunting, or healing.

Many ceremonials involved altars—painted in dry, colored substances such as sand, ochres, meal, petals, or pollen, upon the floor of the ceremonial chamber, or erected in wood or stone and embellished with brush designs.[165] Although earth altars did not contribute directly to painting techniques, they did furnish simplified, balanced motifs rendered in flat, harmonious colors, usually outlined. The dry pigments were strewn on a ground of sifted sand. Examples of such altars from the Pajarito Plateau, as reconstructed by the Museum of New Mexico, depict the Avanyu and tiered, semicircular clouds in soft colors of red, yellow, green, black and white on grounds of yellowish sand.

Earth altars of more recent days displayed similar symbolism. Some of those at Acoma represented clouds, serpents, lightning, and masks.[166] Zia designs included formally balanced cloud charms, healing charms, and those of snake symbolism.[167] At Zuñi, in the Kiva of the North, one very large circular altar some twelve feet in diameter represented twenty-four figures of the Salamobiya (Kachina personages) surrounding a sacred pool and encircled by a feathered serpent. Colors of blue, black, yellow, and red were laid upon a white ground of sand sprinkled over yellow.[168]

Hopi earth altars were elaborately developed and were present in most nine-day ceremonials. The Antelope altar showed four zigzag lightning-like serpents issuing upward from a cloud bank in colors of yellow, green, red, white, and black.[169] The Powamu sand mosaic was exceedingly beautiful with a stylized sun face radiating light and vegetation.[170] Kachinas, fields of grasses and blossoms, squash, corn, and animals with breath-of-life lines were other motifs of Hopi earth altars, all done in flat, outlined color. One of the simplest and most beautiful of Hopi earth paintings was that of large semicircular clouds and rain drawn in delicate lines of white corn meal at intervals on the trail by which the Flute priests ascended, and still ascend, the mesa from the sacred spring during the Flute Ceremony. In certain Hopi rituals, women painted earth altars.[171]

Earth paintings commonly appeared in association with upright altars which usually consisted of an arrangement of vertical boards decoratively notched and ending at the top in terraces representing clouds or tablitas of Kachina heads. Such altars were ceremonially decorated in earth-color symbols of corn, clouds, lightning, and various water-associated creatures. A predominant color of altars was malachite green, upon which designs were painted in flat stylizations, outlined with strong bands of color.

In the Hopi villages, upright altars often took the form of a small stage proscenium with other altar components such as prayersticks and sand mosaics under and in front of it. These structures were of wood, or of native cotton cloth stretched upon a wooden framework. The Niman altar at Walpi offered a striking

Figure 31. Hopi. *Water Serpents' House.* N.d., prehistoric type. Altarpiece for Palulukonti ceremony. Earth tempera on native cotton cloth. Field Museum of Natural History photograph.

example of this type in which successive tiers of painted cloud banks and lines of falling rain were flanked on either side by depictions of ornately headdressed Sun Kachinas.[172]

Indeed, painting upon cloth is old to the Hopi, who employed screens of impressive size in a number of ceremonies. One used in the dramatization of Palulukonti consisted of a heavy cotton cloth reaching from one wall to another and

91

from the floor almost to the vigas.[173] It was decorated in earth-color renderings of Kachinas, birds, clouds, lightning, rain, and sun discs in a skillfully organized composition. It was suspended by loops from a framework of poles and when not in use was rolled up and stored. A painting of comparable size was that which occupied an entire side of the Mungkibva from floor to roof as an altar screen. It was of heavy native cotton stretched upon a framework and was so ancient that its smoke-blackened colors were scarcely discernible.[174] A painted screen was also provided for the Wutzi (puppet-like figures representing Corn Maidens) play in which a corn-grinding ceremony was enacted. A smaller screen served for the Soyal Ceremony.[175] Its decorations, representing germination, were of masked figures, corn plants, sun, serpent, and seeds-in-ground.

Painted stone slabs and ceramic tiles also were used as or in connection with altars. A rectangular slab from Chevlon, painted in red, yellow, black, and white, displayed three triangles, each topped by an abstract bird.[176] This was said by Fewkes to recall "a sand mosaic such as are used in modern presentations of Hopi ritual."[177] Mortuary slabs from other prehistoric sites attested through their rain symbolism that the deceased became rainmakers. At Awatovi, among slabs bearing many fructifying designs, butterflies and dragonflies decorated some, while clouds terraced in yellow, red, white, and green, outlined in black, revealed rain motifs on the inner faces of stones, two and a half feet square, forming a box.[178] Suns, birds, and masks decorated slabs from a fourteenth-century site at Point of Pines, Arizona. Hopi tiles depicted Kokopelli, clouds, seeds, and corn, among related figures.

Prayersticks, often referred to as pahos, carried in ceremonials, interred with the dead, and erected in shrines and altars, were bearers of many expressions of water symbolism.[179] Some were simply painted with plain colors or with contrasting bandings; others took the form of small Kachinas with minutely painted little faces. The most elaborate pahos were actually wooden slabs, some more than three feet in length, which were used in certain rites. These revealed some of the best examples of pre-modern brushwork in their systematically stylized symbols of rain, corn, and various Kachinas. Corn was abstracted into crossbar areas containing dots; figures in dance attitudes were drawn with exaggerated heads, front-view masks and bodies, and side-view, dwindling legs. All paintings were broadly rendered in flat earth color, strongly outlined. Some pahos were said by the Hopi to have been hewn before the time of iron axes.[180]

Painted buckskin and buffalo hides functioned to some extent in Pueblo ceremonies. Some of these containing rain and hunting symbolism served as altars. One hide from Santa Clara shows a central, yellow sun surrounded by drawings of antelope, hunting equipment, dance tablita and staff, terraced and semicircular

92

Figure 32.   Hopi. *Telavi Kachina and Corn*. Nineteenth century. Earth tempera on wooden dance wand. The Brooklyn Museum. Cat. No. (7184).

Figure 33. Hopi. *Paiakyamu Kachina*. Nineteenth century. Painted wood kachina doll. The Brooklyn Museum Cat. No. 04.281(5525).

clouds, and a surmounting varicolored rainbow. The composition is somewhat scattered and is clearly symbolic rather than decorative. A slightly more formally composed painting upon a large hide from San Ildefonso depicts an elaborate star in the center, flanked by two tablitas, a bow and arrow, and a large golden crescent. Above these are two circle-inscribed stars and a red and black tablita. At the edges of the hide lie long groups of lines along which are strung chevron, triangular, and scrolled motifs. A buckskin used in the Hopi Lalakonta Ceremony has rain clouds painted in black and the edges fringed to represent streams of rain.[181]

Hide shields frequently show a mixture of Pueblo symbolism and Plains influence in their designs; details such as sun faces, rainbow bands, hand prints, and prey animals are Pueblo in style while the general layout suggests Plains shields. Certain Hopi ceremonial shields of unique design are fashioned of hide cut in the shape of large faces and painted with eyes and abstract facial markings representing clouds and rainbows.[182] They are adorned with feather tufts at either side to complete the mask appearance. Hides are stretched upon wood framework and painted to represent moisture tablets or sun discs, as worn in Hopi ceremonies. Ceremonial shields of the Zuñi are elaborately painted in turquoise, red, yellow, white, and black.

Ceremonial regalia bears painted symbolism in related themes. Masks of wood and hide, covering the entire head, are the most distinguishing features of certain ritual costumes. They represent a wealth of motif ranging from esoteric abstractions of cosmic features to rather naturalistic representations of life forms. Heavenly bodies and meteorological powers, giant monsters and tiny insects, the winged and earthbound and water-present creatures, the basic food plants, and purely conjured beings are typical mask subjects. Among scores of such forms are Sun in a rounded helmet from which long feathers extend outward like rays, Spider Woman with white crescent eyes painted on a black face, and white hair of raw cotton, Hummingbird with golden beak, and Chipmunk with yellow stripes; fertility bearers with clouds clustering on cheeks and corn emerging from foreheads; heads carved and colored to suggest gourds or deer or eagles; mythical faces with snapping beaks and seed-filled, goggle eyes. Bright colors of the masks are offset by black-hair bangs, crow-feather ruffs, or evergreen collars. Kachina dolls, carved of cottonwood and painted in imitation of beings represented by masks, copy the larger forms in miniature.

Symbols on tablitas, the terraced board headdresses worn in dances, carried aloft the rain symbolism in abstract sky signs, plants, and water-associated life

95

forms.* Some of these include a thirty-inch expanse of intricately designed and organized motifs brushed in flat color and outlined in contrasting tones upon blue, green, white, black, or yellow backgrounds.

A serpent is painted along the hems or on the body of cotton dance kilts worn in the Snake Dance and the Buffalo Dance. Other painted designs appear on Hopi *pota*,[183] ceremonial objects of canvaslike cotton cloth stretched on circular frames.

Rattles, drums, grinding sticks used in the Basket Dance, rain staffs, and many other ceremonial items also have painted decorations. In painting all such things, various patterns and techniques were developed to augment art practices that were to extend into a later day.

PAINTING FOR NONCEREMONIAL USE

Spanish documents testifying that Indians were "expert in the art of painting"[185] tell of houses painted on the inside.[186] Such paintings were unlikely to have been much different from those in Pueblo houses today inasmuch as the terraced and triangular dado designs in red clay, executed on light plaster on the inner walls at Mesa Verde before A.D. 1300, have close counterparts in modern Pueblo homes.

"Thousands" of painted white-cotton mantas[187] and others of painted hide were described as well.[188] Coronado in a letter to Mendoza writes of the first American Indian painting commissioned for non-Indian use:

> I commanded them to have a cloth painted for me, with all the animals that they know in that country, and although they are poor painters, they quickly painted two for me, one of animals and the other of the birds and fishes . . . the artist did not spend more than one day in painting it. I have seen other paintings on the walls of these houses which have much better proportion and are done much better.[189]

Also listed in the same shipment of gifts to the viceroy that included these paintings, are "two mantles . . . almost painted over."[190]

When missions were built, Indian artists helped to decorate them. Certain of these paintings were ceremonial in a sense, yet they may be considered rela-

---

*A circular tablita with painted rainbow design, "most likely Pueblo," together with some ninety-six ceremonial objects (circa 1698-1775) with "forms and designs motifs" suggesting similarity to earlier Puebloan examples and some late Navajo ones," were recently found in northern New Mexico.[184]

tively apart from Pueblo rituals. An example of existing work, perhaps similar to the original, is in the mission of San José de Laguna, built in 1699. Here rainbow and triangular symbols in green, yellow, red, and black decorate the altar, and mural patterns said to represent tombs are painted along the length of the room. The semicircular and terraced clouds of these paintings are wholly Indian, but the doves perched upon green sprays at intervals among the clouds are more naturalistic than usually seen in Indian art in the pueblos.

At Zuñi, the Church of Nuestra Señora de Guadalupe, built in the plaza in 1775-80, was murally decorated by Zuñi artists, who, as Frank H. Cushing said, "scrupled not to mingle many a pagan symbol of the gods and wind, rain and lightning, sunlight, storm-dark and tempest, war-bale and magic, and, more than all, emblems of their beloved goddess-virgins of corn-growing, with the bright colored Christian decorations."[191] Most pueblo churches have interior walls painted with the traditional terraced dado in red or pink earth color. At Santo Domingo, figures of horses, birds, and floral and abstract motifs stand out brightly upon the glistening white of the church portal where they are renewed and varied from time to time.

Other paintings done on buffalo hides for church decoration frequently showed a curious blending of Indian symbolism and Spanish religious art. Perhaps the oldest known of these is a painting on softened buffalo hide, "La Madre Dolorosa," done circa 1675, by a Nambé Pueblo Indian and now in the Carl S. Dentzel Collections at the Southwest Museum. The picture, representing the upper figure of a larger than life-size Madonna, is rendered in earth colors and vegetable dye of reds, indigo blue, white, and black. Although the face and hands are executed in the essentially flat, outlined manner of most Pueblo painting, the work in general reveals uncertain attempts at imitation of Spanish Colonial naturalism.

Another such painting, more characteristically Pueblo, hangs above the altar at Laguna. In it are typical Pueblo four-point morning and evening stars, rainbow, and a few terraced motifs together with non-Indian representation of such figures as sun and moon and the whole surrounded by a purely Spanish border. Bandelier in 1882 photographed one hide painting so used at Galisteo, which was done by an Indian artist in 1808 to represent Nuestra Señora de Begonia. He termed such paintings "artistically worthless," but curiously considered that they indicated "progress" over the decoration of pottery.[192] In experimenting with the strange art, the Indians apparently sought additional protection from enemies and greater assurance of abundant harvests.

97

Figure 34. MA-PE-WI, Zia Pueblo. *Zia Potters.* Ca. 1925. Gouache. Indian Arts Fund.

HISTORIC PUEBLO POTTERY PAINTING

Pottery painting traditions of the preceding centuries brought to the historic pueblos a mastery of techniques and a luxuriant reserve of styles and motifs which became intensively specialized in each of the pueblos by the time the modern school of painting began. The few specimens of pottery recovered from the earlier years of the historic period prove that design systems evolved slowly and conservatively, retaining elements and arrangements with infrequent innovations. Interpueblo borrowings have been comparatively slight in historic times and non-Indian influence in decoration negligible. It has been only within the present century that pottery has been made to a great extent for non-Indian use, but, while increasing the interpueblo borrowings of popular techniques, this fact has hardly minimized each pueblo's adherence to its own design systems and elements. Of the twenty-eight remaining pueblos, eleven still produce pottery in notable amount. Eight of these will be considered here.

Even though, until recently, most painting has been done on utility ware such as water jars, storage jars, and food bowls, its predominant purpose has been one whereby prayers for rain are rendered constantly active. Seeds, plants, water creatures, bird emissaries, lightning, clouds, and rain symbolize the motivating ideas of decoration, and they are multifariously expressed within the various pueblos. Aside from some Hopi use, the human figure, as man or supernatural, has been a negligible element in historic Pueblo ceramic art.

What has been said of interpueblo borrowings applies less to the Hopi than to any other pueblo, for trends in Hopi choice of motif have been strongly influenced by potters of other districts. Of the seven Hopi villages once making pottery, only three—Sichomovi, Walpi, and Hano—carried ceramics into modern times. Zuñi migrations brought Zuñian motifs to the first two, and eastern immigrants were responsible for the Tanoan epoch—a two-hundred-year period of Rio Grande influence—at Hano.[193] During that time, the rain and Kachina symbolism brought westward by the Tanoans dominated much of the pottery design. But in 1895 one of the principal Hano potters, Nampeyo, a Tewa woman, began to revive prehistoric Hopi motifs.[194] At that time, she and her husband, Leson, went to the archaeological camp at Sikyatki and copied designs with pencil and paper supplied by Dr. Fewkes. Thereafter, to the present day, the pre-Columbian designs and their derivations have prevailed in Hopi pottery decoration through Nampeyo's influence. Many new variations have been added in the past half century but old Sikyatki design elements—serpent, parrot, butterfly, feather, and triangle—and compositional schemes are basic in the most characteristic Hopi wares of recent times.

The pottery of Zuñi indicates long-ago influences from the Gila Valley in the free-flowing scrolls and the small animated life forms which are distributed

Figure 35. NAMPEYO, Hopi. *Fertility Design with Feather and Cloud Motifs.* Ca. 1910. Polychrome Sikyatki-type pottery olla. Indian Arts Fund. Cat. No. 410.

99

Figure 36.   Zuñi Pueblo. *Water and Plant Symbols with Scroll Patterns.* Nineteenth- or twentieth-century pottery olla. Red and Black on White. Indian Arts Fund. Cat. No. 7. Laura Gilpin photograph.

through the larger, heavier units of its black and dark-red-on-white motifs. These elements give to the designs a spontaneously facile quality even though the general compositional schemes conform to formal conventions. Schemes often take the arrangement of decorative bands about the short sloping necks of wide ollas, with one to three horizontally banded divisions below, usually cut at opposite sides by vertical panels or by rosettes. Meanders, terraced or scrolled, or repeated units of triangle-created volutes move horizontally within the bands as do figures of small chapparal cocks and ducklike fowls with long curling tails. Vertical panels contain arrangements of scrolls issuing from central rectangular or circular units. The rosettes are large, radiating multipetaled flower forms surrounded by cloud-scalloped circular borders.

Other compositions, utilizing hached forms and old textile-born elements, involve large-unit geometric motifs not confined within bands, and also a characteristically Zuñi creation, "House of the Deer," a prominent device in which a deer with white rump spot and traditional breath-of-life line from mouth to heart stands within a scroll-decorated semicircle.

Large wide bowls with boldly painted single bands, and smaller ceremonial bowls, are notable at Zuñi. The latter are low and open with cloud-terraced rims and paintings of aquatic life forms and water-associated creatures, within and without. Dragonflies, tadpoles, frogs, and feather-crested, short, fat serpents are depicted somewhat in the Hohokam and Mimbres spirit upon these vessels.

At Acoma, where graceful and intricate designs are meticulously painted in black, red, brown, orange, and yellow on grounds of bright white, the decoration is lighter, more delicate and more sedate than that of Zuñi. Survivals of numerous ancient designs are sharply hached or flatly brushed in the circular, rectangular,

Figure 37. MARY HISTIA, Acoma Pueblo. *Whirling Cloud Motifs*. 1962. Black on White, orange ochre base. Collection of Mr. and Mrs. Reginald Gregory. R. Gregory photograph.

101

or terraced-triangular units. They are arranged along horizontal bands or are repeated or alternated as space-breaking motifs around a jar, giving a classic effect. Freedom and informality of line prevail in bird and plant forms. Fat-breasted, parrot-beaked birds with flowing crests, dot-surrounded eyes, and bodies marked with abstract devices of clouds and eggs descend airily upon twigs or clouds, or alight along the undulating curves of a rainbow. The so-called Rainbird or Thunderbird, with double head and tail, elaborately ornamented body and outstretched wings, is occasionally seen on Acoma ware. Plants are painted with grace and spontaneity in full-blown blossoms, cloud-tipped leaves, rounded seed pods, and berries dotted along bending stems. Imaginative use is made also of abstract cloud and leaf motifs in repeated units of all-over patterns.

Zia's painting is strong and free, its composition of design elements perhaps the most adroit in polychrome ceramic art of the Rio Grande pueblos. The red and black patterns which conform beautifully to wide curves of the buff-slipped vessels use few straight lines, but rather the curves suggested by curvature of surface, thus producing a rhythmic sweep of movement in which the painted form and the substantial plastic form unite completely. This unity is frequently achieved through selective placing of pairs of curving or arching rainbow bands. Bodies of jars are usually treated as units above a deep red base, or as wide bands below a narrow orifice border. Blocked out areas contain horizontal volutes, cloud terraces, birds, or feather devices. Birds perch lightly upon plant stems, clouds, or feathers beneath or atop the rainbow.

Zia birds are distinctive with their frequently elongated legs, exaggerated crests upon diminutive heads, and their great alert round eyes, lifted wings, and extended tail feathers. Plants, also, are characteristic in their variously simple designs stated in emphatic brushwork. As at Acoma, berries are spaced along either side of slim stems and leaves are identified with clouds, but flowers are broadly done with single brushstrokes often indicating buds or petals. The ancient eye-in-cloud motif, and the pointed triangular cloud which occasionally becomes a leaf, are repeatedly used on Zia pottery.

At Santo Domingo, the conservatism of the pueblo is reflected in the formality of ceramic design. The geometric patterns are sedate and almost starkly classic, but their variety within narrowly dictated conventions is nothing less than amazing, as Chapman has demonstrated in his extensive study.[195] Variations upon basic motifs seem to have exceeded the ordinary inventiveness of man and to have rivaled the inexhaustible diversities of nature.

102 The decorations in black, or red and black, on cream reveal the persistence

Plate VII. RUTH WATCHMAN, Navajo. *Navajo Sun*. 1934. Design in sandpainting
style. Tempera. Collection of Dorothy Dunn.

Plate VIII. WESLEY NASH, Apache. *Gan Dancers*. 1951. Tempera. Ruth and Charles de Young Elkus Collection.

Plate IX. Unknown Sioux artist. *Sun Dance Lodge Ceremony*. Ca. 1875. Watercolor. Museum of the American Indian, Heye Foundation.

Figure 38. Zia Pueblo. *Parrot with Flowers, Clouds, and Rainbow.* Nineteenth- or twentieth-century pottery olla. Red and Black on Buff. Indian Arts Fund. Cat. No. 599. Laura Gilpin photograph.

of very old motifs. They are mainly geometric or are natural elements, such as cloud, leaf, or feather, frequently abstract in a degree which renders them geometric. In other instances plant forms approach naturalism in informal arrangement, although only slightly in styles. Lively birds and quadrupeds appear in a delightful spirit of fantasy, but they are relatively infrequent.

Schemes of composition include paneled bands on the exterior of bowls and, more rarely, circle-conforming designs within bowls; paneled bands on the outside of jars, marked off by double lines above the red base; repeated or alternate units in a single area above the base. Within the panels, elements are organized into motifs which are repeated upon verticals or diagonals in static or dynamic arrangements. Negative painting has been notably developed at Santo Domingo where, in certain designs, the usually black constructional or divisional **103**

Figure 39. Cochiti Pueblo. *Cloud Designs with Plant and Life Figures*. Nineteenth-
or twentieth-century pottery bowls. Black on Cream, red base. Indian Arts Fund. Cat.
Nos., l. to r., 735, 757, 1570. Laura Gilpin photograph.

104

lines become white spaces while the ordinarily light background areas become black geometric forms.

In the ceramic art of Cochiti there is richness of poetic philosophy such as is seldom equaled in any other pueblo. Cosmic signs and symbolic earth forms achieve a synthesis that transcends the uneven brushwork and the seeming disregard for aesthetic spatial organization. Here, the idea is always uppermost, and decorative quality often appears deliberately disregarded in order to project symbolic intention. Compositions are more likely to lack unity in a purely visual sense than to possess it; apparently unrelated forms often seem to be floating in wide space on the generous curve of an olla or on a storage jar; units placed as if to balance are frequently completely out of scale. Pigments are confined to austere black-on-white and technique often is comparatively inept. Yet, there is unity in composition through emotional content, and quality in brushline through sensitivity of rendering.

In these designs, both thunderbolts and young, tender corn leaves spring simultaneously from a cloud bank and the cumulonimbus cloud blossoms from the tassel of a matured cornstalk. Clouds and leaf sprays revolve on a swastika motif about the interior of a meal bowl. Birds wear seeds on their wings and clouds on their tails, or raindrops and corn leaves where birds of ordinary imagination wear only feathers.

Tesuque has had a fine tradition of line motif freely brushed in black upon the white backgrounds of its red or brown-based pottery, although it has been but little upheld in recent years. Buoyant meanders move briskly about the vessels in curves, frets, or zigzags, topped at intervals with sprouting trefoils and other foliage motifs, or interspersed with spontaneous units centering about a seed pod, star, or flower form. The energetically advancing lines seem to go where they will; the composition follows as predominantly line pattern, producing an effect strikingly original yet somehow related to certain ancient designs of the Pajarito Plateau.

San Ildefonso pottery designs until recently were produced in black-on-red, or black-and-red on cream white. It has been only since about 1920 that the beautiful matte-and-polished black ware introduced by Maria and Julian Martinez has become almost completely in vogue in the pueblo.

San Ildefonso pottery of all types definitely employs various motifs descended from the Pajarito Plateau. The Avanyu—horned, cloud-capped, seed or feather bearing—persists as a figure of design, as do also the seed pod and the triangular cloud, stepped or plain. The polychrome ware is particularly varied.

105

Wide encircling bandings dividing neck and body areas contain geometric designs built upon verticals, diagonals, or occasionally upon spirals in a manner very old. Other more naturalistic elements appear in motifs such as the semicircular cloud built up in a diminishing series as at Cochiti, or individually ornamented with raindrop, seed, stream, or related symbols. Clouds again appear as scalloped borders at the bounding edge of a larger band of decoration, or in leaflike points as faraway rain. The feather symbol, and birds with cloud elements continue as important designs. On the whole, San Ildefonso ceramic painting shows a command of composition and of fine brush technique. It exhibits the classic appearance of intelligently planned and carefully executed patterns commensurate with long proved standards of beauty and symbolism.

Figure 40. Maximiliana Martinez, San Ildefonso Pueblo. *Deer Design.* Ca. 1914. Polychrome pottery olla decorated by Crescencio Martinez. Collection of Richard M. Howard.

A SUMMARY OF PAINTING MATERIALS AND TECHNIQUES

Clays, sandstones, and ores were the main sources of pigments which no doubt were prepared and applied in basically the same manner as paints which have been universally used from ancient times. Color substances were separated from impurities, ground, combined with water, fat, or mucilagenous agents and applied to stone, wood, hide, bone, plaster, clay, or cloth by brushing, spraying, stippling, or other means.

Hematite, mainly, produced the warm colors—sesquioxide of iron reds and purples, and the limonite browns and yellows in ochres, sandstones, and arenaceous clays. Copper carbonate furnished malachite greens and azurite blues. Other minerals and various plants also provided hues for paints.

Color substances have appeared in prehistoric Pueblo burials,[196] were noted by Spanish explorers,[197] and reported by virtually every investigator of Southwest Indian art. Among recent records are listed:[198] black from hydrated manganese oxide, carbonized corncobs found in ruins, corn fungus, lignite, sphalerite and galena, shale, an unidentified black clay, chimney soot, charcoal, and Rocky Mountain bee plant (Peritoma serrulatum) commonly called guaco. Brown came from jarosite and dark brown from burnt lignite.

Yellow also came from jarosite, pollens, and from juices of flowers from shrubs. Red was made from sumac berries; pink "katcinas' clay" was identified as hydrated silicate of alumina. A pink stain was boiled from wheat and sunflowers, and purple was extracted from juice of stalks and husks of black corn. According to most authorities, white was supplied from kaolin and gypsum, but there are instances of other whites: marl, decomposed chalky limestone, and a satiny talc-bearing white sandstone from Acoma.

In 1933-37, experiments were made in the Santa Fe Indian School Studio with most of the earthen substances listed above and with others which have always been available to Pueblo artists.[199]

From earliest times, great importance was attached to color. Pigment was ritually procured and processed for use in rites and in painting ceremonial objects.[200] For instance, yellow and pink were collected from shores of a sacred lake near Zuñi and stored in chunks to be dispensed by head men of the pueblo as needed.[201] A certain red used at Isleta was found in a rock on Nahorai, highest peak of the Manzano Mountains, and was taken out only in necessary amounts by youths appointed by the moiety chief.[202] Fragments of ancient pigments found in burial sites were sought by the Hopi for their unusual efficacy.[203] Color grind-

107

ing was often elaborate, requiring hours of labor from specially appointed people.[204] Eagle feathers, abalone shell, coral, turquoise, and other fetishistic substances were occasionally ground with pigments.[205]

Colors were ground with stone pestles in stone mortars or on slightly hollowed stone slabs after the color-bearing substances had been pounded and soaked. Much color was used as ground, but it was also stored in balls, cakes, or powder for future use. Mixing was done in paint cups of pottery and stone and upon stone palettes, or sometimes in gourds. Such utensils dating from ancient times have been located in innumerable sites. In some cases they have been buried with the dead as offerings and still retain traces of color.[206] Attached sets of two or more globular paint pots of black-on-white or of later decoration were often quite beautifully made. Such were found in Sikyatki,[207] and at Zuñi a large group of little bowls with terraced rims were painted with aquatic forms and meander bands in the manner of larger ceremonial vessels.[208]

Vegetal pigments were usually extracted by pulverizing or boiling. Guaco black, used for painting on light-slipped pottery in the Rio Grande region, was made by boiling the entire plant until a tarlike residue could be formed into cakes.

Water was the main mixing agent for tempera paint, and to it were usually added adhesive substances which were also at times used alone. Yucca syrup[209] was combined with pigment for a glossy paint, and cows' milk[210] was sprayed onto a dry painted surface for a bright gloss. Egg binder[211] produced a typical egg tempera; eagles' eggs[212] were sometimes used. Melon or squash seeds[213] were chewed with saliva for painting masks and helmets, and piñon gum[214] was boiled and mixed with blue and green copper carbonates. The latter mixture was strained through a sieve of shredded yucca.[215] Oil paints were made by combining pigment with animal fat or oil of piñon seeds.[216]

Brushes for fine work were yucca strips chewed to shreds at one end. For covering large surfaces, such as in painting walls, a brush was made by covering the hand with a sort of glove of sheep or goatskin with the hair side out.[217] Paint was often put in the mouth and brushed with the tongue or sprayed by oral blowing.[218] The hand frequently served as a brush, or a fingertip as a pounce.[219] Stippling[220] was done by means of the frayed end of a small stick or a yucca brush, and a dark mass of color was occasionally scratched with a sharp stick.[221] Spattering was accomplished by mouth or by flinging color off a brush.[222]

In the decoration of pottery, yucca brushes were employed far more than any other instrument. Stipple, spatter, scratching, and pouncing occurred almost exclusively on Hopi pottery. Mural painting was apparently brushed. Color upon

108

hides shows the effects of having been brushed, pressed, and rubbed into the surface. Spraying and licking are mentioned mainly for surface coloring of masks and moccasins.[223]

PRECEDENTS ESTABLISHED IN PUEBLO PAINTING
PRECEDING THE MODERN SCHOOL

The styles and motifs of Pueblo painting descended from a unison of Southwest sources. Rectilinear textile designs of the early Anasazi, and life forms and curvilinear patterns of the Hohokam contributed basic elements. Assimilating features from the design perfection of the Mimbres, the geometric conventions of the Great Pueblos, and the free art adaptations and inventions of the Regressive Pueblos, these styles and motifs came into the Historic Pueblos where they were consolidated and advanced and made available to artists of the modern era.

From pure abstraction of triangular, rectangular, and terraced forms, scarcely or not at all discernible as rain symbols, the motifs evolved into ones of greater variety and objectivity through local invention and intrusive adaptations. A bird that was a triangle became a curvilinear creation with cloud-bedecked breast and tail feathers, flowing, leaflike wing, and naturalistic beak and claws. An antelope eventually changed from a rigid, angular-legged rectangle to a softly rounded form in golden coat with white spottings, an appropriate crown of pronged horns, and four realistically articulated legs. Clouds ascended from sharp-cornered terraces to successively heaped semicircles clearly harboring leaves, seeds, and droplets. Yet, with all the tendency toward greater realism, naturalism, as such, was not an objective of Pueblo painting. The style was predominantly abstract and the motif symbolic.

Simple pictographs led into the great specialization of mural painting. Mural figures were painted on large scale in a manner appropriate to wall decoration, for they were flatly rendered in completely harmonious colors in compositions usually well organized within rectangular areas.

Ceramic painting cultivated the disciplines necessary to successful composition. Division and apportionment of areas, and adaptation of lines and masses within sections, developed acute judgment in spatial disposition which was handed down in ceramic record from generation to generation. Such painting also established traditions in fine brushwork through desirability of even coverage and controlled line within limited spaces. Ceramic motif, itself, was practically inexhaustible, for its vast fund bequeathed to the modern Pueblo painter would be limited only by excavation of the last painted sherd from the Southwest field.

109

Painting upon various objects, mainly ceremonial, offered an abundance of imaginative symbolism and a diversity of techniques adaptable to modern painting. Small units of design for depiction in representations of their own settings, and motifs offering themes for experiment and improvisation, contributed elements to the new art.

Devices common to European painting were not needed in Pueblo painting where objective aspect was subordinate to vital idea. In the use of perspective, scientific laws of optics were unexplored, yet convincing spatial relationships were achieved intuitively through relative placements rather than through mechanically determined position and scale. Light and shade usually were supplanted by manipulation of contour through skillful line rendering in situations where suggestion of a third dimension was desirable. Two-dimensional rendering was adequate for most painting. Color use entailed no laws of harmony for natural palettes presented no color relationship problems; the only color restrictions were imposed by symbolic requirements.

The subjects of motif were the subjects of nature, for Pueblo painting clearly showed an art philosophy based on a realization of the relationships within nature, of a "completely living and communicable universe."[224] The corn ear sprang from the cloud and the cloud blossomed from the young leaves of corn; the dragonfly spread his wings upon the sacred meal bowl for he was consort of the spring; the bird carried a cloud in his crest for he was messenger to the sky. Painting operated as an agent for securing good for man and therefore was a necessity. It was not hung on a wall as a beautiful decoration, a display of wealth, or a sentimental record. Rather, its purpose was exemplified in a dado of cloud terraces painted along the walls in order that the fruitful clouds might be a part of the house and ever present in the family as a sort of ensurance.

Pueblo painting was totally lacking in individualistic concept. The individual was never singled out as the producer, recipient, or subject of painting. There were no portraits because the individual man was less important than the plants and animals and the powers necessary to existence which indirectly *were* man. It never would have occurred to a Pueblo artist to sign his name to a work or to be thought of as an artist. He did, however, expect remuneration for his art as a part of the general beneficence of nature toward the entire pueblo. In this respect, his painting was a religious art.

110

NAVAJO PAINTING

Until recently the Navajo have had almost no tradition in painting in its usual techniques. Their first artistic record is in pictographic form.

In and near Basketmaker sites of northeastern Arizona[225] where there are panoramas of earlier drawings, delineations of Navajo beings stand out. Even though many of them are as angular as the Basketmaker figures, these paintings have distinctions which suggest that they are Navajo. In sandpainting-type figures, certain bodily attitudes and peculiar uses of proportion are some of their identifying features. They possess formal schemata different in degree and kind from that shown in the Anasazi pictographs nearby. In apparently later works, life forms move nearer to naturalism, especially in hunting scenes of hunters and fleeing deer incised or painted upon rock walls. Horses enter the later drawings, and, in the Dinetah area, one such scene realistically portrays a man and two horses in action.[226]

Revealing groups of relatively naturalistic, Pueblo-reminiscent Navajo Yei figures have recently been studied among other pictographs dated circa 1550-1775 in the Navajo Reservoir District of northern New Mexico. One depiction of four

Figure 41. Navajo. *Beganiskidi*. Refugee period, ca. 1700. Detail from sandstone petroglyph. Cuervo Canyon, Largo Wash, northwestern New Mexico. H. L. Hadlock photograph.

Yei, painted in lively designs of geometrically ornamented kilts and full-feathered masks, appears in six colors. Other Navajo subjects include buffalo with breath-of-life line, deer, owl, abstract ceremonial designs, and planetaria.[227]

The Navajo have done painting on ceremonial objects for unknown years[228] using red, yellow, blue, black, and white mineral pigments mixed with yucca juice. They have decorated prayersticks, notched wands, and masks, somewhat in the Pueblo manner.

For example, one group of designs on prayersticks from the Shooting Chant, Prayerstick Branch, indicate the character of this art. These small surfaces incorporate motifs of nicely judged spaces and horizontal lines, zigzag lightning, deep-waved sun tracks, alternate opposing diagonals and parallels of lightning and rainbows, and repeated units composed of rectangles, arcs, and acute angles (snake houses, moon phases, and deer tracks). Another set of prayersticks from Shooting Chant, Sun's House Branch, shows symbolic serpents, lizards, and a monster, executed in formal patterns of zigzags, horizontals, cross-lines, and abstract life forms.

Such objects were painted for specific rites, but the more permanent paraphernalia, such as the Pueblo-form masks and screens were renewed with new paint from time to time. The screen of Sun's House was refurbished in much the same manner as screens of Hopi ceremonials.[229] In fact, certain Pueblo characteristics prevail in these paintings as they do in many instances throughout Navajo art and ceremony.* Yet, although Pueblo tradition may have suggested the form and technique, even some of the subject, it scarcely controls the style and seldom the intent of Navajo painting; these are distinctly Navajo.

Symbolic elements and methods of abstraction extend from such painting into modern work, but it is the sandpainting, or drypainting, which has given most enrichment to modern Navajo painting, for this art form has been more in-

---

*Kroeber compares sandpaintings, meteorological-fertilization symbolism, mythology, and legends;[230] Alexander finds Navajo borrowings from Pueblo mythology and art;[231] Fewkes mentions Hopi versions of "Man Eagle" and certain sandpaintings, ceremonial personages, and feathered rainbow;[232] Haeberlin lists faceted prayersticks, yucca suds, pollen symbolism, mask forms, and nine-day ceremonies;[233] J. and M. Stevenson cite respectively, Zuñi medicine ritual[234] and Zia erasures of sandpaintings;[235] Bandelier observes obliteration of ceremonial paintings in all pueblos except Jemez;[236] Parsons summarizes findings and includes Hopi Antelope-altar painting as like that of Shooting Chant.[237] Remote common source for sandpaintings is indicated in widespread usage from Asia to the Plains, the Southwest, and Middle America:[238] Likenesses to Navajo patterns and motifs appear in the Borgian and Fejervary Codices, the Tibetan Mandala, and in earth paintings and ceremonial murals of India.

tricately and multifariously perfected by the Navajo than by any other people. To so much as enter into a discussion of sandpainting here seems almost futile, yet the art must at least be outlined for it certainly wields an influence upon the thought, conscious or subconscious, of any serious Navajo artist of today.

The sandpainting is the visual embodiment of Navajo religion—as nearly as it is ever fixed in graphic symbols. For a few hours the painting holds, among the shifting patterns of songs and active ritual, a definitive yet ephemeral statement of the ideas which motivate the ceremonial. There could be no more living form of painting. Its light and dark lines and its colored areas stream through the fingers of the artists to lie for a brief time upon the smooth, light bed of sand on the hogan floor or, more rarely, upon a softened buckskin. In these moments it serves the patient as a seat of curing or strengthening while the chanter performs his rites, then it is gathered into a blanket and ritually returned to the wind and earth outside the ceremonial hogan. The sandpainting embodies "the spirit of Indian art," says Alice Corbin Henderson, "difficult to explain because it is so different from our modern individualistic conception of art. It belongs to a world where expression is subservient to the 'idea'—where the forms of art are never collected or hoarded as such, but the idea or image is tenaciously held and preserved through centuries."[239]

Sandpaintings are contained in their completeness only in memory by a few men of the tribe who have had the generosity, the patience, and the mental capacity to learn them bit by bit from a master chanter. Now the paintings are dying, one by one, for the press of the modern world is overwhelming them, and, if it were not for the careful recordings of a few painstaking and appreciative people, they would be lost forever. In Santa Fe, the Museum of Navajo Ceremonial Art stands as a monument to the fine art of the tribe as well as a uniquely significant contribution to the art of the world.

There are many sandpaintings—more than five hundred different ones have been recorded and no doubt many more could be, even now. They relate to a galaxy of rites which serve a complex yet basically simple religion, one which in fact has many points of counterpart in the diverse religious systems of the world.

Clyde Kluckhohn summarizes the religion as one whereby harmony within an individual and between that individual and other people or supernatural forces can be maintained or restored.[240] Gladys Reichard is led to conclude that the Navajo religion operates for universal harmony as monism rather than theism, and that Sun as a central deity is an agent of this monism who assists man to his final destiny.[241]

113

Navajo ceremonials, many of nine days' duration, are known by such group names as Holy Way, Evil Way, Life Way, Blessing Way, and, in addition, there are War and Game ceremonials, all of which are subdivided into other groupings.[242] For instance, Holy Way, said by some Navajos to be most important of all ceremonials, contains the Shooting Chant which further embraces Hail Way, Water Way, Red Ant Way, Big Star Way, and other aspects. And, in addition to the Shooting Chant, Holy Way includes the Mountain Chant, Wind Chant, and four other groups of chants. Altogether, some fifty-eight ceremonials have been classified, each containing subclassifications. Some seem to be much older than others. Pueblo influence has come strongly into the God Impersonators subgroup of Holy Way, for there are beings like Kachinas, seasonal restrictions, and numerous sandpaintings in connection with it.

Sandpainting is a vital part of many ceremonies. In a study of the Shooting Chant alone, forty-four paintings are recorded. Holy Way employs sandpaintings throughout the rituals, and, during one phase, as many as twelve paintings may be made in a single performance. Certain paintings cannot be made in summer months without being restricted. Some paintings operate to ward off evil forces and influences, while others are made to maintain favorable conditions or to heal damage done by evil agents.

The paintings are made in sets—one or two designs each day (comparatively seldom at night) during the course of a ceremonial. They are known by different names and they are of many sizes varying from twelve inches or so in diameter to fully twenty feet across. Several artists work upon a painting, and the larger designs necessitate the skill of more than a dozen men who kneel for hours at the edges of the drawing, working outward upon the sand-covered area. They smooth the background with long weaving battens and lay out straight edges of the Yei and other long figures by snapping a taut string to mark guidelines in the sand. They mentally gauge large areas and measure certain smaller spaces by palms and spans, but the composition in its entirety is fixed in the composite memory of the group from which it emerges in a manner wonderful to see. The chanter is in quiet command of the operation.

Dipping into their pine-bark trays of sand-weighted pigments, the painters precisely deposit small streams of color which flow as evenly between thumb and forefinger as sand through the neck of an hourglass. They draw figures, then clothe them according to tradition. Only in minor decorative notes, such as motifs on kilts and pouches, is personal fancy allowed free play. To rectify an error, a painter covers it over with sand and starts afresh, but mistakes are seldom made.

Figure 42. KEATS BEGAY, Navajo. *Making a Sandpainting*. Ca. 1936. Tempera. Collection of Dorothy Dunn.

The color range is almost the same as that used in Pueblo paintings. Red, yellow, and white are from pulverized sandstones or from ochres powdered and given body with plain sand. Black is of root charcoal, sometimes enlivened by minute quantities of warm colors, blue is a mixture of black and white, in reality a gray but which appears as blue in use, and less common colors such as brown and pink are also mixtures of basic colors. Grinding is done on stone metates and pigments are stored in leather pouches. Other colors, customarily used on buck- **115** skin in drypaintings, are made from pollens, meal, and pulverized petals and leaves. Colors have symbolic significance varying with use. As employed in direction, they are usually thus: white is east, blue is south, yellow is west, and black is north; blue is the zenith, also, and black and white spots the nadir. These designations differ upon occasion, with black for east and white for north. Usually, the face of the sun is blue, that of the moon, white. Abstract symbolism is also implied in certain colors, such as blue for peace and happiness; white for day, hope, and beginning.[243]

Figure 43. Navajo. *The Place of Emergence and the Four Worlds.* Pollen painting from the Blessing Chant of Bitahni Bedugai. (Reproduction by Ted Claus.) Museum of Navajo Ceremonial Art.

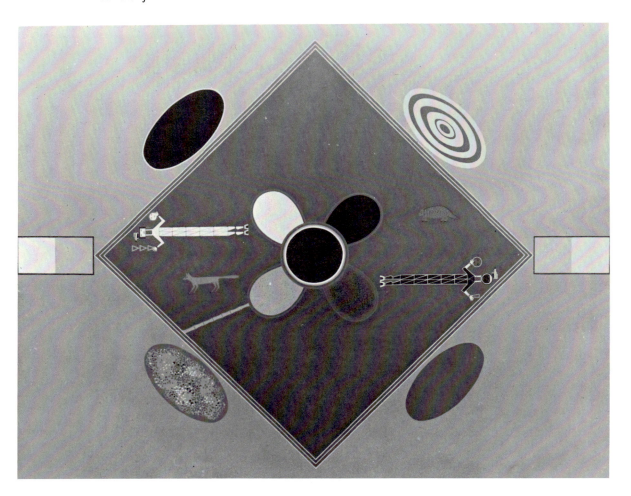

Composition of the paintings invariably satisfies the intuitive sense of order and balance. Four units about a central motif; rows of tall figures standing above a rainbow band; growing forms of plants radiating from the center; or horizontal units extending at intervals across the background are prevalent schemes. Others involve delicately rendered asymmetry and occasional all-over patterned sections filled with small forms. The whole is often encircled, save for one break, by a rainbow or a serpent. In certain designs a framing device is composed of four long serpents, arrows, or other extended motifs. Spaces seem as carefully considered as occupied areas. Particularly in balanced compositions, they are as remarkable as the positive patterns.

Elements which make up the compositions are abstract in varying degree. The tall, slim Yei, the elongated red and blue rainbow, and esoteric monsters are perhaps most abstract, while many of the animal figures are more naturalistic. A great diversity of creatures, plants, and powers appears in the paintings—bear, serpent, lizard, gila monster, weasel, bluebird, porcupine, mountain sheep, and horse are among the animals, although the horse is very uncommon. The sacred plants of corn, tobacco, bean, and squash extend in stylized pattern from long, thin roots. Thunder beings, sun, moon, stars, milky way, lightning, rainbow, seed-filled cloud, mountains, sacred pools, Mother Earth and Father Sky, the Female Rain and the Male Rain are prominent subjects. Relative prominence of figures is determined by the immediate intent of certain paintings—whether to heal, to ensure rain, to ward off enemies, or some other purpose.

Of seven large pollen paintings used in the Blessing Chant of Bitahni Bedugai, the last symbolizes "The Place of Emergence and the Four Worlds." The worlds radiate in varicolored oval forms from the central black circle of emergence. A rainbow-bordered blue square represents the great floodwaters of the time. Sun, in blue mask, and Moon, in white, preside at east and west while naturalistic Coyote and Badger seem almost intrusive in this purely abstract company. Towering above the flood are the Four Holy Mountains and the oppositely located houses of White Shell Woman and her sister, Changing Woman, two principals of the Navajo Creation Myth.

The sandpainting holds in its richly productive systems of design and abstract symbolism potentials for far greater contributions to modern Navajo art than have usually been recognized. Through the sandpainting, Navajo medicine men have presented forms and ideas which have meanings far beyond the confines of their reservation. Such meanings await only to be called forth in a manner appropriate to more extended appreciation to become a delight to many. Attempts **117** to fix the evanescent quality of the sandpainting in permanent media might seldom advance beyond ethnological importance, but an imaginative incorporation of Navajo motifs of universal significance, as well as those of obscure abstraction, in new and enduring form could offer much to creative art.

APACHE PAINTING

Early Apache painting has left few records, but these are symbolic ones, rich in meaning. Apache symbolism is primarily of the sun, with the moon, stars, lightning, winds, fire, water, and lesser characters such as serpents and centipedes ranking in importance. Drawing is angular in the main with only such obvious curves as those of sun, moon, rainbow, and wheellike motifs. It is an art of dynamic, jagged motion, more dissonant than harmonious. It lacks the order of Pueblo ceramic painting or the organization of Navajo sandpainting, but it has a remarkable system of its own which can be defined only as Apache in its aliveness, restlessness, and its authoritative, forceful quality. It is an art which declares that it is related to the angular motifs of basketry but even more so to the angular patterns of the Apache dance.

Few Apache pictographs have been identified, but some of them identify themselves through their unmistakable tribal characteristics. One such group is to be found in the Guadalupe Mountains of southeastern New Mexico where designs have been pecked and painted. These are of sun symbols, masks, angular life figures, serrated borders, and geometric forms. The back of one cave in Slaughter Canyon is covered from floor to ceiling with pictographic paintings, many of which are of obvious Apache origin. Another such gallery is in Boardtree Canyon. H.P. Mera, who first investigated these sites, remarked that the pictographs in this area are unlike, save for casual similarities, those associated with Basketmaker and Pueblo sites, but implied that they are prehistoric.[244] Colors of the paintings are the usual range of ochres, black, white, and one instance of green. Crumbling remnants of pigments were found at several of the sites.

Among hundreds of pictographs recorded and exactly sited by Herbert W. Yeo in south-central New Mexico, some are strongly Apache in appearance.[245] These are mostly petroglyphs, but others are painted in red, red-orange, and gray in forms of suns, stars, masked figures, rows of triangles, and zigzag meanders.

Apache designs have been added to those of the Anasazi in numerous sites of the latter. Ceremonial figures with sharp-pointed headdresses, rainbows with top

118

Plate X. Big Lefthanded, Navajo. *Feather Dance*. 1905-1912. Tempera on mummy cloth. Katherine Harvey Collection, Museum of Northern Arizona.

Plate XI. KYLESDEWA, Zuñi Pueblo. *Helele.* Ca. 1920. Watercolor. Museum of New Mexico.

arc serrated, suns with deep sawtooth rays, wind crosses and the like mark them for Apache among the works of others. In one group of pictographs near Zuñi,[246] both Apache and Navajo characters are distinguishable.

A curious resemblance exists between such Apache drawings and certain pictographs in California. From Mallery's reports,[247] starting in 1896, to the findings of current investigations, basic contacts or influences of some sort clearly seem indicated in the two arts.

Something of the impressive nature and extent of the Far Western pictographs is now being disclosed by Campbell Grant, of the Santa Barbara Museum of Natural History, and Charles La Monk, of the Southwest Museum, Los Angeles, whose reproductions of some of these works are among the most exciting views of prehistoric American art recently offered.

These studies reveal a profusion of abstract designs, many painted or drawn in earth yellows, reds, blues, and greens, depicting angular humanoid figures, serpentine and centipede-like creatures, long denticulate and serrated constructions, suns, concentrics, pinwheels radiating like fireworks, and a galaxy of fantastic characters. Apparent Apache reflections of many details of this art are sharpened by the fact that Grant's studies, sans comparisons, point to ethnographic evidence of comparable puberty rites and sandpaintings among tribes once dwelling in certain pictograph locales of California.

Apache traditions and myths are like those of the Navajo in instances, and in some respects similar to those of the Pueblos.[248] The Apache also make sandpaintings, and paint designs upon objects employed in ceremonials by mythological personages.

Elaborate headdresses are painted for the Gan.* These godlike figures, comparable in general concept to Navajo Yei and Pueblo Kachinas, are principally water beings, having powers over springs and streams. They appear in various ceremonials, especially puberty rites, wearing high fantastic headdresses of symbolically notched wooden slats shaped in large fan forms, or tall verticals ending in points above a horizontal base. Styles vary with groups. They are usually painted white with characteristic Apache symbols in strong colors of red, yellow, blue, black, and orange. Wands and staffs are similarly painted.

Paintings decorate other wooden objects such as drums, flutes, and tall cylindrical fiddles. Colors are flat and usually outlined. Primary colors and black occur most often on grounds of white, yellow, or natural shades. Symbols seem

*Called Kan or Ghost Dancers by Bourke,[249] and popularly known as Crown Dancers, Devil Dancers, Mountain Spirits, or Fire Dancers.

120 Figure 44. Apache. *Suns and Ceremonial Personages*. Late nineteenth century. Painted deerskin. Arizona. Smithsonian Institution. Cat. No. 395,563.

painted for definite purpose rather than for aesthetic compositional effect in any ordinary sense, yet each whole scheme is usually one of arresting design.

Sandpaintings, although on a much simpler scale in every respect as compared with the Navajo, accompany certain Apache ceremonials. During mid-September races of the Jicarillas, a sandpainting is made within a leafy cottonwood bower, and the racers themselves are painted with earth-color symbols. In connection with Jicarilla healing rites, sandpaintings with abstract animal motifs are made on the floor of the ceremonial tipi. Sun, moon, cross-of-the-four-winds, serpent, and lightning symbols, and figures representing mythical beings also occur in various sandpaintings. A sandpainting is drawn each day during the Jicarilla Bear Dance, a curing rite for those who suffer from "bear or snake sickness," [250] and figures symbolic of the deities of the tribe are drawn upon the sand by medicine men of the Arizona Apache. [251]

Paintings in oil or watercolor on hides appear to have been formerly very important for they are described in early records. [252] A few examples on small hides remain from the late nineteenth century, and others have been made since that time. These are mostly upon buckskin in flat, outlined colors of blue, yellow, red, orange, green, and black. They depict Gan and other beings, the symbols of sun, lightning, rainbow, wind cross, birds, feathers, and insect personages such as centipedes and butterfly caterpillars. The designs, like those of the sandpaintings, reveal Navajo and Pueblo similarities in certain larger concepts. Painted hides showing such motifs often served as garments in medicine rites or as "mantles of invisibility" in fortifying the wearers against enemies. [253] Ceremonial deerskin boots and caps also bear typical painted designs, as do leather medicine sashes and hide shields.

Several good specimens of paintings on deerskins from the western Apache depict Gan wearing customary headdresses. One shows the Gan flanked on either side by a row of four crosses, raindrops and lightning borders, while he carries two radiating suns in the center of his body. Four Gan on another hide stand at four points around a central sun. Other figures of these hides are corn ears, very abstract birds, a serpent with breath-of-life line, and serpentine beings suggestive of fire or lightning. Contours are impressed in firm, dark lines which are filled in with hematite reds, ochre and brighter yellows, dark blue, and black, with some areas appearing as if sized.

More naturalism occurs on later hides. One rather literal interpretation of the Gan in an initiation dance, is painted in pink, blue, yellow, and black color, apparently water based, on doeskin.

121

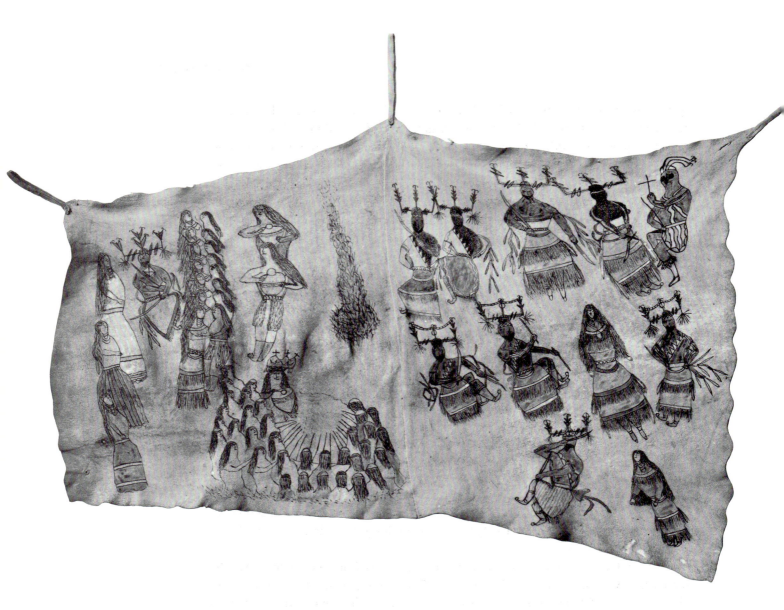

Figure 45. Apache. *Initiation Ceremony*. Nineteenth century. Painted doeskin. Smithsonian Institution. Cat. No. 270,076.

The peculiar symbols of this art, in both their vivid quality and their characteristic style, have much to add to modern Apache painting. In large adaptations they offer abstractions of unique interest, while in small forms they furnish intriguing notes of miniature decoration to more representational scenes.

HISTORICAL BACKGROUND

The Plains Indian, as popularly known, is not the Plains Indian of actuality. Only the closing chapters of Plains history are those generally recorded, and they have been greatly exaggerated and romanticized. The Plains Indian of late historic times has been the Indian of folklore and fiction, of the textbook, of song and drama, and the inevitable caricature to the extent that he has become the stereotype of *the* American Indian, the "Noble Redman," at home and abroad. The wars, the buffalo, the tipis, the vivid figures in streaming warbonnets, the dashing rides on the wide-open prairies have combined to present a singular attraction in vicarious freedom and bravery and adventure that has had a wide appeal.

Yet, the characterization thus revealed is a much distorted one, for its portrayal of Plains life includes but a brief episode in the whole long drama of the vast area of grass-covered, rolling prairie lying east of the Rocky Mountains from lower Canada southward into Texas.

In reality, countless bands and tribes moved through and within the Plains region for thousands of years before the white man came. The historic Plains cultures are relatively superficial in comparison to those that have gone before.[1] In fact, the traits with historic depth within many of the known Plains cultures seem Woodland, dating from a time when such Plains culture as there was existed as a margin at the fringe of the area. The almost exotic culture, superimposed upon that immediately preceding the Conquest, which evolved during the last tragic scenes of Plains history, was instigated largely by the European invader. His in-

4. The Plains

truding horses and firearms provided the artificial stimulus to a quick brilliance of culture upon the Plains which was all too soon followed by a sudden blackout.

In searching for clues as to what actually happened in this immense and challenging region, we find that the Spanish Conquistadores, the early explorers and traders, and the western pioneers left various records of their transient views of the Plains, but that only recently have archaeologists begun to unearth fragments of bygone cultures which are contributing to a basis for scientfic study of the area.

Three main periods of Plains history shape roughly from the studies so far. Consideration has already been given the early bison and mammoth hunters who scattered their distinctive projectile points when they occupied the area in remote ages. Many of their habits of life may have been perpetuated by the succeeding buffalo hunters up to the time of the Spanish arrival; however, there is no way of knowing whether the area was occupied continuously or only intermittently by nomadic hunters during its long prehorticultural history.

Investigations such as those of W. D. Strong and W. R. Wedel show that much later than the early hunters, but before the Conquest, a second type of life, in addition to purely hunting cultures, became prevalent in some sections of the Plains.[2] This life was manifested in a series of horticultural pottery-making and semihunting cultures.

One of the archaic groups of the central Plains appears to have been Algonquian of Northeastern affiliation. Overlaying this are such early cultures as the Nebraska and the Republican with characteristics of the southeast Woodland

Figure 46.   Unknown Sioux artist. *Mythical Thunder Bird*. Ca. 1876. From battlefield in Little Big Horn area, Montana. Watercolor on duck canvas. West Point Museum. No. D-7424.

area evident in ceramic forms, effigy heads, symbolic designs, and Gulf shell artifacts.[3] * Various succeeding groups led a fairly sedentary life in earth-covered pithouse villages and other settlements mostly along the Missouri River and its tributaries. Although hunting continued to provide a part of their livelihood, these

* Recent studies corroborate early Plains evidence of Southeastern influences including that of the "Southern Cult" (p. 15) which "spread not only to [other Eastern areas but to] peoples dwelling beyond the Mississippian cultural frontier, and as discrete elements far out into the Plains."[4]

people cultivated corn, beans, and squash, and, in general showed characteristics more typical of eastern areas.

The Spaniards saw the last of this old order upon the Plains, for the third period of Plains cultural history began fairly soon after the arrival of Coronado in 1541. Journeying up from the Tiguex villages of the Pueblo country in search of the fabled settlements, the Conquistadores found both nomadic hunters and semi-sedentary villagers in the Plains.

The hunters, roving at large, whom the Spaniards called Querechos and Teyas, may have been the Plains Apache and Shoshoneans.[5] The account to Mendoza, the Viceroy, describes them thus:

> The Indians are numerous in all that land. They live in rancherias in the hide tents. . . . They always follow the cattle, and in their pursuit they are as well sheltered in their tents as they could be in any house. They eat meat almost raw, and much tallow and suet which serves them as bread, and with a chunk of meat in one hand and a piece of tallow in the other, they bite first on one and then on the other, and grow up magnificently strong and courageous. Their weapons consist of flint and very large bows. . . . They kill them (the cattle) at the very first shot with the greatest skill. . . .[6]

The account also describes the dog travois, "great trains of them used by the *vaqueros* in hauling their belongings from one hunting site to another."[7] The nomadic existence is further remarked upon by Castañeda:

> These folks live in tents made of the tanned skins of the cows. They travel around near the cows, killing them for food. . . . They do not make gourds, nor sow corn, nor eat bread, but instead raw meat—or only half cooked—and fruit.[8]

Castañeda was greatly impressed with the vast herds, saying that the amount of the cows "already seemed something incredible" and that in twenty leagues one saw "nothing but cows and the sky."[9]

Villagrá, too gives an account of the hunters:

> The men also saw in these regions many of the vaqueros who inhabit these regions and who hunt those cattle on foot. They are well-built, intelligent people who live in tents made of the skins of the buffalo. So skilled are they in the art of tanning, that even after these skins have become wet they dry as soft as linen or fine Holland cloth.[10]

This is the type of life which was no doubt already very old upon the Plains by the time the Conquistadores arrived, and how far beyond the bounds of the Spanish adventures it extended, no one can say.

127

Eastward in the Plains, the Spaniards found Caddoan peoples living in flourishing villages in 1541. Researchers indicate that Coronado's Quivira[11] was in central and eastern Kansas and its inhabitants were the Wichita,[12] while his Harahey, to the north in Nebraska, was the home of the Pawnee.[13] These and other village dwellers raised corn and various crops along the river valleys. "They had plenty of kidney beans and prunes like those of Castile, and tall vineyards," according to Castañeda.[14] They made pottery, tanned hides and painted designs upon them with bone brushes.[15] Members from these eastern settlements moved westward along the rivers hunting the buffalo, returning seasonally to their permanent homes or banding together to found more western and northern villages. Thus, for example, "the Arikara of today were probably the Pawnee of yesterday, who in turn disappeared into the riddle of Caddoan origins in the Southeast,"[16] while the north-dwelling Mandan and Hidatsa were among the Siouan peoples who apparently moved up and down the Missouri River for many centuries before the dawn of history in the region.[17]

Figure 47. Unknown Cheyenne artist. *Buffalo Hunt,* detail. Ca. 1890. Watercolor on muslin. Livermore Collection, Denver Art Musem. Cat. No. JL-3/PS-35-G.

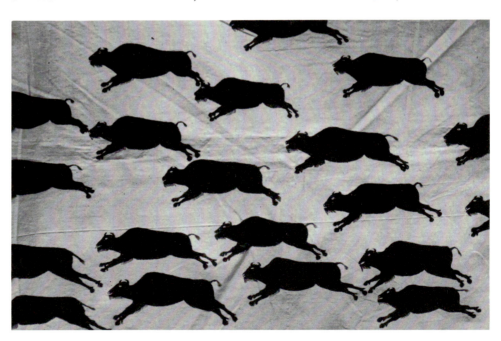

128

In Castañeda's account there is found what might be a hint of early traffic between the Plains and the Southeast, of which these movements may have been the westward extension:

> That they [the Querechos] were very intelligent is evident from the fact that although they conversed by means of signs they made themselves understood so well that there was no need of an interpreter. They said that there was a very large river over toward where the sun came from and that one could go along this river through an inhabited region for ninety days without a break from settlement to settlement. They said that the first of these settlements was called Haxa, and that the river was more than a league wide and that there were many canoes on it.[18]

Soon after these first Spanish observations, the Plains scene began to change. Within the next century after the Conquest, horses in increasing numbers came into this natural grassland habitat and were taken over by Indian hands.[19] A new Plains culture began to emerge at a rapid rate. The dog-traveling hunters, with slight modification of equipment, hitched horses to larger travois, mounted others and began to widen their range. Some of the village tribes either took over the horse and became nomads themselves or were pushed further and further north by the horsemen. Long before 1700 most of the tribes then in the Plains were mounted.[20] There was "turmoil and strife" accompanied by extensive tribal dislocations and cultural readjustments which continued beyond the middle of the eighteenth century.[21]

The Sioux,* the Cheyenne, and the Arapaho, three of the most typical tribes of late Plains history, were comparative latecomers to the Western scene. They had been horticultural Woodland people dwelling in the central Minnesota area prior to their entrance upon the Plains.[22] Their movement out of this location to the Missouri River during the late seventeenth and forepart of the eighteenth century seems to have been caused by the Chippewa, Cree, and Ojibwa who had obtained firearms from the French traders.[23] The Sioux, however, maintained ties to their Minnesota home, as late as 1797 claiming land as far as Sandy Lake.[24]

---

* More properly Dakota ("friends" or "allies"), largest division of the Siouan family. The name Sioux, used by early voyagers and trappers, originated in the Algonquian and Ojibwa *Nadowessi* ("rattlesnake," "enemy," "hated foe"), pluralized *Nadowessioux* by the French. Jesuit missionaries used "*Nadouessi*" as early as 1632.[25]

The name Sioux,[26] approved by Gallatin in 1836, as used here refers to the Dakota, one of Dorsey's eleven and of Wissler's sixteen divisions of the Siouan linguistic family. Other Siouan tribes are designated by name best known, such as Mandan, Crow, Omaha ("against the current; upstream").

129

The Sioux had agricultural traditions that reached back to a much earlier time than when Duluth, in 1678, and Hennepin, in 1680, found settlements of them farming in the Mille Lacs region of Minnesota.[27] They and other members of a large Siouan family apparently had lived in and around the Mississippi Valley from prehistoric times. Their combined population made it the second largest stock north of Mexico, being exceeded only by the Algonquian.[28]

Several investigators have engaged in tracing connections and the early locations of the Siouan peoples.[29] Through studies of dialects, it appears that there were, at the time of the European arrival, two large and two small areas of Siouan occupation.[30] The first large area lay along the eastern skirts of the Appalachians, between them and the Atlantic coast from the falls of the Potomac to the Santee River in South Carolina. The De Soto and Pardo documents reveal that Siouans once occupied all the present territory of South Carolina, and place names show that they also lived in parts of North Carolina and Virginia.[31] The first contact between Siouans and Europeans goes back to 1521 when two Spanish vessels touched upon the coast of South Carolina.[32]

The second large body covered the vast extent of country west of the Mississippi, reaching south to the mouth of the Arkansas River and north to the Saskatchewan. The Winnebago, first encountered by Nicollet in 1634 near Green Bay, Wisconsin, were cut off from the main body of the western Sioux only in late times.[33] The two smaller areas of Siouans were located around Biloxi and the Yazoo River in the present state of Mississippi. The language of the Tutelo and Biloxi of this region was found to be most related to that of the Sioux of the Plains and to be the older language in form.[34]

Of these four areas, John R. Swanton and Roland B. Dixon say that "the several Siouan groups suggest in their situations a broken semi-circle and it is therefore not surprising to find that their traditions point to a central region within this."[35] They include in this traditional region Illinois, Indiana, Southern Wisconsin, and Western Kentucky. A part of this area is that occupied in early times by people responsible for the Oneota phase of Mississippi Valley culture which is beginning to be correlated with that of the Chiwere Sioux.[36]

Other studies have advanced the idea that there had been an old common homeland of the Siouan groups in the central region and have tended to extend "the domain of the Siouan tribes of the east farther west and that of the Siouan tribes of the west farther east at a not remote period."[37]

Some investigators have located Siouans in the Ohio Valley at one time,[38] and one has gone so far as to associate "the majority of the great earthworks" in southern Ohio and northern Kentucky with Siouan peoples.[39] In relation to this, it might be noted that unidentified tribes raised burial mounds in the Baldhill area of North Dakota, some containing fragments of painted bison skull, also bone and stone tools daubed with red ochre.[40] Initial explorations of Dakota mounds have yielded ceramics, effigy pipes, and birch and copper work such as associated with eastern mounds.[41] Effigy mounds are "abundant in North Dakota."[42]

After the arrival of Europeans, firearms were apparently the main cause of the westward migration of the Sioux. The Five Nations of the Iroquois had become warring and powerful after they had obtained firearms from the Dutch around 1650, and they had stalked westward, "killing and devastating" almost to the Mississippi.[43] They have been called "pitiless destroyers" who were the "great agents in the expulsion and extermination of the eastern Siouan tribes."[44]

The withdrawal of the buffalo from the eastern range seems to have had little to do with the westward movement of the tribes as has sometimes been suggested. Buffalo were in the Piedmont region as late as 1730 and in Ohio and Tennessee until after the close of the French and Indian wars.[45] The agriculturists of the East had never depended upon the buffalo to any great extent.

When the Sioux who had settled in Minnesota were driven out by their better-armed neighbors, they moved southward across the Missouri. Entering the Plains, they soon forsook their pursuits and adopted the horse and the life of the nomad hunter-warrior. Certain of their fundamental traditions remained on in ceremonial life and social relationships, but the forceful, upsetting aspects of their new life finally obscured most of the old ways.[46]

Less is known of the pre-Plains history of the Cheyenne and Arapaho who are of the great Algonquian family of the northeast, although their own extensive origin traditions of wanderings from a "cold country in the north and northeast" are recorded.[47] It seems that these tribes, like the Sioux, had in later times established villages in the northern Mississippi Valley where they first came in contact with the French in 1656. There they had engaged in the pursuits of horticultural pottery makers until they were intruded upon by the Cree and other enemies armed with European guns. They had been pushed out of their earth-lodge settlements into the Plains ahead of the Sioux.[48]

For a time they underwent a transition period in which they built villages along the Missouri, Platte, Hart, and Cheyenne rivers wherein they pursued their old customs with modification.[49] Excavations have revealed marks of the older Cheyenne culture such as earth lodges, grain caches, and pottery, and of the contact phase, including horse bones and articles of European manufacture.[50] But **131**

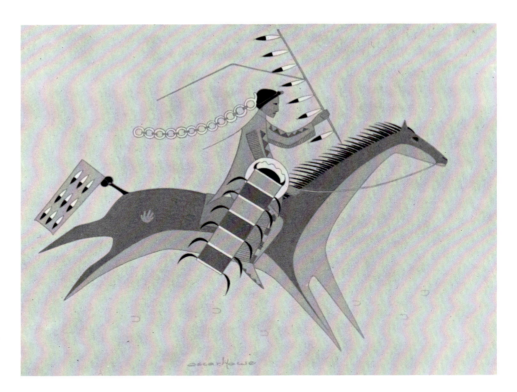

Figure 48.   Oscar Howe, Sioux. *Sioux Rider.* 1959. Tempera. Joslyn Art Museum Collection.

the last of their villages appear to have been abandoned by 1780.[51] They had been terrorized by the warring Sioux, and plagued by the smallpox epidemics which swept the Plains in 1772 and 1780.

Within a century the Cheyenne and Arapaho had completely abandoned the sedentary life, and had replaced it with that of nomadic, predatory hunters. They had adopted the tipi, the horse and travois, and roamed westward to the Rockies. They and the Sioux had intermittent wars until they made a final peace in 1840-41.[52]

Toward the close of the eighteenth century, bands of Cheyenne and Sioux tribes met the Kiowa in the Black Hills and drove them out. The Black Hills had been the Kiowa home when the tribe was first encountered by Europeans in 1732.[53] They had come into that location from their traditional home at the headwaters of the Yellowstone and the Missouri rivers. Beyond this old home, their traditions and calendar histories do not extend, but indications are that their affiliation was with peoples west of the Rocky Mountains rather than with those eastward. The Kiowa are classified as belonging to the Shoshone branch of the Uto-Aztecan family and are said to have lived just west of the Black Hills in the seventeenth century.[54]

According to James Mooney's map, Lewis and Clark found the tribe in eastern Wyoming in 1805.[55] A few years later the Kiowa were in Colorado near what is now the Fort Lupton region where they lived along the Platte for a time, then they gradually pushed southward across the Cimarron into Oklahoma which has been their home country since 1832. They traded extensively with the Pueblo Indians while raiding others as far south as Durango in Mexico.[56]

Thus, insofar as is known, the principal Plains tribes of this study—the Sioux, the Cheyenne, the Arapaho, and the Kiowa entered the historical scene in the Plains. They were four of the several tribes which combined to produce the most spectacular phase of American Indian history.

The heyday of the historic Plains occurred in the brief, vivid years between the advent of the horse and the time when white settlers began to arrive in such numbers as to really make their presence felt. This was roughly a period of three

Figure 49. WILMER DUPREE, Sioux. *Buffalo Calling*. 1935. Tempera. Margretta S. Dietrich Collection.

hundred years for the Plains as a whole; considerably less than that for certain tribes. This span of time comprised what Clark Wissler called the "Horse Culture Period,"[57] and during it there evolved the over-all pattern of Plains culture that is so well known, but which we shall investigate here from the standpoint of its bearing upon the development of Plains painting.

Although the horse accelerated and intensified the nomadic life of the Plains Indians, the great buffalo herds constituted the core of these people's independent existence. The buffalo was the dominant common interest of the various Plains tribes, and it furnished all their major material needs—meat for food, hides for tipis, robes, and receptacles, and materials for many other necessities.

Most tribes had ceremonies for calling the buffalo, and for organizing and conducting communal hunts. The latter usually took the form of a surround wherein many hunters on swift horses under the direction of skilled leaders would ride round the herd, bunching animals up and shooting them one by one. Sometimes the impounding would be accomplished by encircling the herds with grass fires. Hunters occasionally disguised themselves as buffalo by covering their bodies with robes and manes when they wanted to approach individual animals. Buffalo dances were thought to entice game.

Supplementing the buffalo, there were other common economic interests of the Plains tribes. All sought the lesser game—elk, deer, rabbits, waterfowl, and the natural vegetal foods—plums, cherries, wild berries, seeds, roots, and bulbs. Clothing, cut and fitted from skins of bear and elk was worn by each tribe and was decorated somewhat the same with fringes and quills or beads, teeth or shells. The most desired possessions were horses, the "ancient sacred dogs,"[58] for they were the means to many coveted ends. Horse stealing was an honorable pursuit and

Figure 50.   Unknown Sioux artist. *Running Battle for Horses,* detail. Ca. 1870. Watercolor on muslin. Smithsonian Institution. Cat. No. 345,994.   **135**

one of the principal causes of warfare between tribes.[59] Contests for ownership of the wild herds as well as outright thieving took place between rival camps.

Principles of manly rivalry, bravery, and self-sacrifice governed warfare throughout the Plains. "The willingness to risk life for the welfare or honor of the people was the highest test of character."[60] In warfare, it was usually the touching, not the killing or scalping, of an enemy which was deserving of the highest honor of battle. Warriors carried long poles with crooked ends, the coup sticks, with which they counted coup upon their victims by striking them.

Rudolph Kurz, a native of Bern and an early artist-traveler in the Plains, observes that:

> to kill an enemy from a distance bespeaks no courage, is not regarded as the deed of a hero, is not accredited as a "coup"; on the other hand, to strike down a foe in hand-to-hand combat requires force, skill, bravery, and cunning.[61]

He says that a scalp was taken only as proof of combat when there were no witnesses, but that the hero must have touched the fallen enemy with either his hand or his weapon. The practice is believed to have held from the time of hand-to-hand combat before the advent of missiles.[62] Danger and difficulty were regarded above the amount of damage inflicted upon the enemy. Taking articles such as warbonnets or weapons from an enemy was also considered an honorable deed.

Among other honors of distinction was the ability and willingness to give material possessions to others.[63] A man was not so much respected for the number of objects he owned as for those which he bestowed upon others. Giveaway ceremonies were tribal occasions of great interest wherein one member would try to outdo another in the amount of horses and goods he gave to the less fortunate members of the group. He "who wishes to be exalted among his people must be liberal."[64]

Out of the hierarchy of deed honors there arose a sort of heraldry which was one of the principal sources of Plains art. The warbonnet was indicative of social rank, and the eagle feathers, buckskin strips, beads, horns, and other materials of which it was made were symbolic. Elaborate ceremony attended its making. Regardless of rank, no man might make or purchase his own warbonnet for it was made by fellow tribesmen.[65] Maximilian, said of the warbonnet:

> If a warrior is distinguished by many deeds, he has a right to wear the great feather-cap, with ox-horns . . . This cap composed of eagle's feathers, which are fastened to a long strip of red cloth, hanging down the back, is highly valued by all tribes on the Missouri . . . .[66]

He told also of the exploits which merited the horizontal feather and the upright feather worn in the hair. One was allowed to wear an eagle feather for each heroic deed: "Porter les plumes parcequ'il compte coup."[67]

One might also have symbols of his feats of generosity and bravery emblazoned upon his robe, ceremonial shirt, tipi, shield, or even upon his horse. Honor names were conferred for certain exploits. These distinctions could not be gained unjustly or by favoritism. All deeds had to be proved by witnesses before the council of war chiefs. A man was in disgrace if he sought to display insignia which he had not justly won. Catlin gives an account of this strict code.

> . . . in this country where, of all countries I ever was in, men are the most jealous of rank and standing; and . . . every man's deeds of honour and chivalry are familiarly known to all; it would not be reputable, or even safe to life, for a warrior to wear upon his back the representations of battles he never had fought; professing to have done what every child in the village would know he had never done.[68]

Tribal organization, ceremonial beliefs, and practices differed with tribes, although a few were held more or less in common. Tribes were organized into societies, clans, and gens, with each group being responsible for order within itself. A camp circle in which there was designation of location of tribal tipis was usually observed. The principal Plains deities were encompassed in Wakan tanka, Wakanda, or its equivalent.[69] Such names were given to the idea that all life is one and related, that man's physical existence is sustained by natural forces pervading the universe, and by other forms of life. Wakanda assumed many different forms, for it was a quality rather than a definite entity. The sun, moon, stars, winds, the cedar tree, the eagle, even a man, especially a shaman, might be Wakanda. Manifestation of the sacred power might be through so small a token as a bird feather, symbolizing the winged communion between man and unseen powers, or it might be through a vision. Thus, there was no supreme overruling and decidedly personal being among the observers of Wakanda. It assumed any form or action by which man's spirit and power might be supplemented.

Among the Sioux there were "the great sacred ones"—the sun, sky, earth, and rock as high-ranking deities; moon, wind, and the winged-one, the mediators, next in rank; then the inferior beings such as buffalo, bear, elk, and so on through many life forms.[70] Fire, thunder, and the morning star were important deities among certain tribes.[71] The agricultural Pawnee and Mandan gave the Corn Mother a prominent place, and the Omaha, one of the Siouan tribes, continued

137

Figure 51. Sioux. *Battle Scene*. Before 1876. Oil on buffalo hide. Musée de l'Homme, Paris.

to honor corn in ceremony, song, and legend after the tribe became predominantly a hunting one.[72] The use of earth altars and of sacred bundles, usually containing corn, which persisted in some tribes evidenced an underlying adherence to older religious beliefs and practices.

Of all the sacred ceremonials which were perfected during the period in the Plains, the Sun Dance was the outstanding one. It was performed annually in all but a few tribes. The Sioux, Kiowa, Cheyenne, and Arapaho all held Sun Dances. Although most interpretations of the dance included an apparent torture element, they were focused in dramatic ceremonies performed by several men around a central pole within a leafy enclosure, the Sun Dance lodge.

The time was in summer. The Kiowa celebrated their dance, the Kado, "when the down appears on the cottonwoods,"[73] and the Cheyenne theirs, the New Life, "when the grass has reached its full growth."[74] The exact time varied with tribes.

The Mystery Tree from which the dance pole was to be made was sought as an enemy and ceremonially felled, stripped, dragged in a procession to the dance site, and erected there by distinguished tribesmen. In its top fork were placed sacred bundles, offerings of cloth; buffalo, human, and bird symbols, and gifts to the sun.[75] Earth altars were prepared, songs rehearsed, and ceremonial articles painted.[76]

The dancers, after months of ritual preparation through fasting, smoking, sweat baths, rubbing with wild sage, and other rites, were made ready in most observances by having their bodies painted and thongs laced through the flesh of their chests for fastening themselves to the pole. Then they danced, gazing at the sun, until the skin gave way. The Kiowa observance had no torture, since they considered it to be an evil omen.[77] Those who participated in the dance did so in fulfillment of commitments made during a period of anxiety, usually when in battle;[78] others may have taken vows to pray to Wakanda.[79] In any case, it was a great honor to be a participant, and there was no thought of pain or martyrdom but rather a zealous generosity toward the entire tribe in the attitude of the dancers. Even though there were comparatively few dancers, scores of persons took part in the preliminary and attendant ceremonies, and hundreds more were observers in the great encampment. It was a time during which alliances and agreements were made with visiting tribes.

In the Cheyenne Sun Dance, paints and painting were important throughout the ritual.[80] Paint was "symbolic of the earth," and all colors were symbolic, as suggested in their names of cyclone paint, dream paint, hail paint, and the like. Drypaintings of sand were part of the earth altar, and there were many patterns of body painting in which the hand was used as both palette and brush, or by other means such as patterning a pink-painted body by slapping all over with young willow boughs dipped in contrasting paint.[81]

There is variance in regard to the meaning of the Sun Dance. According to Red Bird, a Teton Sioux,

> The Sun Dance was our first and our only religion. We believed that there is a mysterious power greater than all the others, which is represented by nature, one form of representation being the sun. Thus we made sacrifices to the sun and our petitions were granted.[82]

139

Bushotter, another Teton, said that the purpose of the ceremony was a prayer for cure of epidemics and famine, for success against the enemy, and for plentiful food.[83] Two anthropologists' interpretations are Clark Wissler's which holds the Sun Dance to be a supplication to the sun for "divine guidance,"[84] and George A. Dorsey's which terms it a ceremonial of rebirth or renaissance.[85] The last Sun Dance among the Teton Sioux was in 1881.[86]

Other dances such as the War Dance, dances of the Soldier Societies, Hoop Dance, Grass Dance, Rabbit, Buffalo, Dog, and several other animal dances were typical Plains ceremonials which might be considered minor rites in comparison

Figure 52. Unknown Sioux artist. *Ceremonial Encampment, Sun Dance.* Ca. 1890. Crayon, ink, and pencil. Hazen Collection, Smithsonian Institution. Cat. No. 154,064.

to the Sun Dance, yet which had important meaning in the tribal ceremonial patterns. In all the dances there was a correlation between social and religious organizations, and the accompanying arts—music, drama, and painting. The Grass Dance included drypaintings.[87]

Increasing use of the horse created additional leisure for sports, games, and other diversions. The more important characteristic sports were organized and interwoven with social and religious practice so as usually to take the form of a ceremonial in which feasting and fasting, singing, dancing, and symbolic painting had important parts.

In the mores of this period of the Plains, there are to be found traces of ancestral cultures in such manifestations as the Sun Dance, the exaltation of self-sacrifice, wearing of the warbonnet, and use of earth altars with paintings, and sacred bundles. In symbolic and occasionally objective ways such practices, when focused to attention in art,[88] appear related to the Southeast, and even to Middle America.*

The phenomenal development during the Horse Culture Period, although prompted by Europeans, advanced virtually independent of them, for there was little contact between Europeans and the Plains Indians from the time of Spanish encounters until after the Louisiana Purchase. Such contacts as there were usually were in the interest of commercial gain to the white man. A few early traders and travelers such as Pierre La Verendrye had ventured through the region and had written accounts of it before Meriwether Lewis and William Clark entered in 1804, but the Lewis and Clark journals gave the first vivid glimpses of many aspects of the Plains in the full flower of their culture.

Clark wrote of the nomadic life, of old villages deserted for the hunt.

> . . . the Party returned and informed us that they Could not find the Indians, nor any fresh Sign, those people have not returned from the Buffalow hunt. Those people haveing no houses no Corn or anything more than the graves of their ansesters to attach them to the old Village, Continue in purseute of the Buffalow longer than others who has greater attachments to their native village.[89]

*Among similar features are warrior and self-sacrificial celebrations; circular dances around tall, top-decorated ceremonial poles; almost identical feathered headdresses, feathered and painted shields, ceremonial fans, sunburst bustles and arm and leg ornaments of feathers; symbols for names or speech associated with figures of persons; bannered and feathered war staffs; man-eagle personages; profile figures with front-view torsos; triangle, rectangular terrace, and crescent design elements.

141

The journals described hunts and the stealing of horses. Lewis told of horses being held in such high regard that they were put in the lodges at night for protection, and that they were often painted with distinguishing designs:

> . . . they frequently paint their favorite horses, and cut their ears in various shapes. They also decorate their manes and tails, which they never draw or trim, with feathers of birds, and sometimes suspend at the breast of the horse the finest ornaments they possess.[90]

Lewis and Clark also told of tribal honors, tribal divisions, the trade and barter between tribes, and noted that the sign language seemed to be "universally understood by all the Nations we have yet seen."[91]

Soon following Lewis and Clark were John Bradbury, H. M. Brackenridge, and S. H. Long. Then came the Austrian, Maximilian of Wied, and the Swiss artist, Charles Bodmer in 1832, who traveled extensively through the Plains for two years and made admirably detailed records of their observations. The two artists before mentioned, Rudolph Kurz, a friend of Bodmer, and George Catlin, sketched and studied in the area soon afterward. Catlin went up the Missouri River in 1834, and Kurz began a six-year exploration in 1836. All these men left, in addition to general observations of the people they traveled among, some valuable information concerning Plains painting which will be noted later.

By 1850, the California gold rush made the Plains a thoroughfare, and settlers began to move into the territory, making life miserable for the Indians from then on. To the newcomers, the Indian owners of the land were "wild savages," enemies to be feared and annihilated. One sure way to subdue them was to exterminate the buffalo, and so the great herds were slaughtered by the thousands, their hides and tongues hauled out by the wagonload and sold down the Missouri for a token. Where the settlers and traders could not do the work fast enough, the United States Army liquidated the vast herds.[92]

In the more remote parts of the Plains, the old, free life went on a while longer, but by 1880 the accessible herds had been almost completely destroyed and their once proud and independent followers had been corralled upon government reservations. Establishment of reservations had begun in 1855, and in 1871 Congress had declared all Indians subjects of the United States.[93]

The Sioux were scattered on several reservations in the Dakotas and Wyoming. The Northern Arapaho, the mother tribe, had remained on the Wind River Reservation in Wyoming, and the southern division of the tribe had united with the Cheyenne in Oklahoma. The Arapaho Tribe had been separated ever since

142

the overland route had permanently divided the buffalo into north and south herds in 1849.[94] The Kiowa homeland had been in Oklahoma since 1832, as indicated by their annual Sun Dances which were held there from that date until the last one was stopped by government troops in 1890.[95]

When settlement upon reservations was fully accomplished, the great days of the Plains Indians had ended. The buffalo, the staff of life, were forever gone and there was no replacement for them which remotely approached adequacy. For a suddenly bereft people, there remained only bewilderment and desperate frustration.

There were a few feeble uprisings among the Indians in protest of the acute suffering. Many of the people turned for a time to the strange Ghost Dance religion which seemed to offer one last hope in its fanatic doctrine of the defeat of the white people and the return of the buffalo. Various "messiahs" arose to carry the message of hopeless hope to the demoralized Indians. Wovoka,[96] a Paiute from Nevada, was the best known of these, although the movement of defiance dates from Popé at the time of the Pueblo Rebellion in 1680.[97] Leslie Spier relates the Ghost Dance to the Prophet Dance of the interior plateau area of the Northwest, which demonstrated an old belief in the impending destruction and renewal of the world.[98]

Adherents to the Ghost Dance cult practiced hypnotism and performed frenzied circle dances which ended in utter exhaustion and trances. They chanted "messiah songs" and wore "bulletproof" dance shirts and dresses made of buckskin, painted with symbols of sorcery—evil birds, dark stars, spider webs, black crescents, and like omens—which were believed to be absolute protection against the superior weapons of the enemy.

To subdue the uprisings, the federal government mobilized troops near all the reservations which were under the influence of the movement, and there followed a long series of battles.[99] With the devastating Battle of Wounded Knee, in 1890 on the Oglala Sioux Reservation in South Dakota, the cult of the Ghost Dance and the magnificent spirit of the Plains Indians were broken with finality.

PLAINS PAINTING

A spirited and vigorous art, unique in history, grew out of the Plains experience. In keeping with the roving culture, it was a portable art which was at first recorded upon the broad surfaces of the hides of buffalo and other large

143

Figure 53. Unknown Dakota artist. *Warriors and Hunters*. Ca. 1800. Oil on buffalo hide, robe. Collected by Friederick Kohler. Museum fur Volkerkunde, Berlin. Cat. IV B202.

prairie animals. It was more of a personal and materialistic art than that of the Southwest, for it was largely by and for the individual, recording and proclaiming his tribal and intertribal relationships—his exploits in battles, hunts, and his participation in ceremonial celebrations. Whereas in the ancestral days of Plains tribes the people may have been concerned with man-to-God relationships, they later had become more interested in man-to-man associations. Plains painting, although deeply religious in some instances, was not primarily for appeasement or supplication of unearthly powers, but rather for demonstrating personal achievements to gain prestige within the tribe and to proclaim invincibility before enemies. There was less meaningful symbolism in this art than is found in one of purely religious motive. It was dynamic and restless, the art of people on the move who gained their livelihood by contest.

Nearly all that is known of Plains painting has been learned since the beginning of the nineteenth century. The earliest paintings mentioned in historical records were perhaps quite different in subject and design from the ones now known as Plains paintings. Materials and methods, however, were probably much the same in early days, for hide paintings were made in Coronado's time. During the tour of Cibola, Coronado found painted buffalo hides that had been brought down from the Plains country. In a letter he wrote to Mendoza in 1540, Coronado mentioned the fact that painted buffalo hides were sometimes worn by the Cibolans: ". . . and they have painted mantles like the one which I send Your Lordship."[100] Explaining the source of these mantles, he said, "They inhabit some plains eight days' journey toward the north. They have some of their skins here very well dressed, and they prepare and paint them where they kill the cows, according to what they tell me."[101] Some of the mantles Coronado found in Cibola may have been painted by the Pueblo inhabitants who had learned the art from the Plains Indians.

Mention of painting in the Plains was made by La Verendrye in his journal. He gave vermilion to various tribes during his travels of 1733-34, and observed savage tribes which use horses and carry on trade with [the Mandan] . . . bring "coloured buffalo robes" among the Mandan in 1738. He also noted that "several dressed skins . . . painted in various colours."[102] He termed the Mandan "sharp traders" in exchanging their own robes for powder, kettles, axes, knives, and such items.[103]

Clark described painting in the tented camps:

> . . . the Scioues Camps are handsom of a Conic form Covered with Buffalow Roabs Painted different colours and all compact & handsomly arranged, Covered all round an open part in the Centre for the fire, with Buffalow roabs. . . .[104]

145

He mentioned other "Buffalow Roabes, the flesh Side Painted of Different colours and figures."[105] Of one robe he said:

Figure 54.   Unknown Sioux artist. *Tipi Group*. Ca. 1890. Crayon and ink. Hazen Collection, Smithsonian Institution. Cat. No. 154,064.

I went on Shore on landing I was received on a elegent painted B. Robe & taken to the Village by 6 Men & was not permitted to touch the ground untill I was put down in the grand Councille house on a White dressed Robe.[106]

Among the articles Lewis and Clark sent President Jefferson, Clark listed:

1 Robe representing a battle between the Sioux & Ricaras against the Minetares and Mandans.[107]

When Bradbury visited among the Plains tribes along the Missouri in 1809-11, he said of one host, "he spread a very finely painted buffalo robe for me to sit on,"[108] and Brackenridge, in 1811, compared the designs on Arikara robes with pictographs he had seen further east:

. . . the chief exhibited to me a number of dressed buffalo robes, on which he had painted his different battles. The design was exceedingly rude, such as I have seen on the rocks of the Ohio. To represent the path of a horse or foot-men, he had simply represented their tracks.[109]

Long was more generous in his accounts, 1819-20, of the arts than were most of his predecessors in the Plains. He described beadwork and leatherwork among the Omaha, and of painting he said:

Their art of painting is very rude, yet they manage to give some idea of a battle, by graphic representations in colour, on a bison robe. In the same manner are depicted the various animals, which are the objects of their hunts. These robes are also decorated with blue, red, and black broad lines, forming various designs; indeed it is very common to see a robe thus ornamented, worn by an Omawhaw.[110]

At the termination of the dance, Sharetarish [a Pawnee chief] presented Major O'Fallon with a painted bison robe, representing several of his own combats with the enemy, as well as those of his friends, all of which he explained to us.[111]

After describing methods of tanning hides, Long's account mentioned color tracings:

When the process of dressing and tanning are completed, and the inner surface of the skin dry, figures are traced upon it with vermillion, and other showy colours.

These are designed as ornaments, but are sometimes a record of important facts. The story of a battle is often depicted in this way, and the robe of a war-

147

rior is frequently decorated with the narration, in pictures, of some of his exploits.[112]

With the coming of Maximilian and Bodmer, Plains painting was really studied for the first time. Maximilian's accurately detailed descriptions and Bodmer's meticulously specific drawings, made over a two-year period, grow more valuable with passing years as the classic source of information on the Plains of exploratory years. The animated and colorful heraldry set forth upon buffalo hides had reached its highest state of development in their day. They found painted hides common in all Plains tribes among which they traveled. Typical of Maximilian's descriptions are these:

> . . . representations of their warlike exploits, in black, red, green, and yellow. The figures represent the taking of prisoners, dead or wounded enemies, captured arms and horses, blood, balls flying about in the air, and such subjects.[113]
> Other robes are painted with a reddish-brown ground, and black figures, especially of animals; others have a white ground, with representations of their heroic deeds in black, or in gay colours, with the wounds they received, the loss of blood, the killed, the prisoners, the arms they have taken, the horses stolen (the number of which is indicated by the number of horse shoes), in black, red, green, or yellow figures, executed in their yet rude style of painting. The nations on the Missouri are all in the habit of painting such robes; but the Pawnees, Mandans, Manitaries, and Crows, are the most skilful in this art. Another mode of painting their robes is, to represent the number of valuable presents they have made. By these presents, which are often of great value, they acquire reputation and respect among their countrymen.[114]

Maximilian remarked upon the prevalence of art ability:

> . . . they are not deficient in talent for drawings, music, etc., this is quite manifest at first sight. Several Mandans not only took much pleasure in drawing, but had a decided talent for it. The hieroglyphics are well known, which the Indians employ instead of writing . . . .[115]

The work of Mato-Tope, a Mandan, was highly praised by Maximilian, and some of it was reproduced in Bodmer's *Atlas*,[116] where Plate 55 shows two warriors in hand-to-hand combat in a striking pattern of balanced opposition. The design is skilled in its counterplay of verticals, diagonals, and horizontals; and the lack of naturalism not only accents the vigor of the figures but renders the

148

painting arrestingly decorative. Bodmer, in his own drawings, shows details of robes painted with battles and different exploits, and some with a sun design.

Robes were mentioned not only as being universally worn as clothing but as the main items of barter between the Indians and the fur companies. "A robe handsomely painted is equal in value to two not painted. . . .[117] The Company gives value of six to ten dollars for such a skin."[118] On the other hand, Maximilian observed that "The vermilion costs Indians very dear, for the Company supply it from their stores at ten dollars a pound."[119] In Maximilian's estimation, robes were "painted better" earlier in the century, [when it was] "possible to obtain one for 5 musket balls and some powder."[120]

Paintings on tipis and parfleche bags were noted also, and women were mentioned as being skilled in the dyeing and painting of buffalo hides.

In the studies of Kurz and Catlin, accurate representation of ethnological aspects of the Indian subjects has been largely sacrificed to these artists' interest in individual interpretation and academic style. However, many items of interest can be gathered from their drawings and remarks. Catlin, whose work included many portraits, observed that "The art of portrait-painting was a subject entirely new to them, and of course, unthought of."[121] He considered the Indian drawings inferior, yet was impressed by the number that were made, and particularly by paintings on tipis which, he said, "render them exceedingly picturesque and agreeable to the eye."[122] The work of Mato-Tope interested Catlin to the extent that he attempted to make detailed sketches of some of his paintings. He also mentioned other hide paintings, most of which depicted battle scenes "very ingeniously, though rudely pourtrayed."[123]

Kurz made schematic drawings of designs he saw on robes and told of their meaning as tokens of honors earned through battles fought, gifts bestowed, or brave deeds performed in the hunt. He described the "gaily painted tents,"[124] and told of one instance of seeing a painted tree in Blackfoot Indian Country:

> . . . It is a large cottonwood, on the trunk near the foot of which an Indian cut away the bark and, on the bare wood, sketched different figures in vermillion and chrome yellow . . . a sun, a hand, an enclosure, and the forms of different animals were meant to record, so it seems to me, adventures on a hunt . . . .[125]

In his characterization of Plains painting, Kurz analyzed the Indian's style from the viewpoint of a strict academician:

> Here we find the beginning of the representative arts among the Indians. Apart from his liking for pompous show, for ornamentation, . . . the Indian's

149

Figure 55. Unknown Sioux artist. *Abstract Designs*. Early nineteenth century. Oil on buffalo calf hide, girl's robe. Peabody Museum, Harvard University. Cat. No. 53,124.

principal aim in decoration is colored outlines or contours; the human figure is only a secondary matter.

Therefore, though no one can deny that the Indian has artistic sense, from time out of mind he has made no advance in his art. His manner is stereotyped—hallowed, so to speak, through the ages—like heraldry.[126]

Following these records of earlier art in the Plains, hide paintings in their several forms began to arouse appreciation, at least as extraordinary works, among increasing numbers of travelers from the East and from Europe who collected them. Most of today's museum specimens were obtained in the latter part of the nineteenth century, after government troops had been sent into the area. The Smithsonian Institution's collections of Plains paintings were acquired partly through army personnel.

Figure 56.   Unknown Mandan artist. *Inter-Tribal Battle in 1797*, detail. Oil on buffalo hide, robe. North Dakota. Collected by Lewis and Clark, 1804. Peabody Museum, Harvard University. Cat. No. 53,121.

FORMS AND STYLES IN PLAINS HIDE PAINTING

Robes and Linings. The most typical Plains paintings are those on large hides which were used as robes, or as tipi linings. There are two main classes of such paintings: abstract geometric designs and life scenes with life figures. Rarely do these combine.

Abstract designs were the prerogative of women.[127] Greater in number in surviving examples than those with life figures, these paintings show the oldest development. They more than likely had some antecedents in Woodland and other pre-Plains patterns of long ago, such as were later evolved in weaving and quillwork, and upon painted robes and fitted clothing associated with the Cree of Saskatchewan, Naskapi of Labrador, and some other northern groups.

These motifs seem unrelated to the life subjects, for they are formal, quiet, **151**

usually balanced symmetrically, in effect classic. Certain conventional plans* predominate in the arrangement of abstract designs. These are basically simple, involving geometric elements—circles and arcs, hyperbolae, triangles, rectangles,
and straight lines.

One such pattern involves a radiating motif drawn as on a set of concentric
circles occupying the center of the robe, aptly described by Catlin as "a most
wonderfully painted sun."[128] It is actually made up of scores of close-set triangular
elements which occasionally symbolize feathers in Plains art, but do in certain
examples convey the strong impression of radiating force. When the geometric

*J. C. Ewers, in an analytic and statistical study of 134 hides, actually classifies abstract de-
signs into five divisions such as Border-and-Box, Bilaterally Symmetrical, etc.[129]

Figure 57.   Unknown Plains artist. *Sun Design*, detail. Nineteenth century. Oil on
buffalo hide, robe. Denver Art Museum.

152

components of the circle take the form of high isosceles triangles, the design may suggest the orderly circular arrangement of the crown of the warbonnet, which may have prompted "feather and circle" as one name for the pattern. The design is ordinarily large enough to cover the back of the wearer of the robe. It seldom appears without a border, which may be simple or ornate. Colors, as in all abstract designs, are primarily red, yellow, blue, and green, applied evenly and flat, and often outlined with glue size.

Large rectangular or hyperbolic units composed of geometric details appear as focal interests in other layouts. Borders surround these, schematically following the contour of the hide.

In certain patterns, no centralized figure appears, but linear arrangements alone form the skeletal plans of designs. These are mainly sets of parallels running lengthwise of the hide, or stemming at right angles from base lines. Upon these, abstract or apparently nonobjective units are intricately detailed.

The most striking aspect of all the abstract paintings on dressed hides is the contrast in scale and texture they produce—the discrepancy between the delicate tracery of the designs strung out like beaded bandings or weblike applique, and the bulky, broad backgrounds of the thick hides.

Life figures*, represented in varying degrees of objectivity, seem more suited to the hides. Most of these paintings are direct, in drawing and dynamic in action, often giving the appearance of all-over patterns of great animation. Figures are two dimensional, without sky-earth backgrounds, and are flatly painted in selections from red, yellow, blue, green, black, brown, and more unusual colors, sometimes outlined in dark paint. Men and horses are the chief subjects shown in battles, raids, and epic events. Councils, tribal ceremonies, and visions are other subjects. Game and various animals frequently were painted on hides, according to Long and Maximilian.

Hides painted thus usually served to illustrate individual experiences and exploits of the men who painted them. They were displayed as badges of distinction when worn as robes, each artist designating himself in the paintings by the totem on his shield, the characteristic color and markings of his horse, or in like ways. Members of tribes and bands might be distinguished by facial markings, clothing and hair styles, or differing weapons and riding gear. There is seldom anything in the actual drawing of figures that would serve to differentiate one from another.

*Ernst Vatter scientifically analyzes and classifies details of figures in Plains hide paintings in a study which shows this art in a different but interesting light.[130]

Figure 58. Unknown Mandan artist. *Animals and Various Figures of the High Plains*. Oil on buffalo hide, robe. North Dakota. Collected by Maximilian, Prince of Wied, 1833. Museum fur Volkerkunde, Berlin. Cat. No. IV B205.

In a single hide, one painter may show himself in various actions—counting coup upon a fallen enemy, driving a herd of stolen horses, and riding off in a war party; yet the whole effect is one of a scene of many horses and many riders combined.

154   Action dominates the battle scenes where bands of warriors ride against those of enemy tribes. With tails of warbonnets streaming, breechcloths and ban-

ners sailing, feathers flying from long lances and crooked coup sticks, bows and arrows high in hand, the Plainsmen ride forth on galloping horses. This aspect of the Great Plains has never been better painted than in works of this period and that immediately following.

More tranquil beauty is evident in horse-stealing scenes where upwards of a hundred horses may appear on a single hide. Some groupings in these are exceedingly beautiful in their flowing compositions and spare line. Horses, especially in the later hides, are bright blue, green, orange, red, or other hues contrary to

Figure 59.   PRETTY HAWK, Yankton Sioux. *Capturing Horses*. 1864. Oil on buffalo hide, tipi lining. South Dakota. Peabody Museum, Harvard University. Cat. No. 84,298.

nature more often than they are natural colors. But through vital line alone, powerful realism is achieved. The very lack of detail gives pungence. A great number of horses may be indicated by a multitude of pictographic hoof prints in some instances, and, in others, top-view hoof tracks attached to the lower extremities of legs may represent horses' hoofs. Deliberate distortion is often obvious in such exaggerated features as elongated necks and legs of galloping horses. Faces and figures of men are largely schematic, with details of eyes, mouths, fingers, and other parts often omitted or merely suggested.

In paintings of tribal ceremonies, most seen in later works, such subjects as the Circle Dance, the great Sun Dance, gift bestowals, and rites of the warrior societies appear. The Sun Dance, in its several phases, affords a wide variety of subjects in itself—the tree preparation, lodge erection, camp circle, and the dance about the ceremonial pole. Such works are not primarily biographical but are mainly tribal records. They are bright, decorative compositions with stylized figures and patterns, naive perspective, pictorial yet unnaturalistic.

Paintings of visions and dreams are difficult to classify because of their present rarity and their diverse content. They are both abstract and more or less representative. Certain ones seem to be illustrated legends; others are combinations of mystic symbols and fanciful life forms. Sky figures and plant growth, as seen in dreams as "mystery objects," occasionally appear in them, seeming related to a former agrarian life. If there is any surrealism in American Indian art, some of it is here in these obscure designs that appear psychological in character. Designation of the paintings was by such names as *Cedar Tree Vision, Ghost Vision, Thunder-Being Vision, Eagle Vision,* and through them men offered prayers or became eligible for certain cults, societies, and personal recognitions.[131]

Styles in hide paintings containing life figures changed from predominantly pictographic drawing and sparse color in the earliest known examples to the more detailed renderings of later years. A painting of the time of Lewis and Clark, when compared to one of those at the close of the buffalo era, presents marked contrasts. The one is a dynamic all-over pattern of men and horses most selectively painted down to essentials in brown-black outline and small touches of vermilion, yellow ochre, and green; the other, a semirepresentational dramatization in much detail and far broader color range.

Names of artists who painted on hides are mostly lost, but, among a few who escaped oblivion are: White Bird, a Northern Cheyenne; Pretty Hawk, a Yankton Sioux; Silverhorn (Haun-goo-ah) and Yellow Nose, both Kiowa; Sharetarish, an Omaha; Washakie and Katsikodi, both Shoshone; Mato-Tope, the Mandan; To-tay-go-nai (Standing Buffalo), Ponca; and American Horse, Oglala Sioux.

156

Calendars. Other hide paintings are the calendars or winter counts. The Sioux counted their years by winters and said that a man was so many snow seasons old, or that a number of snow seasons had passed since a certain occurrence. Calendars consist of pictographic drawings in dark outlines with small spots of color, arranged spirally or lineally. Each symbol represents some main event of each winter, thereby keeping an annual record. Thus, a pictographic shower of meteorites indicates the "stars-fell winter," a schematic man covered with dots representing smallpox denotes the "all-sick-winter," and so on. None of the calendars is thought to extend further back than the seventeenth century. Few have been preserved although indications are that they were once quite prevalent.[132]

The count made by Lone Dog, a Yankton Sioux, is considered to be somewhat of a key record in that several other winter counts found in Sioux territory correspond to it.[133] It is painted in black and red on a large buffalo hide, and represents the history of the tribe over a period of seventy-one years, beginning in 1800. Horses, buffalo, tipis, people, and many events are represented in a manner remarkable for the amount of meaning conveyed in so few lines.

American Horse worked in 1879 on a winter count which he said had been begun by his grandfather and extended by his father.[134] Among other known makers of Sioux counts upon hides were Bo-i-de (Blaze), Little Swan, and White-Cow Killer.

The Kiowa calendars, more detailed in that they show both years and moons, are said to have been made by religious leaders who brought them out during certain nights in winter camp to be exhibited and discussed in the circle of warriors about the tipi fire. The Anko (in the middle of many tracks) Calendars—one covering twenty-nine years from 1864, and the other, a period of thirty-seven moons—were first drawn in pencil and later painted in colored inks upon a single, large, white buckskin.[135] Vertical bars, with annual symbols attached, extend in a procession across the skin. Crescent symbols are arranged in an arc around the verticals to represent "leaf moon," "geese-going moon," "little moon of horns dropping off," and the principal occurrences in each of these and other moons.

W. J. McGee, who had a chance to see many of the calendars, says of them:

> The germ of painting was revealed in the calendars . . . of the Siouan Indians. The pictographic paintings comprised not only recognizable but even vigorous representations of men and animals, depicted in form and colors though without perspective. . . . To the collector these representations suggest fairly developed art, though to the Indian they were mainly, if not wholely, symbolic;

157

for everything indicates that the primitive artisan had not yet broken the shackles of fetichistic symbolism, and had little conception of artistic portrayal for its own sake.[136]

Tipi Covers. Tipis had covers of painted hides, and often the same battles, hunts, and other events painted on personal robes were depicted upon them. Personal "mystery decorations" representing visions and dreams, when painted on tipis, are said to have been invocations on behalf of the household among the Omaha.[137] Corn plants similar to those painted by the Pueblos were also painted by the Omaha who spaced five or six life-sized stalks around the Sacred Tents, thus showing adherence to agrarian influences. Some tipi covers were decorated with unit motifs and borders, or borders alone. Buffalo, bear, antelope, birds, pipes, suns, and crescents were among motifs so used in symbolic fashion. Occasionally, a single unit, against an all-over background of horns, claws, tracks, or stars appeared on a tipi. Borders were wide and heavily painted when used as the only decoration. Bold geometric shapes, particularly circles and triangles, accented the band at intervals. Some tipis were painted with several tiers of horizontally running patterns.

At large tribal events, such as the Sun Dance, the varied displays on tipis were seen to advantage. Tribal bands, and families within the bands, were distinguished by their tipi markings and their respective locations in the great camp circle. It was at such times that heraldic displays of brave and generous exploits were best set forth in the tipi paintings.

Colors in these designs emblazoned on hides stood well against the severe Plains weather—the whipping blizzards of the prairie winter, driving rain and hail, or the scorching winds and unshielded sun of summer—for they usually were mixed with the rich fat of buffalo suet and rubbed well into the skins, and were renewed from time to time.

Clothing. Fitted clothing of deer and elk hide frequently was decorated with both life and geometric motifs, particularly that for wear upon ceremonial occasions. Before the advent of commercial beads, decoration was only of painted designs with such additional adornments as ermine tails, wisps of hair, elk teeth, cowrie shells, polished bone segments, claws, quill embroidery, feathers, and fringes. Painted black and white stripes were used strikingly on some of the men's costumes, and spiritedly drawn contest scenes appeared on warrior shirts, or more formal rows of figures extended out upon the sleeves or down from breast

158

to lower edge on either side of a long shirt. Mystic signs and totemic devices were also painted to proclaim the prowess and character of the wearer and to hint of fetichism.

Shields. Shields, important among the equipment of the Plainsman, offer the source of some of the most interesting and productive studies of Plains painting, for on their small surfaces were centered symbolic life forms and abstract designs of rich meaning and frequent beauty. They were made of heavy rawhide cut in single or double discs or stretched upon a hoop of stout, hard wood, about two feet in diameter. Painting was rarely done directly upon the rawhide but usually upon a tanned skin which was drawn over the rawhide as a cover.

With the same colors and techniques used upon robes, men painted on shields their tribal, band, or personal totems, their representations of powers believed helpful in hunt or battle, or brief indications of certain personal achievements. The Kiowa formerly had about fifty shield patterns, and all warriors carrying the same pattern constituted a close brotherhood.[138] However, judging from the great variety of existing examples of shield patterns, one is inclined to believe that individual fantasy largely ruled the making of these designs. It is possible to search among scores of museum specimens and find few patterns alike, although tribal differentiations of designs are usually discernible upon comparing groups of examples. For instance, Arapaho shields show a predominance of central patterns—a buffalo, a sun, a tree—surrounded by circular arrangements of consecutive small triangles, or revolving rainbow bands, or groups of radiating zigzags and straight lines; while those of the Crow usually give a heavier, all-painted appearance wherein the shield is marked asymmetrically into several differently designed divisions which contain abstract or life forms, or solid color areas.

Some outstanding design motifs noted in a cross-section of Plains shields were: birds with profile heads and outstretched wings such as are commonly called Thunderbirds, forked lightning, highly stylized buffalo of all colors, bear and bear tracks, fish, rain clouds done somewhat in the manner of Pueblo clouds, trees, zigzag and undulating lines, bullets in flight (dots on the end of oscillating lines), suns, moons, crescents, four-point stars, rainbows, triangles, concentric circles, and stripes in multiple arrangements.

Parfleche Articles. The women painted decorations on parfleche boxes, bags, and other utilitarian receptacles which are common among all Plains tribes except the Osage.[139] They pegged out raw hides which dried stiff and hard. They marked

159

the designs in outline and painted them with bold, flat colors, among which red, blue, yellow, green, and black are the most popular. They are entirely geometric, and often obscure in such a degree as to seem nonobjective. Triangles, rectangles, dots, crosses, bands, and lines are the basic elements of these motifs; there are rarely curvilinear elements.

Leslie Spier analyzed two hundred forty-four examples of parfleche designs, checked them for technique, colors, use of space and mass, widths of line, and structure, and tabulated the results for comparison.[140] His study emphasizes the multitude of variations in the over-all similarities of the many designs. Robert Lowie also analyzed a group of parfleche paintings—Cheyenne, Crow, and Hidatsa—and classified them as to layout, such as "transverse border stripe," "central diamond," "X figure," "framed central triangle," etc., and as to color, unit arrangement, and nomenclature.[141] He demonstrated that they involved a highly developed system of design, but he decided that most of the motifs had no symbolic significance as used. Wissler, however, cited the Arapaho as having given

Figure 60. Unknown Cheyenne artist. *Lines and Triangles.* Nineteenth century. Oil on rawhide, bag. Southern Plains. Field Museum of Natural History. Cat. No. 97120.

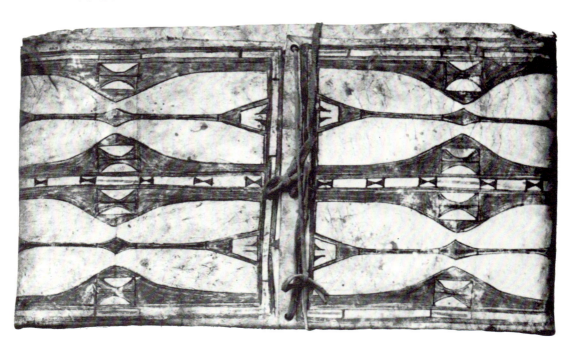

geometric designs a symbolic value, although he found, in general, that symbolism in parfleche designs is relatively rare. He observed that the Dakota and Arapaho, in some cases, used a common geometric figure to symbolize different objects, and concluded that "there is no necessary connection between the life history of a decorative design and the object it symbolizes."[142]

MATERIALS AND TECHNIQUES IN PLAINS HIDE PAINTING

Although most paintings were done on buffalo hide, the skins of elk and deer were sometimes used. Hides to remain supple, were softened and lightened through a rigorous tanning process, then were laced into frames for painting. Tipi covers of large design were painted after the hides had been arranged and sewn in a cone pattern covering the tapering framework of the lodge. Stiff rawhides were painted for parfleche bags and boxes.[143]

The palette[144] available before the appearance of commercial colors included iron oxide reds, yellows, browns, and purples; charcoal, graphite, bone, and soot black; copper carbonate green, gray-blue earth, chalk white, and several vegetable colors. The latter included red from savoyenne root and buffalo berries, purple from chokecherries, yellow from lichens, green from the juice of young poplar leaves, and black from the helianthus. There were colors from other sources, depending on the locality. "Crimson coloured earth" was used for paint on the upper Missouri, according to Lewis.[145] Shooter, of the Sioux, said to have been "a thoughtful man and well versed in the old customs," commented upon the native paints thus:

> A man ought to desire that which is genuine instead of that which is artificial. Long ago there was no such thing as a mixture of earths to make paint. There were only three colors of native earth paint—red, white, and black. These could be obtained only in certain places. When other colors were desired, the Indians mixed the juices of plants, but it was found that these mixed colors faded and it could always be told when the red was genuine—the red made of burned clay.[146]

On the Standing Rock Reservation, the Sioux found yellow ochre which they powdered finely for yellow paint and burned to produce a vermilion.[147] The women mixed the ochre with water, formed the paste into balls and baked them by placing them in a preheated hole in the ground under an intense fire of oak bark. A red paint was then made by pulverizing the baked clay. Similar prep-

161

aration has been reported from other tribes. Prepared earth paints contained in bladders and skin pouches were valued items of trade among tribes.[148]

Vermilion was apparently the first commercially prepared pigment used in the Plains. Between the times of La Verendrye and Lewis, it was often mentioned as a favorite gift item, and one much sought in trade. Lewis told of having given paint to a Mandan chief and of having distributed it among Sacajawea's people.[149] "Paint" then usually referred to vermilion.

By 1880, most colors were procured through traders. Although commercial pigments were expensive, the Indians preferred them because they were brighter, clearer, more easily prepared and applied. In addition to vermilion, the most common traders' colors were red lead, chromate of lead yellow, Prussian blue, chrome green, ivory black and lamp black, Chinese white, and oxide of zinc. They came as powder or in "crude masses" and were prepared as needed.[150]

Traders' paints were sold "in small packages not much larger than a paper of needles and the price of one of these packages in the last century was the value of twenty-five cents."[151] The Indians used their old color names for the prepared paints, calling them "red earth," "green earth," etc. Late in the nineteenth century, colored inks, cake watercolors, and crayons were also available through trade. Both inks and watercolors were applied to buckskin and buffalo hides.

In preparing dry pigments, either native or commercial, powders were mixed with adhesives. Animal fat, usually buffalo suet, was used with pigment in making oil paint, being well rubbed into the hide to insure permanence and richness.[152] Perhaps the most common method of fixing color was that of boiling beaver tails to obtain a glue which was mixed with pigment and brushed into the hide.[153] Paint thus made adhered well and was true and clear in hue. Glue was also made from the liquor of boiled hoofs and hide scrapings. The Kiowa used the mucilaginous juice of the prickly pear as a fixative for yellow ochre. The Sioux also mixed pigments with birds' eggs.

Figures in geometric designs, painted with color dissolved in a water base, were glossed over with glue size to make them permanent. Areas, borders, and outlines which were to remain uncolored, were often covered with glue size or albumen which protected those portions from the soil and handling and caused them to appear comparatively lighter with time.

The painters ground their colors in shallow stone mortars and mixed them in sections of horn, in turtle and clam shells, cuplike stones, and gourds. For applying paints to hides, they used brushes made of pieces of porous buffalo bone— sections from the hip and knee joints, ribs and other flat pieces of bone.[154] The

162

thin edges were used for making lines and the flat sides for spreading color. Painters made other applicators by chewing the ends of sticks to make them fibrous, and by tying tufts of antelope hair to wood handles.[155] Thin strips of wood served for pressing tracings of glue size or color outlines into the hides, especially for abstract designs.

Few colors appear in the oldest known robes, and those largely outlined in black. Maximilian describes robes of the early 1830's as having figures outlined in black on a background tinged with red or brown.[156] The custom of filling in outlines of both geometric and life forms with various flat colors became prevalent throughout the Plains area until the close of the buffalo era. Thus, by midnineteenth century, styles and techniques had been established which were to strongly influence the painting that followed and which persisted well into the modern period.

TRANSITIONAL PAINTINGS AND DRAWINGS

With loss of the buffalo, a few paintings similar to those formerly made on hides of those animals were produced on cowhide, rarely obtainable. Other works in imitation of the old were painted on cloth and infrequently even on a blanket. Such materials were salvaged from the army as well as procured from traders by men who seized upon the new materials as strange but necessary makeshifts in the continuance of their art.

Tipi covers and inner decorations formerly made of hides rapidly changed over to canvas and other heavy cotton. When frame houses began to replace native shelters, painted canvas and muslin hung in them as did the hide paintings in the tents of old. At least, the comparatively flimsy new materials permitted the portrayal of entire ceremonials and lengthy scenes of free-galloping riders, and processions of warriors and horses, along yards of surface.

One typical painting on muslin by a Sioux artist shows a spirited long panorama of horses galloping in two ranks, one above the other, with riders in war trappings chasing enemy horses and counting coup upon captives. The rendering is flat and stylized in the manner of hide paintings, and is graceful and forceful in action.

Two canvases by Short Bull of the Oglala Sioux are of the Sun Dance in the late seventies. Both display imaginative perspective wherein a top view of the dance lodge is surrounded by formally placed side-view tipis in a camp circle. Much rhythm is indicated in orderly repetition of compactly placed dancers. Detail on tents and costumes is clearly defined, and is almost severely formal.

163

Figure 61.   SHORT BULL, Oglala Sioux. *Dakota Sun Dance*. Ca. 1890. Watercolor on canvas. Pine Ridge, South Dakota. American Museum of Natural History.

An exciting, long, action drama is the work of Tatanka Yotanka, better known as Sitting Bull, renowned defender of the Sioux Nation, who used the canvas liner of a cavalry blanket to depict autobiographical events of horse stealing and tribal skirmishes. His drawing in lemon yellow, iron oxide red, indigo, and Prussian blues, is animated, direct, and well grouped, making an admirable mural-like piece. At one end there is lettered the artist's presentation of the painting to Dr. Frank Powell, U. S. Army physician, 1880. Only the high cost of insurance on this painting prevented its placement as a mural in the lobby of a new California post office, but it is now glass-encased in the Dentzel Collection, Southwest Museum.

Kills Two, Jaw, Eagle Shield, No Heart, Swift Dog, and Old Buffalo are among other Sioux men who painted on cloth. Each had his own style of doing two-dimensional figures in vermilion, indigo, yellow, black, and occasional touches of secondary colors. Their subjects were dances, hunts, battles, horse-capturing scenes, and various incidents of camp and prairie. Of these, Jaw's and Kills Two's show the most skill. Kills Two is said to have constructed horses by first drawing the hoofs, then erecting the body form upon them.[157]

One of the most distinguished groups of Plains paintings on cloth is that in the West Point Museum, U. S. Military Academy. The superb beauty of one of these pictures would be difficult to dispute. This is an uncommonly large work, about 70 by 70 inches, on sewn widths of muslin, now well browned with age but giving the appearance of old Chinese silk. The charmingly composed groups of horses and warriors, sensitively rendered in soft reds, yellows, and blue-greens, actually present an effect reminiscent of a Chinese painting. Although no record of artist, tribe, or date remains, it is quite evident that this work is one of the oldest of its kind.

Also especially notable at West Point are three battle scenes painted in 1894-95 by White Bird, a young Northern Cheyenne who as a boy in 1876 had participated in engagements with Major General George Custer's troops. The paintings, from the Captain R. L. Livermore collection, all are on unbleached muslin, in flat, outlined colors. The largest, a 68-by-98-inch panorama titled *Battle of the Little Big Horn*, schematically depicting the terrain and principal action of the event, is drawn in black pencil or sharp crayon, filled in with light shades of primary colors and gray that appear to be crayon or some other very evenly rubbed-in dry pigment. Scores of small figures of men, horses, and tipis are done in the style of late nineteenth-century hide paintings, and are grouped in a manner most meaningful documentarily.

165

Figure 62. Unknown Plains artist. *Indians in Combat*. Ca. 1870. Watercolor on muslin. West Point Museum. Art. No. 1030.P5. Acc. No. 277.

The two smaller pictures, each about 2 by 2½ feet, are in every sense fine art. Both are scenes of spectacular action, one *Reno's Retreat,* and the other *Custer's Last Stand*. The former, despite its melee of men and horses, is strikingly composed; the other sacrifices unity to events, yet its high-spirited components are fascinatingly interrelated through force of drawing alone. Direct outline is a strong feature of both these paintings, and appears to have been done in inks of indigo and sepia. Few details appear within the outlines; men's faces are schematic, with a triangle, almond, or simply a dot, for the eye. Attention is concentrated on whirlwind motion. A comparatively wide range of fill-in colors, from

Plate XII. George Keahbone, Kiowa. *The Mud Bath.* 1935. Tempera. William and Leslie Van Ness Denman Collection.

Plate XIII. FRED KABOTIE, Hopi. *Hopi Corn Dance.* Ca. 1925. Tempera gouache. Bayou Bend Collection, Museum of Fine Arts of Houston.

fairly bright yellows, reds, and blues, to pale yellow, orange, and gray, is accented by spottings of solid brown-black and dark indigo.

Figure 63.   WHITE BIRD, Cheyenne. *Reno's Retreat*, detail. 1894-1895. Watercolor, crayon, and ink on muslin. West Point Museum. Art. No. 1209.Z4. Acc. No. 408.

Other paintings from the Livermore Collection are in the Denver Art Museum. Outstanding among these battle and hunting scenes, is a long panorama, *Buffalo Hunt*, wherein a galloping herd of black-silhouetted animals is pursued by a few hunters as wounded beasts lag or lie behind. The concise drawing conveys powerful action, and the thick tempera paint gives flat, sharp contrast to the near-white muslin background.

Paper, also, from about 1870 on, became more and more sought for painting. Biographies, winter counts, rosters, and pictures or subjects depicted on hides and canvas were made on rough manila sheets or foolscap—a grayish or light yellow paper. Lined ledgers, of the sort traders and army quartermasters used in keeping accounts, were prized by erstwhile hide painters for expressing ideas burgeoning in a tumultuous era. Drawing books were rare indeed, but occasionally were supplied by individuals interested in the work of certain artists. Pencils, colored crayons, water colors, inks, and vegetable juices all were utilized as media in the new works.

Winter counts, following schemes of those painted on hides, show pictographic symbols for major events of successive years. An example of such counts is that contained in the work of Battiste Good, a Sioux born in 1821, who painted in a drawing book with six colors.[158] He said that his counts followed exactly the old record purporting to show events in cycles from purely mythical times around A.D. 900 to 1700, and in annual symbols from 1700 to 1800. The bulk of representations in his supposed time span is obvious fantasy, but the last part seems correlatable with other counts. Good's drawing is unusual in that it portrays not only objective events but more abstract conditions such as pain, fear, good, possession, hunger. For instance, he indicates pain by a tortuous line inside or alongside the figure of a human being, letting the symbol stand for pain suffered during the season of "smallpox-used-them-up-again winter," or "many-women-died-in-childbirth winter," or "died-of-whistle winter" (a time when food poisoning caused many deaths). Most of the counts concern intertribal strife, horse stealing, hunting, weather, and government relations ("first-issue-of-goods winter," etc.). The remarkable quality of the accounts is their effectiveness in conveying such extensive and varied meanings in starkly simple drawings.

Rosters of members of bands within tribes are also recorded by pictographic devices. In such rosters, each man's head is drawn in profile with an object depicted above and attached by a line to indicate, somewhat in the manner of Mexican codices, that the man possessed a certain name. In the Plains, a man usually acquired by merit the name of the creature or natural force or singular state of being which his personal abilities, attributes, or achievements best represented—High Hawk, Fire-Thunder, Fast Elk, Great Buffalo, Whirlwind, Strikes-an-Enemy, Gives Many, or the like.

Some rosters also reveal ranks of members by the inclusion of exploit markings. *Red Cloud's Census* and the *Oglala Roster* are two of these.[159] The *Census* was drawn about 1880, in crayon, on seven sheets of heavy manila paper, apparently by several different people, for the drawing on some sheets shows more skill than on others. The *Roster*, representing eighty-four members of the band, is done on a single sheet of foolscap in colored pencils and watercolor. Both depict figures in the manner of hide paintings.

The most remarkable drawings and paintings made on paper are those mainly autobiographical in nature. Done in direct pencil lines and colored in crayon or watercolor, these paintings stand alone among Plains art. To those who made them, they were not for display as were the paintings on hides and cloth, nor for any utilitarian purpose as were the calendars and rosters, but were expressions by individuals mainly for themselves. They welled from the art impulse suddenly dammed against barriers thrown up by the invader, and they sprang from nostalgia and defiance—a wistfulness for the old days and a protest against the new. These works filled countless pages with impressions of childhood, adventures of youth, ceremonials and exploits of manhood, and battles against the enemy, the

Figure 64. Unknown Southern Plains artist. *Fight with Cavalry and Mountain Guns*. Late nineteenth century. Watercolor and crayon. Smithsonian Institution. Cat. No. 166,032.

"Long Knives," as the federal troops were called.[160] In the face of defeat, these paintings did not admit defeat but showed the white enemy vanquished, even dismembered and bleeding. Such violence against native foes had seldom appeared in Plains art.

Many of the works remaining from this period were originally collected from the artists by army officers stationed in Indian territory. One outstanding book of drawings* saved in such a way is that made by a Cheyenne artist while a prisoner at Fort Robinson, Nebraska in 1878-79, and later carried with him into battle following his release. It is filled with drawings in pencil and crayons of a few colors, and it is a poignant statement of deeds of the artist and his tribesmen in times of strife. The drawing is much the same as that on later hide paintings—grouping of horses and riders done in free line with buoyant spirit, and battle scenes where troops with firearms send bullets against dauntless men armed mainly with bows and arrows.

A letter which has been preserved along with the book is eloquent in regard to this work:

Post of San Antonio, Texas
Sept. 21, 1889

My dear Joe,

Only the canvas covered book has any special history, the book with the bullet hole in it. It was, or rather the pictures were, drawn by a northern Cheyenne Indian while in confinement at Fort Robinson, Nebraska, during the winter of '78, '79. I was then Post Adjutant. I endeavored to get the book but its owner and maker refused to part with it for any price. So I gave the matter up. It purports to depict the deeds of several of the Northern Cheyennes during their famous march from the Indian territory to the Wyoming territory.

The outbreak of the Cheyennes is well known, and [as] a consequence of the outbreak, I got the book in this manner. Four troops of the 3rd cavalry, A, E, F, and H commanded by Captain Wessels who by the way was severely wounded, surrounded the hostiles and charged upon them killing all the bucks and unfortunately in the melee, some women and children, but previous to the charge I saw an Indian with the book pressed down between his naked skin and a strap around his waist; another strap went between the middle of the book and around his shoulder.

I turned to Private Laselle of H troop who was near me and said, "I want that book if we come out allright." Several others of the enlisted men heard me

* American Museum of Natural History specimen No. 50.6619.

Figure 65. Unknown Northern Cheyenne artist. *Drawings in Prisoner's Notebook.* 1878-1879. Pencil and crayon. Fort Robinson, Nebraska. American Museum of Natural History. Cat. No. 50.1/6619.

also. When the fight was over, and as the dead Indians were being pulled out [of] the rifle pit, they drew out finally my Indian with the book, apparently dead; the book was injured to the extent of a carbine ball through it and was more or less covered with fresh blood.

This fight took place near Bluff Station, Wyoming Territory, January 22, 1879. The Herald of the 23rd, 24th, or 25th will give an account of the same. The muster rolls of Troop "H" 3 cavalry on file at the Adjutant General's office will tell you of the fight also. This first was the closing one of a series [of] fights with the Indians and they perished to a man.

In haste,
Frank

High Bull, another Cheyenne, killed in battle in 1876, left his autobiography of wars and exploits as a pencil and wax crayon record in a small ledger. A tribal fellow, Spotted Wolf, circa 1889, contributed a ledger full of pencil, ink, watercolor, and crayon drawings of geese, hunters, myths, weddings, and intense scenes of battles with soldiers. Tich-ke-matse, drawing in watercolor and ink on foolscap, **171**

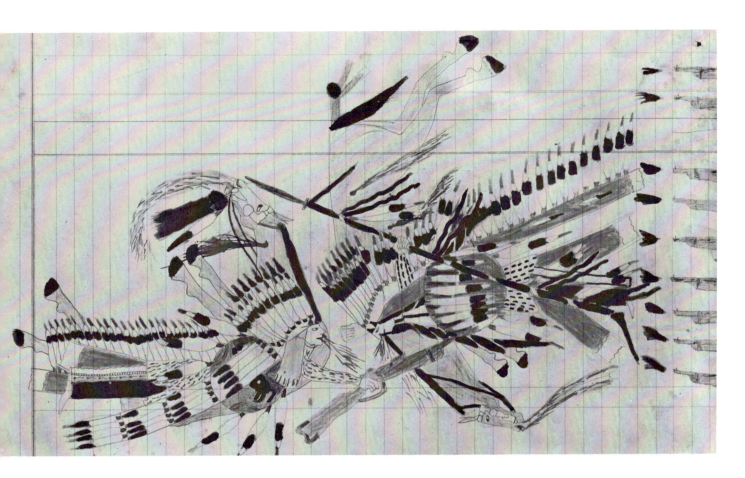

Figure 66.   SPOTTED WOLF, Cheyenne. *Warriors Dying in Battle.* 1889. Watercolor and crayon. Smithsonian Institution. Cat. No. 166,032.

manila, and cardboard, carefully depicted Cheyenne ceremonies, animals, hunts, soldiers, American flags, and forts. Largely anonymous Cheyennes of the same period, 1879-80, salvaged ledgers entitled "Monthly Return of Quartermaster's Stores," and "Property Return Issues to Indians," in which to record some lively views of keenly observed aspects of Plains life. Drawing firmly over lines and type, they left their impressions in both old and more naturalistic style. Howling Wolf, while a prisoner at Fort Marion, Florida, filled a drawing book for Miss Eva Scott (later Mrs. Fenyes) in 1877 with "Scenes from Indian Life." His sharp, fine, small drawings in bright crayon and ink, darkly outlined, adhere to former Plains styles and also explore some innovations. *Medicine Tent, Council of War*, and *A Wild Turkey Hunt* are some of the twenty-nine titles written on the still white, crisp paper of this charming book.

172   Among other Cheyenne prisoners inadvertently distinguishing themselves through their art at Fort Marion, was a young man named Making Medicine. In one collection, he has some forty works in two 9-by-12 drawing books. One is stamped "Ordnance Office. Received Sept. 15, 1875," and the other is accompanied by a note from a former owner observing that, "This is a specimen of the Indian idea of art, although rude and simple, with a little instruction, I think they would draw nicely." How well this artist draws, may be judged by the sharp, sure pencil and firmly laid crayon, the strongly individual style in the consistent angularity and economy of line, the selective yet intricate detail. Birds, buffalo, dancers and wrestlers, and social occasions of Making Medicine's home country are subjects of his choice rather than battles. He honors his captors with a delightful "Sailing Party" where white sails of pleasure craft carry army men and strange Floridans on the blue waters along the forested coast. This picture, while stylized, is quite different from his other works.

Figure 67.   MAKING MEDICINE Cheyenne. *After the Turkeys.* August 1875. Pencil and crayon. Drawn while a prisoner at Fort Marion, Florida. Bureau of American Ethnology, Smithsonian Institution. Cat. No. 39-a.

173

Buffalo Meat, a fellow tribesman and inmate, offers a book of sixteen drawings of bright-blanketed processions and herds of fleet animals, among other works. One such, a herd of antelopes, graceful and rather realistic, covers a page. Two hunters are in pursuit as a blue fox steals along below. Buffalo Meat's pencil evenly outlines vermilion, yellow, cobalt, and black crayon patterns in

Figure 68. BUFFALO MEAT, Cheyenne. *Procession of Men with Blankets and Fans.* Ca. 1875. Pencil and crayon. Drawn while a prisoner at Fort Marion, Florida. Smithsonian Institution. Cat. No. 4656.

which he occasionally uses overlay to produce grays and a varied color range.

Two books of drawings by Wo-Haw (Beef), a Kiowa, also were made during imprisonment of the artist. Several of the forty-eight pictures represent Fort Marion and environs of St. Augustine, Florida, where Wo-Haw was a prisoner from 1875 to 1878, but most of the drawings are of allegorical and tribal scenes of battles, hunts, and ceremonies. The drawing, done in definitive pencil outline filled in with colored crayon, exhibits more naturalness and anatomical features than that of the hide paintings. Line arrangements and placing of color masses result in the good composition, which is also evident in Wo-Haw's watercolors on single sheets.

Zo-Tom, another Kiowa prisoner at Fort Marion, drew scenes from "The Life of a Kiowa Red Man" in a 6-by-10 sketchbook, also for Miss Eva Scott, in 1877. The two-dimensional drawings and those showing some experiments in perspective, all are sensitively done in several colors of crayon and a black lead pencil. These include *Bride and Groom, Running from an Enemy*, a school class with prim mistress, prison scenes, and views of home on the plains.

Further works by Zo-Tom, also completed in prison, are similar to the above and are titled by Captain Richard Pratt who escorted twenty-seven Kiowa among seventy-two chained prisoners to Florida.[161] Zo-Tom, along with Wo-Haw, and others of their company mentioned here, were among those "showing much artistic skill" in the school started in Fort Marion by Mrs. Pratt who had "interested a group of St. Augustine women in the young savages" of her project. According to Harper's Weekly Magazine of May 11, 1878, the pupils instructed the ladies in archery in exchange for their kindness.[162] Incidentally, this pioneer school led four years later to Captain Pratt's founding of the famous Indian Industrial School in Carlisle, Pennsylvania.

Fortunately, and due to the awareness of many concerned in the matter, a surprising number of sketchbooks and drawings from the Fort Marion episode are known to have survived. Names of two other Kiowa artists who contributed to the total are especially noteworthy—Bear's Heart and Etahdleuh Doanmoe (Dgoanmoe) (Edwin Etadleuh). The former painted companies of prisoners, school classes and church meetings, boats, buildings, and trains, using very fine lines and smooth color in a small distinguished sketchbook. Thus he revealed, in sometimes slightly Egyptian perspective and a considerable adherence to the old Kiowa style, the influence of his alien environment.

Etahdleuh did rather impressionistic views of Kiowa villages and buffalo groups as well as watercolors of horses and riders which were decisive and expres-

Figure 69.   ETAHDLEUH DOANMOE, Kiowa. *Man and Woman Riding.* 1879. Watercolor. E. P. Upham Collection, Smithsonian Institution. Cat. No. 290,844.

sive. One very admirable series of drawings, in indelible and black ink, crayons,
and watercolors on large roster pages, pictures various bright groupings, and particularly conveys the tall dignity of Kiowa soldiers with their long lances, in their
fine outfits accented by bone breast plates and vests decorated with elk teeth.

Of course, not all Kiowa who drew were prisoners. Of those who left works,
most were anonymous, with classification other than tribe unknown, and sometimes not even that except from identification through the painting content. This
176   is true with other tribes, especially those more remote at the time, such as the

Blackfoot from which at least one individual opus of this type can be identified. This is a small Spencerian booklet filled by an exceptionally gifted artist whose freely drawn equestrian figures are remindful of those in hide paintings.

The Sioux are represented in a large number of latter nineteenth-century watercolors and sketches in crayon, most of which are unsigned. One typical museum catalog entry reads: "Dakota. Anon. on 65 sheets, 92 drawings, around 1876." Such a group of Sioux works is that in three small drawing books in the Hazen Collection, Smithsonian Institution. One of these, a little eight-page booklet, circa 1892, contains some exceptional drawings in pencil and colored crayons, all in essentially two-dimensional manner. Other than the more usual subjects of horses, warriors, and the Sun Dance, are scenes of skinning the buffalo, of tipis in encampment, Indians buying goods, and of lovers meeting. The en-

Figure 70.   Unknown Sioux artist. *Buying Goods*. Ca. 1890. Crayon, pencil, and ink. Hazen Collection, Smithsonian Institution. Cat. No. 154,064.

campment scene is particularly interesting in its use of decorative lines to represent low background hills and far horizon.

Every sort of paper served for this art. Some of it was cut into uniform size and sewn together with long stitches into various booklets, apparently the work of the artists themselves. Blotting paper, trimmed to about 4 by 8 inches, constitutes the relatively few sheets in one little hand-bound book crudely covered with calico. In it are sketches in pencil, crayon, and indelible ink, some showing figures with personal names designated by association with animals attached by lines as in the old rosters. A miniature book, only 3 by 5 inches, entitled by someone "By our Special artist Roan Eagle," is partially filled with quite clearly drawn figures of buffalo, dogs, elk, mountain sheep, antelope, love scenes, and many single riders on horseback. Media are inks and water-based colors for which plant juices apparently served as pale pigment in some areas.

Rudolf Cronau, a German who traveled in the Plains in 1880-83, collected a remarkable assemblage of paintings. These works are now mounted in a handmade portfolio, about 24 to 18 inches, containing seventy pages, including a foreword, titles, and occasional brief notes in Cronau's own script. A number of drawings were obtained from prisoners of war at Fort Randall, others from Sioux artists at different places on the Standing Rock and Pine Ridge reservations, and a few from itinerant members of other tribes—some apparently from the Northwest coast. The pictures are executed on foolscap, manila, and various papers with pencil, crayon, and watercolor. The Plains works, almost entirely Sioux, present a wide range of subjects handled with similarity of style—selective lines, flat color, animated figures strong in realism yet lacking much naturalism. Besides the usual warrior, hunting, and raiding scenes, characters and episodes from Plains mythology afford insights into little-known subjects such as the Wakinyan, or Thunderbeings. There are also pictures of bears, deer, elk, mountain goats, and antelope which recall Pueblo styles, and of ceremonials such as masked Deer and Buffalo Dances, intertribal rites, the Sun Dance, weddings, and processions. A few landscapes shown as aerial-view pictorial maps also are included. Interspersed are some succinct scenes of army-Indian battles. Hardly a name appears among the whole of these very interesting sketches, but "Sinte" is written on a few, especially those of mythological figures; and "Kanri-belo-ka" appears on several large watercolors, perhaps the finest of the lot. Cronau published some of these and similar works in Germany.[163] The original portfolio is now in the American Museum of Natural History.

178 Elsewhere, a few Sioux pictures are signed by such names as Na-co-is-ta,

Figure 71.   Unknown Plains artist. *Deer and Buffalo Dance*. 1880-1883. Watercolor. Cronau Portfolio, American Museum of Natural History.

Nupa Kte (Kills Two), and Teji-mo-ni (Walking in Light), although most signatures are in translations such as Red Hawk, Red Dog, Eagle Crow, Roman Nose, White Magpie, and the famous Sitting Bull, who as a young man, around 1870 drew his pictorial autobiography in a lined U.S. Infantry roster. The original is lost, but a Sioux copy verified by Sitting Bull remains. Some seventy years later, Matthew Stirling unraveled this mystery as far as is likely to be done.[164] How-

179

ever, the record, as it now stands in sepia ink and chalk tints, is a considerable work of art in its own right. *Steals Horses from Crows* and other horse groups show lines and masses in motion in a most incredible manner involving the keenest observation and forthright expression.

Figure 72.   TURNING BEAR, Brule Sioux. *A Sioux Dance.* 1880. Crayon, watercolor, and pencil. Fort Omaha, Nebraska. John Hay Collection, American Museum of Natural History.

Turning Bear, name of a Brule Sioux chief who was also an artist, is a signature virtually unknown but which deserves notice. While a prisoner at Fort Omaha, Nebraska, in 1880, this man proved himself an artist of unusual ability. One of his pictures, made in crayon and watercolors for Captain Leonard Hay of the 9th Infantry, is a balanced, all-over composition of high animation. Twenty-six dancers in war regalia and costumes, similar to those worn in the modern Taos Pueblo Horsetail Dance, appear in five rows flanked by spectators. Their whirling, kicking exuberance is contained in the center by the horses and people advancing from either side of this large picture. Aside from carefully designed rendering of costume detail, the drawing is rather schematic yet immensely realistic in effect.

Another Sioux painting of impressive size and quality now hangs in the Museum of the American Indian. It is done in outlined watercolors by an excellent miniaturist. His multiple small figures of encamped tipis and clustered participants offer one of the most evocative interpretations of the great Sun Dance.

The most extensive work known to have been done by a Plains artist during the closing decades of the nineteenth century (and which continued into the twentieth) is that of Tatanka Cante Sica, or Amos Bad Heart Buffalo as he was commonly called. He was an Oglala Sioux who lived his early manhood during the last days of the most characteristic period of Plains history. His father and his uncle had fought Custer in the Battle of the Little Big Horn, and so vividly had their accounts been given the younger Bad Heart Buffalo that he was able to portray the entire battle in its every detail from layout of the field to the sequence and aspects of encounters. This pictorial history, known as *The Amos Bad Heart Buffalo Manuscript*, was discovered long after the artist's death by Miss Helen Blish who made an exhaustive study of the drawings and paintings of the document and the circumstances surrounding them. Unfortunately, this admirable three-volume report[165] has never been published; however, the drawings and paintings have been handsomely reproduced in color with brief notes.[166] Taken together, the Blish manuscript and the Szwedzicki reproductions form an invaluable and distinguished document.

The drawings and paintings, originally done in an 8-by-12-inch ledger with brush, crayon, pen, and pencil, depict the Sioux's plan and action, and the final results of Major Reno's rout and Custer's "Last Stand" in the Battle of the Little Big Horn. There are maplike drawings of the battlefield, battles, capture of cavalry horses, processions of warriors, details of maneuvers and participants, the ending procession and rituals, and a final self-portrait of the artist upon his horse. There are 417 plates in the ledger (240 regular pages and 177 inserts), some of

181

them patched. Script in Lakota dialect occupies 9 of these, leaving 408 of drawings; 355 are in 4 or more colors. In all, 8 colors are used—red, yellow, blue, green, purple, brown, gray, and black. Some of the plates show very fine brushwork, others are sketchily done. The drawing combines stark pictography with near naturalness. The industrious quantity and brilliant organization of the work are its most amazing aspects.

On the whole, the work as art does not measure up to that generally achieved in the era of hide paintings. It lacks the clean-cut directness of style and the frank disregard for naturalism found in the older paintings, although it outranks most of the latter in subjective qualities. Aside from the artist's clever use of pictography, in which he describes hundreds of warriors and animals at a glance, his drawing seems to have had chance influences from non-Indian sources, yet it is predominantly Sioux in character and it is an undeniably unique and admirable accomplishment.

Helen Blish, who is best able to speak for the work, offers her own description of *The Bad Heart Buffalo Manuscript*:

> The first fact that impresses one is the great number of the drawings, their wealth of detail, and the inescapable evidence of hours and hours of painstaking execution. Then comes the realization of the artist's ability of the recorder—his naively effective use of balance, color, rhythm, spotting, and perspective; his feeling for decoration; his varying uses of impressionism; and his development of conventionalizations. But finally one is impressed by the thoughtfully critical attitude, the ingenious and far-reaching conception of the work, and especially the maturity of mind and breadth of vision which prompted the young Indian to undertake, of his own accord, the careful accumulation and preservation of data of such historic and cultural significance as this. He is one of the few who could stand aside and view the life of his people objectively, who could stand by in appraisal and with the poise of a critic.[167]

At the time he enlisted as a scout in the U.S. Army at Fort Robinson, 1890-91, Bad Heart Buffalo bought the ledger in which these drawings and paintings were made. According to Helen Blish, the artist was interested in native histories, both recorded and unrecorded, and had finished a symbolic winter count (now lost) of the Oglala Sioux, covering three years, when he decided to do a more detailed account of battles, rituals, and ceremonies that were largely unrecorded yet vastly meaningful to his people. It is said that he filled at least three ledgers with such drawings, but of these only the one manuscript remained.[168] This passed into the possession of his sister Dollie, Mrs. William Pretty Cloud, who cherished

NE HA KIJE

Plate XIV. NEHAKIJE, Jicarilla Apache. *Bear Dance*. 1935. *Tempera*. Margretta S. Dietrich Collection.

Plate XV. Eva Mirabal, Taos Pueblo. *Picking Wild Berries*. 1940. Tempera. Margretta S. Dietrich Collection.

the book so much she insisted that it be buried with her. Amos Bad Heart Buffalo painted up to the time of his death, at the age of forty-four, in 1913.

In summarizing Plains painting, perhaps the most significant fact that stands out is that here a representational and wholly individualistic art evolved from a totemic fetishistic one. In the days of painting on buffalo hides, such an art was in the making—an art for demonstrating thoughts and events from man to man in a manner beyond totally symbolic communication from man to God; an art for expressing the importance of the ego as well as the importance of the group. The autobiographical records of bravery, prowess, and generosity in battle or hunt or social relationship all went into the forming of a new attitude toward art.

This attitude was heightened with the new media at a time when Plains freedom was being destroyed by the conqueror. Actions which were being stultified found vicarious expression in paintings in ledgers and on oddments of paper or cloth with the traders' paints and crayons. Here was the birth of a new Indian art—one solely for the individual, an art for art's sake.

Figure 73. Unknown Plains artist. *Mythical Encounter*. 1880-1883. Cronau Portfolio, American Museum of Natural History. Watercolor.

The Rise of the Modern School

No definite date can be set as the beginning of the modern school of American Indian painting although it is generally conceded to have begun with Crescencio Martinez of San Ildefonso Pueblo, and, through him and his followers, to have spread to other groups and tribes. However, there were modern beginnings in several places before the San Ildefonso movement began.

Certain instances of artists working in modern media of pencil, tube and dry colors on paper and cloth for purposes other than ceremonial or tribal are in the records from the middle of the nineteenth century on. Probably the earliest reference to such work among the Plains tribes is that concerning a Cheyenne artist which is contained in the journal of Lieut. J. W. Abert, 1845:

> The next morning I went out to pay Captain Fremont a visit. Mr. Kern, the artist who accompanies his expedition, showed some sketches by "Old Bark's" son, in which he had represented himself killing some Pawnees with the lance. The execution was quite good, and exhibited considerable feeling for design and proportion.[1]

Early Pueblo works are mentioned by 1881 by Capt. John G. Bourke: "Bought of a young [Jemez] boy, a couple of pictures, cleverly done, representing the Zuni or Moqui Coyamasés dancing."* From such indications as these, it can be deduced that there were many more artists working toward the modern school

* From Bourke's journal, in Lansing B. Bloom, ed.: "Bourke on the Southwest." *New Mexico Historical Review*, Vol. 13, No. 2, 1938, p. 228.
For the two references, I am indebted to John C. Ewers and Richard Howard respectively.

5. The Early Modern Painters

than ever got into the records, and that Indian painting in the modern manner was earlier and more widespread than has been generally believed.

Paintings done in modern media by Plains artists mentioned in the preceding section certainly predicted the modern school, and no doubt are a part of it. Attempts at classification of this art are indeed arbitrary. Drawings and paintings done in ledgers and on nondescript and cast-off pieces of paper and cloth purely for the satisfaction of the individual were essentially not unlike recognized painting of the modern school.

The fact that most works were sporadic and done in vulnerable circumstances, resulted in their largely escaping notice and consideration as works of art. Too, these paintings although they may have been filled with vitality, good drawing, and frequently precious art qualities, were usually not thought of in the popular sense as pictures, so they went into oblivion, a forever irreplaceable loss to world art.

A few of these early productions which inspired some measure of recognition as art found their way into government and museum publications fairly early. In bridging the time between obscurity and recognition, some of these might serve here as indication of the full appreciation all remnants of this remarkable art are sure to receive, as in a recent Milwaukee Museum publication in full color of thirty-six works selected from one hundred sixteen drawings in ink and crayon by some twenty-seven Sioux artists.[2]

One of the first such publications illustrates in line drawings a series of eleven paintings made by a Dakota artist, Running Antelope, for Dr. W. J. Hoffman to whom interpretations of the work were given.[3] The artist, who had been chief of the Uncpapa Dakota at Grand River, painted scenes depicting events in his own life. The original sketches, made in a large drawing book with watercolors, illustrate different deeds in the life of the artist. Each drawing shows Running Antelope on his horse, and usually with his eagle shield. He indicates a variety of horses and costumes for himself, but his face is always depicted in the same way, with a vertically striped band from chin to bridge of nose. Rather than to attempt representation of personal physical characteristics, the artist uses this symbolic device alone to distinguish himself. His signature is a small running antelope, very like those drawn in the Southwest, which is shown under the horse he rides. The simple stylized drawings exhibit some feeling for arrangement. One, especially, is reminiscent of Egyptian perspective in the placing of rows of figures one above the other to indicate depth.[4]

Another publication presents selections from a series of paintings somewhat similar to those of Amos Bad Heart Buffalo, although the attendant report observes, "It is impossible to reproduce now this mass of drawing on any scale which would not be too minute for appreciation."[5] This group was made in 1881 for Dr. Charles E. McChesney of the U.S. Army, who obtained interpretations from the artist. Red-Horse, a Dakota at Cheyenne River, South Dakota, did this stylistic record of the Battle of the Little Big Horn on forty-one sheets of manila paper averaging 24 by 26 inches. The plates,[6] some in color, give a fair idea of the character of the original paintings now in the Smithsonian Institution. One shows the camp in abstract composition of three horizontal sections with vertical and opposing diagonal lines, very few of the areas in mass.[7] The battle scenes are lively depictions of men and horses in profile. Red-Horse had a natural gift for composition, as is seen in the successful handling of large numbers of riders within a compact area.[8] There is nicely detailed design in the warriors' trappings, and a lovely combination of soft tones in the areas of turquoise and yellow ochre, with spotting of black and vermilion. Both men and horses are seminaturalistic, with slight variation in contours.

Some interesting and variously conditioned reactions of artists and others to such works are recorded along with the pictures.[9] A Dr. Capitan, who had asked Omaha Indians to make drawings for him, exhibited them in 1883 in the Jardin d'Acclimatacion in Paris. He said concerning them, "It is singular to note that by the side of very rudimentary representation of human figures the pictures of horses are drawn with a certain degree of correctness." And, another observer, Richard Andree, publishing his opinions in Vienna in 1887, remarked that "The redskins east of the Rocky Mountains . . . are, however, very productive in fig-

188

ure drawing; nay, that art has advanced to a kind of picture writing. . . ." which, disadvantageously to the Indians, he compared with Australian drawings.

Garrick Mallery, however, had noted "many pictures in existence at that time," that "skill in drawing was observed by traders," and that "the idea of testing the artistic ability of Indians in several tribes, occurred to [himself] and to many other travelers, who generally have been surprised at the skill in free-hand drawing and painting exhibited." He cites Crevaux, a French voyageur who distributed pencils and "saw those savages, who are accused of being absolutely ignorant of the fine arts, all draw with extraordinary facility." Mallery added, "It would seem that the Indian had about the same faults and decidedly more talent than the average uninstructed persons of European descent who make similar attempts." Here he compares a drawing of two warriors on horseback, made by an "Apache Indian" (appears Cheyenne) at Anadarko, Oklahoma in 1884, with illustrations of thirteenth century German knights[10] and notes "a striking similarity," adding that, "doubtless still better examples could be obtained to compare the degree of artistic skill attained by the several draftsmen." Mallery refutes the legend that Indians were afraid of Catlin's representations by stating that the "Indians themselves drew figures in all views and parts."[11]

Navajos, too, were observed to be experimenting with colors and paper during this period. R. W. Shufeldt, writing in 1885-86, told of Choh, a Navajo youth of twenty-two or twenty-three, who lived near Fort Wingate, New Mexico, who drew intently on wrapping paper at the trading post at one of the counters where he acquired red and blue pencils from time to time. In describing Choh's work, Shufeldt made such remarks as these:

> . . . flaming red frogs with blue stripes down their backs and sides, with still more pretentious birds, will be found on every piece of paper that comes beneath the hand of this untutored artist. . . .

> His figures of Indian men and women are particularly worthy of notice, and one in watching him carefully can gain some idea of the relative importance that he attaches to the various parts of their war and ordinary trappings through the emphasis with which he depicts some of them. . . .

> . . . not much of a naturalist [as] delineations of birds and animals will testify. . . .

> . . . gaudily dressed chief riding at full tilt upon his Indian steed. His work seems rather above the average Indian artist, but as *I had seen many of*

189

their productions before and watched many of them while they executed them, I paid no special attention to this additional example of an old story. (Italics added.) [12]

What did impress Shufeldt, unfortunately, for it was the only example illustrated in his report, was Choh's effort at drawing a locomotive which was done childishly with crude attempts at light and shade, although scarcely any effort toward perspective. Shufeldt called it "good work for an untaught Indian," and added, "When we come to consider really how low they are in the scale of civilization, it is an astounding production."[13] Choh, it seems, drew several locomotives, "all from memory," even though the station was fully three miles from his home.

One wishes the author had given the Indian subjects preference in his illustrations—the "flaming frogs," the "pretentious birds," and the figures with their "war and ordinary trappings."[14] If these and some of the works of Choh's contemporary tribesmen had been recorded, they would be an invaluable link in the history of Indian painting and of American art.

It should be noted that around Choh's time some quite modern-looking mural paintings (in terms of the present) were being done on walls of certain pueblo houses. Watson Smith shows an 1899 photograph of murals in a large "room (not a kiva) at Zuñi." While these paintings must have had ceremonial significance, they clearly point toward the styles and some of the subjects and techniques of modern murals made outside the pueblos for public enjoyment.

These avant-garde though traditional works of Zuñi artists depict seminaturalistic animals, some of them three and four feet high, in a slightly animated procession along the walls at about eye level. Deer, antelope, rabbits, and other large and small quadrupeds touch a narrow base line while a large eagle with wings spread flies aloft. All appear to be painted in flat color with some indications of outline.

Early modern works, recorded by the U.S. Government, reached unusual excellence in a group of Hopi paintings made in 1900 for Dr. Fewkes, who used them in a study of Hopi Kachinas.[15] This group of paintings, bound in four volumes and now in the library of the Bureau of American Ethnology, is known as the *Codex Hopiensis*. It undoubtedly is one of the most important collections of aboriginal art in America. In Fewkes's account of the work he says that the idea of using Hopi paintings in this manner was suggested to him by then currently published Mexican codices, especially the celebrated manuscript of Padre Sa-

Figure 75. Zuñi Pueblo. *Procession of Animals.* 1899. Murals assumed to be in earth color tempera. Interior of a Zuñi house, not a kiva. After Smith (528). Peabody Museum, Harvard University photograph.

hagun,[16] and Chavero's *Lienzo de Tlascala,*[17] "lately (1892) published by the Mexican government."[18]

Fewkes found "several Hopi men competent to paint a collection of the kind desired, and finally chose for that work Kutcahonauu, or White-bear, a man about thirty years old, who was believed to be the ablest of all who were considered."[19] Fewkes says that the artist had picked up a slight knowledge of English at the Keams Canyon, Arizona, school and that, although he may have had some little art influence there, "this modifying influence is believed to be very slight, as the figures themselves show."[20]

Kutcahonauu's uncle, Homovi, who had never been to school, "drew some of the best pictures, the technique of which is so like his nephew's that it is safe to conclude that the drawings of the latter are aboriginal in character,"[21] according to Fewkes. The bird Kachinas—eagle, owl, cock, hummingbird, etc.—were painted by him. Another Hopi, Winuta, drew a few of the pictures. He, like Ho-

191

movi, had never been to school. Fewkes believed that "the pictures here reproduced and described may be regarded as pure Hopi, and as work little affected by the white teachers with whom of late these people have come into more intimate contact than ever before."[22]

"Paper, brushes, pencils, and pigments" were supplied by Fewkes who "left the execution of the work wholly to the Indians."[23] During the course of the painting the artists were at one time discouraged by gossip of sorcery which spread through the village, but they were reassured by Fewkes.

Of the paintings, Fewkes says, ". . . they show the ability of the Hopis in painting, a form of artistic expression which is very ancient among them. . . . As specimens of pictorial art the pictures here presented compare very well with some of the Mexican and Mayan codices."[24]

In this delightful group of paintings can be seen most of the conventions of modern Pueblo painting which have carried through to the present day. In the main, there is lack of perspective, of anatomical "correctness," and of light and shade. The paintings are flat and stylized yet they show great vitality. Potential action is evident even in the perfectly balanced, motionless representations. Animation is largely effected by color vibration and bold patterning.

Most of the figures are drawn with full-view heads and shoulders, with the rest of the body in profile, although a few have profile heads. In the case of these, both eyes are usually shown if they are of the globular sort, one of them extending from the center of the forehead. If essential features of a Kachina would ordinarily be obscured by a front view, as with *Kokopelli*, bearer of seeds, who has a traditional bulge in his back, a complete profile is attempted.[25]

Foreshortening is avoided although some feet and certain mask beaks are indicated as front view by actually drawing them more or less top view. In one instance a kneeling figure, *Huik*,[26] is drawn with legs turning out from the knees at right angles to the body. Considering the right-angular character of the costume details, shoulders and arms, this arrangement is much more pleasing than the stumpy effect that actual foreshortening would have produced.

Outlines are used around the main body of each Kachina and usually to separate the larger color areas. Pencil lines are left for this purpose in some instances although a heavier outline in black paint is more common. Color is used both in full intensity and in a semblance of earth tones, producing a lively appearance. The paint, transparent water color, so much thinner to handle than their native tempera, presented a problem in technique to the artists who had obvious difficulty in applying it. However, the accidental variation of color seems in keeping with the naivete of the drawings.

192

Heads, or rather masks in most instances, receive more attention than any part of the figures while hands and feet are insignificant. Masks are proportionately much larger than the rest of the body, with every symbolic detail meticulously represented.

Great care is evident in accurate drawing of details of costumes such as finely patterned embroidery designs of kilts and mantas, with even the intricate weaving and braiding techniques often represented in belts and sashes. Texture is rendered in fur, feathers, and hair, sometimes minute to the extent of painting individual strands of hair, or the guard hairs of the fur of pelts worn as part of the costume. Sashes and other parts of the garments are placed in such a way as to display all their important symbolic features regardless of the arrangement they might take in life.

A number of Kachinas are drawn in pairs, conveying the musical quality of the dance rhythm so often achieved in Indian painting by slightly varied repetition of line, pattern, and color. The figures of *Aya and Letotobi*[27] show how the painters avoid the dullness and static of exact repetition by using almost imperceptible differences. Other pairs are placed in opposition, as in the figures of *Tatacmu and Paski*,[28] and employ a strong countermovement of balanced masses and line directions. This, too, is one of the favorite devices of the Pueblo artist which has been used from the early days of textile and ceramic design. Opposite figures are seldom exactly reverse-duplicated, although they give the general appearance of being so. Vitality exists in the delicately calculated or perhaps intuitive variation.

Trees, clouds, and corn which appear with some Kachinas receive the same unnaturalistic treatment as that of the human figure, and indeed the same treatment they reveal in paintings of the present day. Clouds are like those in ancient pictographs. Trees are drawn with symmetrical branches, and corn with balanced ears and leaves. Roots and pollen are painted as important features of the corn.

A yellow antelope, in profile, with white neck bars and rump spot, and front-view pronged antlers, is very characteristic of all Pueblo antelopes. He might be considered one of the parent antelopes whose many offspring throughout Southwestern painting closely resemble him. The pictographic antelopes looked much like him, too, and those on the early pottery.

While there is a simple dignity about the drawing of all these Kachinas, clownish humor emanates from the *Koyimsi*,[29] or Mudheads. They are successfully portrayed as clever, friendly little pranksters, but the *Paiakyamu*[30] are drawn with a severe sort of humor, almost repellent. *Paiakyamu and Kaisale Mana* appear exactly as their contemporary impersonators.

193

Paiakyamû.   Kaisale mana.

Figure 76.   Hopi. *Paiakyamu and Kaisale Mana*. 1900. Watercolor. From original
in *Codex Hopiensis* of J. W. Fewkes, Smithsonian Institution. Cat. No. 4731.

In most respects these paintings are clearly forerunners of the modern
Pueblo school. Dr. Fewkes, in preserving them, made his most distinguished contribution to American Indian art. Without his art-discerning eye, which noted
each small detail of beauty throughout his studies in several branches of anthropology, our knowledge of the early modern phase of Indian painting would be at
a great loss.

194   Following the *Codex Hopiensis*, the next known work of the early modern school was that of Api-Begay, a Navajo whose colored drawings were discovered by Kenneth Chapman in 1901 near Pueblo Bonito. The artist had drawn some of the Navajo ceremonies on pieces of the trader's cardboard boxes with red and black pencils and had left a few of his pictures at the trading post where Dr. Chapman found them. Api-Begay was sought out at his hogan by Chapman who encouraged him by giving him a wider range of colors* and offering to buy some of the drawings. Unfortunately, Pueblo Bonito was a long way from Santa Fe in those days, and it was impossible for this encouragement of the drawings to be continued, but Api-Begay did complete several colored sketches for Dr. Chapman. This artist, like Choh, was an example of the undoubtedly many Navajos who demonstrated their artistic abilities when they had a chance at even the simplest materials.

An unknown Navajo of this period is said by Katherine Harvey to have been a prolific painter, an old man, whose works were collected by a reservation trader, Mr. Murphy, around 1902. This artist's dynamic, fragile impression of a *Feather Dance*, in pale orange, gray, and varied whites, with touches of black, on fine brown cotton cloth, is the oldest picture in the delightful collection made by Miss Harvey.

In 1908, four very good crayon drawings of Hopi Kachinas made by pupils at Sherman Institute, Riverside, California, were sent to the Smithsonian Institution where they were given a note of approval for the archives by Dr. Fewkes, referring to his own report on such works. Also, appended was a letter from Miss Anna Israel, of Sherman Institute, terming the work good "for untutored savages"—curiously, almost identical with Shufeldt's estimate of Choh's efforts some fifteen years earlier. Actually, these Hopi drawings are indistinguishable from their counterparts of today, and are among the rarest works of American art.

Alfredo Montoya, an earlier artist than Crescencio, is now recognized as having painted at San Ildefonso before the major art movement began there. Some of his paintings were obtained by Mr. and Mrs. Fred Henry of Denver while they were at the field camp of the School of American Research at El Rito de los Frijoles in 1908-1909.[31] Alfredo's painting is in the style later made famous by the San Ildefonso group which he, although a young man at the time the Henrys knew him, did not live to join in its great development. In 1941, Mr. and Mrs. Henry gave two examples of Alfredo's work to the School of American Research

*Dr. Chapman says, "These were colored pencils; Prang's. They were just out and the first set I had ever seen."

Figure 77. ALFREDO MONTOYA, San Ildefonso Pueblo. *Deer and Antelope Dancers.* 1908-1909. Watercolor. School of American Research. Cat. No. B1 59/72.

to be added to its priceless collection of foundational works of the modern school.

H. J. Spinden speaks of Alfredo Montoya's work and mentions that the artist had sold paintings in Santa Fe during the period when his home village of San Ildefonso "was at its lowest economic ebb."[32] Dr. Spinden also states: "In 1909-1912, while doing ethnological work in the Rio Grande Valley, [I] obtained several drawings from natives of Nambe and Cochiti covering gods and ceremonies. These, like the drawings collected by Fewkes, and other drawings met with occasionally as wall decorations in sacred chambers or as pictographs on cliffs and boulders, have a close similarity to the work now [1930] being produced on paper in water-color paints."[33]

Olive Rush—later to become one of the Southwest's leading painters—also bought Indian paintings and colored drawings at an early date, among them a number from Tesuque Pueblo which were made in 1914. She says that on some of her first trips to the pueblo she found a few of the men painting, among them, Pan-Yo-Pin (Tomas Vigil), Juan Pino, the Elder, of Tesuque, and Ce-Komo-Pyn of Santa Clara are three of the artists represented in her collection of early works.

Thus it seems that the modern school of Indian painting had diverse and gradual beginnings which were brought to focus in the work of Crescencio Martinez and his followers.

197

Through the series of paintings that Crescencio Martinez, Ta-e (Home of the Elk), did under the sponsorship of the School of American Research of Santa Fe, then directed by Edgar L. Hewett, and through the subsequent influence this important work had upon other capable young artists, he probably deserves the title of founder of the modern school of American Indian painting, although, as shall be noted, some opinions differed from this. At least, the modern school became locally recognized as such during the brief but influential course of Crescencio's painting career.

At the time of his death on June 20, 1918, a victim, "probably [of] pneumonia," during the influenza epidemic, Crescencio was still a young man.[1] He was an unusual Pueblo type, perhaps because of Navajo descent on the paternal side, rather tall and lean, with an uncommonly long head like a Basketmaker's, and clearly defined, angular, sensitive features.[2] In his native San Ildefonso Pueblo, he had been a decorator of pottery, working with his wife Maximiliana, sister of the later renowned Maria Martinez. He had also worked intermittently for Dr. Hewett and the School of American Research in the excavation of early Pueblo sites in nearby Pajarito Plateau. While doing so, he had shown a thoughtful interest in pictographs and paintings in excavated sites, and had told Dr. Hewett that he himself could paint.

It was during one of the field camps, in the summer of 1917, that Crescencio brought some of his paintings to Hewett, who, immediately recognizing the artistic and ethnological values of Crescencio's work, asked him to make more paintings. In fact, soon after this encounter, Hewett furnished paper and paints and engaged Crescencio to "produce, in watercolor, pictures of all the characters that

6. Crescencio and His Followers

appear in the summer and winter ceremonies" of his pueblo.[3] By the end of the year this pioneer series was completed, and, of Crescencio's subsequent paintings, Hewett says:

> In January 1918, he gave me a careful explanation of all the cardinal figures and costumes as he understood them and I commissioned him to paint a complete series of designs. The first twelve he finished and delivered late in winter. These he signed. The last ten were finished in the spring. He lacked only one (the second eagle), of finishing the commission. He completed the first eagle just a few days before his death. It was his last work.[4]

These works, now preserved by the School of American Research, Santa Fe, comprise what Dr. Hewett called *The Crescencio Set*. The paintings, entirely ceremonial in subject, are of groups and single dancers, also of drummers. They have a brooding quality, with little ease in the drawing but, rather, a careful hesitancy. There is an over-all sombre, serious mood, even sadness, in the characters; no gaiety in the dancers, yet the painting is light and delicate. The figures, with long heads like Crescencio's own, often appear as translucent as the puppets in a Chinese shadow play. At times they seem to be clothed in gauzy stuff, wrinkled and loosely hanging on the nimble, elongated bodies, fragile yet enduring. They are charged with life and vitality, graceful stepping, never at rest.

All the paintings are in transparent watercolor, displaying the varying intensities of hue common to that medium. The artist shows a preference for pale and greyed colors with brilliant, full-intensity hues in smaller areas. Dark, rich blues appear in manta hems, and clear bright reds in sashes and embroideries.

199

Figure 78.   CRESCENCIO MARTINEZ, San Ildefonso Pueblo. *Eagle Dance.* 1917. Water-color. Millicent A. Rogers Foundation.

Blacks are usually grayed; there is nothing heavy about Crescencio's work. His outlines are not traced in the customary black but are drawn in pencil only. Detail is minutely handled, with stitches in knitted leggings and woven belts, or texture in feathers, fur and hair finely indicated. Hands and facial features are all delicately drawn with an almost ascetic quality. In all, it might be said that Crescencio's painting, although obviously concerned with a certain amount of naturalism, is symbolic and other-worldly in character. If an attempt were made to compare it with another art, its closest likeness in style and mood might possibly be found in the melancholy and mystic art of Medieval Europe.

Other paintings, similar to this set, were bought from Crescencio by Alice Corbin Henderson and Mary Austin. One of these, *Mountain Sheep Dancers,* painted in 1918, is now in the collection of the Indian Arts Fund, Santa Fe. Other paintings by Crescencio are in the collections of the Millicent Rogers Foundation in Taos, the Mesa Verde National Park Museum, and the American Museum of Natural History.

While Crescencio was at work, other young artists were doing some of their initial painting. Several of these, too, soon began to use the room and materials

200

provided by the School of American Research at the Museum of New Mexico.[5]
Seven boys still in school received encouragement after class from Superintendent
and Mrs. John D. De Huff in their home at the Santa Fe Indian School.[6] Among
the latter were Ma-Pe-Wi, first signed Velino Shije and also known as Velino
Herrera,* of Zia, and two Hopi boys, Fred Kabotie and Otis Polelonema.[7] Awa
Tsireh (Alfonso Roybal) of San Ildefonso, a nephew of Crescencio, and Ma-Pe-
Wi were given commissions at the museum, to be joined later by the two Hopis.
Ma-Pe-Wi also continued at the Indian school, and Awa Tsireh painted both at
home and at the museum studio, selling his paintings to the museum and a few
of the townspeople. Like Crescencio, these artists painted without having re-
ceived formal instruction. Hewett says of Crescencio's and these artists' work:

> No one knew how he came by his remarkable ability. He had been taught
> nothing about drawing or color and, with no preparation or practice at all, did

*Many of the artists have more than one name. That most used by each in signing his paint-
ings will appear first or alone in the text.

Figure 79.   FRED KABOTIE, Hopi. *Snake Dance.* 1919. Watercolor. Collection of Jens
Jensen.

Figure 80. MA-PE-WI, Zia Pueblo. *Winter Dance.* Ca. 1935. Tempera. City Art Museum of St. Louis.

his work with accuracy and precision. Those who followed him, inspired by his example and by the appreciation accorded his work, have shown the same singular talent.

[These young Indians] were simply protected from learning art by our methods and enabled to go on in their own way in which no one can teach them.[8]

More artists, mainly from San Ildefonso, began to join the ranks of the new school. A few had been quietly working for some time; others had simply followed the lead of those who had begun to paint. Important among them were Julian Martinez (Po-ca-no), Richard Martinez (Opa-Mu-Nu), Oqwa Pi (Abel Sanchez), Soqween (So-kwa-wi, Encarnacion Peña), Tse-Ye-Mu (Romando Vigil), Wo-Peen (Luis Gonzales), and Quah Ah (Tonita Peña), a San Ildefonso girl who had gone as a child, after her mother's death, to live with an aunt who resided in the pueblo of Cochiti. Quah Ah had been painting since she was six years

202

old,* but at this time began to make known her work with the San Ildefonso group. These twelve, mainly, formed the nucleus of artists upon whose work the new school developed in the Pueblo region, although there were notable beginnings in a few other pueblos, particularly Zuñi, Tesuque, and the Hopi villages, which contributed to the larger development.

Dr. Hewett unhesitatingly places Crescencio in the lead of the entire group. "In this native American school the name of Crescencio Martinez will stand as

*Quah Ah, according to Alice Corbin Henderson, credited Miss Esther B. Hoyt, a teacher at San Ildefonso, with having encouraged her and her sister, Alfonsita, and Alfredo Montoya to paint in the pueblo day school. Miss Hoyt told the children to think of the dance in the plaza and of how they felt while dancing, and to paint that.

Figure 81. Tse-Ye-Mu, San Ildefonso Pueblo, *Bird with Fertility Symbols*, detail. 1924. Watercolor. Riverside Museum.

the first artist of record,"[9] he says, and further speaks of Crescencio as the one "to whom more than to any other one person was due the renaissance of painting in watercolor as a medium instead of the aboriginal earthen colors."[10] Awa Tsireh was "his succesor," and Kabotie and Ma-Pe-Wi were the other two "most noted" Indian painters in Hewett's estimation.[11]

Other early followers of the development of the modern school seem to doubt that Crescencio should be given all the credit for founding the new school. Dr. Spinden says, "The first Indians of the Southwest to make a display on their own initiative of water-color drawings of the local dances and mode of life were Crescencio Martinez and Alfredo Montoya, no longer ago than 1917* . . . [they are] now dead, but the school they started still carries on."[12]

Alice Corbin Henderson, who had bought work from Crescencio in 1916 and from Awa Tsireh a year afterward, says of the latter's work in relation to the new school:

> I thought as I looked at the drawings, that they pointed a new direction; and, indeed, Alfonso's example proved to be the start for a genuine new development of Pueblo art. Other Pueblo artists, turning from the decoration of pottery, began to record their more realistic impressions of the life about them, and soon there was veritably a "new school" of aboriginal watercolor artists, whose work was exhibited side by side with that of their white confreres in the Art Museum at Santa Fe.[13]
>
> . . . This new development, in fact, represented no "break" but was merely an extension of the centuries-old art tradition of the Pueblos. The transition, that is from the dwellings, through the symbolic pottery designs, to these more realistic but still highly conventionalized drawings of human forms was purely natural progression and sequence.
>
> What Awa Tsireh did, by his example, among the Pueblos was simply to release a whole store of latent visual impressions not previously recorded in any purely visual way. . . .
>
> [He] first projected the image of this new form of art among the Pueblos.[14]

According to Mrs. Henderson, Awa Tsireh's maternal grandfather was a full-blooded Navajo who, when a baby, was left behind after a raid and was adopted in the pueblo. His mother was one of the finest potters of San Ildefonso, as was his aunt, Tonita. In addition to these women, Mrs. Henderson says that one of Awa Tsireh's early influences was a "wise teacher" at the St. Catherine's Indian

204   * For earlier date, see p. 195.

School, Santa Fe, who let him draw as he pleased. Mrs. Henderson herself was very fond of Awa Tsireh and gave him much encouragement. Once she showed him a book of Japanese prints at which he looked thoughtfully, and, as Mrs. Henderson relates, "brushing his hand lovingly over a page, said simply: 'Made good.' What more can an artist say of another artist's work, or wish to have said of his own?"[15]

Of Crescencio's work, she said, "Alfonso's uncle, Crescencio Martinez, following his nephew's example, also made watercolors, before his death."[16]

Whatever claims can be made for the different versions of the beginning of the modern school, it can certainly be said that the time was ripe for a new Indian art expression to burst forth, and that several artists, more or less simultaneously and spontaneously, began to paint in the new manner. Of these, Crescencio will, in all likelihood, stand as the symbolic, if not the actual leader.

Certainly it would be difficult to distinguish among these earlier artists as to the fineness and unique interest of their individual accomplishments, yet a brief consideration of the work of a number of them, in addition to Crescencio's, might differentiate some of the individual styles which were emerging within the larger patterns taking shape in the new development.

Awa Tsireh is the stylist, the maker of beautiful, orderly patterns. His work is completely decorative—decorative realism. He achieves the utterly impersonal, unified, selectively stylized character of the Pueblo ceremonial. The figures in his paintings are always players, actors—never real people—giving an exaggeration, a dramatization of life in strikingly colored scenes. They are unit patterns in the whole pattern, formalized, with no hint of portraiture or effort at naturalism. The doll-like faces are set in oversize squarish heads with strong, square jaws and birds' eyes. Hands and all details are precisely drawn. Each feather is stylistically represented; each costume symbol and sash fringe is minutely done. In the larger ceremonial paintings, where often dozens of figures are brought into play, the artist creates rhythm and orderliness by an almost exact repetition of shapes and attitudes. Much differentiation in color spotting and design of small details keeps such groups from seeming regimented.

One of Awa Tsireh's favorite arrangements combines figures of human beings or animals with plants and abstract forms under a wide-arching rainbow above which, at either side, cloud terraces extend. The animation in life forms— the loping deer, the arch-tailed skunks, or the puppet-like dancers—presents a striking contrast to the formal, static beauty of the rainbow-cloud backdrop, giving a true theatrical effect. In these paintings the spaces frequently appear to be

205

Figure 82.   Awa Tsireh, San Ildefonso Pueblo. *Bear with Fawn.* Ca. 1925. India ink. Denver Art Museum.

mechanically measured and the arcs seem to be described by a compass, yet upon examination, slight variations can be found to prove that the pottery decorator's skill is responsible for the precision.

Awa Tsireh's drawing is usually two dimensional and flat although at times it shows that foreshortening is no problem to him. He occasionally combines three-dimensional with two-dimensional effects without clash, and often he uses accurate foreshortening together with an unusual kind of his own, producing a two-dimensional appearance. His line quality is extremely sure and exquisitely clean. Vigorous action is seldom seen in his work although when it does appear it never dominates the picture. Speed is held, by pattern and design, in the middle of the paper.

206

Much of Awa Tsireh's art shows a preference for vivid color, often the clear bright hues of India inks which he frequently uses pure. What might easily be garish color is set in gemlike brillance against deep, rich blacks, balanced area for area throughout the composition. In the 1917-20 stage of his work, Awa Tsireh forsook his stronger tones for softer hued watercolors outlined in pencil. These examples have a certain charm and delicacy that his bolder work lacks. In them he depicts not only ceremonials but subjects of genre, such as pottery making scenes.

One phase of his earlier work was given to abstract painting of fantastic birds, reptiles, and composite mythical monsters, done in complex design and scintillating color. Some aspects of these seem to be largely inventions of the artist, but on the whole, they undoubtedly had their origin in the esoteric beings of Pueblo mythology for, with all their obscurely involved symbolism, they clearly carry the marks of the rain cult—the Avanyu, stepped and terraced clouds, triangular fertility motifs, leaves, field symbols, and various water signs.

Ma-Pe-Wi has proved one of the most inventive and prolific of all the Indian painters. His invention may not cover as wide a range as that of the one or two other artists, but it is more intensive within a field he has chosen for himself. He is at once a naturalist, in the sense that Indian painting can be considered naturalistic, and a symbolist, and he is unique in his strong handling of naturalism and complete abstraction in the same composition, causing them to play upon and emphasize one another.

In his paintings of ceremonial and genre, Ma-Pe-Wi's figures are the people seen in the pueblo with all their differing characteristics; they are filled with warmth and life. Pottery makers, men working in the fields, buffalo dancers, corn dancers, Koshare, and the entire Pueblo pantheon are convincingly portrayed in their traditional functions. The earlier work of this type, more naive and done with less finesse, has more intriguing interest; the later painting is a marvel of technique which frequently overpowers the content. Its flawless brushwork, profusion of realistic detail, and exceedingly natural rendering of textures are amazing. The oily blue of turquoise, the hard-twisted wool of woven belts, brown crispness of buffalo manes, ceramic texture of ollas, the soft burnish of heavy silver are all his with seemingly no effort.

Much of this same tendency to naturalism is carried into Ma-Pe-Wi's hunting scenes where spirited huntsmen on well-groomed ponies pursue powerful buffalo. Here again there is purer design and decoration in the earlier work; however, in all his hunting scenes, Ma-Pe-Wi incorporates some classic symbolism representing

207

clouds, sun, terraced mountains, plant forms, or pictographic derivations. A succession of arcs, from which vertical lines drop as falling rain, mounts upward in the sky area of such paintings, and a base line, decorated with cloud or earth terraces, frequently extends across the lower portions. It is often in these hunting scenes that the artist's varied and ingenious interpretations of Pueblo legend and philosophy appear. He has a command of symbolism and a deep insight into its meaning. For all his skill at naturalism, it is in this imaginative employment of symbolism that Ma-Pe-Wi excels most. Some of his finest work utilizes abstract symbolism of sky, field, and forest with stylized plants and animals in purely creative scenes. It is here that one sees a strong kinship with certain of the most modern approaches to painting—those of emphasizing subjective values through interpreting exterior forms in relation to their basic meanings and original sources.

Kabotie is the most versatile of the painters, equally adept in recreating the unearthly quality of Kachinas, the formal pattern of Hopi ceremonials, and the informality, warmth, and intimacy of everyday pueblo scenes. He does varied illustrations, also, in which he shows himself to be a gifted analyst. In these he often does three-dimensional representation as successfully as an academically trained artist, evincing masterly draftsmanship, perfect proportion and anatomical "correctness," adroit perspective and foreshortening, thus proving, as Ma-Pe-Wi, that he can render naturalistic realism when he wishes, yet he does so with great originality and economy of means. And, too, he gives in these illustrations free rein to his wide range of interpretative power, creating the moods of humor and happiness, sadness or terror, of beasts and human beings in myriad situations.

It is undoubtedly in painting Hopi ceremonials and ceremonial participants, especially the Kachinas, that Kabotie reaches his highest art. His performers are not men dressed as gods; they are gods. Perhaps nowhere in the work of the modern Indian artists is the man-to-supernatural link, as interpreted by ceremonial impersonation, conveyed with such conviction as in Kabotie's art. Symbolic realism transcends representationalism—far and away, and painting becomes as persuasive as the dancers in life. It is morbid, fecund, weird, exhilerating, as the case may be. The figures stand out against the white or dark grounds of the paper, subtly rounded to produce the effect of the solid, wooden bulk of Kachinas or the uncanny forms of anthropomorphic and zoomorphic creatures. They are filled with vitality and potential action, emanating power.

Kabotie's composition is usually formal, conforming to the ceremonial patterns, or it is in other instances an organization of contrasting elements in which formal characters combine with incidentals and properties such as exquisitely

208

Figure 83. OTIS POLELONEMA, Hopi. *Preparing for the Buffalo Dance.* 1919. Gouache. Indian Arts Fund.

rendered melons, ears of corn, baskets, ollas, fir trees, and cottonwood boughs which appear as unusually potent still life.

Otis Polelonema is a strong artist and a true primitive. These facts jump straight to the eye. Much of the charm of the paintings is inherent in their straightforward and rugged naivete. They reflect the artist's ability to override rules to the direct creation of his own techniques and devices in the matter of such bugaboos as perspective, light and shade, and color theory. He masters them all, and how delightfully.

Polelonema's early works show Hopi interiors, and Hopi rituals in the brilliant sunshine of the Arizona mesas. Kachinas of multiple descriptions, and dancers, medicine men, farmers, brides, potters, clowns—all in the bright colors of actuality—people his pictures.

209

Figure 84. QUAH AH, Cochiti Pueblo. *Corn Dance.* Ca. 1930. Tempera. Museum of
New Mexico.

Quah Ah's art is an art of radiance and tranquility. It is possessed of delicacy and grace, and much music. It is unequalled at conveying the dignity, the
serenity, the great earnestness and wholehearted sincerity of the Pueblo ceremonial and the Pueblo people. Quah Ah's work is not ever spectacular or striking, but
it is completely unpretentious and authentic. She might be called a conservative

210

painter for she has set her own standards in keeping with tradition and has adhered to them through the years so consistently that, even beyond her death, she has never been superceded as the dean of Indian women painters.

Quah Ah's ceremonials conform to established patterns and yet they lack the impersonal, formal approach usually observed in ceremonial painting. Her dancers are conventional yet they are very living people. Her singers sing the most lustily of any in Indian paintings, the heavy women dance lightly on their toes, the drummers beat powerful rhythms from the big, resonant drums, and the staff bearer sways his weighty emblem of fructification over the heads of the dancers. Her Koshare appear not as spirits but as men disguised as spirits. There can be no deception in Quah Ah's painting but only straightforward, simple representation which amounts to realistic illusion in its own way.

She paints the cheerful contentment and peace of normal Pueblo life into her home scenes. Especially delightful are the groups of pottery makers in which Quah Ah demonstrates the craft and achieves convincing ceramic quality in the large ollas, always faithful in their decoration to traditional symbolism.

The artist shows more tendency to experiment in color than in any other aspect of her work. She sometimes uses bright colors in large areas emphasized by strong black outlines, black and white accents, and brilliant stripes. In other paintings her corals and turquoises gleam among softer colors and the staid blacks and whites. She frequently prefers transparent watercolor to the more generally favored tempera, and she carries her fresh, free watercolor treatment into work in oil.

Julian Martinez's watercolor painting was definitely a minor activity as compared to his brilliant achievements as the decorator of the pottery of his wife, Maria, yet, fine in its own right, it had a noteworthy influence upon other painters of San Ildefonso and upon many succeeding younger artists. Julian promoted a San Ildefonso *Deer Dance* style in which the dancers are shown in forward-bending attitude, usually with one foot swinging out backward. The figures are drawn in an extremely sure, incisive manner, the snow-white shirts outlined with such fine, unwavering brushlines as appear to have been done with a silver stylus. Deer, antelope, and mountain sheep are thus represented singly or in the entire hunting ceremonial. Tse-Ye-Mu is one of the main exponents of this style, adapting it in a bolder, more massive manner than Julian's. The style has had many interpreters throughout the Pueblo area in the past forty-years.

Julian introduced the Avanyu, variously improvised, into watercolor painting. He had used the motif in classic form upon pottery and, given the wider range of modern watercolors he carried the serpent figure to fantastic developments, incor-

211

porating it in mythical birds, dragon-like monsters, and other odd creatures. Several San Ildefonso artists painted individual variations of the motif in the twenties and thirties, and, in simpler version, it has appeared in the work of Ma-Pe-Wi and many younger Pueblo painters.

Another motif which Julian was influential in introducing is a certain equestrian figure which seems to be a Pueblo adaptation of the Plains warrior. In paintings of this subject, the riders often appear in warbonnet, buckskin, and other

Figure 85. JULIAN MARTINEZ, San Ildefonso Pueblo. *Hunter and Deer*. Ca. 1925. Tempera. Katherine Harvey Collection, Museum of Northern Arizona.

Plains-type clothing, and they usually carry shields and war or hunting equipment. The horses are stylish pintos or are plain, flat-colored steeds painted in a formal, somewhat rigid manner suggestive of carrousel ponies, quite unlike the angular, dashing horses of the Plains.

It is a matter of conjecture as to whether Julian or Awa Tsireh is responsible for the advent of the skunk in the new painting, but Julian uses this highly decorative animal most delightfully in many of his compositions, thereby establishing it as a fully respectable subject in Pueblo art.

Richard Martinez (Opa-Mu-Nu) is a versatile, poetic painter with a far and perceptive view of the Pueblo World extending from old Pajaritan mythical creatures to scenes and ceremonies of his native San Ildefonso. Although he stamps the character of his own environment upon each painting, he endows each form and rendering with a sort of magic inventiveness, even to the dancers whose dress and motions are regulated by convention.

The ceremonial subjects thus keep within the restraint of custom while possessing the ease and grace of unconfined movement and pattern. The artist paints small selective groups from larger ensembles—usually two to four figures which dance in space or beneath an arch of sky patterns. His single figures of eagle-, buffalo-, or deer-men move within an encirclement of rain and plant motifs, or are flanked on either side by symbols of the hunt or field.

Martinez's views of the plaza never become literal. In one, for instance, the small silhouette of a kiva serves as a magnetic center for various energies. Tracks of men and deer describe the life about it and entering into it. A spruce tree rises to shelter it on either side, plumes of Avanyu curl up toward it from the sacred spring, and rainbows bend down around it from clouds and sun. Far from being a complex picture, it is one of the simplest.

Animal and hunting scenes are equally perceptive, with sometimes a surprise of humor in a sedate setting, but it is in his inventions of bird- and avian-related beings that Martinez's originality reaches its height. All these he creates in tempera paint with characteristic freedom and fluidity of drawing and brushwork. The birds range from a broad-patterned turkey feeding in a windblown cornfield, beyond hunter hawk with rabbit, songster perched on fantastic flowers, airy snowbird mistily encircled by palest clouds, to omnipotent eagle with heart of sun and tongue of lightning within an aura of thunderbolts. Bird-related creatures take form in the feathered serpents. They become obscure in abstractions that combine pre-Columbian symbols with the artist's imagery growing out of them. These compositions are the most modern in appearance of all Martinez's works, and the most

213

Figure 86. SOQWEEN, San Ildefonso Pueblo. *Avanyus of East and West Fighting*. Ca. 1920. Gouache. Bayou Bend Collection, Museum of Fine Arts of Houston.

remarkable. Some elements in them may well relate through vanished trails to Sikyatki and Chevlon.

Soqween's painting of this earlier period has a sensitive, delicate character somewhat reminiscent of the art of Crescencio. It inspires a deeper response than

Plate XVI. CHIU-TAH, Taos Pueblo. *Taos Round Dance*. 1938. Tempera. Margretta
S. Dietrich Collection.

Plate XVII. Rufina Vigil, Tesuque Pueblo. *Mass at Fiesta*. 1936. Tempera. Collection of Mr. and Mrs. Max Kramer.

the more decorative aspects of Pueblo art usually do. This effect appears to result from his painting technique more than from any other factor, although his projection of emotional quality depends also on expressive drawing and intuitive composition. The paint never is smooth and flat but shows the uneven textures of varied mixtures and pressures through which he has directed his brush. His strokes of white paint on brown buffalo manes become the cold whiteness and softness of snow rather than decorative spots on a dark ground. And so does the paint in the other areas respond to its particular association beyond form.

Serpents and birds, especially turkeys, are Soqween's subjects, too, as well as are the performers of every public ceremony. They are stylized and even decorative, but they are moreover alive in a manner of their own. One of the finest of these works is of warring Avanyus, lashing in a tremendously forceful pattern of curving horns and sailing clouds. Here again, even in this commanding composition, the paint itself produces an effect of power and direction. This painting, one could say, should stand well in any contemporary show.

A number of young men at Zuñi, most of whom were necessarily anonymous in the early days when painting of modern aspect was forbidden there, were founding the Zuñi branch of the modern school while the above named artists were workin and around Santa Fe. A few names on earlier works did appear—Quetaque (Jefferson Yatock), Cheyatie, Newmi, Lawasewa, Pyler, Kylesdewa, Lamina, Hiuwa, and Bessetola—as opinion became somewhat more liberal.

Theirs are strong paintings of elaborately costumed masked impersonators and complex ceremonies. The works are bright, at times vivid, in color, large in motif, usually sketchy in detail and representation of textures. Slight action seems indicated in them, yet they are dynamic and mysteriously forceful. Unlike the work of the eastern pueblos, these mainly impressionistic paintings frequently contain suggestions of Matisse-like backgrounds and an unusual perspective in house interiors and in indication of diminishing figures. In the painting of the Shalako and other masked performers, the Zuñi artists favor a combination of front, three-quarter, and side views in a single figure. In general, the work shows a closer affinity with that of the Hopi artists than with that of the eastern pueblos, although it is quite distinctive from any other art.

From a consideration of all these representative styles and characteristics, it can be observed that several trends were in progress and certain conventions were formulating. In the main, the style of the new painting was more symbolic than naturalistic, although there were some leanings toward naturalism through

215

invented devices. There was little concern with modeling, foreshortening, and perspective, but, rather, an emphasis on realism gained through skillfully rendered line and suggestive color. Keen observation and intuitive understanding of nature

Figure 87.   PYLER, Zuñi Pueblo. *Interior of Shalako House*. Ca. 1920. Watercolor. Bayou Bend Collection, Museum of Fine Arts of Houston.

were always evident. In ceremonial paintings, the formal arrangement of the dance more or less dictated the composition. Freer arrangements appeared in genre subjects of occupations and home activities. Symbolic elements coupled with more naturalistic forms furnished the basis for some highly dramatic presentations of hunting episodes, woodland scenes, and, less commonly, ceremonial motifs. Skill controlled the execution of minute detail, and textures were convincing and varied through suggestive brushwork.

Watercolor paint was both transparent and tempera, although the latter, nearest the consistency of native earth color paints, was favored. Colored inks were occasionally used with brilliant results but they did not gain great popularity among the artists. Palettes differed widely with the painters, ranging from greyed tones to full intensities, with bright colors appearing more often. Garish color was uncommon. Outlines, varying from pencil gray to dead black, usually surrounded all major areas.

Pottery decoration had conspicuous carry-over into painting through motifs and technique. Not only the stylization and ingenious composition, the outlines and flat color areas, but actual motifs were often adopted from ceramic art. The Avanyu, terraced and semicircular cloud designs, bird figures, plant units, and rainbow bands were among the motifs taken over from pottery.

Although the new painting did not have the strictly religious intent embodied in most of the pottery decoration, it clearly possessed much of the same spirit of the older art, and, in its use of symbolism, remained quite conservatively true to precedent. In fact, these paintings usually were made for direct gain, yet never at the expense of tribal standards of dignity and good taste.

Influential conventions and mannerisms perfected by individuals in the new school were manifested in such figures as Ma-Pe-Wi's balanced cornstalks and spruce trees, and his successive-arc cumulus clouds, Julian Martinez's ponies, deer dancers, composite serpents, and skunks, Kabotie's Kachinas and still-life elements, Polelonema's experimental perspective, Awa Tsireh's rainbow-cloud backgrounds and his theatrically conceived dancers, Richard Martinez's abstract life forms, Quah Ah's bright-blanketed choruses, Soqween's decorative naturalism, the Zuñi group's impressionism, Crescencio's religious concept of ceremonial painting.

It can also be noted that, from the work done thus far, five major divisions of painting subjects had been established in the Pueblo development of the modern school: 1) ceremonial, 2) hunting, 3) genre, 4) fauna and flora, and 5) abstract compositions.

217

The Kiowa branch of the modern school of Indian painting began at about the same time that Crescencio and the San Ildefonso group were founding the new schools in the Pueblo region. Like that of the latter group, the Kiowa's initial work was encouraged by a few appreciative individuals.

The first of these was Susan Peters,* who, in 1917, had gone out to the Kiowa country as a field matron in the United States Indian Service, with headquarters near Anadarko, Oklahoma. Mrs. Peters had at one time been a student of art and had done some painting of her own, so she had not been long in her new position when she began to notice that several young people on the reservation were making attempts at drawing with whatever materials they could find. She became greatly interested in their efforts and decided to help them.

The following year Mrs. Peters organized what she called a fine arts class and invited all those who wished to paint to join it. The mayor of Anadarko took notice of this pioneering project and offered to provide a room for the class to use as a studio. Mrs. Peters bought the painting materials herself, for no adequate equipment was furnished by the Indian Service. Soon, twenty-three painters were enrolled, among them Monroe Tsa Toke (Tsa-to-ke, variously spelled). Stephen (Steven) Mopope, Spencer Asah, James Auchiah, and Jack Hokeah. They worked mostly unadvised but Mrs. Peters gave them what technical help she could. The opportunity of having materials and the stimulation of working together through Mrs. Peters' thoughtful provision and suggestion eventually resulted in such an

218 *The account of initial work of the Kiowa School is based on conversations with Mrs. Peters and with a number of the artists.

7. The Founding of the Kiowa School

improvement in the artists' work that some of them began to sell their paintings.

Mrs. Peters had heard of the New Mexico developments and decided to go over to see for herself what was being done by the Indian painters in the Pueblo area. She took time out from her field matron's duties to go to Santa Fe where she carefully examined the results of the new movement. Whatever ideas she thought might be helpful in her work with the Kiowa group she took back to Anadarko. It was not her intention to transfer techniques or styles but to observe, for the good of her own project, how common problems arising in the two new developments were being met at Santa Fe.

During the ensuing decade, more artists advanced their work to exhibition quality, and a few, having grown to college age, had achieved such stature in painting ability that Mrs. Peters decided to help, and to obtain aid for, them to enter the University of Oklahoma. She made arrangements with Prof. O. B. Jacobson of the art department for their entrance in January 1928. Tsa Toke, Mopope, Asah, Hokeah, Auchiah, and one young woman, Bou-ge-tah Smokey, first entered the art classes of the university through this arrangement.

At Norman, the young artists came under the influence of both Jacobson and Prof. Edith Mahier who immediately realized that here was remarkable talent. Jacobson says that, "Encouraged and stimulated by the friendship and sympathetic interest [of the professors] they have perfected their art until their work has acquired national attention."[1]

No scholarships had existed at that early date for Indian art students; however, L. H. Wentz, of Ponca City, became aware of the work and provided the equivalent of nominal scholarships for the artists, thus giving them freedom for

219

Figure 88. Tsa Toke, Kiowa. *The Cormorant*. Ca. 1940. Tempera. William and Leslie Van Ness Denman Collection.

full-time art work at the university from January through May. Jacobson describes the results of their work during that period as "astounding."[2]

Work by the group was within a short time exhibited in several museums of the United States, and, by summer of 1928, it had made its debut in Europe at the International Congress of Folk Arts in Prague. In 1929, Prof Jacobson published a portfolio of Kiowa painting in France.[3] Under his sponsorship, Kiowa painting gained a wide notice during the next two years, then, in 1931, it joined the Exposition of Indian Tribal Arts for a two-year tour.

Within the next few years, there were numerous group exhibitions and one-man shows of Kiowa painting. Anadarko continued as home base for many of the artists, and there Mrs. Peters never failed to advise and assist them. She repeatedly made the long trip to Gallup, New Mexico with exhibits of their painting for the Inter-Tribal Indian Ceremonial, and managed sales and collected prizes for them there and elsewhere. Through her continued efforts on behalf of this art which she quietly fostered from the beginning, Mrs. Peters encouraged younger painters to join the group from time to time, and extended interest to Oklahoma tribes other than the Kiowa.

220

Another source of appreciation and support to the Kiowa artists was Mrs. William Denman, of San Francisco, perhaps the most consistently discerning collector of Kiowa paintings. Since the early days when she became acquainted with Mrs. Peters' work, Mrs. Denman followed the accomplishments of Kiowa artists.

Kiowa paintings are inspired by ceremonial dances such as the War Dance, Medicine Dance, Dance of the Dog Soldiers, Hummingbird and Eagle Dances, Hoop and Feather Dance; the Peyote Cult; singers, flutists, drummers, war and hunting parties, legend, ritual, and genre.

In comparison to contemporary work of the Pueblo School, Kiowa painting, in general, appears broader in treatment, heavier in color and stronger in color contrasts, more uniformly stylized, and more emphatically decorative. Many paintings are of single figures or small groups; large ceremonial compositions are seldom seen in work of this period. Seated and rear-view figures, and portrait-style heads are fairly common in Kiowa painting, whereas they are rarely found in paintings of most other tribes.

The works of Hokeah, Mopope, Auchiah, and Asah seem at first glance very much alike, yet, upon more careful examination, many individual differences appear. There is something about many Kiowa paintings which strongly recalls figures in Mexican codices. Especially is this true of Hokeah's work. His boldness in broad handling of the brush and simplicity of detail; certain attitudes of dancers and the manner of drawing hands and feet, feathers, fans, and bells; and the utter lack of emotion in his painting are reminiscent of figures particularly in the Tonalamatl of the *Codex Borbonicus*[4] and in the *Codex Nuttall*.[5] His dancers are theatrical, and are conventionalized with a sameness which at times verges upon stencil-like monotony, yet they are arresting and powerful.

Mopope's painting has more emotional quality, greater delicacy and differentiation, pleasanter balance in the strong tones and more frequent use of lower values to offset solid blacks and intense spottings of white. The faces have mobile variation and less of stereotyped rigidity, expressing diverse moods. Detail is finer yet not comparable to that of most Pueblo painting.

Auchiah creates fascinating color contrasts; for example, he plays brilliant red and white against dull yellow, blue, and full intensity black to gain a surprising vitality. His gay color gives certain animation even to figures in repose, and added liveliness to those in action.

The character of Asah's work is contradictory; at times it is very stiffly stylized, as in his formal ritual scenes, at others, it is possessed of unusually light

221

222 Figure 89. JACK HOKEAH, Kiowa. *War Dance.* Ca. 1930. Tempera and silver paint. Bayou Bend Collection, Museum of Fine Arts of Houston.

grace and suppleness, especially in the single dancers which seem alive and convincingly moving.

Bou-ge-tah Smokey's painting shows a naive charm and a more naturalistic conception than that of the above artists. Her subjects evince a greater interest in genre than in ceremonial, and her more hesitant technical handling does not detract from the straightforwardness of her compositions.

Of the Kiowa group, Tsa Toke stands most apart, related, yet individual. His art has depth and sensitivity, stronger realism, and almost none of the straight theatre and poster boldness which characterize modern Kiowa painting in general. With a few adroit brushstrokes, he conveys character—an aged, pensive face of a tribal matriarch, the lean, shrewd features of the Plains warrior. Yet in his decorative realism he does not forsake imaginative symbolism. His Peyote ritual motifs,[6] simple yet emanating vitality, have power to evoke the mysticism of the cult. In different mood and flowing line, groups of the artist's ceremonial men move rhythmically through repetitive units, communicating the shifting patterns of the dance forms. Tsa Toke knows how to put color to specific use—a full palette of strong intensity for depictions of animation; muted grays or simple blacks and whites for concentration upon religious mood in inscrutable ritual. As Mrs. Denman has said, "Tsa Toke's work seems to show that he felt deeply, with a subconscious relationship, what he painted of the tribal life of his ancestors."

Fully aware of the importance of this remarkable outgiving of heretofore latent talent, several other unusually appreciative people joined earlier sponsors in a concerted effort to encourage the development of the modern school of painting together with Indian art in its various forms, and thus they initiated the Santa Fe movement. It was an enterprise founded on intelligence and goodwill of the finest kind. Santa Fe, culturally rich and, in those days, peacefully beautiful, had been the place chosen from all America by these people as their home. Here were internationally known artists—painters, poets, musicians—scientists whose work related to the arts, and others creative in their active appreciation.

Mary Austin, who was one of them, spoke of members of the group as "people with the training which would enable them to evaluate the decorative art of the New Mexican aboriginals," and she particularly mentioned Kenneth M. Chapman, to whom "we owe most of the light we have on Pueblo aesthetics."[1]

The Santa Fe movement was twofold: it helped to bring arts forth from the obscurity that had been caused by stupid, sometimes apparently vicious, policy at the hands of government agents and by the broadside impact of an alien culture; and it formulated and advanced methods by which remains of the finest examples of the arts that had gone before might be rescued and preserved from increasing destruction.

The movement began as an immediate campaign of calling attention of the public to the unrecognized treasure of Southwestern Indian art through voicing pleas for its continuance. One of the first statements came from two pioneer Southwestern artists, Ernest Blumenschein and Bert Phillips, founders of the art colony in nearby Taos. Believing that good deeds should begin near home, they

8. The Santa Fe Movement 1919-1932

gave an eye-opening address in Albuquerque early in 1919. In their joint talk, "Appreciation of Indian Art," later published in the *Evening Herald*,[2] Mr. Phillips said in part:

> There are many gifted artists among the Indians. Their conceptions are as individual and full of racial character as those of the Japanese, and should be cultivated as such. I have seen paintings done entirely without instruction that were wonderful; the composition, the color, the whole feeling, splendid; and yet absolutely Indian in character.
>
> There is a great future in Indian art; of this we artists are confident. It will be recognized and appreciated and will prove of definite commercial value. Already the artists are buying paintings of the Indian artists.

And Mr. Blumenschein said:

> If in the adoption of a "higher" civilization the Indian gives up his own remarkable gifts to the world, the loss will be irreparable. The art of the Indians is not only beautiful, but it is unique . . . the aboriginal American has actually contributed more to the arts than two hundred years of "civilized" occupation of North America has produced.

In the same year Natalie Curtis, author of studies of both music and decorative arts of the Indian, then living in Santa Fe, wrote:

> It seems a curious fact that in the long contact of the white race with the strikingly indigenous people of America, we have never recognized the art-crafts of the Indian as an asset to the nation's culture and a stimulus to our own industries. We echo Europe, whereas we might develop a decorative art truly American.[3]

Also, during this year, several more new painters appeared among those under Superintendent and Mrs. De Huff's personal encouragement at the Santa Fe Indian School.[4] Noteworthy among them were two San Juan boys, Manuel Cruz and Guadalupe Montoya, and "a Taos boy" who did a "native and primitive drawing."[5] Works by these and other artists were shown in two exhibits at the Museum of New Mexico.[6] The first group was purchased by Mabel Dodge Luhan, then Mrs. Maurice Sterne, who lent the pictures for further display.[7]

Following these local exhibitions, plans moved toward larger showings of Indian art. The leader in this cooperative effort was John Sloan, whose summer studio was in Santa Fe and who was then president of New York's Society of Independent Artists which held an annual exhibition at the Waldorf-Astoria Hotel. It was he who planned the introduction of American Indian painting to the critics and public at the time of the March-April 1920 show of the Independent Artists, as a feature of the exhibition. This provided the first opportunity for people to see Indian painting displayed on a par with that of other contemporary artists. It was the first time, in fact, that Indians had been presented to the nation as *living* artists.

John Sloan wrote from the exhibition to Sheldon Parsons, then art director of the Museum of New Mexico, describing the great interest shown.[8] Art critics immediately recognized the quality of the work. Characteristic of their comment was that of Walter Pach who called the paintings "primitives in the true sense of the word," and further stated:

> Effect of instinct is at once apparent if we consult the older arts of the Indian: the great paintings on skin, the pottery with its decoration, the katchinas or dance effigies, the textiles, and so on. Always one has a sense of the Indian frankness . . . his lyric, epic, or humorous quality entering only unconsciously to give a certain tone to the scene and to make the justness of his vision the more convincing, for no art so spontaneous could fail to bear with it the impress of the artists' mood.
>
> Drawing of detail is of fair-fineness, even where the ensemble is most massive. The richness of the whole is worthy of a great Oriental school, but this work is different from the Oriental and nearer to us: it is American![9]

Mr. Pach had urged recognition and preservation of Indian art in a previous article in which he spoke of the purity and the austere beauty of Indian painting, "quite worthy of a European primitive."[10]

Two other noteworthy exhibits of 1920 were those sponsored by two of Santa Fe's distinguished poets. Mary Austin made arrangements with the Ameri-

226

can Museum of Natural History in New York for paintings from San Ildefonso Pueblo to be shown,[11] and Alice Corbin Henderson with the Arts Club in Chicago for an exhibit of Awa Tsireh's beautiful miniatures. Among other paintings shown simultaneously with Awa Tsireh's was a group from Ananda Coomaraswamy. "Thus East meets West at this exhibit which is further enriched by Czechoslovak water colors,"[12] observed a reviewer, who no doubt saw many similarities in the styles and techniques of the eastern and western Indian paintings.

Sponsorship of a more personal kind was being given by another Santa Fean, Olive Rush, the artist who was to have one of the greatest influences upon the development of modern Indian painting. As has been mentioned, Miss Rush had already gone as early as 1914 to out-of-the-way places in the pueblos to seek unknown and little known painters doing small watercolors and crayon sketches of pure Indian quality, and to give them her quiet, strong encouragement to continue creating in a manner wholly their own. In addition to purchases of beginning works already noted, Miss Rush later bought several early attempts of Quah Ah, Awa Tsireh, and Julian Martinez.

In 1921, popular demand brought a return appearance of the Pueblo painters at the Independent Show. Many favorable comments were made in the New York press at the time, and the Independents enthusiastically made the claim that "these Indian paintings are the greatest art produced in America."[13]

Soon after the New York show, the Indian artists participated in a large, all-Southwestern exhibit which the General Federation of Women's Clubs sponsored at Salt Lake City. Of the Indian paintings, it was said by a reviewer that they were "The most unique feature of the entire exhibition . . . they represent the most purely American art yet produced."[14]

By 1922, visitors to Santa Fe had joined the movement. E. H. Cahill gave an appreciative description and critic's appraisal of Indian painting, and also told of the beginnings of the modern school. Underlying his entire paper there was urgence for recognition and understanding. He called the paintings "works of art in themselves, valid for all time," and contrasted their method with that of the European who would handle masses of light and shade while the Indian would concentrate on what the artist knows. He further said:

How really fine was the American Indian civilization—for it was a civilization—and how many things it has added to our Caucasian world is beginning to dawn upon us . . .

The ability of any race to create an art as great in its originality and its simple power as this Indian water-color art is proof sufficient that it is far from its period of artistic senescence.[15]

227

Another summer Santa Fean, Rose Dougan, set aside a fund from which the income was to be distributed by the Museum of New Mexico during the week of the Fiesta as prizes for Indian artists and craftsmen to encourage them to raise their standards in the continuation of their own typical arts.

This was the first year of the annual Indian Fair, then held in the armory, but in most years since, under the portál of the Palace of the Governors where craftsmen and artists display their products. Painting prizes of the first fair went to Fred Kabotie, Velino Shije, Antonio Garcia, and a Zuñi painter who signed himself George C.[16] Dr. Chapman led in the organization and assemblage of this exhibition which continued thereafter.

The following month, October of 1922, saw the opening of Amelia Elizabeth White's Gallery of American Indian Art in New York City.[17] Miss White thus extended to the East the dynamic influence she had brought to the Santa Fe movement. Exhibitions of only the finest Indian paintings and other arts were to be shown in the gallery, making it an authentic and unique contribution to the many faceted art of New York City. Later, with the encouragement of Mrs. John Sloan, Miss White was to multiply this influence immeasurably through gifts from her private collections to many museums.

During this year, too, Dr. Hewett had called the attention of artists nationally to Indian painting through his address before the national convention of the American Federation of Arts in Washington, D.C. He told of the work thus far, and of the promising outlook for a great revival and development of Indian painting. "We have demonstrated in the Southwest that the aesthetic spirit of the people lives and responds to friendly encouragement," he said.[18] John D. De Huff, who had worked far ahead of his time in Indian education, also gave a talk before an educational convention in which he spoke for government recognition of Indian art through Indian schools, and pointed out the "distinct loss to the world at large" which would ensue from an indifferent policy.[19]

The New Mexico Association on Indian Affairs was organized in 1922 with William and Alice Corbin Henderson, Francis Wilson, Margaret McKittrick, Martha White, Gustave Baumann, and Sara McComb as its prime movers. Soon the Association became actively concerned with Indian art through its arts and crafts committee which made selections, did judging, and provided prizes for arts exhibited during various fiestas in the pueblos.

The Santa Fe Movement gained momentum and power with the establishment of the Indian Arts Fund in the autumn of 1923. Kenneth Chapman had led the way. Withdrawing from archaeological work by degrees, he had been a one-man force for a good many years in searching out specimens of the fast-disappearing post-Spanish Pueblo pottery of earlier days, and recording their painted motifs. He realized that, while prehistoric wares were lying in comparative safety in various ruined sites, pottery in daily use was disappearing by the minute, and along with it a wealth of irretrievable ceramic painting.

A few people, Dr. Harry P. Mera, Frank Applegate, Mary Austin, Alice Corbin Henderson, Andrew Dasburg, Elizabeth Shepley Sergeant, and one or two others, realized the importance of the work and saw that it needed immediate support to be effective on any scale. It was the cooperation of these people that established the Indian Arts Fund expressly "to revive the Arts and Crafts of the Indians by giving them free access to the choicest specimens of their tribal handi-work. To educate the people of the United States as to the value of America's only surviving indigenous art."[20] The small organization, incorporated in 1925, has since operated with no salaried employees and with no inducement over and above the altruistic purpose which prompted its inauguration.

Never relaxing in their efforts to acquaint the public with the importance of Indian art, the writers of Santa Fe continued to tell of it. At about the time of the establishment of the Indian Arts Fund, Alice Corbin Henderson addressed American colleges and universities through a compelling article in *Poetry* of which she was associate editor. In what she titled "A Plea for the Study of Indian Culture," she said:

> Again, our artists are endowed with scholarships to enable them to study classical or archaic Greek or Roman art in Italy or Greece; but where is the scholarship to send young art students to Arizona or New Mexico to study a living art of design as unique as that of Greek or Etruscan vases?[21]

And, through her own fine discernment, she conveyed the thought that "An appreciation of Indian culture implies a background of general culture."

Mrs. Henderson regarded the artists with a warmth of understanding, for she knew them well. Even before Crescencio's sponsorship by the Museum of New Mexico, she had noticed his art. In the summer of 1916, Crescencio and his wife were employed by the Rocky Mountain Camp Company whose headquarters were old La Fonda in Santa Fe. They lived and worked in the courtyard stables, Crescencio caring for the horses when he was not painting at a little table in the courtyard. Here, Mrs. Henderson, coming in to leave her horse, watched Crescencio paint and sometimes she bought his pictures. She said some of these works, now in the Indian Arts Fund Collection, "grew in the stable while the horses fretted under the flies."

229

Awa Tsireh also received her personal encouragement, from the summer of 1917 when she first saw his pictures at El Rito de los Frijoles. She had gone there with Dr. Ananda Coomaraswamy, artist-philosopher of India, who "had noticed the alliance of this work to that of East India and Persia" and that the horses had the "alert vitality which only primitive artists, or Orientals, seem to be able to give to the drawing of animals."[22] Awa Tsireh, in the years that followed, often brought paintings to the Henderson home where Mrs. Henderson herself would purchase or would send them to Chicago for exhibition. She wrote of this young artist's work in 1925: "Awa Tsireh's drawings are, in their own field, as precise and sophisticated as a Persian miniature. The technique which has produced pottery designs as perfect as those of an Etruscan vase has gone into his training," and she asked for a more intelligent understanding of work such as his in order that "the whole fabric of Pueblo art may not only be preserved, but may be encouraged to develop along its own lines—to no telling what achievements."[23]

There were two significant exhibits in 1925—one at the Arts Club, Chicago,[24] was assembled and presented by Miss White; and the other, also in Chicago, was a one-man show by Awa Tsireh at the Newberry Library[25] where his meticulous brushwork must have been in perfect harmony with the minute detail of miniatures in fine old Books of Hours and other manuscripts in the rare collections there.

The Santa Fe movement was strengthened as it progressed by addition of new members to the original supporting group from time to time. One of the most capable and constant friends the Indians of the Southwest have ever had came to live in Santa Fe in 1926. Mrs. Charles H. Dietrich had already become acquainted with many Indian people and with Indian painting through her several previous visits to the area. Her purchases of early watercolors by Quah Ah were to mark the beginning of one of the world's finest collections of modern Indian paintings, and her encouragement of the initial watercolor art at Zuñi was to lead into the individual encouragement of scores of artists in the years following. Mrs. Dietrich had not been long in Santa Fe before the New Mexico Association on Indian Affairs claimed her as its president, the position it never allowed her to leave except in an emeritus capacity during her last years. Under her leadership, the Association became nationwide in its influence, not only in maintenance of fine standards in the Indian arts, but also in betterment of health, economics, and various crucial problems affecting the Indian Southwest.

Influences from the Association and the entire Santa Fe movement, together with results of certain contemporaneous efforts on behalf of the Indian in other localities, finally reached Washington. An impartial commission from the Institute

Plate XVIII. Quincy Tohoma, Navajo. *Riders Resting.* 1937. Tempera. Margretta S. Dietrich Collection.

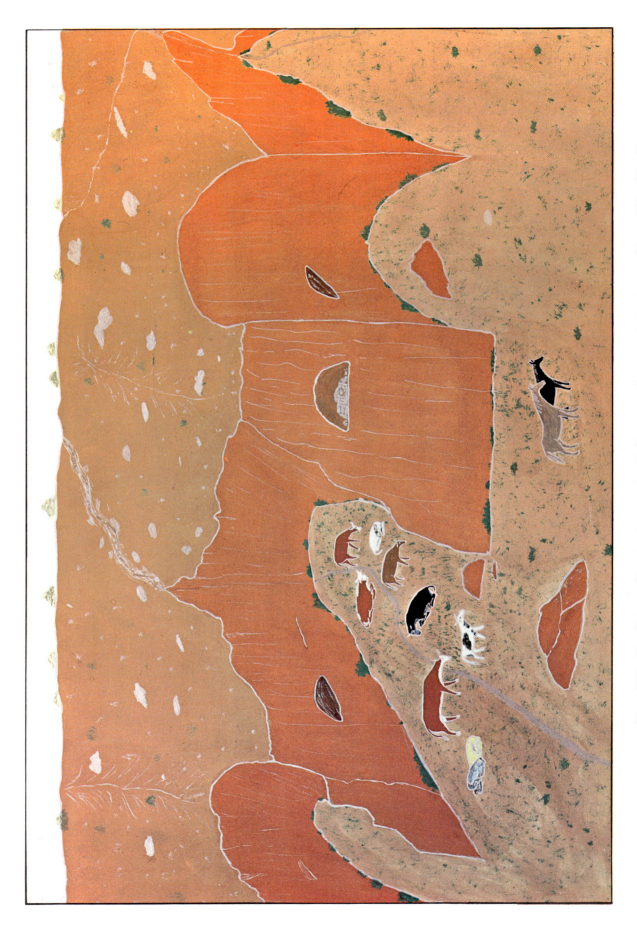

Plate XIX. Ned Notah, Navajo. *Canyon de Chelly.* 1936. Tempera. Collection of Mr. and Mrs. Max Kramer.

for Government Research, appointed by the Secretary of the Interior, Hubert Work, began in 1926 to make a thorough investigation in the field of Indian administration, which resulted in dynamic changes in government policy affecting many aspects of Indian Service, including the arts.

During the following year, the Denver Art Museum opened its main gallery to an exhibit of Indian art including the Anne Evans Collections of paintings, later shown at the University of Colorado.[26] The musuem at this time announced plans to establish an Indian arts collection. Throughout the ensuing years, its program for Indian art appreciation became internationally known through its authoritative and clear Indian Art Leaflet Series[27] and traveling exhibitions inaugurated by its first Curator of Native Arts, Frederic H. Douglas.

An exhibition in New York, too, marked the season of 1927. It was held at Corona Mundi,* International Art Center on Riverside Drive where "the paintings made a tremendous impression upon the Eastern public, and their spontaneity of conception and real beauty of color, and design, has been praised in the Eastern press."[28] An unusually large number of artists, some new names appearing, was included in the showing: Fred Kabotie, Awa Tsireh, Tse-Ye-Mu, Quah Ah, Otis Polelonema, Oqwa Pi, Pan-Yo-Pin, Ma-Pe-Wi, Julian Martinez, Santiago Coriz, Cipriano Chaves, and Crescencio Martinez. The show was so well received that associates of *The Nation* asked that it be displayed during a dinner honoring the American Indian where there were many tributes to those who had helped "in inspiring the American Indian to this new effort at creative work and of again infusing his fine imaginative spirit into the sum total of America's creative fire."[29]

This year of wide recognition of Indian art witnessed the most successful Indian Fair that had ever been held in Santa Fe. Exhibits were finer and were participated in by more artists, including painters from the Kiowa branch of the modern school. The prize lists were longer because of a substantial increase in the Indian Fair endowment fund. The Museum of New Mexico, during its sponsorship of the fair, had done much to raise the general level of exhibits. Following the Museum's precedents, an arts and crafts committee assumed responsibility for the fair with Kenneth Chapman continuing as advisor and judge.

It was 1927, also, that saw the incorporation in Santa Fe of the Laboratory of Anthropology, a direct outgrowth of the Indian Arts Fund. The year before, John D. Rockefeller, Jr., had visited Santa Fe and was impressed by the work done by the organization in its collections, then housed in the basement of the

*Now the Riverside Museum.

231

Museum of New Mexico. He asked how the Fund had obtained such amazing results. Dr. Chapman said that the name *The Indian Arts Fund* had been chosen because it frankly "sounded like money," and that members had obtained subscriptions by every fair means possible. Mr. Rockefeller recognized the need of a home for the rapidly expanding assemblage of choice pottery, paintings, silver, weavings, and other arts which even then covered the shelves and much of the floor. He offered a grant for the creation of a laboratory in which the collections could be exhibited and studied.

In 1928, formal announcement of Mr. Rockefeller's $200,000 grant for the erection and equipment of the first unit of the Laboratory of Anthropology was made, and his offer of further gifts proportionate to scheduled amounts from other donors was outlined.[30] John Gaw Meem was to design the building for which a fifty-acre site had been given by Senator Bronson M. Cutting and the Misses Martha and Amelia Elizabeth White of Santa Fe. Many of the leading names in anthropology were among the board members and trustees of the planned institution. This new home, commensurate with the beauty and potentiality of the objects it was to house, and adequate for future extension of conservation and research definitely oriented toward art as well as other aspects of the study of man, was indeed a great prospect.

Meanwhile, in the same year, Indian painting exhibitions gained further attention from art critics. In Dallas, where a showing by ten Pueblo artists was sponsored by the Dallas Art Association, Alexander Hogue, of the *Times-Herald*, spoke of a "sophisticated art," and of the nine-year movement which had aided it, and observed the futility of the Indian artist who deserts such achievements for inferior work in an imitative manner.[31] Nearer home, twenty-four watercolors from the School of American Research displayed in Roswell, New Mexico, received an appreciative review in the *Southwestern Dispatch*.[32] A San Francisco exhibition was acclaimed and perceptively detailed in the *Chronicle* whose critic termed the paintings "amazingly Oriental in treatment, resembling Persian miniatures."[33]

In the next two years there were exhibits in Madrid,[34] in Prague at the International Congress of Folk Arts,[35] and at the Brooklyn Museum.[36] Included in these exhibitions were Miss White's collection of Pueblo painting and a few works of the Kiowa group. Dr. Spinden arranged the Brooklyn exhibit to suggest origins of certain motifs of the paintings by including examples of pottery, Aztec hieroglyphs, Kachinas, and tablitas. It was an unusually meaningful and delightful exhibit, the idea of which might well be used again and again in different places.

232

Dr. Spinden wrote from long and knowing experience of the paintings and of the *Codex Hopiensis*, one volume of which was lent by the library of the Bureau of American Ethnology to accompany the modern works: "The American Indian is truly the Great Symbolist," whose art exists not only to express an idea of beauty but to "win invisible friends and block invisible enemies in the mystical hinterland of his life."[37] Paintings in the exhibit showed the original freshness and vital drawing of the works of this period. One by Ma-Pe-Wi, *Hunting Deer and Turkeys in the Snow*,[38] depicted a high rainbow, and winter clouds sifting snow on symmetric hills. In the foreground, deer fled from hunters while two turkeys standing thigh-deep in the snow seemed unperturbed. This was a classic example of the stylized realism that might be considered a forerunner of much of the later, younger artists' work.

The Hall of Indian Arts was installed in the long entrance room of the art gallery of the Museum of New Mexico in 1930. Here was hung a large, representative selection of paintings made by Crescencio Martinez, Ma-Pe-Wi, Awa Tsireh, Fred Kabotie, and others while under the sponsorship of the museum in the beginning days of their painting. This occasion marked the first time a permanent exhibit of Indian painting was displayed equally with collections of non-Indian works, and it gave observers a chance to see how well this indigenous art ranked in beauty and interest with other modern art in adjoining galleries. It also provided a constant reference point for the Indian artists themselves, particularly the younger generation.

Oqwa Pi's San Ildefonso paintings went, in 1931, on a tour of many centers including Yale and Stanford universities, the Joslyn Memorial Museum, Omaha, the Museum of Modern Art, New York, and the Milwaukee Art Institute, whose bulletin notes:

> His paintings exhibit a fresh immediacy in color and movement of true aboriginal art: A wonderful simplicity, combined with the depth derived from that conventionalism which is the expression of ancient race experience.[39]

The Santa Fe movement arrived at two consummate achievements in 1931—the dedication of the Laboratory of Anthropology on September 1,[40] and the opening of the Exposition of Indian Tribal Arts at the Grand Central Galleries in New York on December 1. Thus, the Indian Arts Fund collections went into their well-deserved home at last where they could be adequately seen and appreciated, and where their high standards might have an inspirational influence upon arts to

233

come; and the Exposition's assemblage of Indian art, superb in content and arrangement, opened in inauguration of a two-year tour of leading art centers "to gain recognition and a wide discriminating market for the Indian artists and thus encourage them to continue their own native arts within the best of their traditions."[41]

THE EXPOSITION OF INDIAN TRIBAL ARTS

The Exposition of Indian Tribal Arts[42] was conceived and executed by some of the leaders of the twelve-year Santa Fe movement and assisted by many others, including the Secretary of the Interior and the wife of the President of the United States. John Sloan was president of the exposition and Miss Amelia Elizabeth White was chairman of the executive committee.*

Some fifty museums, colleges, and private collectors of the nation enthusiastically lent items for exhibition. Again there was a splendid cooperative effort, nationwide this time, "for the purpose of stimulating and supporting American Indian artists by creating a wider interest and more intelligent appreciation of their work in the American public at large, and to demonstrate to the country what important contribution to our own culture the Indian is making."[43]

Not since the Indian Congress at the Trans-Mississippi Exposition at Omaha in 1898[44] had an effort been made to present the American Indian as a functioning, vital member of the national scene until this remarkable modern exposition opened in New York. It brought to fulfillment that earlier gesture toward a much merited recognition which had so soon been nullified by indifference and neglect. Never before had the Indian been completely recognized as a full-statured artist in several fields.

In the *Introduction to American Indian Art* which accompanied the Exposition, John Sloan and Oliver La Farge said in part:

> The Indian is a born artist; possessing a capacity for discipline and careful work, a fine sense of line and rhythm, which seems to be inherent in the Mongoloid peoples. He has evolved for himself during many thousands of years a

---

*The Hon. Charles Curtis, Major General Hugh L. Scott, the Hon. Charles G. Dawes, Walter L. Clark, Edward C. Delafield, and Mrs. Roberts Walker were its other officers. On its board of directors, twenty-three in all, were such names as Frank Crowninshield, Mrs. Charles H. Dietrich, F. W. Hodge, Oliver La Farge, Mrs. Eugene Meyer, Mrs. John D. Rockefeller, Jr., and H. J. Spinden.

form and content peculiarly his own. We white Americans have been painfully slow to realize the Indian's value to us and the world as an independent artist, although his work has already won recognition abroad.[45]

With John Sloan as its president, it was natural that the Exposition should give an important place to painting among choice selections of ceramics, silver, textiles, and sculpture. Artists represented by paintings were: Crescencio Martinez, Awa Tsireh, Ma-Pe-Wi, Otis Polelonema, Oqwa Pi, Fred Kabotie, Tse-Ye-Mu, Quah Ah, Wo-Peen, Pan-Yo-Pin, and the Kiowa group—Tsa Toke, Mopope, Hokeah, Asah, Bou-ge-tah Smokey, and Auchiah. The first prize of one hundred dollars was awarded Awa Tsireh for *Koshare and Rainbow*, reproduced on the cover of the *Introduction*.

To give a sampling here of critical comment on the Exposition and the critique of painting might provide an indication of the measure of esteem won by the Indian artists through this revelation of their work. *The Art Digest* said: "Probably never before has an exhibition been given so much space in the newspapers and periodicals."[46]

No one wrote more understandingly of the painting than did John Sloan himself:

> These paintings are astonishingly modern in spirit, yet they represent the evolution of the Indian's own traditions and are not borrowed from the white artist. In these pictures we see the object combined with the artists subjective response to it—a union of material and technique in a pattern both symbolic and intelligible. . . . Simplicity, balance, rhythm, abstraction, and virility, resulting from discipline, characterize the work of the Indian today . . . .
>
> The Indian artist deserves to be classed as a modernist; his art is old, yet alive and dynamic. . . . His work has a primitive directness and virility, yet at the same time it possesses sophistication and subtlety. Indian art is at once classic and modern.[47]

Of the Exposition itself, Mr. Sloan said:

> "As an art show the Exposition is of the greatest importance to Americans. As an Indian show it is unique, and will, I predict, prove to be of great importance to the Indians themselves."[48]

An editorial in the *New York Times* observed:

> In the picturesque richness of Indian craft now brought to our doors . . . the visitor may discern a yet comparatively untapped source of decorative inspira-

235

tion. While we have had our eyes turned to Europe with momentary vogues this authentic native American art has been overlooked. . . . [It contains] a Greek-like classic simplicity and at the same time . . . examples of design that the most famous contemporary artists might envy.[49]

Cyril Kay-Scott, quoted in the *International Studio*, deplored America's European eclecticsm and its ignorance of its own "unique and rich heritage of primitive art,"[50] while Liston Oak, authoring the article, noted the persistence of this ancient art as "perhaps unique in history," and that "the materials, the medium used, has come with the white man, but the art, the aesthetic, is native."[51]

Walter Pach, one of the first American critics to appreciate the significance of Indian art, observed that museums here are unable to compete with those of Europe in ancient art but are ahead in Indian art, and that we should not lose or waste it as we have our natural resources. He said in the New York *Times*:

> The Exposition of Indian Tribal Arts is organized for this very purpose, to conserve what is left—and there is a great deal left—of our heritage of Indian art. . . . It is to be hoped that it will contribute to a better understanding of the aboriginal American and wider recognition of the Indian as an artist.[52]

An *Art and Archaeology* review by Rose Berry which considered all aspects of the exhibition remarked, "No one thing of this Inter-Tribal Exhibition will tell as much, however, as the painting—modern painting, too."[53] Quah Ah's "Spring Dances" was praised as best in the show.

Herbert J. Spinden wrote in the *Introduction to American Indian Art*:

> It is not too much to say that Indian youths have astonished the world of art by the spontaneous beauty of their paintings which follow a tradition of good taste.[54]

And in the *International Studio*, Spinden again wrote:

> . . . the Indian proves himself to be bold and versatile in the use of line and color. He does not restrict the subject matter of his drawings to mere realistic commentary on the things that obviously surround his life. Nor on the other hand is he content to make much use of decoration that is purely geometric and devoid of meaning. Instead, he uses consistently the mode of decorative realism and joins the elements of aesthetic appeal with those of intellectual appeal.[55]

236   In *Parnassus*, Dr. Spinden said further:

Figure 90. RICHARD MARTINEZ, San Ildefonso Pueblo. *Plumed Serpent.* Ca. 1925. Tempera. Denver Art Museum.

. . . a strange new world of aesthetic conventions spreads itself before us . . . which we have never imagined in the childhood of our European tradition. . . . we discover that the moving forces are the same hopes and fears which animated the Greeks, and which should animate any people who have enough imagination to create an immaterial universe.[56]

Edward Alden Jewell, in the New York *Times*, noted:

One feels the influence of this vast background in the modern watercolors, which relate quite as distinctly to ancient work in basketry and blanket weaving as to the drawings in line and color that embellish eighteenth or nineteenth century buffalo hides . . . we find strikingly similar use of massing, though here

237

Figure 91.   MA-PE-WI, Zia Pueblo. *Buffalo Hunt.* Ca. 1930. Tempera. Indian Arts Fund.

compositional elements seem to have been brought to more conscious formal development. Also intensified in this modern work is the effect of movement, reaching forceful utterance in a watercolor like "Buffalo Hunt."[57]

Comparing Indian painting with that of other schools, Mr. Jewell added:

Indian abstraction is seen to be something radically unlike that of any of the modern European "isms." The Indian artist would not know what to make of cubism or futurism; yet he knows a great deal about simplification and stylization, methods of working that have sprung directly from the employment of symbolic

238

forms. Unless one be very learned indeed, one cannot hope to trace all the bewildering symbolism to its source. But it is easy just to accept it as aesthetic material, especially since so much genuine artistry has gone into the business of giving life to these strange and fascinating forms.

In his fidelity to tribal convention, the Indian artist seems closer to the Far East than to the Occident, where so much more stress has always been placed upon individual performance; where art fashions come and go with each generation, taking root in an ever lengthening perspective, yet at the time representing response to immediate social moods that often prove of fleeting significance.[58]

Catherine K. Bauer, in the *New Republic*, said:

Primitive art—and above all American Indian art—is communal art. The seeming discipline of the artist's imagination is . . . the clear result of the individual's sense of participation in something larger than himself. . . . The Indian artist may perhaps best be distinguished by his feeling for physical purity —the purity of abstract perfection and of extreme economy of means. This geometric quality is present alike in the simplicity of his forms, in the rhythmic reiteration of his dances and patterns, and in the laconic neatness of his symbols.

There is something fine in this severity, this directness and strict economy of design and form.[59]

More from a sociological standpoint, Eunice Fuller Barnard wrote in the New York *Times*:

Lo, the poor Indian—first a savage foe, to be conquered or bought off, then the unregenerate ward, to be proselyted and pressed into our alien ways—begins to emerge, before our newly opened eyes, as artist. For this exposition is only a conspicuous demonstration of the new attitude which for the past decade has been growing, especially in the Southwest, toward the Indian and his works. Our problem child, so to speak, who through the centuries has amazingly and successfully resisted our sternest efforts to civilize him in our image, is suddenly seen to be, in his own, a kind a genius passing our full comprehension. . . . [His works] are being recognized not as curios or exhibits for a museum of natural history, but sophisticated achievements in design.[60]

The originality of the Indian's achievement as artist was best summarized by Royal Cortissoz in the *Art Digest*:

239

There was no connoisseur to patronize or stimulate him. There was no common denominator of aesthetic taste, in our sense of the term, to guide him. He erected his own standard of what we can only regard as a native feeling for what was right and fine.[61]

Such were the comments which followed the Exposition of Indian Tribal Arts throughout its two-year tour of art centers of the United States under sponsorship of the College Art Association. By the end of the showing, Indian painting, and Indian art in several of its forms, had won a respect and an admiration such as it never before had received in its native land.* Insofar as painting was concerned, a new art had been established and a new school of American painters had been recognized.

*The exhibition, also shown in the Venice Biennial Exposition, "was acclaimed the most popular exhibit among all the rich and varied displays assembled."[62] John Sloan and the committee were praised for "siezing the psychological moment for presenting this truly indigenous art to a large public."

240

The next phase of the Santa Fe movement, insofar as painting was concerned, centered in an oncoming group of artists and new art experiments in the United States Indian School where some seven hundred youths from about twenty tribes were in residence. A change was taking place in all the Indian schools, but particularly in this school, which had been designated the arts and crafts center for the entire Indian educational program.

It has been mentioned that mounting demands for recognition of Indian rights and culture had led to an investigation by the Institute for Government Research. That the demands had been fully justified was well documented by the Institute's comprehensive and enlightening report in 1928. In regard to Indian arts, the report specified and criticized wasted opportunities of government agencies in their lack of encouragement of the arts. It deplored the "general policy [which] has been to make a white man of the Indian rather than to encourage things native,"[1] and it recommended a new approach:

> The survey staff has been impressed by the possibilities of the development of native Indian art. . . . It would seem that, encouraged and developed, it would not only add materially to the economic resources of the Indians, many of whom are in great need, but it would also furnish them the opportunity to make a distinctly Indian contribution to our civilization which would appeal to their very proper racial pride.[2]

The logical place for the government to begin encouragement of the arts was in the Indian schools. The new Commissioner of Indian Affairs, the Hon. Charles J. Rhoads, made a wise choice for his director of education in W. Carson Ryan,

9. The Santa Fe Movement 1932-1937

then a professor at Swarthmore College, who formulated and put into effect some vigorous educational policies based on immediate and long-range needs of the Indian people. Dr. Ryan had not been in office long before an about-face in the schools' attitude toward Indian art was evident.

The role of arts and crafts center fell naturally to the Santa Fe school because of its location in the midst of the appreciation generated by the Santa Fe movement, its nearness to sources of most of the surviving indigenous arts, and its good fortune in having at its head Superintendent Chester E. Faris whose long and distinguished career in the Indian Service had won an unusual respect from the Indian people.

THE FIRST MODERN INDIAN MURALS

It was due to the imagination of Mr. Faris that the School's initial mark of distinction was attained in the first modern Indian murals ever painted beyond tribal bounds. By 1931 the new arts and crafts building had been opened and classes had started to advance in crafts productions, but nothing had been done in painting. In the spring of 1932, Mr. Faris had an idea that the recognized painters, together with some of the students who would like to have a chance at such work, might paint figures upon the walls of the large, unattractive room in which the students dined. He was aware that many problems would be involved in such a venture, so he sought the advice and help of Olive Rush, one of the Southwest's leading artists, whose attitude toward her painting was in many respects like that of the Indian artists toward their own.

Several adult artists were invited from the pueblos, and one from the Kiowa area, to talk over the proposal. Julian Martinez, Tse-Ye-Mu, Richard Martinez, and Oqwa Pi came in from San Ildefonso Pueblo. Jack Hokeah, of Oklahoma, represented the contemporary group of Kiowa painters. Students who wished to cooperate in the project were Miguel Martinez (Oqwa-tu), son of the famous Crescencio, and Juan Diego Martinez, son of Maria and Julian of San Ildefonso; one Hopi boy, Riley Quoyavema; one Zuñi, Tom Weahkee; and four Navajos, Edward and Alex Lee, Paul Tsosie, and Albert Hardy Begay.

Together, these artists, Olive Rush,* and Louise Morris, whom Miss Rush had asked to assist in the work, discussed plans for procedure, for it was to be a cooperative project throughout. From the first, Miss Rush considered her own participation comparable with that of a conductor "directing an orchestra wherein all members are brilliant players." (No small contribution on her part, however.) The entire group considered the low-ceilinged, sprawling room with its narrow-windowed walls cut by doorways at opposite sides. How could the murals gain final unity? First, the artists would paint the walls a light, warm, neutral tone, absolutely matte, and then decide later about colors to be used upon it by each artist. What subjects would be best to paint? All agreed to bring in small paintings and sketches for consideration by the group.

A day or so later, when the paintings and sketches were brought in, they were almost all of ceremonial and dance subjects, and it was with some difficulty that Miss Rush induced the artists to reserve one wall for paintings of everyday activities. From the Navajo sketches, which largely represented sandpainting designs, the group took up the suggestion that a rainbow from one of the designs be elongated to extend entirely around the room, above all the paintings and just below the ceiling, with its head and feet on opposite sides of the entrance door. This would make for a stronger unity, they agreed.

Most of the painters had never used commercial oil colors, and perhaps none of them had ever made a large drawing. In many cases this project presented entirely new problems in painting, yet it had much of traditional precedent to build upon. Olive Rush said of the painters:

244   *This account of the project is based on innumerable visits with Olive Rush, and upon her own diary of the development.

With the sure instincts of artists and that blessing of childlikeness natural to them, they meet their problems with almost no hesitation or fear; and because it is a part of their lives, their art expression has the ease of the singing of birds. This is a precious thing, and he must move softly among them that would help them adjust their art to our modern world.[3]

Laying in their trial drawings, the artists worked in charcoal from their detailed watercolors, or from preliminary sketches which were soon discarded because they were only slightly done in pencil. They drew freehand, without use of cartoons, improvising as they went, from ideas set down suggestively in the smaller works. As this initial drawing progressed, they would stand back individually or in groups, and criticize it for composition, scale, or motif, without using these unknown terms. They had a natural feeling for harmonizing one's work with that of all the others, and of appropriate placing and distribution of styles and subjects.

Miguel, from his drawings of horses, made a trial charcoal sketch on the wall. He stood before his panel troubled, looking back and forth from it to some drawings which had been laid in by other artists on the opposite side of a doorway. He seemed loath to continue the drawing, and Miss Rush asked why. He replied that it was not good to put a horse there, and he erased the horse and sat before the blank space in serious contemplation. Finally he walked up, swung in, with one confident sweep, a large semi-circle, then turned and said, "How is that?"

"Well, what is it?" asked Olive Rush.

"The Plumed Serpent. It should be there."

"Yes, an abstract figure would be better there because there is an abstract design on the other side of the door."

Hokeah, who had also condemned the horse, agreed for the same reason.

In another instance, Julian proposed a drawing of a girl accompanied by a procession of skunks. After a good-humored consultation, the group joyously ruled the skunks out of the main dining room into the hall where they made a gay and appropriate approach toward the door.

As the drawings were finished, the painters began to experiment with their new color medium. Their first tendency was to use paint straight from the tube. Miss Rush soon saw that this would make the walls appear disunified, and that a little control in the interest of harmony would be necessary here. So she helped with the mixing of a uniform palette in amounts sufficient for each section of the project. In this palette there was ample range for each painter to make abundant

245

individual choice and yet harmonize it with the over-all color theme. Some of the artists chose low colors, others brilliant hues, a few showed preference for black, grays, and white, with small areas of color, and the Navajo painters selected the nearest approximation to the earth tones used in the sandpaintings of their tribe. Some members were in doubt about using variations of basic colors rather than the same hues throughout. "They seemed a little puzzled as to whether it is good decoration to have colors vary slightly, and I want them to realize that it is," Miss Rush said at the time.

Cooperative effort was so strong in the mural project that it led to composite character in some of the paintings. Certain panels were the joint work of several artists, and all the paintings underwent reciprocal and cooperative criticism throughout their successive stages. Composition of the whole was a natural growth, and in the end seemed effortlessly right. Without set scheme or formal plan, the murals had attained certain unity and coordinate beauty. There had been no need for centering of composition in a room where there was no head of the table but where all were equal. The general movement was toward the corners where it was caught up and turned back in ingenious ways or arrested by an abstract design of perfect balance.

Olive Rush said, "The place has a gay and exhilarating look; it was done in that mood." The murals are bright without gaudiness, bold with restraint. Some show lively action; others, quiet, balanced design. Color plays in harmony across the walls; no dead blacks or too bright whites appear anywhere. All the blues are compatible, from deep sapphire to palest turquoise, and there are related strong reds and soft reds, vivid greens and grayed greens, and so on through the color range.

The many individual compositions present striking differences. Delicate, obscure abstraction prevails in the sandpainting designs with their esoteric Yei and improvisations upon natural forms, while stylized naturalism rules the massive paintings of potters and moccasin makers and water-bearers. One hunting scene has dash and high spirit, one has quick action stopped short, and another is almost pastoral in its serenity. The main action of the entire room is in the first of these where a hunter with streaming hair rides a spirited, rearing black horse and takes sure aim at a lynx who wears the life symbol upon his rich yellow coat.

On either side of the entrance door, two other hunters and their prey face one another. At one side, six brown buffalo with brilliantly patterned manes trot in a diagonal before the the hunter who rides an abruptly halting pony. All is extremely stylized here—the bare-bodied hunter in green breech cloth; the decorative buffalo

Plate XX. HARRISON BEGAY, Navajo. *Creation of North Mountain.* 1957. Tempera. School of American Research.

Plate XXI. ALLAN HOUSER, Chiricahua Apache. *Apache Warriors*. 1937. Tempera. Collection of Mr. and Mrs. Alden C. Hayes.

Figure 92.   Oqwa Pi, San Ildefonso Pueblo. *Buffalo Hunt*. 1932. Mural in oil. Santa Fe Indian School. James Watson photograph.

bearing upon their manes the sacred Avanyu, terraced and semicircular clouds, feather symbols and lightning; the pony painted like a wooden horse with dark gray mane and tail and a few white spottings.

On the opposite side of the door a quiet hunting scene shows two dove-gray deer loping gently ahead of a musing hunter on a black-and-white horse. Here a relationship among all the creatures gives the impression that these delightful deer are perfectly safe. The hunter, a pattern of red brown body and white buckskin, carries a white shield decorated with clouds, and his gentle pony is purely Pueblo with none of the wild speed of the Plains horse.

The abstract designs vary from near-static to extremely dynamic. There are quiet, regular cloud patterns; Rainbirds of low color in balanced masses, Thunderbirds of scintillating hues and whirling, radiating motion; and a green serpent which looks like a deep-water monster lashing his tail and spitting lightning barbs in stormy movement within a rainbow circle.

Two shinny players brightly interchange orange reds and turquoise blues and step on tiptoe as in a ballet. Two ponderous deer dancers move stealthily along the back wall toward an antelope dancer in ochre coat. These seem neither men nor animals but wholly supernaturals. The bold and immobile Kiowa dancers

247

might have been intruders here, yet they are not. Midway, on opposite walls, these two Aztec-like eagle-men are aloof yet not altogether strange in this room which predominantly emanates the spirit of the Pueblo world.

"Along with interest and movement, the room seems actually to have acquired light, and the walls seem to emit light and life from an inner source. There is an indwelling power, as might be expected from a people who recognize and revere strength of spirit in all natural things," was Olive Rush's own comment upon the completed murals.

These remarkable paintings, created with great enthusiasm, had been completed in but six weeks. All had been done easily, happily, without hurry, although in a medium new to the artists. The form was new, also, for never before had Indians attempted to adapt their tribal arts to modern architecture. Indeed, here was an art form new to the world. "One may not predict how far it will carry us—an expression so fresh and vital,"[4] said Olive Rush.

"What shall we paint next?" asked the artists. In answer, the group decided to form the Mural Guild. They moved into an old chapel nearby, and, with Miss Rush's help, prepared some large canvas panels for further works of mural size. Paintings related to those in the dining room emerged upon these canvases—buffalo hunts of heroic size from the skillful brush of Ma-Pe-Wi who had joined the guild with several others; the deer of Julian Martinez and of his son, Juan Diego; Quah Ah's small dancers and choruses grown to almost life size; Hokeah's eagles bolder than ever; ancient pottery designs reborn in scale and color; and abstract bird designs representing the whole sky complex of the Southwest through imaginative variations of symbolic sun and storms, lightning, rainbow, swelling rain cloud and rising fog.

Before the summer of 1932 was over, an exhibition of these impressive panels had been prepared for showing in the Corcoran Galleries, at Rockefeller Center, and at other Eastern galleries. In August some of the canvases, paint still moist, had gone to the Inter-Tribal Indian Ceremonial at Gallup, New Mexico, where they were seen by thousands of travelers at this crossroads of Indian America. Soon afterward, murals were invited to the Century of Progress Exposition, Chicago. Paintings on canvas applicable to walls were made for such exhibitions.

Word of the new art soon appeared in national journals. *The Literary Digest* mentioned artists "who regard art as a community affair and who frown upon individual ambition, [and of the] free expression and utter absence of self-consciousness" of the art.[5] Mary Austin, in the *American Magazine of Art*, noted that the

248

Indians are natural muralists whose paintings "would never be on the point of falling off the walls as the work of too many moderns does."[6] She spoke of native training that through generations had enable artists to adjust complicated designs to the surface of pottery, and suggested that the change from watercolor to oils presented no particular problem because nobody ever had told the Indians it would be difficult. She added advice to observers:

> . . . no mistake could be worse than to approach the work of these Indian artists as mere curios. They represent, as much as any painting does, the use of ancestral material to express the profoundest present insight. They are essentially modern in the successful use they make of abstraction as well as thoroughly native in all their implications.[7]

The *Art Digest* told of the growth of the new work,[8] and Olive Rush herself offered accounts of it,[9] including that in an issue of *Theatre Arts* given over to the drama of the Indian. She spoke of the great vitality of Indian art, of its strength and simplicity, its nobility of line and mass peculiarly fitted to wall painting, and of its fertile symbolism, and added:

> More than to paint the body of nature, the Indian loves to glorify her power, and to express in symbols her evanescent quality, her bright gleam. . . . His growth is enormously helped rather than hindered by his symbolism, for as we find an infinity of words with our little alphabet, so he creates endless compositions from his living symbols.[10]

THE INDIAN PAINTING STUDIO

In August 1932, when the Exposition of Indian Tribal Arts, nearing the end of the first year of its tour, had won critical acclaim for Indian watercolor painting, and when the mural projects and the fine crafts productions of the Santa Fe Indian School had already begun to receive recognition, there were yet no painting classes at the school. Dr. Hewett's statement:

> The purpose now is to broaden the experiment by extending the same opportunity and encouragement to other individuals and tribes until it is made a fair demonstration of the ability of the race and the possibility of reviving a power that has been submerged, dormant through generations. . . .[11]

249

had not been put to the test as official policy in this art-aware school, nor in any school in the Indian Service, ever.

However, a plan for a painting studio at the Santa Fe school had been in the making for four years through specialized field and art studies.* By August 1932, it was ready to be put into effect. The plan had been proposed to the director of Indian education the year before, but it had appeared as if no new position would be established for such work. The nation was in the midst of a depression and budgets were being cut in Washington.

Determined to try to establish the Studio through any means available, D came, after the completion of her studies in the Art Institute of Chicago, and outlined the proposal to Superintendent Faris. He was interested, through puzzled as to how the work might be undertaken in the absence of a regular civil service position such as all members of his staff held in their respective fields. After giving some thought to the matter, he said, "We have a vacancy in one of our fifth grades; if you think you can handle that work in addition to your painting classes, you might write the Washington office at once and apply for that position. Meanwhile, until we see what happens, we do have a small fund for odd labor. Do you want to begin the work as a laborer?"

Thus, in the light of the school's fine achievements in mural painting and crafts, and the high standards set by older artists through encouragement of the Santa Fe community, the new painting studio opened, although unofficially, in the Santa Fe Indian School on September 9, 1932.

THE SETTING FOR THE WORK

The crafts classes occupied all the workrooms in the new arts and crafts building, so the display room was temporarily assigned the painting classes as a studio. It, of course, had no studio equipment, although there were two large display tables. The carpentry shop agreed to make drawing boards in order that students might work somewhat individually at the crowded tables. Drawing and painting materials avaliable through the school warehouse were quite limited: manila and glazed paper, pencils, chalk, charcoal remaining from the mural work, large limp brushes, boxes of eight watercolor paints of a type used in the elemen-

250 *Made by the writer of this account, referred to as D, who considered herself as an artist-researcher and guide rather than as teacher in the formal sense.

tary grades, and a few tube watercolors which were soon discarded because of poor quality. Better supplies were a year away through the "Annual Estimate Catalog."

Forty students, between the ages of fifteen and twenty-two inclusive, enrolled in the painting classes which were elective for all except nine graduate girls, mostly from Plains tribes, who were "special art" students planning to become teachers. This group was required by the head of the arts and crafts department to attend painting classes. For the others, enrollment was made flexible through a school office provision that any student who wished to do so might drop the course at the end of a six weeks' trial period. The schedule and assignments of members of each class were made by the department head. Some students, because of other commitments, were allowed less time than others, the periods ranging from fifty minutes to, for two students, a half day.

The majority of Studio enrollees were from Southwestern tribes—the Rio Grande Pueblos, the western Pueblos of Laguna, Acoma, Zuñi, and the Hopi; and the Navajo, and Apache. There was also a small representation from the Plains and other tribes outside the Southwest area. The Southwestern students were the ones for whom the original Studio plans had been made; a central school of arts and crafts had not been proposed four years earlier when D had begun the research necessary for founding the Studio. This all-tribal school was a development of a few months by national headquarters. However, D tried to make the best provision possible for the unanticipated non-Southwestern students until detailed plans for them could be worked out.

In addition to painting classes, several groups of design students came and went each day, for design was required by the department head of all crafts students—those studying silversmithing, woodwork, weaving, embroidery, beadwork, and the like. Unfortunately, the schedule made it necessary to run several painting and design classes concurrently, yet most of the painting students were cooperative and worked as well as possible while being surrounded frequently by more formal classes. Actually, the attention which D could give the painting students, after requirements of the design classes and an entire fifth grade were fulfilled, was definitely at a minimum. (During the first year, a half day each was devoted to the Studio and to the fifth grade in its regular classroom activities, the latter work having been made official in October through D's civil service appointment.)

251

OBJECTIVES AND ATTITUDES

The objectives of the Studio were the following: 1) to foster appreciation of Indian painting among students and public, thus helping to establish it in its rightful place as one of the fine arts of the world (a continuation of certain preceding aspects of the Santa Fe movement), 2) to produce new paintings in keeping with high standards already attained by Indian painters, 3) to study and explore traditional Indian art methods and productions in order to continue established basic painting forms, and to evolve new motifs, styles, and techniques in character with the old and worthy of supplementing them, 4) to maintain tribal and individual distinction in the paintings.

In order to accomplish these objectives, the broad plan of procedure was 1) to determine, insofar as possible, each student's personality, interests, abilities, the backgrounds of his tribal art and its relationship to his individual art and the general arts, 2) without teaching in the formal sense, to create a guidance technique which would provide motivation, clarification, and development for each individual student's painting process.

The attitude of the classes presented the first problem, for there was an element in it which stemmed from the fact that some students expected the schools to provide quick training in the accomplishments of the modern non-Indian American which they thought would enable them to cope with the latter upon equal terms. The students all wanted to learn, and the more difficult a subject appeared to be, the better they liked it and the more enthusiastically they worked at it. When they had the good fortune to encounter, in any of their various studies, a teacher of superior imagination and education, they were happily willing to attend as many hours of overtime classes as he would give them. Many had acquired the belief that things Indian had no place in the schools, but rather that they should be learned only at home and kept there.

For generations preceding the Rhoads administration Indian schools had fostered a cleavage between Indian and non-Indian culture, so it was not surprising that there existed a strong carry-over, among many students, from former attitudes toward the supposed complete superiority of the superimposed culture. Aside from individual efforts of a few creative and courageous members of the Indian Service

252

Figure 93.   Lucy Richards, Sioux. *Sample of Daily Work*. 1893. Pencil. Pine Ridge
Agency School, South Dakota. Smithsonian Institution. Cat. No. 168,515.

253

personnel,* the only "Indian arts" encouraged in most Indian schools had been through outright copy or in psuedo manner of Longfellow, Cadman, Russell, Remington, and Dallin—and usually these resulted in exceedingly poor imitations. The schools had equipped Indian young people for life neither in the dominant culture nor in their own.

A major emphasis, in most subjects, upon learning modern ways was healthful and necessary, but total exclusion of everything native had caused confusion for many students. Fortunately, there was in nearly all of them an underlying appreciation of native culture, much more readily accessible in some than in others. The urge to get completely away from Indian backgrounds in schoolwork, or in all living, was usually much stronger in students other than those from the Southwest because they had been forced to turn completely to the dominant culture for means of earning a livelihood.

In such circumstances, it had not occurred to most students to think of their native art as *art*. Indian art was something accepted without thinking about it, as a part of everyday life, whereas *art* was some sort of composite of magazine and book illustrations, posters, calendar scenes, catalog illustrations, caricatures, literal portraits, chromo mural and easel paintings, and the overpopularized "Indian heads" and "Noble Redman" scenes. Very few students had seen good examples of academic art. The concept of the universal fine arts of which their own is an integral part was utterly unknown to any one of the students in the entire school.

This was a concept which would have to be acquired gradually—absorbed in the course of fully appreciating, first of all, Indian art itself as art, and then as an art that extends beyond the bounds of Indian culture into the whole culture which belongs to everyone for the knowing. To offset the attitude of wanting to learn only academic and commercial art, it would be necessary to tap the latent force of group pride and put it to work. Obviously, such action would have to be undertaken slowly and understandingly. The process would have to allow for freedom of the individual wherein he might be given to realize something of the broader values and possibilities of his native art and to choose to develop them under Studio guidance, or to withdraw at will and thus have no compulsion of direction.

---

*Early encouragement of Hopi pupils at Sherman Institute, the De Huffs' personal aid at Santa Fe, and Miss Hoyt's guidance at San Ildefonso, have been mentioned. Also, at Carlisle Indian Industrial School, in the early 1900's, Angel De Cora, an excellently educated Winnebago girl, held classes in creative Indian design.[12] Other instances were noted by Lewis Meriam: "At the time of our survey (1926-27) a few progressive teachers had broken away from past principles and were letting the children practice their native arts."[13]

BEGINNING WORK

D had no idea to what extent pro-academic art notions dominated the imaginations of the students until the sheets containing the outcome of their first efforts were in her hands.

In an attempt to ascertain something of the interests and abilities of the prospective classes, she had given each student a large sheet of manila paper, a stick of charcoal, a piece of cloth, and had said, "I'd like to have you show me some of the things you care to draw. Sketch anything you wish. Don't worry about making mistakes; erase and try again."

This request had not been met with general enthusiasm. A few members of the classes had seemed to resent being asked to draw something before being taught anything, but most of them had worked earnestly and had tried to do their best. Several had sat rather unhappily before blank sheets not knowing what to draw. To them, D had quietly made individual suggestions such as: "If you can't think of something you'd like to draw, you might make a design, or an animal, or a dancer, or a hunter, or a woman working."

In going about the class, D had purposely made as few comments upon the work as possible for she wanted to see what the students would do alone. Only to the ones who seemed entirely at a loss as to how to proceed had she offered any suggestions. Some students had worked directly as if they knew what they wanted to do, others had seemed uncertain, erasing successive attempts and starting over.

Several samplings were thus taken in order that the preliminary pattern of individual interests and aptitudes might be clearer. The result was that the forty students indicated interests in approximately the following proportion: animals and plants in more or less naturalistic manner, 13; Indian heads and other psuedo-Indian subjects drawn with attempted light and shade, 6; life drawings of Indian character and subject, 5; invented designs incorporating some Indian motifs, 5; classifiable tribal designs, 4; portrait-type drawings of non-Indian subjects, with attempted light and shade, 3; naturalistic landscape, 3; cartoons in the manner of stereotype Indian caricatures, 1.

As compared to non-Indian groups of similar age range in D's experience, there was indicated a high incidence of drawing facility. Of the total number of students, such ability was indicated about as follows: excellent, 8; above average, 19; average, 9; fair, 4; poor, 0.

Supplementing these indications, informal conversations revealed that perhaps about twelve of the forty students actually expected to do Indian painting.

Figure 94. ALLAN HOUSER, Apache. *Early Sketch*. 1934. Charcoal. Studio records.

Most of these had seen paintings done in their home villages even though at that time scarcely a score of practicing modern Indian painters could be named throughout the Arizona–New Mexico area. Four or five students had done some painting. All the others had enrolled with the expectation of having objective, step-by-step academic instruction in "how to become a painter" with emphasis upon

256

one aspect or another. One Plains boy, a graduate of Haskell Institute, had come to the Santa Fe school because he supposed the new arts and crafts department would teach advertising design and cartooning. Another Plains boy had come in a "special art" capacity and was interested mainly in portrait and landscape painting. The nine "special art" teacher-training girls definitely expected lessons of a "methods" nature, as in public school art of formal tradition. Several of these girls also wished to paint individually.

The immediate questions which arose from this situation were: What could be a uniform starting point for these equally deserving people of such varied needs and interests? What might be objective enough to enlist the attention of those who expected regimented lessons, and yet be basic to subsequent work in Indian painting or any painting which might eventually be chosen by them? What could be done with the few materials at hand to provide a common experience, helpful to all, in which all might share and from which individual, free work might stem?

The simple answer lay in the common need for understanding and ably handling painting materials. The coarse brushes which would have to be replaced later for finer work would serve for color mixing and elementary brushwork, while the available transparent water colors, with a few temperas supplied, would suffice for initial mixing experiments.

D explained to the students that, although some of them had handled color, there were endless things to learn about it and that some experiments might reveal new and interesting facts. They then tried mixing colors—any colors—for the consistency which would produce as flat and even a coverage as possible. Individual advice was offered where needed and efficient tool handling habits were encouraged where they had been lacking. As students completed this practice with satisfaction to themselves, they were asked to arrange the colors in rainbow sequence while working for more and more even application within controlled areas. This was in order that they might think for themselves of the natural relationships between colors while further refining their application technique.

In subsequent periods the classes studied graying of colors through an understanding of color complementaries which was accomplished without emphasis on theory or even the term. Students discovered color complements for themselves by gazing at a large spot of color then at a white space until the complement appeared. They were interested to see how color balance is based on the natural reaction of the eye. D told them that they might discover how these opposite colors could subdue one another, even destroy one another to the extent of produc-

257

ing dead black. Many experiments followed in which color intensities and values were explored. Colors were juxtaposed, balanced, grayed, neutralized. Earth-color tones were produced by lowering intense hues. Blacks were created by cross-mixing pure, bright colors, and variation in blacks and whites were obtained by subtle combinations. Most of the students seemed to enjoy these experiments and some began to indicate individual tendencies in the choice and use of color.

Another basic color practice was in the drawing and arrangement of brush lines upon large sheets of manila paper in which texture, rendering, and design were improved and freedom and invention developed. Each student used not one but many sheets. An abundance of creative, flowing line designs in striking color appeared during these exercises.

After the sessions of color handling the classes experienced a similarly foundational use of pencil, chalk, and charcoal. They made pictographic life drawings of circular, elliptical, or angular elements. They used no models (as D had done in her own life classes), but rendered action and proportion informally through memory and imagination. "Try to think of these figures as doing all sorts of things that people and animals might do." The quality of vitality, rhythm, and even spirit of many of these simple drawings was amazing. Again, large numbers of drawings were made, and many more by some students than by others.

Although a few of the older members thought this work childish, most of them seemed to appreciate its purpose and did it with earnestness and enjoyment. Several of those who had had difficulty in thinking of what to draw on the first occasion proved to be free and inventive in this approach.

Throughout these beginning studies, as in all the work that followed, D watched each sheet develop under the hand of each individual. She did this in as unobtrusive and quiet a manner as was possible, under the community-table setup, in order that the painters should not feel they were being critically observed. She individually commended art tendencies and gave advice, not manual aid, where it seemed needed. Thus, if a color persisted in being cloudy, too thin, too thick, or streaked in application, if lines were ragged or edges were undesirably hard or blurred, she could suggest means of improvement. In everyone's work she found at least one feature to commend, and the standard of worthiness for commendation was always the best she had seen in Indian art as known in relation to fundamental fine qualities of painting in general.

More detailed figures were next attempted. D gave colored chalks to the classes and asked them to try to draw some of their pictographic figures singly or in groups as if engaged in some activity as they might appear in a painting. "Make as many arrangements as you like, lightly with charcoal, then choose the draw-

258

Figure 95.   Po-Ve Pien, Tesuque Pueblo. *Sketch for Playing Shinny.* 1936. Charcoal and chalk. Studio records.

ings you like best and complete them with colored chalk. If some of you would rather draw the figures direct, without pictographs, do so."

Most of the students drew schematic figures first and erased them in progress; others drew directly. When, after a few sessions, enough good chalk drawings had appeared, D suggested that anyone who wished might take a sheet of watercolor paper and, using the chalk drawing for reference, make a similar, direct drawing for a painting.

259

Figure 96. Po-Ve Pien, Tesuque Pueblo. *Playing Shinny*. 1936. Tempera. Collection of Mr. and Mrs. Max Kramer.

For the Southwest students, this transition from foundational to more specialized work seemed fairly easy, but for the others it presented a problem. What were they to draw; who were their pictographs to become? They were encouraged individually to try to show some of their own tribal subjects but most of their efforts were weak and uncertain. The majority of these students had forgotten, or had never known, or seemed uninterested in their tribal backgrounds. These people would have to have provisions less than they deserved but the best that could be immediately offered under the impromptu circumstances of the Studio's beginning.

260

The Oklahoma boy made some fairly good and very earnest attempts to draw activities and events from his tribal sources. He would have much preferred academic art yet became interested in trying to see what he could do in the Indian idiom. The Northern Plains boy was definitely not interested in trying to paint in an Indian manner and therefore he was encouraged to study lettering and to draw designs for school papers, posters, and signs, which might be in line with his commercial art interest and yet not too intrusive in the major art class activities. It was suggested to the teachers-in-training that they might illustrate Indian stories and legends or draw any Indian activities they may have seen. Whereas the Southwest artists were encouraged to paint their own best-known tribal subjects, these girls might prepare to make use of intertribal material in the schools.

From the chalk sketches, drawings for tempera paintings began to take shape. The preceding studies seemed definitely to have made most of the students more facile than they were in the initial survey. They seemed freer to make trial drawings and color tests. In time, everyone drew directly with pencil on trial papers, and eventually more than half the class made drawings directly upon watercolor paper with very few revisions. The predominant subjects which they chose were home life, hunting scenes, and various ceremonials.

Two Hopi boys, and one each from Acoma, Zuñi, and San Juan, excelled from an early date, and two Santa Clara girls, sisters, soon began to distinguish themselves through steady and intelligent work. Others with particular talents took more time in discovering their special abilities. Frequently from some fragment of their sketchwork, D could suggest to them where their emphasis might be placed in order to develop peculiar aptitudes and original ideas. Originality was constantly sought and encouraged. Certain paintings made by the less technically skilled were often superior works because of imaginative use of traditional motifs or invented ones.

Any production which revealed copy of unworthy exotic influences was discouraged, not by forbiddance, but by suggestion of a variety of choices of tribal elements which might make a particular painting more authentic and interesting. In line with policies of the Indian Fair,[14] borrowings in tribal motifs and styles, if such did not occur in real life, were not usually encouraged at this early stage of the students' development. Details of costumes, properties, activities, and symbolism were considered for appropriateness in particular settings. Here, again, fitness was determined by customary usage, past and present, insofar as known, among the Indian people themselves. If non-Indian and out-tribal influences might be intelligently used after the young artists were well familiar with their

261

own tribal source materials, the decision to do so would later be in the hands of the artists themselves, particularly after they had left school.*

As all the activities had progressed, the best examples of drawing and painting were hung in the Studio where they could be studied, compared and commented upon by informal groups of students talking among themselves. Names began to appear, even though to these admirably non-individualistic people it seemed superfluous to write one's name upon a painting. In time, it came to be understood that to have one's work exhibited meant commendable achievement, and thus a real incentive to improvement. Although very profitable trips were made to the Laboratory of Anthropology and the Museum of New Mexico for the

* A case in point was the work of Paul Goodbear, Cheyenne, a young professional whose painting showed conformity to then current general art styles.

Figure 97.   Oscar Howe, Sioux. *An Early Painting.* 1935. Tempera. Studio records.

Plate XXII. T'o-Pove, San Juan Pueblo. *Women Getting Water*. 1935. Tempera. Margretta S. Dietrich Collection.

Plate XXIII. HA-SO-DE, Navajo. *Wolf Man*. 1960. Tempera. Ruth and Charles de Young Elkus Collection.

purpose of studying work of their elders, the students found that it was this gradually heightening standard which they were creating for themselves within the Studio that was most vital to their work.

At the end of the semester, most of the painting was technically rough, yet several promising new trends in style and content were discernible, and it was the latter fact which would count most in the long run. Technique, which seemed to interest the students more, would develop with practice.

By the beginning of the second semester, the majority of students seemed to have become genuinely interested in developing their painting upon Indian precedents; however, there were still in the classes, in which some new students had enrolled and from which none had asked to drop, a few who were not wholeheatedly cooperating in the activities of the Studio. Some who had at first been opposed to the procedures were working out an admirable adjustment and were actually producing some good painting. Others, mainly from one small group of those for whom the classes had not been planned, but who were required by the arts and crafts department head to attend, were so plainly disappointed at the lack of objective, formal lessons that they were not only doing poor work themselves but, by their negative attitude, were causing tensions in the class which were affecting the work of some of the students who now wanted to pursue only Indian art. If time and facilities had allowed, these understandably dissenting members might have had a class of their own in which a wealth of background materials and intensive guidance might have at least given them a new understanding of their native art; yet, under the pressing circumstances, the only hope for better adjustment was for deeper channeling into the more objective crafts-design classes their desire for completely formal work. And indeed such resulted in creative productions in textile pattern, block print, and silver, beadwork, pottery, and embroidery design which were exhibited with paintings at the school year's end.

At about this time the head of the arts and crafts department indicated that she considered the accomplishments of the painting classes unsatisfactory. "The students have no standards; we don't want little things, we want big things," she said. She suggested a more objective approach and that models might be used.

This point of view was understandable, for there were the successful dining-room murals, admired by all, and there were the established patterns and wholly objective methods, supported by abundant material supplies for embroidery, weaving, and other crafts so admirably used in this capable crafts teacher's own classes. The goals and the slowly developing plans of the Studio were not readily

263

Figure 98.   CAROLINE CORIZ, Santo Domingo Pueblo. *Textile Pattern from an Acoma Pottery Motif.* 1934. Tempera. Studio records.

evident; most of the results thus far did appear amateurish and small and inconsequential as compared with other recent art activities of the school.

If the Studio classes might have begun at the mural level, as had the few students who had enjoyed the good fortune of working with a group of acknowledged masters of Indian painting in making the dining-room murals, enthusiasm about beginning to do Indian painting might have been high from the first, for *there* was painting of impressive size and beautiful ensemble in which the smaller contributions of the amateurs were happily incorporated in the preponderance of work by the experts. There was painting new in scale and purpose, in the honored oil medium, which was admired daily by visitors who came, even from distant places, to see it.

But, for the Studio, big things were temporarily out of the question where there was so much groundwork to be laid and so little time and material to accomplish even that. The Studio was indeed on trial, with no indication whatever of official recognition. Although D's half day as a fifth-grade teacher was official, her Studio work remained entirely extracurricular and voluntary. Only Kenneth Chapman, who made visits to the school in the capacity of arts and crafts consultant, and Helen L. Kinnick, a supervisor from the regional office of the Indian Service, understood and offered encouragement to the efforts of the Studio at this time.

In compliance with the request that had been made, models were tried, but utterly without success. It required only two sessions to fairly demonstrate that drawing from models was completely worthless to the project and considerably confusing in the Studio.

To meet the interest in academic art, the department head arranged for an instructor from the state university to come up at regular intervals in the second term to teach a night class in portrait painting. This class was attended mainly by "special art" students and one or two Southwest students who had not enrolled in the Studio, but a few students who had begun to make progress in the Studio also enrolled. The outcomes of this effort are not of consequence here except wherein they affected the Studio. A few "special art" students definitely transferred all interest from the Studio to the academic class. Other students enrolled in both classes became noticeably retarded in their progress in Indian art, although they seemed to be basically more interested in the latter. Studio artists not in the academic class seemed only mildly interested in it and were apparently uninfluenced by its work. The night class was discontinued after a few weeks.

As the winter advanced, Studio exhibits steadily increased in size and in artistic calibre, and, by the end of March, they were beginning to make a good

265

showing. The students had been supplied with marginally adequate paints, papers, and brushes until these necessities could be obtained through official channels. Painted with better media, and now correctly mounted, the best works began to take on a somewhat professional appearance. Even so, there were still a few members of the classes who doubted the value of the work.

It was near the end of March that Frederic H. Douglas, curator of Indian art at the Denver Art Museum, paid a surprise visit to the Studio and gave it the first open professional approval it had received. He very carefully went over the exhibit and other paintings and made enthusiastic remarks before the students as he pointed out various features of the compositions. He said that he would like to have some of the work for the Denver Art Museum. Without being aware of it, Dr. Douglas raised the Studio morale incalculably.

A few days later, Olive Rush paid her first visit to the Studio and also immediately recognized the accomplishment. She asked if some of the artists would like to help with the new portable murals which the recently reassembled Mural Guild was preparing under her direction for Chicago's Century of Progress.

Soon afterward, it seemed a great event when two masonite panels and some oil paints were brought into the Studio, for the entire class entered vicariously into the work which was actually done by three artists chosen on the basis of sketches to do the painting. Miss Rush and Dr. Douglas had definitely brought a higher degree of reassurance and pride into the Studio.

This new buoyancy did not last long for D, however, for on April fourth she was told by the school principal that there seemed to be no hope for the establishment of a civil service art position which would enable the work of the Studio to continue after May. D would have been willing to continue without the official art position, but the principal indicated that this would be irregular. It would be best, he said, that D plan on dropping the work at the term's end.

However, there was such a press of activities with the first annual Santa Fe exhibition of Indian painting about to be hung by the Studio, and the first modern Indian marionette play about to be staged by the younger pupils, who had also completed illustrations for a book of Navajo poetry,* that there was little time to doubt that the very momentum of all this creative work would carry it on.

When, with the encouraging help of the curator, Mary R. Van Stone, the exhibit was hung in two alcoves of the Art Gallery of the Museum of New Mexico,

* *The Colored Land,* written and illustrated by Navajo Children. Ed. by Rose K. Brandt. N.Y.: Charles Scribner's Sons, 1937.

the artists gained a new pride in their work. Many Santa Fe artists and art patrons became acquainted with this younger supplement to the development they had been fostering among adult Indian painters. They offered immediate backing through their favorable comments and their purchases. (The school administration designated fifty per cent of sales amounts for the arts and crafts fund; fifty per cent for the artists.)

Olive Rush wrote a critical review for the *Santa Fe New Mexican* in which she stated:

> Lovers of decorative and colorful painting will not wish to miss the exhibit shown at the Art Museum this week . . . boys and girls from all over the Indian country have again proven their mettle—that they need only the opportunity to work through their own various forms to come through to brilliant racial expression.
>
> This requires on the part of the teacher not only a wise encouragement of native methods and tendencies, but a most acute discernment of individual creative effort. It is for her to tread softly a path she must pursue with courage and caution; it is for her to forget all rules she has learned in the schools not to commit the blunder of teaching one race the point of view, or the method of attack, of another race.
>
> . . . One surprise was the discovery that the Hopi students have long had, in their Wützi, a delightful sort of marionette; and in the first alcove, number one shows a pair of Wützi, framed in by the stage-setting arrangements used in the Hopi country. Zeyouma, the painter of this picture . . . is again the author of the most amusing watercolors of mudheads to be seen anywhere. He has these little clowns going through legendary games and antics, with a naive feeling for line and composition that sets them above mere illustration. Other Hopi painters are Dahouta and Joshongeva giving us brilliant color in the cactus dancers, flute, and snake dancers, Katchinas of several orders. We shall hear of these painters again.
>
> The Velarde sisters, Pablita and Po-ve of Santa Clara, find their best expression in picturing the people of their pueblo at their daily tasks, women making pottery, or husking corn, or winnowing wheat—all beautifully expressed; while Valle of Acoma delights in painting the spirited Acoma birds of tradition. From San Juan comes Sa-Pa with a sheaf of delightsome animal and dance drawings. Reba Yarlotte from the Crow reservation, and Domak, a Chippewa girl, show their first attempts at painting, and the list includes others quite as well worth seeing.[15]

Following this exhibit, the Studio joined other classes of the arts and crafts department in an exhibition at the school. During this showing, the New Mexico

268 Figure 99. AGNES BIRD, Chippewa. *Woman Stripping Birch Bark.* 1935. Tempera. Collection of Dorothy Dunn.

Association on Indian Affairs awarded prizes to Joshongeva and to Sa-Pa for their paintings, and, from this time, throughout the years of the Studio's work, the Association gave unfailing support and encouragement. The Association's president, Mrs. Charles H. Dietrich, through her personal interest in Indian painting and the Indian people, became one of the Studio's most understanding and helpful friends.

SECOND YEAR

A week before the opening of school in September, an event occurred which was to determine the life or death of the Studio. Rose K. Brandt, Supervisor of Elementary Education, Office of Indian Affairs, who had known of D's work for four years, came to Santa Fe from Washington. In an examination of the Studio's accomplishments and a conference with D, Miss Brandt assured her that she would try to bring about official establishment. She asked D to outline fully her objectives and to send them to Dr. Ryan, Director of Indian Education, Washington. In the meantime, the Studio was to continue, and on full time. "I am going to bat," she said.

Within a few days the Studio moved from the arts and crafts building to a small elementary classroom in the academic building where activities would still be crowded but students could at least have individual small desks, and the design and painting classes could be conducted separately.

The Studio enrollment more than doubled this year, with several more students from outside the Southwest. The added half day (no longer devoted by D to regular classroom teaching) made it possible to have much better organized classes than those of the first year. Work began along much the same lines as the year before, with the initial surveys showing a much greater interest in Indian painting. More individual time could be given the academically inclined students to help bring about their adjustment to the work of the Studio. With a strong nucleus of artists from the preceding year, the problem of enlisting interest in Indian art was comparatively simple. A spirit of cooperation and appreciative attitude prevailed from the start.

Time was available this year for a number of creative projects in addition to regular painting and design classes. The first of these was the painting of earth color murals in the Studio. Hunting and preparing colors was an activity in which all could engage. Even visitors became interested in the search, and the Studio

269

soon had a stock of clays, sandstones, and color-bearing ores from all over the Southwest.

These substances were pounded, screened, soaked, and the pigments extracted from them and ground. Various adhesives such as eggs, melon-seed extract, and glue were tried in the mixing of a heavy tempera suitable for use on dry plaster. Colors were named for the areas in which they were found: Acoma red, Domingo purple, Laguna white, Picuris brown, Hopi green, La Bajada yellow, and so on. They constituted a lovely range of harmonious colors such as the Indians had always used in painting.

For the murals, selections were made from smaller sketches, then enlarged, freehand, in charcoal upon the walls. The painters were so much interested in this

Figure 100. Po-Su-Nu, San Juan Pueblo. *Basket Dancers.* 1933. Earth color on plaster. Collection of Mr. and Mrs. Max Kramer.

activity that they did most of the work in their free time on Saturdays and at night, filling the walls above the blackboards with panoramas of dancers, hunters, animals, and of people at work.

One Navajo boy, in particular, worked almost every night until dormitory call. He needed very little guidance, and that mainly in the initial mechanics of untried new media, for he possessed a remarkable, even rare, talent. Everything he undertook to draw flowed into a thing of grace and beauty under his brush. He seemed never to find enough time to state all he had to say—spirited ceremonial dancers, fleeting deer and racing horses, bears, hunters, shepherds, weavers, gamblers, and all the *dramatis personae* of the remotely beautiful Navajo scene. In seeing this art, one would wish that he might stand between it and anything

Figure 101. ANDREW TSIHNAHJINNIE, Navajo. *Sketch for Antelope Hunt.* 1933. Charcoal and gouache. Studio records.

Figure 102. Andrew Tsihnahjinnie, Navajo. *Antelope Hunt.* 1933. Mural, oil on canvas. Santa Fe Indian School. Ernest Knee photograph.

that would ever intrude upon it or change it in the least from its natural course.

In the early winter, the Studio again received an unusually helpful visitor. This time Moises Saenz, Minister of Education of Mexico, came with his keen insight and his great warmth of personality which caused the students to honor what he said about their painting. He urged that the Studio be allowed a much larger, lighter place, and said of its work:

> I feel that Indian art has so much to contribute to American civilization, as well as great values to the Indian himself, that much time and encouragement should be given to it in the schools. . . . Indians need little technical training of the kind given in ordinary art schools . . . merely time, materials, encouragement to do the thing they know . . . keep hands off in technical instruction. . . . Give the art of the Indian currency in the world at large.[16]

272

Soon afterward came H. D. C. Pepler, of Ditchling, Sussex, England, who saw in the paintings a renascence of long-suppressed artistic power. He arranged for an exhibit to be sent to the Royal College of Art, London. At about the same time, another exhibit was arranged for the Museum of Fine Arts of Stanford University by its director, Pedro J. Lemos who had been pioneering for several years to bring about recognition of Indian art in the nation's schools.

On December twelfth, the Studio was officially recognized when D received a civil service appointment as "Teacher of Fine and Applied Arts." In creating this position, by authority of the President, the Office of Indian Affairs had done much more than to recognize the Studio, it had recognized Indian painting for the first time.

When the Works Progress Administration's art projects were begun in Santa Fe, the Studio was invited to participate. Andrew Tsihnahjinnie and Pablita Velarde signed for making oil mural panels and smaller paintings in watercolor. They worked in the Studio but had a fortunate opportunity for professional association with Kenneth Chapman, Raymond Jonson, Datus Myers, and several other Santa Fe artists in the project. Tsihnahjinnie painted animals and Navajo hunting scenes, and Pablita Velarde did home activities of her native Santa Clara Pueblo. Their paintings were exhibited at the Laboratory of Anthropology along with those of other New Mexico artists and afterward at the Corcoran Gallery in the national showing. This was the period when Tsihnahjinnie was doing his most distinguished painting in both tempera and oils, and his work on the WPA Project was among the best that he has produced to date.

Another large project of this school year was that of the science murals. The question had risen from several sources: "Can Indian painting function for the school or must it exist apart in the Studio?" The science class suggested an attractive experiment in correlation of the Studio and the laboratory through its offering of rich content for pictorial presentation. Here was a chance for the modern-yearning Indian young people to see how well their amazingly *modern* traditional motifs might unite with some of the most advanced ideas of the modern world.

The tenth-grade students in the science classes had gone, as much after hours as in regular sessions, to frankly ask a willing and capable science teacher to tell them more about the stars and the weather and the biological facts of their existence: "What makes an eclipse and snow and rain? Why are some people well and others sick? Why do some people have light skins and others dark, and what were men before they were men?" It seemed no one had ever tried to tell them the basic answers before, but now these young people were informed as straightforwardly

273

and clearly as modern science could set forth the facts. Was there a conflict with tribal ideas? In specific items, yes; in fundamentals, surprisingly little, the students said. In fact, the new information resolved and clarified some of the mysticism of the older beliefs.

Could not a part of the conflict between the old art and the new be resolved in the science murals by showing in them that many elemental concepts of art and science are neither old nor new but eternal and commonly shared?

In the preliminary discussions of the murals it was decided that astronomy, geology, biology, physics, and chemistry should be represented. Because the work would have to be done mainly outside school hours by students common to both science and art classes, volunteers for the paintings were chosen on the basis of their interest in particular subjects as well as upon that of their technical ability.

The artists made tryout sketches with colored chalk on large sheets of wrapping paper. They organized, revised, eliminated, and simplified. To be roundly informed, but not to copy, they made abundant use of their textbooks, encyclopedias, dictionaries, portfolios of Indian design and specimens in the Laboratory of Anthropology, the science teacher's notebooks, and of each other's ideas. When they drew upon the walls with charcoal, they simplified their designs still further until these were at last devoid of any but the most significant ideas.

The painting was done in earth colors the artists had prepared themselves. The natural harmony thereby achieved would have been much more difficult to obtain with commercial paints. Unity was also strengthened by the placing of each subject in relation to the whole group. Each artist was aware of the relation of his mural to the larger unit both in content and design.

On the walls the arrangement of the murals begins with *Astronomy*, represented by the earth's solar system in which a bright sun dominates the planets in a pattern of major and lesser rays of light. *Geology* follows, portraying time and life upon the earth in symbolic, varicolored bands of rock strata, each containing fossil and skeletal designs showing the evolution of animals from the beginning of multicellular life to the higher mammals. Many of the motifs were taken direct from Mimbres pottery design, others were created.

The next three murals are concerned with two branches of biology and a unifying design depicting the interdependence of plants and animals. *Zoology* presents, through abstract forms, animal life from the lower orders to the higher, from sea prominence to land prominence. *Botany* shows a similar sequence of plant life from the mosses, ferns, and palms to such modern forms as yucca, giant cactus, Indian paintbrush, and aspen. A completely abstract composition be-

274

tween these two panels represents the carbon cycle and the principal factors—light, soil, water—necessary to life. Waves of color symbolize carbon dioxide given to plants by animals on one side, and oxygen given to animals by plants on the other side.

Opposite these biology paintings are two vertical panels. Facing *Zoology* is one analyzing growth upward from an exquisitely designed single cell to the many-celled organisms. The amoeba subdivides and develops into many; then follow creatures exhaling the traditional breath-of-life symbol, then larger forms, and finally a huge Avanyu. The same cell pattern carries through to show continuity and evolution. Facing *Botany* is the panel similarly delineating the growth of plant life from the single-celled algae to multi-cellular plants. The simple algae subdividing into spirogyra are followed by mosses, ferns, and a flowering yucca. The same colors and basic motifs are carried through to maintain relationship.

To indicate that all life is controlled by the elements of weather and climate, *Physics* follows in a powerful representation in Hopi design of storm, wind, rain, cloud, rainbow, and lightning, with electricity in oscillating bands underlying all. And the final mural, *Chemistry*, portrays all matter as ultimately composed of electrons and protons. In elliptical orbits of spectrum colors, electrons whirl about the protons in a simple dynamic design. This mural was painted a decade before the atom was to be taken apart in nearby Los Alamos, yet its direct statement surely remained with the members of this science class to that later day.

The artists who painted the science murals were: *Astronomy*: Robert Thompson, Laguna; *Geology*: William Sarracino, Laguna; *Biology*: Andrew Tsihnahjinnie, Navajo; *Biology*: Riley Quoyavema, Hopi; *Biology (Botany)*: Pablita Velarde, Santa Clara; *Biology (Zoology)*: Po-Qui (Teofilo Tafoya), Santa Clara; *Physics*: Lewis Lomayesva, Hopi; *Chemistry*: Bennie Manzanares, San Juan.

While these special projects were in progress, general work within the Studio was expanding rapidly. Exhibits were advancing in quality and numbers, and from them selections were made to send to invited showings in other cities. In the Studio, the exhibits were increasingly meaningful to the young artists who were becoming ever more critical of the work of their fellow students and of their own. A general understanding prevailed that to copy from one another was unethical but that to try to raise the standard of one's own work to equal that of the finest painting on display was a worthy effort.

The artists from the Southwest area, through the broadening of subject from memory and research in the Laboratory of Anthropology, and through constant refinement of technique, were producing paintings of progressively finer interest

275

and variety. Those from the Plains and other areas were making a sincere effort to equal the Southwest achievements by evolving new motifs from known living traditions supplemented by research in ethnological records. A good proportion of high quality paintings was now being contributed by this group.

By the first of May, there was enough outstanding painting to provide a much larger and more impressive exhibition in the second annual Indian painting show at the Museum of New Mexico. Olive Rush was again asked to write a review in which she stated in part:

> The exhibition . . . fills three alcoves in the State Art Museum. And that it is a matter of more than local interest has already been proven by these young artists who have exhibited this year at the Royal College of Art, London, the Western Federation of Arts exposition in Detroit, the Corcoran Galleries, Washington, and last year at the world's fair. One student, Tsihnahjinnie, has a painting reproduced in the April issue of the American Magazine of Art. They have decorated not only the walls of their school studio, but the Science room as well . . . But the art lover and connoisseur needs no promptings such as these to win him to the side of art rich in design and wild in flavor from various tribes and nations.
>
> Commanding the first alcove is an antelope mural panel; in oil, by the talented Navajo, Tsihnahjinnie, who never fails to lead us into his world of delight. Here to make them fly the better, he has placed a fluttering tip on everything, and a cloud or a feather forms the markings on the neck of the antelope, a rainbow is under the cactus and chamisa. For a watercolor of deer and nursing fawn he shows stylized animals behind very stylized bushes, and an original use of strange color combinations. Then his streamline horses—how different they are from the Sioux horses by Bear Runner. The Sioux have painted horses superbly for generations, on deerskins—on their teepees, and behold Bear Runner with his beautiful "Sioux Horse Dance." He and Chase, another Sioux, show dancers that look strangely Kiowa, but these boys declare them to be strictly Sioux. Tyndall, an Omaha, has been experimenting in abstract landscapes combined with figures and he may arrive at something exceptional when his figures and landscape come together on a common footing—enveloped, as it were, in the same abstract way. These students from the north where the art of their people has languished of late, are to be greatly commended in their effort toward a true tribal expression. Begay paints boys in a wild race. The Navajo girls are showing their mettle, Sybil Yazzie with sensitive charming watercolors of Navajo women on horseback and of women carding and spinning wool, Ruth Watchman . . . with a sand painting design on a ground of sand.

The only girl who is a full-time painting student in the school is Pablita Velarde of Santa Clara who gives us work of great delicacy and charm—watercolors, and a pleasant and rhythmic design of corn grinding.

A San Juan girl, Po-Su-Nu, has a basket dance done in earth color on native ground. The design is a fine achievement through simple means, one great sweep of line for the shoulders of her women, and a clever use of triangles, circles and straight lines for developing her theme. . . . One panel so done (in earthcolor technique) is by Pai-tu-Mu of the humorous mudheads, and another by Valle, a superb Acoma bird. Mirabal of Taos, uses earth colors beautifully, his watercolors are like miniatures, yet he can paint plastu.

There is but one Apache painter in the school, but if there were but one in the world, he could write down the Apache as an artist nation. His name is Ne-hakije, and he has painted a leafy bower that hides an Apache sand painting that will give you a thrill if art can move you. Out from this design of pale stems and green leaves steps an eerie procession of racers—the picture is called "Apache Racers" and is a memory from childhood, one of a series in which he is recording the old Apache customs as he remembers them.

. . . Then there is Po-qui of Santa Clara, an earnest student in his first year at painting, with a deer dance in earth color in which the Acoma whites make a fine design strangely static, amid the sweep and push of movement toward the front.

There are miniatures by James Louis with expressive hands and astonishing detail of embroideries. Eileen Lesarlley, Zuni, aged 15, presents her first painting and it would "stand up" anywhere. Herrera, Taos Dancers, and Vincenti Mirabal, Taos, watercolors of distinction. Yepa, Jemez, pageantry. Nor-My-Se-Ye shows his sense of humor in his great Shalako chattering to a tiny mudhead, and the Hopi, Honyesva, has developed his own technique in watercolor, using a double outline of two shades of the same color, real sophistication again, while in his oil he has shown a clever management of the feathers on the Kachinas.[17]

THE THIRD YEAR

The opening of the third year of the Studio saw an enrollment of more than four times that of the first year and a proportionate increase in students from outside the Southwest. Among the latter, the Sioux, Omaha, Kiowa, Klamath, Cherokee, Salish, Chiracahua Apache, Cheyenne, and Arapaho were represented. Again, new members of this group had come with the expectation of studying only academic art, and again the problem of re-evaluation of Indian art and adjustment to the Studio's program of Indian painting development was undertaken by them

277

(and with success, for only one chose to drop from the Studio during an entire school year). The expanded enrollment presented difficulties in regard to program and facilities, for there were not hours allowed in the rigid general school schedule nor sufficient materials on hand nor seating space to adequately accommodate all students who wished to paint.

Orders for larger amounts and varieties of paints and papers to be purchased from the Studio's own funds were immediately requested through the school office, and all members of the Studio offered to help rehabilitate the old, vacant library building for a new workship if it should be permitted for such use.

A month later the new Studio was ready, even with skylights and individual tables, and separate rooms for various activities—painting, mounting and shipping, preparation of earth colors and cleaning of tools—and cupboards for supplies, books, and safekeeping of finished work. There were greatly expanded areas for exhibits, and space on every hand for moving about freely and spontaneously in the choice of working materials, in consultations, and in all activities involved in the work. Many new supplies had arrived and the students were enthusiastic even though the schedules would permit only a fraction of them to have a reasonable amount of time to paint. Every member had contributed something toward this new home—repairing, sanding, scrubbing, waxing, hauling, arranging, and the like. Students from other departments also had voluntarily helped.

Early in the school year, requests for exhibits began to arrive. The first exhibition went to the Addison Gallery of American Art at Phillips Academy, Andover, Massachusetts. This selection of paintings, as listed in the catalog,[18] was representative of those sent out by the Studio in following months to art museums, libraries, colleges, and schools. It included the following range of subjects and of tribal representatives:

EARTH COLORS

C-Som-Ma-Thya, Santa Domingo, *Abstract Design*
Lomayesva, Hopi, *Hopi Sun and Rain*
Vincenti Mirabal, Taos Pueblo, *Taos Dancers*
Pai-Tu-Mu, Laguna Pueblo, *Laguna Mudheads*
Ruth Watchman, Navajo, *Navajo Sandpainting of the Ninth Day*
Yo-W-Tw, Acoma, *Acoma Bird*

WATERCOLORS

Woodrow Ball, Klamath, *Crater Lake*
Lorenzo Beard, Cheyenne, *Cheyenne Man with Pipe*

278

Cecil Dick, Cherokee, *Cherokee Woman Pounding Corn*
Mary Ellen, Navajo, *Navajo Sandpainting Design*
Ha-we-la-na, Zia Pueblo, *Zia Deer Dance*
Roselee James, Hopi, *Hopi Butterfly Dancers, Hopi Corn Dancer*
Eileen Lesarlley, Zuñi, *Zuñi Dancers, No. 1, Zuñi Dancers, No. 2*
Vincenti Mirabal, Taos Pueblo, *Taos Clowns, Taos Dancer, Woman Plastering Oven*
Mary Montoya, Santa Ana Pueblo, *Santa Ana Hunting Dance*
Nehakije, Apache, *Apache Racers*
Nor-My-Se-Ye, Zuñi, *Zuñi Eagle Dancer, Zuñi Fire Dancer*
O-te-la-te-ya, Cochiti Pueblo, *Cochiti Antelope Dancers*
Pai-Tu-Mu, Laguna Pueblo, *Laguna Sun Dancer*
Po-Qui, Santa Clara Pueblo, *Santa Clara Hunting Dance, Antelope Dancer, Buffalo Dancer, Eagle Dancer, Santa Clara Basket Dance*
Bear Runner, Sioux, *Sioux Sun Dance, Hunka Ceremony*
Juan Suazo, Tesuque Pueblo, *Pueblo Corn*
Calvin Tyndall (Um-Pah),* Omaha, *Omaha Buffalo Dancer, Omaha Eagle Dancers, Omaha Family, Omaha Skin Painter, Omaha Singers, Plainswoman with Travois*
Quincy Tohoma, Navajo, *Navajo Race, Navajo Country*
A. Tsihnahjinnie, Navajo, *Antelope, Navajo Fire Dance*
Twoitsie, Hopi, *Hopi Man with Burro*
Pedro Vallo, Acoma, *Tying Chili*
Pablita Velarde, Santa Clara Pueblo, *Pueblo Kitchen, Santa Clara Corn Dance No. 1, Santa Clara Corn Dance, No. 2, Woman Winnowing Grain*
Rufina Vigil (Sah-wa), Tesuque Pueblo, *Plastering the Pueblo Home*
> OILS
Honyesva, Hopi, *Hopi Kachinas*
Po-Qui, Santa Clara Pueblo, *Buffalo Dancers, Santa Clara*

In early winter, Paul Coze, artist-ethnologist of Paris, visited the Studio and assured the artists that the people of France would be interested in their paintings. He arranged an exhibit to be held at the Musée d'Ethnographie of the Trocadero in June 1935. Dr. Ryan also visited the Studio, and let the students know that he was very much pleased with their accomplishments.

One of the developments which had interested both these men was that of the earth colors. Two new projects in earth colors were carried through this year.

* The artist chose the spelling Um-Pah as the simplest version of his Omaha name, Onpon, Elk.[19]

The teacher of social science had asked that the Studio cooperate in the making of murals for the social science classroom, and D had proposed that three of the students try doing some smaller murals in true fresco for the Studio and one of the residence halls.

Twelve artist-students of the social science classes* cooperated in painting, on three adjoining walls, murals to represent certain Indian contributions to American culture—the interchange of cultural elements in colonial and pioneering America, and the ascendency over the native of the non-Indian material culture in America.

The procedure in making these murals was much the same as that for the science murals. These were also well coordinated in content and unified in design even though the intermittent sessions of work lasted over a period of about four months. One Navajo boy would bring his radio and paint most of his Saturday afternoons, others would work until late at night or on weekends. Some of the best units in the project were enthusiastically made by students who had had some difficulty in becoming adjusted to the study of Indian painting.

The first modern Indian frescos were made by Po-Qui, Twoitsie, and Waka who used earth pigments extracted and ground in the Studio. The successive stages in this difficult technique were observed by the other students for whom it would have been impossible to arrange such work on sufficient scale until a later time.

While these projects were in progress, the majority of artists were engaged in preparing several exhibits and commissions. They had been invited to present the principal exhibit at the Western Arts Association convention in the Stevens Hotel, Chicago. They mounted and crated one hundred paintings to send to this, and, when D was authorized by the Commissioner of Indian Affairs to accompany the exhibit, the students assumed entire responsibility for the Studio for a week. D brought back to them two letters of praise for their show; one from Charles Fabens Kelley, director of the School of the Art Institute of Chicago, and the other from Hugh M. Newman, director of the Chicago Academy of Fine Arts.

Edwin R. Embree, director of the Julius Rosenwald Fund, also had seen the exhibition and had asked that mural panels be painted for the organization's conference room in which mural paintings from several ethnic groups were to be assembled. Yepa, of Jemez, began work on one of these, *A Summer Dance* (Corn

---

*Woodrow Ball, Klamath; Felice Cheromiah and William Sarracino, Laguna Pueblo; Dan Quiver, Sioux; Andrew Tsihnahjinnie and Ha-So-De, Navajo; Po-Qui, Santa Clara Pueblo; Emeliano Yepa, Jemez Pueblo; Allan Houser, Apache; Bennie Manzanares, San Juan Pueblo; Cecil Dick, Cherokee; Tonita Lujan, Taos Pueblo. See Bramlett (57).

Dance), and Po-Qui, of Santa Clara, planned the other, *A Winter Dance* (Buffalo Dance), as a follow-up experience in oil painting after his fresco.

A student from the Omaha tribe, Um-Pah, was preparing his first one man show for the Joslyn Memorial Museum, Omaha, near his home. Because he would soon finish school, he was being encouraged in this practical experience which might lead into further individual exhibits beyond the Studio.

After the Paris exhibit had been sent, the Studio received a cable asking if it would be possible to rush some two hundred posters to announce the showing. Although this request arrived on the eve of the Easter holidays, every member of the Studio volunteered to work Friday and Saturday in order that the posters could be done. Lettering in so short a time was out of the question, so the French announcement was printed by the local press. The students were asked to make broader, sketchier drawings for this purpose; however, many of the paintings were as nice as those sent on for the exhibit, and all were superior works, entirely beyond ordinary poster quality. During the two days of intensive and joyous activity, most of the students on the campus came at some time to the Studio to see what was going on, and some even volunteered to try to help. This one experience, perhaps more than any of the many inspiring activities in the Studio, proved absolutely that modern paintings, springing from Indian tribal sources, could be done wholeheartedly, spontaneously, and without thought of monetary reward. The students had cheerfully made paintings before to give one another, to the school, and to take home, yet never had there been such an immediately voluminous outpouring of artistic effort as for this unseen and practically unknown cause. It seemed to be an unpremeditated gesture of international goodwill.

At the third annual exhibition in the Museum of New Mexico in May, four alcoves of the finest works of the year were hung, and in the long studio building there was not enough room for all the paintings which merited display in the school's arts and crafts exhibit.

Frederic H. Douglas's review of the museum show included the following statements:

> The exhibit of Indian water-colors on display . . . is both an extremely inclusive setting forth of this remarkable modern art development and a monument to the foresight and appreciation of those collectors who fostered the movement in its infancy and to those government workers who have guided it to its present state of excellence. It seems to me that nothing better indicates a new day for the Indian than the fact that the Indian Service, after years of striving to kill the artistic hopes and expression of the Indian has swung full around to a

281

policy of strong encouragement. . . . How successful [the] students have been in gaining far-flung recognition may be gauged by the fact that large exhibitions of work from the Santa Fe Indian School are now on view at the Pacific Arts Association convention in San Francisco, and at the Bureau of Ethnography in the Trocadero of Paris.

A survey of the current exhibit as the last of a long series brings to light some interesting pointers as to the health and validity of the movement. In its inception water-color painting was restricted to some of the Pueblo groups, and for some years it appeared that these groups alone would develop in this direction. But the present show makes very clear the fallacy of this idea, for it displays work in this medium from about twenty tribes, ranging from Arizona to Wisconsin. No cultural group seems to have a monopoly in the possession of skill in painting. Even where it has not been practiced so long the examples shown indicate clearly that the potential ability needs only a chance to rise and shine. In other words, the development of this art proves conclusively that the inborn artistic gifts of the Indian race are strong enough to have survived the attacks of bureaucracy and civilization and to emerge stronger than ever in its new generations. One may demolish manifestations of a culture, but its inner hopes and ideals defy any assault, and find expression somehow.

A second good augury for the future of the movement can be seen in its ability to move forward instead of crystalizing into certain well mastered forms. . . . the artistic urge of these young intellects is too vital to stand still. New forms are ever appearing, not only because of the spread of the art to tribes of other cultures, but among the varied pueblos. . . .

To comment in detail on the present exhibit is a difficult task. Each picture deserves a word for its individual excellence. But with the limitations of space this is not possible. Hence only a few comments may be made on outstanding painters. Feasting at Yeibechai, by Sybil Yazzie is an excellent example of the modern trend toward genre subjects. Singers, by Po-Qui of Santa Clara is an up-to-date variant of the ceremonial picture and exhibits the glowing color so loved by the Indian. Tsihnahjinnie, a Navajo, displays some very original conceptions of animal life, worked out with a very unconventional palette. No. 218 is a striking example of the Hopi mastery of Aryan metric abstract design. No. 31 by Agnes Bird, Chippewa, is one of the first works from the Great Lakes area. True to the art concepts of her people, Miss Bird shows a fondness for plant forms. Apache Devil Dancers, by Allan Houser, is extraordinarily effective, both for its use of white on black and for the immense vitality of the figures. For effectiveness gained by economical means, No. 111 by Um-Pah, an Omaha, is noteworthy. [Five paintings] are very noticeable because of their difference from more familiar Pueblo forms. They are studies of Sioux life in the highly individu-

282

al style of the old plains painted robes. It is a pleasure to see that this art movement takes as well among the plains people as elsewhere. Much fine art will come from this area, with its strong tradition in painting. No. 125 by E. Yepa, displays the work of a painter who clings, at least in his pictures, to a style seen in the first days of the movement. His conservatism is to be commended, for while progress is desirable, a brake is often useful.

Santa Feans should congratulate themselves on being able to see this fascinating art at such close range. May there be many more such exhibitions.[20]

THE FOURTH YEAR

With the foundations well laid by the fourth year, the 1935-36 season was one of refinement and expansion. Administration shifts in both local and central education offices were occurring, and the Studio was left more or less on its own for a good part of the year, pending the fixation of new administrative policies. This was a year of more flexible schedules, greater freedom in choice and procurement of supplies, more specific consolidation of energies toward the most desirable outcomes of the Studio. The top-heavy design classes of former years had levelled off to reasonable hours and enrollments, giving more time for painting, especially to those who had been limited to two or three hours a week. The Studio was less Jack-of-all trades and more specifically devoted to painting.

For students from outside the Southwest, this was the richest year thus far, for D had had the first chance from her institutional assignments to spend the entire summer sketching basic motifs and arranging for exhibits to be sent from museums for each of the non-Southwest groups represented in the Studio. For the first time also, she was able to offer them a store of source material from her own researches in many collections. Dr. Douglas of the Denver Art Museum had outlined her museum itinerary, and Dr. Krieger of the United States National Museum had been particularly helpful in arranging for some of the finest examples of Plains hide paintings and other Plains art to be lent to the Studio from the national collections. Curators of such rich stores of Indian art as those in the University of Pennsylvania Museum, Museum of the American Indian of the Heye Foundation, Peabody Museum of Harvard University, American Museum of Natural History, and the Field Museum, Chicago, had been most cooperative in making research materials available for D's study and use in the Studio.

Such source material was studied by the classes for authenticity of spirit and style, for veracity of small detail, and for skilled control of media as well as for

283

historic content. It was never copied outright by the students other than for study, but its influence was allowed free play in the creation of works following and improvising on traditional idioms as a springboard to future developments.

For the Pueblo, Navajo, and Apache artists, it was a time of delving more deeply into the vast reserves of their tribal arts near at hand, and of broadening their ideas of subject inclusiveness to make for greater versatility and interpretation. By this time, it seemed very much worthwhile to everyone to record and illuminate events which might otherwise be lost forever, and to project little-known designs of the ancients into modern settings through new arrangements and inventive adaptations, and moreover to offer the original contributions of a new generation of artists who were yet maintaining Indian identity in values too precious to lose.

Because the majority of painters had already worked in the Studio, there had grown a fine rapport between student and student and between student and guide. New students were received by everyone with helpful attitude. The younger beginners had a class of their own this year with a graduate of the Studio, Geronima Cruz (Po-Tsunu), of San Juan Pueblo, assisting. The older members seemed as interested in the work of these younger artists as in that of their own age and experience level. Beginners felt free to go to others for advice if they wished. Everyone belonged.

Guidance techniques had evolved into an assumption of mutual understanding between student and guide wherein, for the older students, a minimum of suggestion was necessary. Several artists had advanced to a point where they were almost completely on their own, yet the awareness and approval of the guide were still helpful to their artistic growth. The work of the majority undoubtedly grew better under some measure of individual and unobtrusive guidance. From the beginning, such guidance took the form of simple, quiet discussions between D and each student while the others went on with their work, unheeding. Or it took, upon infrequent occasions, general discussions for the whole class.

In a typical class, fragments of conversations in regard to individual paintings were such as these:

"You're changing your figures. Why?"
"They were too long; didn't look like men."
"Sometimes long men look better in a painting; many artists make them long purposely. I thought your long men seemed to go well with the tall slim trees and the tall staff and the mysterious feeling you were getting into the whole thing. Everything seemed to belong together."

"Shall I keep them long?"

"Do as you like, but don't worry whether or not they look just like men. In a painting, nothing has to be natural."

"Don't you feel that your black is too heavy for those lighter colors? Does this black over here seem to outweigh those pale colors on the other side?"

"Yes, I think so; I can make these other colors brighter."

"That would be too much to change. They are nice colors; could you try to soften your black a little to see if that might help?"

"How about white in it?"

"Try white, or try mixing in the black some of those colors you already have used; make several tests and see which looks best to you—anything for a lighter black that blends in with your other colors instead of jumping out by itself."

"Good. That's something different. You've made a Plains landscape into a design."

"I'm wondering about putting some dancers in here." (Indicating the foreground.)

"Your sketch is nice just as it is. Why don't you paint this one simply as a decorative landscape, then try dancers or hunters or other figures with line background another time?"

"I think this should be on a bigger paper."

"Yes, and wide. It's width that counts in this drawing. You have so many lines going across the paper, you'll get an effect of much bigger, wider space if you emphasize these lines across."

"Isn't that a Zuñi design on this jar?"

"It's one I saw at the Laboratory."

"It's a nice design but does a Zuñi design look as if it belongs with the other pottery designs your woman is painting?"

"Maybe I'll make a Tesuque design on that pot, too."

"Well, how are the sketches you were going to make?"

"Not much good."

"The animals and trees are fine; I think you need to keep practicing the drawing of people. Sometimes it takes a little longer for them. Keep trying. I'd like to see you do a painting using some of these deer and trees which are so nicely designed. You can make many more kinds of trees than you have here, too, a whole forest of them, and other kinds of plants, also."

285

"I don't know what to paint; I'm tired of dancers."

"Why don't you try to think of some everyday happening which would make a nice picture—planting corn, or hoeing it or husking it and throwing it into big piles, all colors; or cleaning the irrigation ditch in spring, or selling pottery at the fiesta, or getting wood from the hills; winnowing grain; making things—the house, rabbit sticks, belts, moccasins, or something else? You can think of many things."

"I'll make a drawing. I know something."

"You are putting your color on nicely, but don't you think your white is lost against the white background? (I'll hold it off a ways and you see how it looks.) Can you mix a speck of something in it to make it show up better?"

"A little brown?"

"That would make a nice warm white which would look fine with your other colors."

"Here are some pictures of Sioux paintings I thought you'd like to see. I think they're so fine in rhythm and action and clean-cut lines."

"Who made them?"

"These are only my sketches but the originals were made by an unknown Sioux artist many years ago. They have been preserved by the American Museum of Natural History in New York."

"I'd like to make some of them."

"It would be a good idea for your own reference. You can learn a great deal from them, I think, even though you want to keep developing a style of your own."

"You put some real character into these horse sketches. The antelopes seem to be too much like Gerald's; these horses are yours. Why don't you make a painting with lots of horses in it?"

"A race?"

"A race would be fine, and there are others you could do well, too—a rodeo or a roundup. Remember when they herd the horses into the corral in the spring —the wild ones, the shaggy ones, red, yellow, and black and spotted? You could make a wonderful painting of that sometime—many, many horses, big and little ones, all sorts of colors."

"Does this look to you as if it's falling down toward the bottom of the paper?"

"Too much white at the top? I can cut it off."

286 "You don't need to cut it off; why don't you try a design over the heads of the dancers—a design of clouds, or rainbow, or birds, or sun, or something else?"

"That's a very interesting arrangement. It seems as if someone were up on a hill looking down on the whole Yeibichai."

"I'm trying to show everything."

"You're succeeding very well but don't you think you should give yourself more room in your final drawing?"

"I'll get a big sheet and draw more people, too."

"How about a big, dark paper? Even black, if you want it. Your fires would sparkle and all those blanket patterns would look bright in the dark. This will be one of your best paintings."

Thus, the guidance and the expression were fluid and continually evolving. At times it seemed as if the two met in perfect understanding and that each was somehow conditioned by the other.

The principal class discussions of the year centered about a study of world art from early days to modern times. Informal talks were accompanied by prints and slides from the Art Institute of Chicago and the Museum of New Mexico for the purpose of giving the students some idea of the relationships between the arts, including that of the American Indian, and to show that there were many periods, schools, and styles contributing to the whole of art. Prof. Kenneth Chapman generously came out to the Studio and presented part of the section on Indian painting, using some of the same material as in his classes at the University of New Mexico.

The students seemed more interested in the subject than the average college group and worked more industriously and happily at their notes and references. The directness and aliveness of Paleolithic painting, the orderly conventions of Egyptian frescos, the stylized realism of art of the Mediterranean centers, the exquisitely detailed rendering of Persian and Indian miniatures, the poetic impressionism of Chinese watercolors intrigued them most. They made comparisons for themselves and at times were amazed at unaccountable similarities such as those between ceramic designs of archaic Rhodes, Crete, and Cyprus, and those of certain modern pueblos—a bird from a Cypriote oinochoe of 700 B.C. and one from present Santo Domingo Pueblo; a deer from a Rhodian jar and one from a Zuñi olla, separated by more than twenty-five hundred years. They found the European paintings of the Christian era more strange to their own, although they awakened to an appreciation of the urgence of expression, the close, rich techniques of the Italian primitives, to the delightsome genre of a Pieter Brueghel or the elemental approach of a Cezanne, or the color, design and dynamism of a Kandinsky.

287

These young Indian artists seemed to gain a new respect for their own art through this study, a new reason for making a contribution of their own. It was as if, to sum up all their statements, they might have said: Our own is of this greater world of art, and it is our privilege to help American Indian painting become known in its rightful, permanent place among all these other arts. Our art is related, yet it is unique, and only we can carry it forward.

This was a year of many exhibits in all parts of the country. One of the principal ones was held at the Art Institute of Chicago at the invitation of assistant director Charles Fabens Kelley. Another was shown in the Gallery for Living Artists of the Brooklyn Museum where Howard Devree saw it and later reported in the New York *Times*: "Their compositions in face of the impingement of the white man's culture have suffered surprisingly little in the loss of native characteristics and afford an interesting comparison with the work of their elders."[21]

Various older artists helped in the preparation of exhibits—mounting, listing, shipping—in order to learn how to handle their own exhibitions when they left school. Those within the area of the Santa Fe school were encouraged to return to the Studio as a base when preparing exhibits, if they wished.

Early in the spring, Nehakije, a former member of the Studio, came down from the Jicarilla Apache reservation with twelve fresh, vivid watercolors. At the Studio, he mounted and prepared them for his first one-man show at the Museum of New Mexico. Before he had left the Studio a year earlier to take over his aging father's work, he had said, "I'm going on with my art. I'll learn all I can about Apache customs and ceremonials and I'll paint them. I'd like to write about them, too. I will send my paintings to museums as I did when I was in school. Maybe next spring I'll have an exhibit in Santa Fe." The care of the cattle and sheep had come first, but Nehakije not only had painted pictures, he had equipped his own studio, experimented with pigments from natural sources, and had written and illustrated a story, "Jicarilla Apache Winter," which he had published in *World Youth*.[22] The *New Mexican* review said of his exhibition:

> His paintings reflect his strength and his imagination. They are the work of an original painter uninfluenced by any school, although there is a suggestion of the Persian in his fine detail, delicate lines, and brilliant color. . . . These paintings are as impersonal as pure abstract, yet they are filled with mood and meaning.[23]

A graduating student, Po-Qui, in preparation for his post-school career, successfully completed a mural commission in the Maxwell, New Mexico, High

School where he painted Santa Clara subjects in oil in the manner established in the Santa Fe Indian School dining-room murals.

The Studio steadily acquired new friends through their visits and through traveling exhibitions. Educators, artists, collectors, and researchers came from all parts of the nation and from foreign countries. Among the latter was Pál Kelemen, of Budapest, who was then engaged in his comprehensive study of pre-Columbian American Indian art.[24] Although more particularly interested in pre-Columbian art, Dr. Kelemen was an erudite analyst of the modern work. He brought the reassurance of a fine critic and scholar to the Studio.

Another who became one of the Studio's most understanding friends was Mrs. William Denman, a member of the newly formed Indian Arts and Crafts Committee appointed by the Secretary of the Interior. She sponsored an exhibition of Studio paintings at the San Francisco Museum of Art, and in succeeding years encouraged Indian artists through her purchases and prizes. From that time until Mrs. Denman's death in 1959 this fine contribution continued.

At the end of this rich and rewarding year, even though many paintings had been sold, there were more than six hundred of exhibition quality from which to choose the annual show. Those selected filled the main galleries of the entire first floor of the Museum of New Mexico. Among the comments of Annette Fassnacht, reviewing the exhibition from the viewpoint of the educator-anthropologist, were:

> This is the twenty-first exhibit of the year. . . . in the Gallery for Living Artists [Brooklyn, New York, the show] was so well received that it was retained there a week beyond the scheduled time. The Brooklyn Museum has arranged to send exhibits of Indian paintings to Prague, Vienna, Budapest, and Warsaw within the coming year. There is to be an exhibit in Cheltenham, England this summer. The Studio's calendar of exhibits for next year is already nearly filled. . . .
>
> Has Indian art at last arrived? It is, rather, that we have at last become able to appreciate an art so mature as that produced by the Indian artists. . . .
>
> Art is a serious business with the Indian. It has always been a dominant factor in Indian culture. . . . a composite of the arts. Such complexity of content has made it necessary for the artist to do much more than copy the outside of things. . . .
>
> These artists have proved that they can venture outside the field of ceremonial life and still keep within the traditions of their art. . . .[25]

A noteworthy event during this final exhibit of the season was Edgar L. Hewett's approval of the paintings. Until this time he had withheld comment as if waiting until enough work had been accomplished to make it clearly evident that the course the Studio had been following was leading to desirable outcomes. Dr. Hewett, of his own accord, examined the exhibit most thoughtfully with D, pointing out what he considered the most significant work and making wise analytical observations. "You are heading in the right direction," he said, "This painting is new, but it is Indian."

Chester E. Faris, who had been superintendent of the Santa Fe school at the time the Studio began, came from another state to see the exhibition and to offer his personal congratulations on the success of the young artists.

In retrospect, one would say this was the finest year of the Studio.

THE FIFTH YEAR

By the fifth year the objectives of the Studio had been realized to an extent which permitted recognition of certain patterns and tendencies within it and in its relationship to other organizations and interests.

It had become clear that the broad capacity in which the Studio was operating was twofold: it was an instrument for guidance and development of artists, and it was an agent for enlisting the interest of the public in Indian painting.

Rapid increase of both enrollments and of public interest made it also evident that further advancement of the Studio's objectives would be determined henceforward not alone by Studio personnel but by the measure of awareness and appreciation to be found in the controlling agencies within the Indian Service system which decided policies either sustaining or destructive to creative effort.

In the particularized patterns within the Studio, the painting itself had begun to indicate both tribal and individual trends in style, technique, and subject. A summary of representative tribal, sectional, and individual painting at this stage revealed the following.

Pueblo. The Pueblo artists painted ceremonials, hunting scenes, and craftsmen of the several villages much in the manner of their predecessors. Certain conventions established by the older painters were frequently followed such as the painting of antelope with golden yellow coat marked by stylized white neck bars, belly, and rump spot, or the framing of dance, hunting, or other seminaturalistic scenes with purely abstract designs of cloud, rainbow, terraced mountain, or plant.

In addition, the younger painters placed a new emphasis upon abstract design from ceramic-derived and invented motifs. There were many new variations upon old sky themes and unrestricted ceremonial symbols. The seemingly endless

290

productivity in this respect attested the strong vitality of the strains of Pueblo art.

No artists before had developed to such an extent the possibilities of all aspects of Pueblo genre in its multifarious scenes from plaza, field, and dwelling, yet these artists did not exhaust this rich source of subject.

An innovation was the purely decorative forest scene unconcerned with human life. Here fantasy in the creative treatment of plant and animal design had free rein. Santo Domingo artists, in particular, carried such patterns to a high degree of specialization because of their pueblo's painting restrictions of which the Studio was aware. Even human figures which had no ceremonial significance were practically taboo in Santo Domingan art, and if they were shown at all they would usually have faces turned away or partly hidden behind some object.

Understood restrictions in other quarters governed the appearance of masked figures. While such beings peopled the paintings of the western villages, they did not appear in works from the Rio Grande pueblos except on very rare occasions. There were no rules and nothing was ever said about these limitations; they were simply recognized and respected within the Studio.

Mutations occurred in the use of media and devices. Color became entirely unpredictable—brilliant turquoise deer, purple trees, ceramic motifs which forsook earthen tones for bright shades, startling uses of blacks and whites. Perspective, when used, appeared similar to that in Egyptian, Persian, East Indian, or Chinese painting. Light and shade, although occasionally employed by the Hopi, was seldom attempted by artists of other pueblos. In any case, light differentiation was not handled in an academic manner but by individual contrivance.

It is interesting to note that, in their developments thus far, the young artists had demonstrated the wisdom of a statement to be made, in the catalog of the exhibition, twenty-four years later by Fred Kabotie as jury member for the 1961 American Indian Artists Exhibition at Philbrook Art Center:

> Basically the old way of painting is the beginning for the on-coming young artist who has not lost contact with the home background, and out of this something different evolves and opens the way to develop into a new style.

Representative artists whose styles were becoming fairly well defined were the following:

Taos. Chiu-tah (Vincenti Mirabal) was first of all a colorist. In his ceremonial scenes of many figures, he frequently put even the paper to work for his color ensembles, using rich dark backgrounds of handmade textures to enhance the vibrant, full range of blended hues. Blanket patterns on stolid figures seemed

291

shimmering and live, flesh tones glowed with warmth, even his blacks were fresh and interesting.

Pop-Chalee (Merina Lujan) was a specialist in minutely decorative woodland scenes of delicacy and sprightliness. Her small alert animals played against a colorful, balanced pattern of leaves, stems, and flowers, as bright-feathered birds darted in and out among the treetops.

Eva Mirabal (Ea-Ha-Wa) had the ability to translate everyday events into scenes of warmth and seminaturalistic beauty. She was an unintentional portraitist, achieving character with a few deft lines. In miniature pattern, she was exceedingly skilled. Animals, genre, and the less formal ceremonials were her favorite subjects.

Other Taos painters who were developing styles of their own were Tonita Lujan, Jerry Lucero, Eloisa Bernal, and Rita Martinez.

San Juan. T'o-Pove (Lorencita Atencio) painted in a careful, straightforward style the genre of San Juan and the Mexican-influenced ceremonials. Incorporated in her works were finely detailed patterns from embroidered and woven designs, or of plant forms brushed in clear, lifelike color.

Po-Tsunu (Geronima Cruz) painted in a similar way with broader, stronger brush treatment and less emphasis on small design. Her art was placid and decoratively literal.

Sa-Pa (Emeliano Abeyta), Santiago Garcia, Manuelita Trujillo, Maria Abeyta, and Rebecca Chavez were other San Juan painters of unusual ability.

San Ildefonso. Popovi Da (Tony Martinez) painted the Deer Dance and Buffalo Dance in a style similar to that established by his father, Julian. He used exceedingly thin, light outlines with stencil-like areas of true, flat color to achieve a clean-cut classic effect. He indicated inventive capacity in developing abstract bird forms from old Pajaritan motifs.

Juan Pedro Pino, Tomacito Vigil, and Suwa (Jose V. Aguilar), three others of the younger painters, were also doing creditable work.

Santa Clara. Pablita Velarde (Tsan) was a steady, serious worker, most adept at scenes depicting potters and homemakers of Santa Clara. Her painting was decorative yet lifelike, with careful attention to authentic detail. In her ceremonial paintings, her resourcefulness often led her to choose the more unusual and little-known aspects for depiction.

Po-Qui's (Teofilo Tafoya's) work was dignified and conservative, save in his portrayal of the Kossa to which he brought sardonic humor. He usually chose to paint various phases of the Buffalo Dance, Corn Dance, or other formal cere-

292

Figure 103. Po-Qui, Santa Clara Pueblo. *Kossa*. 1935. Tempera. Collection of Mr. and Mrs. John Gaw Meem.

monials, imparting to his representations the steady, balanced patterns of the dances through his strong compositional ability.

Kgoo-Ya (Leandro Gutierrez) saw Pueblo events in a robustly original way. He would set difficult tasks for himself such as showing a scene half in light and half in shadow, or one viewed simultaneously from afar and near at hand. Not **293** attempting academic tactics, he invented his own in solving his technical problems successfully.

Among the proportionately large number of commendable Santa Clara painters were others of the Gutierrez family—Juan B., Joe La Cruz, Clarence, and Joseph L.; and three other artists of the Tafoya family—Rosita, Oku-Wa-tsa (Joseph), and Moses. Two of the Silvas, Marcus and Eugene, were also beginning to do work of quality.

Tesuque. Sah-wa (Rufina Vigil) was one of the most versatile of the young women. She painted in a deliberate, independent style all aspects of the life of her pueblo. Equally facile were her renditions of ceremonial, genre, and abstract design. She had great patience with fine detail, and was adept at composition.

Po-ve Pien (Joe Evan Duran) painted games, dances, and work-a-day scenes in clear bright color with naturalness and naivete. Small touches of humor gave a light and happy quality to his pictures.

Others carrying on artistic traditions of the Vigil family were Joe, Pete, and Utimio; and of the Swazo family, Juan and Pat.

Cochiti. Ben Quintana was one of the few who are so endowed that they might one day be masters. At twelve he painted Cochiti ceremonials with a sureness, dignity, and insight that already rivalled the work of artists conceded to be of top rank in Pueblo art. His varied subjects were taken from all walks of Pueblo life and interpreted with rare selectivity and beauty of brushwork. (At fourteen he won, over fifty thousand contestants, the American Youth Prize of one thousand dollars, the largest prize ever awarded an Indian artist.)

Joe H. Herrera (See-Ru) did justice to a fine tradition in his authentically drawn ceremonial subjects. His work was unlike that of his renowned mother, Quah Ah, for his was coolly decorative where hers was warmly natural.

Avelino Arquero was inventive and venturesome, an experimenter with line and strange color. Any subject was his, even landscape which he was able to do in a sort of shorthand brushwork—balanced lines and designed shapes of earth contour, bush, and tree.

Stimone (Justino Herrera), Cipriana Romero, and Joe Quintana also were Cochiti painters of increasing ability.

Santo Domingo. Lorenzo Garcia combined fantasy with naturalism in animal figures to produce paintings of pure delight which held the observer on the borderline between reality and a world of make-believe.

Jose J. Garcia began with fundamental motifs of Santo Domingo ceramic design, and, with added and heightened color, mechanical draftsmanship of his

294

Plate XXIV. Quah Ah, Cochiti Pueblo. *Ceremonial Figures.* Ca. 1930. Oil on wood. Architectural decoration detail, Rancho de la Cañada. University of New Mexico.

Plate XXV. T. Tomassee, Hopi. *Nataska Kachina Group.* 1920. Tempera gouache. Museum of the American Indian, Heye Foundation.

Plate XXVI. GILBERT ATENCIO, San Ildefonso Pueblo. *Sipapu*. 1959. Casein tempera. Collection of Richard M. Howard.

own invention (he chose to use instruments), and juxtaposition of shapes, he produced uniquely decorative floral and bird patterns which might have been used in mosaic or stained glass.

Belardo Nieto's paintings were fantasy and decoration in a crisp and spirited style which would fit into ultramodern settings. Exquisitely drawn and brushed with finesse were his lacy branches on spindling trees, high-prancing, long-necked fawns in exotic blues, and clouds hung like pale, gray webs.

Leo Reano's few formative paintings of his first year were enough to mark his unusual talent for draftsmanship and emotional communicability. His strikingly original style seemed to have burst forth full-fledged, related to no other. He intuitively used distortion for dramatic effects in hunting scenes of wild beauty.

From Santo Domingo, with all its taboos and restrictions, came some of the most original and highly promising art produced in the Studio. In addition to the above painters, C-som-ma-th-ya (Tony Tenorio) and Santiago and Juan Pedro Garcia did work of uncommon potentiality.

Jemez. Emeliano Yepa had a somewhat stilted style which enhanced the formal patterns of ceremonial and small Jemez scenes he chose to paint. His brilliant palette brought animation and a note of daring to his balanced, conservative compositions.

Jose Toledo, the younger, was also establishing his own style with varied subjects which included home interiors, hunting scenes, and dance forms.

Zia. Ha-we-la-na (Marcelina Herrera) could perceptively relate a narrative in a patterned setting. Yet her work was not illustration but visual legend. She touched the subjects of mourning and pathos, which seem all but taboo in Pueblo painting, with grace and understanding. Her drawing was delicate, her color richly alive.

Waka (Ignacio Moquino) brought unusual spontaneity to his ceremonials, hunts, and harvesting scenes. He combined Zia ceramic design with lifelike figures in an individual manner.

Juan B. Medina's art was cleverness and lifelike humor combined with the strictly decorative design of Zia pottery. Under his hand the ancient painted bird forms became animated, and the stiffly patterned plants sprang to life from painted bowls, in such pictures as *Zia Chicken in Trouble, Birds on a Tree, Tired Chicken,* and *Be-Have Yourself.*

Other Zia names of note were Andreita Salas and Jose C. Herrera who were both carrying Zia traditions into inventive works.

Santa Ana. Mary Montoya, with gently drawn scenes such as *Woman Win-*

295

296 Figure 104. JUAN B. MEDINA, Zia Pueblo. *Birds on a Tree*. Ca. 1935. Tempera. Collection of Dorothy Dunn.

Figure 105. Juan B. Medina, Zia Pueblo. *Tired Chicken.* 1937. Tempera. Collection of Mrs. Thomas E. Curtin.

Figure 106. Juan B. Medina, Zia Pueblo. *Be-Have Yourself.* 1936. Tempera. Margretta S. Dietrich Collection.

297

nowing Wheat and *Woman Baking*, and Blas Sanchez with brightly stylized subjects of *Deer, Little Antelopes*, and *Desert* were doing the first modern watercolors of Santa Ana Pueblo.

Laguna. Pai-Tu-Mu (Robert Thompson) used a soft-toned palette to paint elongated, graceful Kachinas and austerely animated clowns. Joseph Martin with a natural fine talent, and Walter Johnson brought such subjects as *At Camp, Forest*, and *Woman in Her House* to balance their interest in ceremonial figures.

Acoma. Yo-W-Tw's (Horace Valle's) paintings were entirely abstract, and usually in earth-color hues. The bird and flower motifs of Acoma provided a working base upon which he invented his own designs in strong, even technique.

Lolita Torivio's work emanated a childlike sincerity and simplicity. She painted a comprehensive range of activities of field and home in lovely color, imparting to them much of the serenity and peace of Pueblo life.

James Louis was skilled in painting brilliant-colored miniature dancers of energetic animation.

Zuñi. Eileen Lesarlley's paintings were of the women of Zuñi, done in a static, decorative style with intricate detail. The woven pattern of a belt, the embroidered hem of an apron, the clustered setting of turquoise in a ring were painstakingly wrought. Her drawing was deliberate, her color bright, set off by stark blacks and whites, her composition as formal as ceramic design.

Dempsey Chopito could paint the impressive Zuñi gods with vital line and color, could combine lively composition with rigid form to convey the mystic power and austerity of supernatural beings.

Tony Chopito, Alfred Dosedo, Jack Bobelu, William Lewis, and Reginald Dewa also had unusual ability to render the emphatically decorative figures of the Zuñi ceremonials. Their flat, bright colors and decisive outlines contributed to the abstract stylization of forms.

Hopi. Tom Jay's miniature Kachinas were brilliant in costume and gay in spirit, for he painted them as in a lighthearted ballet, with shining, jewel-toned color and lilting action.

Walter Joshongeva painted Hopi ceremonial sequences in a manner more natural than the usual effigy-like Hopi figures, yet his painting was not naturalistic in its selection of large elements and finely detailed small units.

Philip Zeyouma was inventive and original in his choice and arrangement of traditional Hopi subjects. His work had a strong individual stamp and could never be mistaken for that of any other Hopi artist. With a light touch, bordering on

298

Figure 107. LOLITA TORIVIO, Acoma Pueblo. *Woman Picking Chili*. 1936. Tempera.
Collection of Dorothy Dunn.

299

humor, he could present the Wutzi, the Koyimsi, and various Kachinas in scenes of merriment.

Eddie Nequatewa was versatile. Two styles were his—balanced, formal decoration, and realism of small and lively Kachinas and Koyimsi. Vivid color and careful pattern were always evident in his works.

Hansen Twoitsie worked in a scholarly manner, going to prehistoric sources for Hopi ceramic patterns and adapting them to easel paintings. When he painted human figures, they were in the genre of earlier days, in earth-keyed palette.

Roselee James, Lewis Lomayesva, Bert Poneoma, Preston Keevama, Robert Lomadafkie, Dahouta, Homer Grover, and Walter (Waldo) Mootzka were other artists each evolving an admirable style of his own from Hopi sources.

Navajo. The Navajo artists had no precedent in modern painting. Obviously the sandpainting designs could not, by their completely religious nature, be the major basis for development of a modern style even though they would provide a rich source of motif to be used in connection with Navajo subjects and for adaptations in pure abstract design. Navajo ceremonials and occupations and the austere beauty of the Navajo country were as productive of interesting subject as anything in Pueblo life, and, since so much of Navajo art had already been developed in conjunction with Pueblo sources, it seemed only fitting that this new art should show a tendency to evolve on lines similar to modern Pueblo painting. Subject alone would make for distinctive flavor and might eventually lead toward a modern tribal style.

As the Navajo artists advanced their work, the general character of technique became that of flat application of color surrounded by outline. Indication of horizon or background was not usual, although a few artists did some interesting experiments in landscape wherein the awsome disparity between the smallness of creatures and the immensity of the Navajo country was rather convincingly stated through ingenious perspective. The most common subjects were ceremonials, games, races and riders, sheep herding, animals, portrayals of crafts workers, and scenes within and about the hogan. With these subjects, motifs from sandpaintings such as rainbow, sun, serpents and other creatures, corn, squash and bean plants would often be incorporated. On the whole, there was much more spirited action and less formality of composition than in Pueblo painting. Colors frequently held to the sandpainting range or were heightened slightly from those tones. Brilliant color less usually appeared.

300

Sybil Yazzie excelled in miniature. Scores of horses and human figures filled her paintings so rich in color and imaginative in statement. Her broadly inclusive ceremonials would shine in the dark or sparkle in the sunlight; she had a gift for selecting the right color hues and values for chosen occasions. Within the larger patterns, her tiny motifs of necklaces, bracelets, belts, hatbands, harnesses, fringes, and like adornments studded each scene with meticulously wrought decoration.

Wade Hadley (To'dachine) deftly painted all manner of plants and animals of the Navajo environment, imparting to them equally warm realism and decorative design. His brushwork was exceptionally fine and surely controlled. His color, which ran to grays, browns, greens, and golds, was never harshly mixed.

Ned Notah painted with such charming simplicity and genuine naivete that his works could be classed as thorough primitives. He would render a challenging view of Canyon de Chelly, or a simple drawing of a child with a sheep, in the same unpretentious and disarming manner.

Keats Begay worked in a related style, painting shepherds and flocks against the deep terra cottas of the Navaho desert. He conveyed the character of the land and its people.

Stanley Mitchell painted small, tightly drawn figures of droll aspect, their little faces differentiated by hair-breadth lines. His was a sparkling palette in which bright reds, purples, and oranges vibrated among clear, light cobalts of enamel-like texture. Dancers, horsemen, silversmiths (he, too, was a silversmith) were his subjects.

Ruth Watchman was a research technician in design. She seemed to care little for painting the pictorial aspects of Navajo life but set for herself the task of studying the patterns of the sandpaintings and of creating a technique whereby characteristic elements of these fleeting designs might be permanently captured. She worked with plaster and sand and true earth pigments until she admirably achieved her purpose. Her paintings were miniature sandpaintings, authentic in design, color, and texture.

Mary Ellen chose for herself another difficult problem—that of painting, side by side in a single scene, the temporal personages of the Navajo world and the extremely conventionalized plants of the sandpaintings. By intensifying colors of the plants and rooting them to earth, while lowering the color values and immobilizing the action of the human figures, she approached compatibility in such diverse components.

Harrison Begay was a prolific and versatile painter. The full range of Navajo subjects was at his command and he approached it all with reserve and good judg- **301** ment. His style was at once decorative and lifelike, his color clear in hue and even in value, his figures placid yet inwardly animated. He was a conservative painter and an inventive one. He subscribed to no innovations except those of his own making, and he seemed to be inexhaustibly resourceful in a quiet, reticent way. Among other things, he invented a dynamic symmetry which he used upon occasion. He was the sort of artist who might go on painting and maintaining his own standards indefinitely, whether he were all alone or among many.

Gerald Nailor was the suave stylist-decorator. His lovely patterns of horses, deer, and antelopes were smartly and proudly drawn with never a thought for natural appearance. Every detail of their design was accomplished with adroitness and polish. If one must use the term in connection with Indian art, his work was sophisticated. Nailor originated plant forms and resourcefully employed small units from sandpaintings for decorative motifs above or below his main figures. A leafy bush would spring from a rainbow fragment or a sacred spring; a Yeibichai moon would light a hunting scene. He set styles which others in and out of his tribal group would surely follow for years to come.

Quincy Tohoma (later Tahoma) painted animals first among his varied subjects. He followed them knowingly into all their wild haunts of the Navajo country in every season—antelopes racing across a sunny mesa, gray deer plodding through deep snow, bear cubs huddled on a windswept mountain ridge. In other paintings, his hunters and warriors rode remarkable steeds such as were never nourished on Navajo grass; his insignificant shepherds herded infinitesimal flocks against gigantic backgrounds of weird red rocks and distant ranges. For depth or roundness or foreshortening, he invented his own devices most convincingly.

Andrew Tsihnahjinnie, in many respects—incisive interpretation, spontaniety of brushwork, originality of color, vigor of draftsmanship and vitality of action—had no equals among the artists of the studio and perhaps few superiors among modern painters. If equanimity and self-confidence were to rule his artistic abilities, Tsihnahjinnie might well be one of America's top-ranking painters. In the brief seasons when he felt freed to paint the things he knew so deeply, without troubled concern for doing otherwise, his work attained a trenchant beauty, unique in modern art.

Ha-So-De (Narciso Abeyta) developed a markedly individual style, although, in his formative period, his admiration for the work of Tsihnahjinnie could be clearly seen. It was a fine influence and used honorably by the younger painter. His paintings of hunt and home scenes were broad in brushwork and flowing in line, at times appearing almost nonchalant. He was never concerned with small

302

Figure 108. ANDREW TSIHNAHJINNIE, Navajo. *Navajo N'da-a*. 1934. Tempera. Amelia Elizabeth White Collection.

detail but only with the sweep and dash of movement in wild, free scenes. His was a positive art.

Other Navajo artists who were emerging with notable works were Amie Duncan, Winnie Chee, Kee Yazzie, and Timothy Begay.

303

Figure 109. Ha-So-De, Navajo. *Children to the Day School.* 1940. Tempera. Museum of Art, University of Oklahoma.

Apache. There were few examples of brushwork in Apache art which might furnish a basis for modern painting, although painting on hides, clothing, shields, and musical instruments furnished some indication of motifs and techniques. Angular designs and unnaturalistic figures painted in flat, outlined colors which characterized early Apache work appeared in the new painting.

The modern expressions produced active life forms rendered in flat, usually outlined color. Ceremonials, hunts, and events of war were favored subjects; homelife scenes were less common. Because of the three distinct tribal areas and relatively few artists from each, it was difficult to draw generalizations in regard to modern Apache painting.

Nehakije* (Steven Vicenti) of the Jicarilla Apaches was the first and perhaps potentially the finest of modern Apache painters. His work was authentic yet imaginative, and it was stated with utmost grace and delicacy. It possessed an elusive fragile beauty, as well as strength. With a palette of whites, grays, and blacks through which dashes of scarlet, ultramarine, and emerald flashed, he painted the quiet, intense participants in Jicarilla ceremonial games and dances, or the tall, erect riders on slim, long-legged horses, waiting, seldom in motion.

Wilson Dewey and Ignatius Palmer painted the dynamic, angular-patterned Gan Dance of the San Carlos and Mescalero Apaches, respectively. Dewey, particularly, succeeded in evoking the characteristic stomp, twist, and stop-short action of the dance pattern. Palmer's figures were done in quieter mood. Dewey also portrayed scenes of the Arizona desert home of the San Carlos in stylized decoration, as well as exotic animals—*Two Green Deer*, for example. Palmer also painted such subjects as *Deer and Flowers* and *Going for Water*.

Two resourceful painters of less technical advancement brought an interesting range of subjects to their early work: Alfred Kayitah, from Mescalero, with such titles as *Cattle Country, Making Shields, Making Masks, Apache Riders, The Big Tipi*; and Walter Balatache with *Apaches Traveling* and *Apache Hunters*.

Allan Houser (Ha-oz-ous) possessed a remarkable balance of artistic intelligence, self-assurance, and industry which enabled him to advance his work from crude drawings to paintings of fine-arts calibre in the four years of his Studio career. Such determining attributes might carry him far in the art world. He had a fund of knowledge of tribal custom and ceremony which he wisely incorporated with research material to present many aspects of Chiricahua Apache life. He be-

* Nehakije was the subject of Malvina Hoffman's *Apache* (bronze) in the Hall of Man, Chicago Natural History Museum.

came an adroit technician, refining his color to exquisite subtleties and brushing it to flawless texture. With incisive outlines and very few flecks of the brush he revealed his comprehension of anatomy and action. He might have stated less with full academic rendering. One thing could, upon occasion, mar his figures, and that was a tendency to caricature.

Plains. The Plains artists had a much more difficult time in bringing their art to the fore than had those from the Southwest; nevertheless, a modern Plains pattern was taking form. The influences of subjects and styles of hide paintings and early watercolors were the most potent in the general conception of their work, while the geometric design of bead, quill, and parfleche decoration exerted a lesser bearing upon composition and incidental motif.

Broader than the subject coverage of these forerunning works, the new painting led into a more detailed treatment of legend, ceremonial, and the genre of both old and recent days. Following the precedent of former art, the new painting was largely two dimensional with occasional suggestion of depth obtained by placement of lines and forms in an unacademic perspective scheme. There was literally no attempt at light and shade in any of the Plains work. Color was more likely to be bright and clear than grayed. It was applied in flat areas and surrounded by outline. Action was the keynote of this art as it had been in the hide paintings, and it was as convincingly rendered through the same command of clean, forceful line.

Of the Sioux artists, Oscar Howe was the outstanding painter. He had the quiet, persevering studiousness which combined with high technical aptitude to make for intellectual achievement in art. His paintings were immediately recognizable as authentic; hours of patient research, of brush practice and color experiments, of thoughtful consideration for compositional effect were in every piece. Yet, with such deliberation, he produced a result of ease and spontaneity. Hunters and warriors interested him rather than dancers, although he did occasionally turn to them and to everyday activities of the camp for subject. He often composed upon large papers which gave range for many riders on galloping, varicolored horses. The general effect was suggestive of the hide paintings but the detail was finer, the color more subtle, and the drawing more representational.

Other Sioux artists were Wilmer Dupree, Oscar Bear Runner, Tony Guerue, and Dan Quiver. Dupree, with originality and selectiveness, based his painting upon a study of historic work such as that of Kills Two and Amos Bad Heart Buffalo. To this knowledge, he brought personal ideas which combined to make mod-

Figure 110. Oscar Howe, Sioux. *Sioux Warriors*. 1936. Tempera. Margretta S. Dietrich Collection.

ern paintings reminiscent of the color and verve of the old styles. Bear Runner relied more upon memory of legends and recent ceremonials for his subjects. He did small groups of dancers or riders in colors ranging from earth browns to bold yellows and blues. Guerue spent most of his time in sketching and experimenting but produced an occasional painting of distinction. One was of a large herd of buffalo with brown bodies and startling white manes, moving across a wide space in the huddled rhythm of a herd upon the plains (now in the art museum of

307

Oberlin College). Quiver was a deliberate and reserved painter who specialized in decorative single figures wearing elaborate ceremonial costumes.

Um-Pah (Calvin Tyndall) of the Siouan Omaha, was a prolific artist of individuality and fine technical ability. A broad range of subjects from his memory of Omaha tradition was at his command, and he interpreted such scenes as *War Dancers, Buffalo Hunt, Moving with Travois, Omaha Women* with fine drawing and cleanly brushed color. He had intelligently transferred an interest in chromo landscape to an original development in stylistic representation of the expanse and terrain of his home country. With ingeniously manipulated line he could spread the rolling hills, the ridges, the canyons and marshes, and the low-growing flora in scenes which evoked the vastness and loneliness of the Great Plains.

Figure 111. LORENZO BEARD, Cheyenne-Arapaho. *Ghost Dancers.* 1936. Tempera. Margretta S. Dietrich Collection.

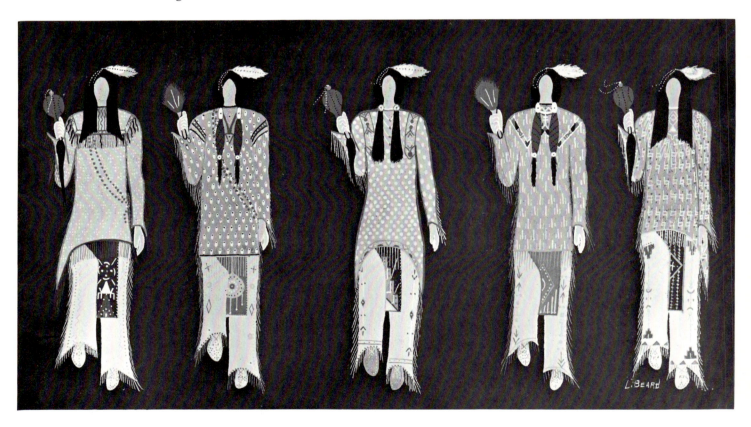

From the Southern Plains came Allan Bushyhead and Lorenzo Beard of the Cheyenne and Arapaho tribes. Both were painters of primarily decorative compositions. Bushyhead favored imaginative, exaggerated design and color in ceremonial dancers, particularly phases and aspects of the Sun Dance and Buffalo Dance. He was painstaking in presenting detail such as beaded motifs and finely patterned feathers. Beard consulted tribal sources of ceremony and legend for creating modern variations upon them. He was a selective painter, shearing details for the sake of pungent simplicity and gaining striking effects thereby.

George Keahbone, Kiowa, coupled his knowledge of tribal customs with research to produce some emphatic paintings obviously related to the Oklahoma Kiowa art movement, yet more individual through having been apart from it. There was as much vigor but less of the overstatement which frequently appears in modern Kiowa painting, and there was more delicacy of detail. Keahbone's work was varied, embodying subjects from single dancers and horsemen to compositions involving herds of animals or complete ceremonials. He brought as much of realism as decoration to his paintings. His fast galloping horses and energetically stomping War Dancers were especially strong in life quality although he handled them in an unnaturalistic manner. Pure bright color combined with rich browns and blacks and staccato whites to accentuate the lively character of Keahbone's work.

Woodland. Cecil Dick, Cherokee, principal exponent of the Woodland Indians in the Studio, was a dramatist whose highly personalized, richly colored paintings of legend and ceremonial episode could, with progressive refinement, lead into works of distinction.

EXHIBITIONS

For the paintings of these artists and others of the Studio, far more exhibition requests came during this fifth year than the existing setup was able to handle. Exhibits went to the following places:

San Francisco Museum of Art
Faulkner Memorial Gallery, Santa Barbara, California
Central Coast Teachers Institute, Santa Cruz, California
Public Schools, San Jose, California
International Children's Exhibit, Santa Rosa, California

309

Figure 112. CECIL DICK, Cherokee. *The Rabbit's Game*. 1935. Tempera. May Carothers Llewellyn Memorial Collection.

Museum of Fine Arts, Stanford University, California
All-American Watercolor Show, New Jersey State Museum, Trenton
The Watercolor Gallery, Goose Rocks Beach, Maine
Syracuse University, New York
Berea College, Kentucky
Witte Memorial Museum, San Antonio, Texas
Hollins College, Virginia
Public Library, Little Rock, Arkansas
Germantown Friends School, Philadelphia, Pennsylvania
Oneonta State Normal School, Oneonta, New York
Clarksville Public Schools, Clarksville, Pennsylvania

Plate XXVII. Talahytewa, Hopi. *Butterfly Dancer*. 1950. Gouache. Margretta S. Dietrich Collection.

Plate XXVIII. JOE H. HERRERA, Cochiti Pueblo. *Pictograph (Creation)*. 1953. Casein tempera. Collection of Dr. and Mrs. John M. Verosky.

Greenville Public Schools, Greenville, Michigan
Roswell Public Schools, Roswell, New Mexico
Seattle Woman's Club at Frederick Nelson's, Seattle, Washington
United States Tacoma Hospital, Tacoma, Washington
University of Oklahoma, Norman, Oklahoma
Western State Teachers College, Gunnison, Colorado
Eastern Arts Association Convention, New York
Southeastern Arts Association Convention, Raleigh, North Carolina
Western Arts Association Convention, Toledo, Ohio
Morris Studios, Cleveland, Ohio
Fred Wilson's, Phoenix, Arizona
National Education Association Convention, Detroit, Michigan
National Association on Indian Affairs Meeting, St. Louis, Missouri
New Mexico State Teachers Convention, Albuquerque
Second National Exhibition of American Art, Rockefeller Center, New York

Typical responses to the exhibitions are these. From Joseph F. Cantieni, Director, Department of Fine Arts, Berea College and Allied Schools, Berea, Kentucky: "We have been proud that we are showing such a collection of good paintings that so many ages and types of people could enjoy. [The Studio] must be doing a tremendous job well."[26] And from Herbert B. Tschudy, Curator of Contemporary Art, Brooklyn Museum, Brooklyn, New York: "The exhibition which you sent us from Santa Fe has been very successful. People of taste and knowledge of art have been loud in their praise of these pictures, marvelling at the ability of the artists, many of them still youngsters, to create a thing which, while retaining the best of their traditions, has the elements which are in keeping with the spirit of the times."[27]

Allan Houser had his first one-man show at the Museum of New Mexico in March.[28] The exhibit included nineteen watercolors, virile in line and finely finished in brushwork, which set forth all aspects of Apache life in versatile manner. It was in every respect an adult exhibition into which the artist had invested four years of continuous, serious work.

The fifth annual Studio exhibition was held in May at the Museum of New Mexico, and Olive Rush, who had so faithfully and perceptively followed the five-year development, wrote of it:

It has been a delight the past week to go into the state art museum where an art so different in aspect from our own blossoms and glows upon the walls of two alcoves. Is it a great art? We are led to so believe from these examples. An exhibit that has won friends for Indian art in centers of culture from coast to coast has

311

been added to the new works done this year . . . and a small part only of the exhibit hangs in the museum, the majority is on the walls at the Indian School. After seeing the museum you will wish to drive two miles south on the Albuquerque road to see more. . . .

To single out examples of this show would be as difficult as unjust. Through the work of youth from 11 to 20 there is not a trace of carelessness, and no lack of keen observation. Not an exhibit here but is arresting in its own happy way. Lively color is the first impression you get and never does it leave you. Color dances and exalts as in "Gift Giving" by Sibyl Yazzie of Rough Rock who has developed a miniature style of great beauty. The horses at the back are sturdy like Chinese pottery horses of the Chou dynasty. Akin to the Persian is Ned Notah's memory of his home "Canon de Chelly," a symphony in reds with cattle small in just proportion to the great red earth on which they live. "Horses Going into Corral" are in rainbow hues, suiting the glory of the horse in the mind of an Indian boy.

Eerie in color as in presentation, are the small animals and dark forests of Pop-Chalee . . . Her scattered, amusing, naive compositions are reminiscent, at first glance, of Paul Klee. Her "Purple Forest" is now owned by the Museum of Fine Arts, Stanford University, and she looks forward to having a studio of her own. . . . There is a night at the studio called "Christmas Eve" by Kgoo-Ya (Leandro Gutierrez), Santa Clara, that realizes well the dark outside and lighted inside of a house. It requires brains indeed to "get away with" a problem like that, of figures bathed in two lights, in one and the same picture.

But while the Indian color recalls the Persian, his command of line links him with the Chinese painters. It is a different line. Chinese calligraphy trains the artist and scholar from childhood in expert line. Later, his philosophy guides its sensitive use in expressing his idea. While the Indian, like ourselves, has not the advantage of the long technical training, he shares something of the mental outlook of the Oriental, his calm, his freedom from the disturbance by the practical that rules our lives. Line, with the Chinese, implies form. "It is form's frontier," they tell us, and it is used to such simplification that it may become abstract, however objective the subject. So, it seems to me, with many of these watercolors. And, like the Chinese, the Indian things in nature have a life of their own independent of man, and are presented in their natural atmosphere with a variety of flowing or staccato lines expressing life and vitality. We seldom find them making a still life, painting a dead animal among bric a brac. . . .

Is it the rainbow god who capers so astonishingly above the galloping pintos in "Antelope Hunt"? Certainly the drama is enacted in a landscape of exploding vegetation, and excitement among the gods seems fitting, whereas, in Gerald's pastoral scenes, in mother and child motifs, a calm god smiles from above, drip-

312

ping water or sunshine as needed. We hope this Navajo boy will keep to the proud Indian beauty, more and more, his eyes on the straight road. It must be hard in a world where garish lights beckon on all sides. He has humor as well as feeling for line. "Tourists" were never depicted so touristy before, never before so funny!

The quaint sense of humor of Juan Medina leads him to animate the well known Zia birds and flowers. "Zia Chickens in Trouble" and "Tired Chicken" present these old friends as well drawn as they are on the pots, and how surprisingly. There is an oval composition of the Basket Dance by a Hopi girl (Rose Lee James), there is a balanced dance composition, very expert, by a 12-year-old Cochiti boy (Ben Quintana) who has a delightful sketch at the school entitled "A Man Fishing."

. . . Jose Garcia's "Birds and Flowers," rich in color, exquisite in detail [is an example of Santo Domingo abstract]. Tony Martinez, son of our friends, Maria and Julian, has a watercolor . . . whose fine lines are all done with the brush. It is pleasant to see Pablita Velarde represented, a former student who now has a studio at Santa Clara and directs the art at the day school there.

Stanley Mitchell, an expert worker in silver, does miniature painting with fine bridles and trappings. One comes upon surprises—an abstract of an arroyo with animals and trees, a threshing at Tesuque, gray animals in a cornfield, black bears under windy trees, home scenes from Acoma of Katchina-making, or of shampooing, with charming detail. "Clearing the Irrigation Ditch" is by T'o Pove who paints in "Women at the Spring" a millefleur background, Southwest millefleur, with no reflection of the French. There are games done differently, Juan Gutierrez has a beautiful formal design of rainbow and clouds and rain over a majestic Buffalo Dance.

Assisting . . . the work to keep it purely Indian and uncommercial, is Geronima Cruz of San Juan, a former student who has charge of the younger pupils. At the studio there is an entire roomful of the work of her pupils, excellent in standard for children so young.[29]

At the year's end, the Studio was awarded the Médaille de Bronze at the Exposition Internationale des Arts et des Techniques, Paris. Thereafter, the students took over the work of the Studio entirely, with Geronima Cruz (Po-Tsunu) in charge.

In years to come, members of the Studio in this founding period were to discover a large representation of their works in many museums throughout the land, and in an even greater number of private collections, and Oliver La Farge was to summarize the Studio development as "a major demonstration of the contribution Indian culture and genius has to make to American life."[30]

313

Continuity and the Expanding View

Figure 113. PABLITA VELARDE, Santa Clara Pueblo. *Santa Clara Women Selling Pottery*. 1939. Mural in casein tempera. Maisel Building, Albuquerque. **315**

Beyond and largely stemming from developments fostered by the twenty-year period of the Santa Fe movement and accomplishments which centered about Anadarko, activities in Indian painting began to occur in other localities and among tribes additional to those of the founding groups.

EXPOSITIONS

Indian painters were key participants in the Golden Gate Exposition at San Francisco in 1938-39 where a selective and representative exhibition of Indian arts and crafts was presented under the direction of the newly established Indian Arts and Crafts Board of the United States Department of the Interior. Murals of tribal subjects were painted by Waka, Po-ve Pien, Popovi Da, and Charles Loloma. Many artists exhibited watercolors.

An event of major importance was the Exposition of Indian Art of the United States presented at the Museum of Modern Art, New York, in 1941 by the Indian Arts and Crafts Board under the direction of René d'Harnoncourt in collaboration with Frederic H. Douglas of the Denver Art Museum and Henry Klumb, architect.[1] Not since the Exposition of Indian Tribal Arts a decade earlier had such an admirable effort been made to present Indian art at its full stature. This was an expertly selected exhibition, widely representative in content and dramatic in presentation which Edward Alden Jewell called "an event of the very highest importance."[2] Examples of painting, from the Awatovi murals to contemporary watercolors, indicated that the finest Indian painting had attained a rank commensurate with that of internationally recognized modern art.

10. Recent Developments

MURAL PAINTINGS

Mural projects were completed by Indian artists in public and private buildings. Mention, however, should first be made of earlier murals and related works done by individual painters at about the time of, or soon after, the completion of the Santa Fe Indian School dining-room murals. Quah Ah painted Cochiti figures for the portal of the James W. Young *Rancho de la Cañada*, Peña Blanca, New Mexico, near her home; and Wo-Peen executed the first extensive individual mural project in his decoration of walls in the Lake Massasoit unit of Springfield College, Massachusetts.

Quah Ah's painting is not actually a mural, but is on the inner side of a heavy beam, an old bridge timber, which supports the *vigas* of the ranch house portal. This work, about 18 feet long and completed in 1931, retains the fresh appearance of the original oils. It depicts a series of dancers and symbolic rain figures, with a wild-pigeon motif at either end.

Wo-Peen's work, commissioned in 1934 at the suggestion of E. M. Robinson of the college faculty, was a pioneering activity in several respects. It was the first time Indian murals had been chosen for buildings outside the Santa Fe region, the first full-scale mural undertaken alone by an Indian artist, and the first time an American college had given direct encouragement to an Indian painter.

The buildings in which the oil murals were painted comprise the campsite of Springfield College and are designed in a modified Pueblo style. For this reason, Wo-Peen's characteristic Pueblo forms of rainbow, cloud, bird, serpent, and Buffalo Dancers lend themselves appropriately to the decoration. The Avanyu, in

Figure 114. Wo-Peen, San Ildefonso Pueblo. *Sacred Flying Water Serpent* (Avanyu). 1934. Mural in oil. Springfield College, Massachusetts.

this instance, representing a literally flying serpent, embodies the artist's most unusual conception of Pueblo symbolism. In asymmetrical curves, the serpent coils around the sun and upward across a cloud bank, lifted on wings part feather, part cloud. The dancers convey movements of the ritual and portray exactly each ceremonial detail of the strong figures.

Murals which undoubtedly stand as the finest achievement of a group of Indian artists since the initial modern mural project, are those commissioned in Albuquerque in 1939 by the architect, John Gaw Meem, for the facade and entry

318

of Maurice Maisel's new trading post, a pleasing building, modern although suggestive of early Southwestern style in its low, simple lines and its light buff color. Mr. Meem had proposed that Olive Rush do the paintings but she suggested that she share the work with several Indian artists. This seemed to Mr. Meem an appropriate idea, for such decoration would be not only compatible with the architecture, but a peculiarly functional part of the building in that it would serve as an introduction to the Indian arts which the structure was to house.

The rectangular courtlike entrance to the trading post provided an ample space immediately above the display windows, yet not too high above eye level, for a series of paintings in casein tempera applied in *fresco secco*. These are widely representative of Southwest Indian life and ceremony from northern New Mexico to the White River district in Arizona. Although varied in subjects and styles, the murals unite in a harmonious continuity of decorative forms along the forty-odd running yards of four-foot panel in an over-all effect of great charm such as is too infrequently seen in art associated with business houses.

In executing the work, Awa Tsireh represented the founding artists who might be considered the old masters of Pueblo painting. All other artists who collaborated were of the Santa Fe Studio group. Popovi Da, Pablita Velarde, and Pop-Chalee painted northern Pueblo subjects, while Ben Quintana, Ku-Pe-Ru, and Joe H. Herrera did Keres motifs. Wilson Dewey and Ignatius Palmer added some of their Apache patterns, and Ha-So-De and Harrison Begay contributed Navajo ones. Olive Rush showed in her own sections of the ensemble how well Indian subjects can be rendered by one who paints in rapport with Indian artists.

The group developed the project in much the same cooperative spirit that had predominated in painting the dining-room murals. The medium and form here again were untried by some of the painters, although several of them had done murals, and had used casein tempera on paper. In this project, they coordinated thin pigments of near transparency upon the natural warm gray of the plaster, giving a fresh, free, watercolor effect throughout.

Approaching the entrance, one sees a long line of dancers on either side. At left is Awa Tsireh's *Corn Ceremonial* of marionette-like dancers lacking any hint of naturalism but brightly bringing the character and spirit of a harvest festival to the heart of Albuquerque. At the right is Begay's quiet-toned, precisely moving procession of Yeibichai dancers giving an almost complementary night-to-day apposition to Awa Tsireh's high-keyed composition, yet strangely in complete balance with it. Begay is a master of subtle variation, and this painting is a good example of it.

319

Moving nearer, one sees the spirited sweep of Ha-So-De's *Navaho Ceremonial Hunt* revealed upon the back wall above the inner entrance. It is reminiscent of a Persian hunt. Stylistic horses with slim legs and flatly rounded flanks carry the dramatic hunters unerringly toward antelopes darting for cover in the dark, shooting sprays of a central bush. Power and boldness and clean-cut pattern are here, stated with whimsical imagination.

Then, up within the entry, on two cross-corner panels at either end of this hunting scene, there are single woman dancers—*Deer Dancer* by Ben Quintana and *Corn Dancer* by Ku-pe-ru. Forward, at both sides of the outer entrance, are the emphatic, angular *Gan Dancers* of Palmer and Dewey. Beside these are Joe H. Herrera's gaily patterned *Butterfly Dancers* and bright *Deer Dancer*, Popovi Da's formally designed *Rain Birds* and *Butterfly Dancer*, and Olive Rush's fresh green corn through which a Pueblo family walks gently.

Within the entrance enclosure, there are two other paintings in which Olive Rush blends her fragile, authoritative style with traditions of the Indian painters. A swish of action in a graceful *Deer Dance* is delicately suggested, and all the poise and dignity of Navajo women on horseback are caught by her light, deft brush. Few artists might be able to integrate their own characteristic style so happily with another as distinctive as that of the Indians. Perhaps this is because Olive Rush is "a poet looking for things of the spirit rather than actualities."[3]

The works of two other women complete the walls. Pablita Velarde, whose forte in this period was Pueblo genre, shows a group of Santa Clara women selling pottery. The inscrutable, stolid strength of character of Pueblo women is contained here in a massive, simple way that is more emotional in effect than passively decorative. Yet, there is decoration, too, in the clothing and pottery, and in the faces—each a different design in itself. The calico dresses are minutely patterned with almost mechanical exactness, and the pottery forms are shaped firmly and painted precisely, as in life.

In a quite different mood, Pop-Chalee does a forest fantasy where little animals frisk about beneath mythical trees. It is pure invention and decoration done with a lively, delicate grace combining something exotic—perhaps the small stylized detail of India, her mother's homeland—with the balanced composition so traditionally Pueblo.

In the same year that these murals were completed, another group of painters began decorating several rooms of the new Department of the Interior Building in Washington, D. C.

320

In the penthouse, which was designed to house a small refectory, paintings in low-keyed oils appear in near life-size upon the neutral tan walls of the three-sectioned room and over the wide entrance ways. Among these, Woodrow Crumbo, Potawatomie, paints ornately illustrative horses and other animals, a buffalo hunt, and a gracefully composed native betrothal. Allan Houser depicts Apache riders and women dancers in finely brushed color, but in concept and drawing beneath his capabilities. Gerald Nailor, who presents ceremonial motifs, animals, hunters, and a Navajo weaver at her loom, leaves his best record in this particular room in a wide panorama above the entrance way. Here, in sandpainting hues, his well-composed, deftly drawn and painted *Antelope with Birds and Corn* makes fine and appropriate decoration. (Incidentally, Nailor soon afterward tried a modified style, depicting tribal events and persons on the walls of the Navajo Council chambers, Window Rock, Arizona, in which he incorporated popular mural modes of the day.)

The most distinguished murals in this penthouse, however, are those by Ma-Pe-Wi in his consistent handling of an entire alcove. They show an inclusive variety of subjects of the Pueblo World, skillfully united here and painted in the same serene artistry Ma-Pe-Wi employs in his watercolors. Especially notable are the Buffalo and Deer Dancers, and the strong, characteristic figures of the Corn Dancer, Koshare, and a drummer. Views of a woman with a child and another with pottery give balance to the action of the animal and dance subjects.

A decoration more successful in general than that in the penthouse is produced by a simpler mural scheme in the arts and crafts shop of the building. In this, two artists relate their tribal subjects in both style and manner. Gerald Nailor and Allan Houser show respectively a Navajo antelope hunt and an Apache buffalo hunt on opposite walls. The paints are nicely coordinated in the soft, warm ochres and oxides of earth colors although the paintings are executed in oil upon canvas-covered walls. The smaller size of these works lends to more intimate handling of the animal and plant forms and to better integration of the compositions of the two artists.

Two Kiowa painters, James Auchiah and Stephen (Steven) Mopope, display impressive panoramas of tribal scenes high at either end of a very large dining room on the lower level of the building. Mopope's *Indian Theme* shows spirited War Dancers moving on either side of a quiet central figure. His colors are lively as are also those of Auchiah who presents dancers, singers, and scenes of the Autumn feast in his *Harvest Dance*. These paintings are in flat color as are all murals in the building except those of Ma-Pe-Wi which show an occasional slight modeling.

321

The first mural commissions undertaken by a Sioux artist were those completed by Oscar Howe in his native South Dakota. At Mobridge, Howe painted ten large oils of Sioux subjects and Missouri Valley history in the municipal auditorium. This is a singular achievement in that the artist's work was virtually unknown in the region at that time, 1942. He was chosen to paint also some symbolic Sioux designs within the dome of the Carnegie Library at Mitchell, and to design panels for that city's auditorium, the Corn Palace. Later, Howe executed a mural, *Origin of Corn*, in Nebraska City, Nebraska, and, in 1958, he designed a mural two hundred feet in length, for execution in ceramic tile on the Proviso High School, Hinsdale, Illinois.

Pop-Chalee painted a spirited panoramic mural of bright-colored ponies in the municipal airport at Albuquerque, and a large, bold pattern of the Giant Zuñi Shalako in the Santa Fe Railroad's ticket office in Santa Fe. Also in Santa Fe, she painted a buffalo hunt, exotic in both color and form, in the Hinkel Company's department store, enlarging the same theme as part of an inclusive presentation of Southwest Indian art by Marshall Field and Company, Chicago, in 1943. She painted a group of five large casein tempera murals in her tapestry-like style, in 1952, for the Arkansas Valley Bank, Pueblo, Colorado.

Four muralists, depicting scenes of warfare, hunt, and ceremonial, have decorated museums—Victor Pepion of the Blackfoot Tribe, in the Museum of the Plains Indian, Browning, Montana; Allan Houser in the Southern Plains Indians Museum, Anadarko, Oklahoma; Woodrow Crumbo, the façade of the museum of the Thomas Gilcrease Foundation, Tulsa, Oklahoma; Crumbo, and Archie Blackowl, Cheyenne, in the Philbrook Art Center, Tulsa, Oklahoma.

Fred Kabotie painted his first murals in the Indian Watchtower, Grand Canyon National Park. In pictographic style, these sketchy but imaginative works shed light on Hopi legends and symbolism.*The Origin Legend of the Snake Priest*, for instance, discloses a prehistoric version of the first navigator of the Colorado River. In somewhat similar vein, Kabotie in 1947 decorated three walls of the Painted Desert Inn near Holbrook, Arizona, with murals in oil depicting Hopi ceremony and history.

Andrew Tsihnahjinnie completed abstract murals in sandpainting motifs for the Westward Ho Hotel, Phoenix, Arizona, and, in 1958, he executed an extensive commission for the Harris Company's store in a new shopping center in Riverside, California. On at least one wall of each department in the large building, the artist almost incredibly adapted Navajo design and characters to the various

322

specialty shops. In the Alessandro Room of the spacious restaurant area, he gave an assignment of the sentimental *Ramona* theme a vigorous Navajo rendering. One of his powerfully drawn long-lined horses and several fantastic, sandpainting-derived plants appear along with clouds and the principals of the legend.

Pablita Velarde finished two mural projects in the late 1950's. The first, depicting Pueblo subjects rather naturalistically in oils, is in the Foote Cafeteria, Houston, Texas. The other, featuring a long horizontal panel of Navajo sandpainting adaptations in earth colors, is in the lobby of the Western Skies Hotel, Albuquerque, New Mexico. The First National Bank of Santa Fe commissioned Miss Velarde in 1961 to decorate a wall in its Los Alamos branch. For this, she painted a *Buffalo Dance* with large-scale figures.

Eva Mirabal painted two murals in the mid-1960's—*Bridge of Wings* for the Pittsburgh Planetarium and *Running Horses* in the library of the Veterans Hospital, Albuquerque.

Figure 115. Pop-Chalee, Taos Pueblo. *Mythical Horses.* 1952. Mural, 10 by 22 feet, in casein tempera. (One of a group of five.) Arkansas Valley Bank, Pueblo, Colorado. **323**

MUSEUM SPONSORSHIP, EXHIBITIONS, AND COLLECTIONS

The Museum of New Mexico continues its pioneering activities in the preservation and encouragement of Indian painting. Some of the finest works of contemporary Southwestern painters are among its continually expanding acquisitions, including the valuable Mary A. Shively Collection of unusual subjects. Offering to Indians the same exhibition privileges as to all artists, the museum invites their participation in general shows, hangs the Indian one-man shows, and circulates group exhibitions statewide and internationally. In 1956, as an extension of its local annual Indian exhibit established twenty-three years earlier, the museum inaugurated the annual Indian Artists Exhibition which invites painters from outside the Southwest. This show is important in that it upholds the precepts upon which the museum's Indian art policies were founded in the days of Crescencio Martinez. That is, it honors Indian traditions and original, resourceful developments of those traditions.

The Philbrook Art Center, Tulsa, has long demonstrated its appreciation of Indian painting by having provided a spacious permanent gallery for a growing collection of Indian works, and through establishing in 1946 the Annual National Exhibition of American Indian Painting in which very substantial prizes are awarded. These actions are in line with the original tenets of the museum when it was founded in October 1939. In view of its premise, as stated by the first director, Bernard Frazier, "that cooperation among all men can be achieved through their opportunities to know and understand the underlying cultures of the world,"[4] the Philbrook Art Center accords to what it considers the best Indian art recognition comparable to that given any worthy art. The museum also circulates many exhibits from its Indian collections. The artists' response to all these provisions is attested in Director Robert Church's introduction to the catalog of their eighth annual exhibition in which he notes the broadening scope of participation from Alaska to the Gulf.

The Denver Art Museum, at its Chappell House center, frequently includes painting in its ever changing and ever dramatic exhibitions of native arts of the world. Here, Indian painting is shown in its relationship to various periods and cultures. This museum was among the first to collect Indian paintings and has a large select store which includes the largest contingent of works by So-qween (Encarnacion Peña) and Richard Martinez. Also, it was one of the first to recog-

324

nize that clarity and sound educational techniques as well as esthetic arrangement are essential to the appreciation of museum collections.

An outstanding assemblage of Indian art is that contained in the Bayou Bend Collection in the Museum of Fine Arts of Houston. It includes eighty-one watercolors by artists of various Southwest Pueblos and of the Kiowa and Omaha Tribes. Some very fine early works of the modern school are among them, and are featured in a principal gallery.

The Museum of Northern Arizona discriminatingly emphasizes Indian arts. It houses some of the most beautifully painted prehistoric and modern Pueblo pottery and one of the finest assemblages of contemporary paintings. Foremost among the latter is the choice Katherine Harvey Collection which is among the most extensive of the major collections and one of the best balanced, dating from 1902 to 1957. The Harvey group contains at least one work by almost all the principal painters of the period, also one or two treasures by early unknowns. The museum has sponsored a Junior Indian Art Exhibition annually since 1934 in addition to occasional shows by adult painters and yearly expositions of Navajo and Hopi tribal arts. In another important function, the museum acts as repository for reproductions and several originals of the Awatovi and Kawaika-a murals.

In Phoenix, Arizona, the Heard Museum frequently shows Indian paintings, and has a group of its own, while the Read Mullan Gallery exhibits a thoughtfully chosen private collection.

The Southwest Museum, Los Angeles, has an outstanding group of late nineteenth-century Plains paintings on muslin and canvas, also some of the finest Hopi ceremonial pictures. A Pueblo oil hung as a mural and various watercolors of the 1930's show some unusual subjects.

The Joslyn Art Museum, Omaha, presented the first showing of Omaha Indian painting in 1935, and recently has included works of Oscar Howe in its Midwest Biennial Exhibition. Five Howes are in the museum's permanent collection.

Also in the Midwest, the City Art Museum of St. Louis and the Cleveland Museum of Art both have fine small groups of Indian pictures hanging in their galleries. The Columbus Gallery of Fine Arts and the Cincinnati Art Museum own important selections of earlier modern works. The latter has eighteen pictures by ten Pueblo artists. The Detroit Institute of Arts and the Dudley Peter Allen Memorial Art Museum of Oberlin College also own Indian pictures. The Milwaukee Public Museum has 116 nineteenth-century Sioux drawings which it has now mounted, exhibited, and published in color.

Two art museums in New Jersey have shown exceptional interest in the con-

325

temporary works. One of the most inclusive collections in the East in is the Newark Museum. Dating from the 1920's, these paintings include outstanding works by founders of the Modern School and the Santa Fe Indian School. A set of twenty-three Onondaga-Iroquois paintings of around 1950 are recent acquisitions. The Montclair Art Museum has featured Indian painting exhibitions which have been heavily attended and owns a number of works. Ma-Pe-Wi, Awa Tsireh, and Oscar Howe are among Indian artists represented in its collections.

The Riverside Museum in New York City owns a comprehensive and rare group of Pueblo watercolors acquired by Mr. and Mrs. Louis Horch in the early 1920's. Julian Martinez, Pan-Yo-Pin, and Tse-Ye-Mu are represented among several artists no longer painting. Early in 1964, the museum presented a remarkable exhibition of thirty works by nine of these artists.

The Corcoran Gallery, Washington, the Peabody Museum of Harvard University, the Art Museum of Cornell University, and the American Museum of Natural History all have modern Indian paintings. The museum of the American Indian, New York, has a large, prize collection of early Plains watercolors and crayon sketches, and no doubt the only Seneca and Shawnee works of circa 1900. Mohawk, Hopi, and Zuñi paintings, of around 1930, are other items of special interest here. Also in New York, the Museum of Modern Art has one excellent early Awa Tsireh—*Green Corn Ceremony*.

A number of museums emphasize Indian arts of their respective areas. The museum of the Plains Indian, Browning, Montana, and the Southern Plains Indians Museum, Anadarko, Oklahoma, display Indian works exclusively. A privately established center, the Thomas Gilcrease Foundation, Tulsa, opened in 1949 "for the purpose among others of maintaining an art gallery, a museum, and a library devoted to the permanent preservation for public use and enjoyment of the artistic, cultural, and historical records of the American Indian." Exhibitions have been shown in the galleries and many Indian painters have works in the permanent collections.

The Friends of the Middle Border Museum, Mitchell, South Dakota, includes Plains paintings among typical items representing the region. It featured a special exhibition of Oscar Howe's art at its opening in 1954, and chose some for permanent display.

Art interests of two distinguished Santa Fe institutions concentrate upon Southwestern arts. The School of American Research, for many years integrated and still closely associated with the Museum of New Mexico, owns the early modern collection of Pueblo painting made by Dr. Hewett, and, through purchase prizes in the museum's annual Indian painting exhibition, has added a chrono-logical succession of outstanding examples. The Museum of Navajo Ceremonial Art, devoted mainly to the preservation and interpretation of sandpaintings and other aspects of the tribal religion, contains also some modern Navajo temperas collected by the founder, Miss Mary Cabot Wheelwright.

Regional by definition, Mesa Verde National Park Museum displays a mural-type work of impressive size in its beautiful Southwestern style auditorium. Done in oils on canvas, this painting adapting a Navajo sandpainting design was made in the Santa Fe Indian School Guild around 1933 by Paul Tsosie. Another large Navajo picture, painted by Gerald Nailor in 1937, depicts high-spirited horses in this artist's characteristic range of subtle matte color. The museum also shows a group of typical Navajo and Pueblo tempera pictures.

Important exhibitions have occurred in San Francisco. The M. H. de Young Museum has accorded recognition to works of Indian artists and craftsmen through its several special exhibitions. Displaying various choice items from Alaska to the Mexican border, the museum also has acquired prize works from these shows as well as from civic donors. Also, in San Francisco, the California Palace of the Legion of Honor has sponsored large retrospective shows chosen from long-established private collections, especially those of the city's most dis-cerning friends of Indian art, William and Leslie Van Ness Denman, and Ruth and Charles de Young Elkus.

All these institutions, particularly the art museums, demonstrating the fore-sight to acquire and display Indian paintings, are thereby evincing the awareness of indigenous arts urged by the eminent critic, Walter Pach in his discussion of *The Museum of the New World*.[5]

SPONSORSHIP OF ASSOCIATIONS

Exhibitions in which the artists personally participate are held each August during the Inter-Tribal Indian Ceremonial at Gallup, New Mexico. Two major prizes and many lesser ones are awarded through the Ceremonial Association for the best paintings by artists of each tribal group. Hundreds of Indian people hav-ing no other opportunity to do so see contemporary developments here, and artists often are influenced by one anothers' work. Thus, the influence of the Ceremonial itself upon Indian art is a strategic one, beneficial according to the selectiveness of the show.

327

Among Indian welfare organizations, the Southwest (formerly New Mexico) Association on Indian Affairs, is unique in its close contacts with Indian painters. Through its long established policy and its continuous efforts in furthering standards in all Indian arts and crafts, the Association awards prizes to paintings during the Santa Fe Fiesta and at summer arts and crafts markets which it instituted and sponsors. It has also at times made awards during fiestas in the pueblos. To artists who live in or market their work in Santa Fe, the Association's prizes and follow-up interest through its Indian Club there have been of practical and inspirational value.

The California League for American Indians, San Francisco, sponsors exhibitions and lectures on Indian art in various California cities.

On a national scale, the Association on American Indian Affairs, New York, conducted and reported a survey of Indian arts in 1959, and has for many years been a strong champion of the artists and their work.

The most influential association of all, with respect to Navajo art, and certainly one with far-reaching horizons, is the Navajo's own Arts and Crafts Guild at Window Rock, Arizona. This unit, operating under the tribal council, encourages, displays, and cooperatively markets superior examples of all Navajo arts, including painting. The enormous guild building here at the tribal headquarters exhibits some of the most distinguished and exciting arts America has to offer.

SPONSORSHIP OF SCHOOLS AND EDUCATIONAL FOUNDATIONS

A number of schools encourage Indian students in the development of native precedents in painting, although the United States government schools do far less than they did in the 1930's, and could have done since in this respect. Here lies the greatest opportunity to creatively implement a wise carry-over of native arts to the changing general culture, as a two-way benefit—one which the Indian people themselves should help to plan and guide. Here also is the main source of oncoming Indian painters without whose realized potential the art dies. Yet, through lack of discernment and awareness in official policy in Indian education for too many years, this opportunity has been all but lost.

At the Santa Fe Indian School, from 1937 to 1962, when the school was converted to a new institution, the Studio remained under the direction of Po-Tsunu

328

(Geronima Cruz Montoya), who maintained through changing administrations a few of the original objectives. Although, because of directives and reorganization beyond Mrs. Montoya's control, exhibitions had decreased to a token of their former extent and quality, the Studio's long established annual exhibition continued through subsequent participation in the national Indian Artists Exhibition at the Museum of New Mexico.

A few of the government day schools, particularly at Jemez Pueblo and in the Hopi area, have been giving some productive attention to painting among the younger students, as has the Albuquerque Indian School.

Schools in the Navajo area enter their best seventh- through twelfth-grade students' paintings in an annual prize exhibition at the Navajo Arts and Crafts Guild. In 1963, five cash awards and ten honorable mentions were given.

Bacone College, Muskogee, Oklahoma, offers guidance to Indian painters through its art department headed by Walter Richard West, a Cheyenne artist. Some notable contributions to the annual Philbrook Art Center exhibition come from painters who have studied at this school.

Two universities aided Indian painters through artist-in-residenceships following World War II. The University of Southern Illinois, Carbondale, sponsored Eva Mirabal of Taos Pueblo, and Dakota Wesleyan University, Mitchell, South Dakota, appointed Oscar Howe as artist-in-residence in order to add to his art that of a regional cultural development centering in the school.

The State University of South Dakota later appointed Howe as professor of art and as a staff member of its W. H. Over Museum, as well as a director in its Institute of Indian Studies. The museum collects and exhibits Plains art.

The University of New Mexico through its art department has widened the horizons of several Indian painters without causing them to diminish their own art resources. Among these are Ha-So-De, Joe H. Herrera, Jose Rey Toledo, and Po-Qui.

Southwestern at Memphis, one of the first colleges to recognize the unusual significance of Indian art, has for years invited exhibits through its selective small museum, and recently has presented lectures on the subject. It hangs paintings from its own collection not only in the museum, but in its president's office and various campus centers. Tohoma, Nailor, Herrera, Howe, and other names of the 1937-55 period are prominent in this group.

The College of Fine Arts, University of Oklahoma, has led all colleges in educating Indian painters and in collecting their works for its fine arts gallery.

The great educational foundations have begun to welcome Indian artists.

329

Fred Kabotie and Allan Houser have completed projects under fellowships from the John Simon Guggenheim Memorial Foundation. The John Hay Whitney Foundation also has made grants available to Indian painters. In 1960, the Rockefeller Foundation provided a supporting grant for a three summers' workshop in Indian arts at the University of Arizona.

The Millicent A. Rogers Foundation, while not essentially an educational institution, does serve in this capacity through its excellent Museum of Southwest Arts in Taos, New Mexico. One of the most selectively representative collections of modern Indian paintings, dating from the 1920's, is housed here.

SPONSORSHIP OF TRADERS IN INDIAN ARTS AND CRAFTS

Some of the traders, on and off the reservations, have taken a personal interest in helping Indian artists to exhibit and market their work. Notable among them is Fred Wilson, of Phoenix, Arizona, who has arranged showings of paintings, including several exhibitions at the Heard Museum, Phoenix. M. L. Woodard, of Gallup, New Mexico, has sponsored a number of painters through his firm's excellent small museum. Also, as board member and sixteen years secretary-manager of the Inter-Tribal Indian Ceremonial Association, Mr. Woodard has personally aided large-scale exhibitions which many of the artists attend annually.

Largely an outgrowth of trader interests, the Scottsdale National Indian Arts Exhibition, sponsored by Indian arts dealers, other businessmen, and civic groups, was established in 1962 for holding annual national exhibitions of Indian arts in Scottsdale, Arizona. Hundreds of painters and some craftsmen compete in this show for many prizes and trophies in a complex hierarchy of classifications.

THE INDIAN ARTS AND CRAFTS BOARD

The Indian Arts and Crafts Board, appointed by and operating in connection with the United States Department of the Interior, exists for the purpose of upholding standards in painting and other Indian arts. Its work is implemented through museums, traders, educators, and special agents.

330

SPECIAL EXHIBITIONS

A comprehensive retrospective exhibition of Indian painting was presented for the first time in a distinguished showing of 115 pictures in the National Gallery of Art, Washington, in 1953. It contained paintings of sixty artists representing ten tribal groups, and dates beginning with works of Crescencio Martinez around 1917 to those of two painters chosen to send their latest works direct from their studios.

Subjects touched upon most aspects of ceremonial and daily life of tribes included, and styles ranged from esoteric abstract symbolism to semirepresentationalism. A small number of works exemplifying some increasing trends toward literal drama and illustration was included for comparison.

In his foreword to the catalog, David E. Finley, the gallery's director, states:

> The paintings in this exhibition, although contemporary in appearance, derive from the ancient Indian tradition, and both in subject matter and manner of execution make a valuable and unique contribution to the body of creative art in America.[6]

Washington critics unanimously commended the show. Leslie Judd Portner in the *Post* mentions "the color of indescribable delicacy, held within a limited range in the individual picture—the colors of sky and earth" and the "restraint and austerity in clean, pure line and subtle tone apparent throughout [producing] not a cold art, but one of strong control."[7]

Florence S. Berryman in the *Star* observes that the paintings "all have a freshness and charm of excellent draftsmanship, bright, mostly high-keyed colors, and the interest of a way of life," and states her opinion that "the paintings most esthetically satisfying are those in which the Indian artists are most 'Indian.' "[8] And the *Times-Herald*'s critic, Gladys Harrison, consolidates reasons for her terming the display "a most enjoyable show."[9]

Most of this exhibition was hung the following summer at the Art Institute of Chicago in the main galleries. The Chicago *Tribune*'s art critic, Eleanor Jewett, describes the paintings as "utterly delightful and refreshingly simple and direct."[10]

Both exhibitions, assembled by the writer of this account, were selected from fourteen museum and private collections. The National Gallery show was a direct

331

result of the perceptive encouragement of Mary Benjamin Rogers who devoted much of her effort in her last years to furtherance of Indian art.

Immediately following the National Gallery exhibition, the United States Information Agency requested that an exhibition be assembled for European travel. During 1955-56, this show[11] of sixty tempera paintings by artists representing eight tribes aroused great interest through its presentation in leading cities of the British Isles and on the Continent from Italy to Finland. Harrison Kerr, dean of the College of Fine Arts, University of Oklahoma selected the paintings from four American collections.

A second exhibition[12] under the same auspices went on tour to Berlin, Muenchen, Heidelberg, and ten other German cities in 1960-61, and it was requested by Austria for the following year.

A memorial exhibition honoring William and Leslie Van Ness Denman occurred in the California Palace of the Legion of Honor, San Francisco, early in 1962.[13] The fifty-seven selections from the extensive group of Indian paintings collected by Mrs. Denman covered a diversity of style and content from early Zuñi and Hopi pictures to those made in 1958.

The Margretta S. Dietrich Memorial Exhibition was presented by the Museum of New Mexico in mid-November through January 1, 1963.[14] Occupying all the first floor, the exhibition comprised seventy paintings by forty-nine artists and encompassed dates from 1921 to 1954. Although these represented little more than a third of the magnificent Dietrich Collection, they offered one of the most impressive displays of contemporary Indian painting on record. Their subjects in tempera and watercolor included ceremonials, hunts, flora and fauna, genre, and landscape, and the styles were both traditional and inventive.

Following the Dietrich exhibition, arrangements immediately went forward through the United States Information Agency for fifty-five paintings from the collection to tour from Athens through Southern Asia in 1963.[15] Most paintings in this and the above-mentioned six shows were made in the Studio of the Santa Fe Indian School or by artists who began their careers there. Fine old works by Fred Kabotie, Ma-Pe-Wi, Quah Ah, Awa Tsireh, Tsa Toke, Otis Polelonema, and others, also were among those catalogued.

A large exhibition of paintings and other Indian arts went to Finland under the aegis of the Finlandia Foundation for extensive appearances in Helsinki and provincial centers, beginning in September 1962. Sponsored also by the American-Scandinavian Society, the tour extended to other principal northern art centers. In the summer of 1964, it was a feature of the fiftieth anniversary celebration of

332

the Danish-American Society in Copenhagen. The display drew largely on collections of the Southwest Museum which cooperated with the Finnish Consul of Southern California in originating the show. Also included were eighteen pictures from the Dietrich Collection.

RECENT TRENDS AND THE WORK OF INDIVIDUAL ARTISTS

In a survey of individual artists, it is readily evident that comparatively few outstanding new names have appeared among Southwest painters since around 1940, although those from the Plains and Woodland areas have been fairly frequent in both appearance and turnover. Hardly any painters of the initial modern movement remain active, although some twenty-five artists of the Studio group of the 1930's and early 1940's continue to exhibit. Among the younger painters, relatively few have demonstrated the artistic calibre of artists dropping out of the older ranks, yet they undoubtedly possess ability comparable to the latter.

World War II had a retarding effect upon Indian artists in general, but particularly upon those in the New Mexico area where concentrated defense projects and the abnormal influx of populations literally revolutionized the economic and social structure of the Pueblo region. Many artists of all tribes went into the armed forces, and some of the most promising did not return—Ben Quintana and Chiu-tah among them. Others became permanently disoriented through lucrative occupations in the nearby defense centers or the more immediately urgent responsibilities at home. Those who did proceed with their art, despite upheavals, met with confusing new influences, but little in the way of intelligent guidance and long-range helpfulness. Much of the painting became stereotyped, imitative, and lacking in its former fresh quality. Comparatively little distinguished new work appeared. The situation was aggravated because, in many instances, the suddenly expanded local market resulted in higher prices for inferior paintings and thus a lack of incentive for artists to do their best work.

Since World War II, with the exception of one brief resurgence, there has been an over-all decline in painting quality with nothing so far to indicate the approach of a florescence such as occurred in the 1920's and 1930's. The main sources of standards for artists in recent years have been the annual exhibitions mentioned above, and even these standards have been aberrant because of variance in the calibre of juries.

333

Particularly in the museum shows, which indicate that actual talent is as abundant as ever, trends toward both eclecticism and deeper resourcefulness are obvious. Although at present the basically indigenous works still outweigh the pictures imitative of popular painting styles of the past and present, the latter are gaining, though seldom in artistic stature.

Thus far, the critics of nationally recognized judgment agree that the Indian painting most precious to the world of art is that most typically native. However, native attributes in painting hold more strongly in some tribes than in others, and among individual artist members of a tribal group. This is to be expected, for, in all groups, natural and intrusive cultural changes have changed the arts—some, almost imperceptibly through generations; others, abruptly indeed. The *tempo* of change is one of the strongest factors in the ideologies and responses of today's painters. Many artists are privileged to have grown up in very old and distinguished Indian American societies, and often are university educated as well, while others are by choice or involuntary circumstance now considerably or completely identified with the population at large.

Among the painters who are the direct inheritors of their native arts, there are those who can understand, interpret, and creatively extend art from the living cultures and deep, rich resources. Through their exclusive knowledge and experience, they alone can truly do this, thereby uniquely contributing to the painting of today and to the enduring art of all peoples.

On the other hand, most of the artists who have lost their ancestral legacies have already begun to indicate by their works that they could most happily develop their careers entirely in the general field. Here they might well profit by the disciplines and rewards, and, moreover, they could choose to be influenced, or not, as any painter might be, by the Indian subjects and designs now widely available.

The following painters are among those active or especially noteworthy in recent years.

PUEBLO

Fred Kabotie, often thought of as dean of modern Indian painting, is less active as a painter than in former years because he serves the advancement of Indian art through teaching and research. In the latter capacity, he wrote and illustrated a remarkable book, *Design from the Ancient Mimbreños*[16] in which he presented, from the Hopi standpoint, his own views of those incredible paintings.

When Kabotie does paint, he continues to be a prizewinner. Among his honors was the Grand Prize at the first Annual National Exhibition of Indian painting at the Philbrook Art Center, 1946. His later work shows increased experiments in third dimension in more academic manner. These lack the force of his earlier inventions through which he is internationally recognized.

Otis Polelonema, whose valued work was seldom seen for about twenty years, returned with painting as strong as ever to win the Anne Evans Memorial Award in 1954 at the Denver Art Museum, followed by the Southwest Association on Indian Affairs Award and the Denman Prize in New Mexico exhibitions. Continuing in a slightly modified phase of the robust coloring and naive yet expressive drawing of his art of nearly forty years ago, Polelonema explores further now the ceaselessly enchanting pantheon of Hopi ceremonial personages, favoring Kachinas of every name and form.

Bruce Timeche, one of the most capable Hopi painters to appear recently, has won several high awards in annual exhibitions at the Museum of New Mexico and the Inter-Tribal Indian Ceremonial, Gallup, New Mexico, annuals. He depicts somewhat representational, authentically detailed figures in both oil and tempera —more successfully in the latter. Timeche is a fine draftsman, and, while adapting the unacademic modeling and foreshortening introduced by his predecessors in the Hopi group, he works for a more formal naturalism.

Peter Shelton (Hoyesva) paints unique watercolors which he rarely exhibits outside the Inter-Tribal Ceremonial. He is at his best in studies of obscure Hopi symbolism. These, he introduces in a quite modern-appearing abstract style which is actually very old, dating back to prehistoric murals and screens. In low-keyed, flat color, his outlined figures appear as intriguing decoration even to observers entirely uninformed of their original associations. Shelton has won the Denman Prize and others.

Lawrence J. Outah's infrequent Hopi offerings place him nevertheless as a versatile painter. His palette ranges from pale to bright, and his style varies in effect from minutely personalized figures to broad and boldly rendered designs. His Kachinas, which sometimes appear Chinese, are especially striking. Masks and all, these supernatural characters have an uncanny lifelike look that seems to belong to neither man nor superhuman being. Outah's art is infallibly original.

Bert Preston (Tenah), another occasional painter, was a regular exhibitor in earlier annuals at the Philbrook Art Center where he won a first prize. His work is traditional in Hopi subject and precisely decorative in its flat-laid color and balanced composition.

335

Figure 116. Suwa, San Ildefonso Pueblo. *Stampede*. 1957. Casein tempera. Southwestern at Memphis.

Raymond Naha is developing resourceful methods in using light and shade to dramatize Hopi ceremonials and dancers. He illuminates scenes in the striking contrasts of a particularly strong palette. Native conventions, however, underlie his painting even though it stands out as daringly different from that of the traditional Hopi school. He received the Indian Arts Fund Award in 1962.

Gibson Talahytewa has a perceptive talent for unintentional portraiture which he employs now and then in expressive miniature figures. Harry Sakayesva, James Humetewa, and Bert Poneoma paint in a simple, broad manner with drawing more casual than that in older Hopi works. These men seldom paint, and their pictures are rarely seen in exhibitions.

336

Other Hopi painters include: Mootzka, a capable artist, prolific in the 1930's; Lomoyosta, Wilbert Taho, Dick Pentewa, and Morgan Saufkie, who have shown occasionally in galleries and exhibitions; George Outie, a former prizewinner at the Philbrook Art Center; and Leroy Kewanyama, a promising younger man who has won awards. Pupils of Fred Kabotie appear now and then at the Inter-Tribal Ceremonial with very good paintings, but few continue beyond school as artists.

San Ildefonso Pueblo's fame as an art center, save for the work of a few men, has diminished in the painting field. One of the main standard bearers is Gilbert Atencio, who has thus far seldom departed from developments of time-honored themes and forms. His crisply drawn and clearly colored renderings of ceremonial and home life have, since around 1947, been favorites in many shows. From that year, in which he won a third prize at the Philbrook Art Center, to his 1961 receipt of two top awards, followed by the Mary Benjamin Rogers Prize in 1963, at the Museum of New Mexico, Atencio has advanced with but one slight deviation in his meticulous and authoritative art. His Kossa, especially, are always superb.

Suwa has pursued a remarkable exploratory career. From the naive and charming expressions of his young student days, his work has led through an interval of rather ordinary efforts in academic classes to a widely expanded realization of his own art. Now, from the deeply developed esthetics of his native San Ildefonso, Suwa draws forth the strong patterns for valid contemporary works. With ancestral forms and ideas, he combines wise choices from his lately acquired skills and techniques. He has evolved for himself an individual expression that partakes of two cultures yet remains inherently Pueblo. Suwa has won the Mary Day Watrous Award at the Denver Art Museum, the Dorothy N. Stewart Memorial Award at the Museum of New Mexico, and a first prize at the Philbrook Art Center, among other honors.

Wo-Peen when he takes time from regular employment to paint, produces works of distinguished beauty. These usually depict Kossa of many moods, or black stallions—rearing, galloping, trailing, or quietly standing, singly or in groups. In whatever position, they are of an aristocratic breed of pure invention. Their strong, classic forms, almost entirely in silhouette, show powerful brushwork in pure black paint, exquisitely detailed by hairbreadth lines and mere touches of palest corals, grays, and golds. The technique is all the more remarkable because it is the work of a right-handed artist who of necessity retrained himself to paint with his left hand. The late Charles Fabens Kelley considered Wo-Peen an Indian artist of highest rank, and, once while in Santa Fe, journeyed to San Ildefonso to meet him.

337

338

Figure 117. Wo-Peen, San Ildefonso Pueblo. *Kossa with Melon.* Ca. 1958. Tempera. Collection of Sterling Christopher Sanders.

Figure 118. Wo-PEEN, San Ildefonso Pueblo. *Rearing Stallion*. 1955. Tempera. Collection of Mr. and Mrs. Max Kramer.

339

Figure 119. Wo-Peen, San Ildefonso Pueblo. *Trailing.* 1939. Tempera. Margretta S. Dietrich Collection.

Soqween and Oqwa Pi of the original San Ildefonso group, have resumed part-time painting after years of work on their farms. Each has won the award of the Twentieth Century Art Club of St. Louis in recent Museum of New Mexico annuals in Santa Fe. In simpler rendition than in his older paintings, Encarnacion's (Soqween's) abstract Avanyus and seminaturalistic dancers remain his principal subjects. Oqwa Pi's ceremonial figures are more rugged than in earlier pictures, yet they retain a naive appeal that is becoming rare.

Popovi Da, in an infrequent picture, shows himself to be an imaginative painter still. Increasingly his interest lies in abstract Tewa design, particularly in decorating the pottery made by his mother, Maria Martinez, as well as by himself. The latter pieces are stunning innovations clearly based on the distinguished ceramic precedents set by his parents. Much of Popovi Da's attention, however,

340

is devoted to promoting and marketing the arts of his family and pueblo. Public service has claimed his time also. He has governed San Ildefonso and has presided over the affairs of the All-Pueblo Council at various times.

Anthony Da, son of Popovi, has shown decided ability in his introductory appearances in annual shows. He is an individual painter of exceptional inventiveness who employs both fantastic and established characters in his compositions. His color is clear and incredible, his brushlines manipulated in unusual contours of natural forms and conjured patterns.

The great Awa Tsireh, until his sudden death in 1955, intermittently painted with his usual finesse and in ever-resourceful variations of his original style for a few connoisseurs. He did not exhibit in his later years. Today his work is prized.

The name of Pablita Velarde remains first among those of Santa Clara Pueblo painters and is well recognized wherever modern Indian painting is known. Her career has undergone a fairly steady development along its own lines from her formative works in 1932 to the present. At first emphasizing the genre of her native village, Pablita's painting has extended to include various art patterns from other pueblos as well as from the Navajo area and several prehistoric Southwestern sites. Casein tempera, oil, and her own mixtures of local earth colors are her media. Native earths, first assembled and prepared for modern use by the Santa Fe Indian School Studio while Pablita was a student there, now constitute her principal medium for *fresco secco*. She more effectively and appropriately employs these natural paints in her abstract motifs adapted from ceramic designs, mural figures, and similar sources than in more naturalistic representations. Another productive avenue for Pablita is Tewa mythology and legend, which she has extensively interpreted in tempera paint. Much of her painting has retained its original strength and naivete. She has received, at least once, most of the major awards in the annual exhibitions.

Po-Qui, who began as one of the most capable Santa Clara artists, has largely forsaken his own painting for service as an art educator. Since taking his degree from the University of New Mexico, he has directed painting in the United States Indian School in Albuquerque, but, when he is free to paint, he shows much the same strong, conservative approach as that in his youthful works. Simplified, massive figures, convincing in character and expressive of Pueblo timelessness, are his usual subjects.

From Santa Clara come also occasional paintings by Marcus Silva, Frank Naranjo, and Marie Sisneros. Michael Padilla is a promising student artist, a double award winner in 1962.

341

Quah Ah, until her death in 1949, continued to be the principal figure in Cochiti Pueblo art and the leading woman painter among Indian artists. Her pictures traveled internationally and entered into every notable collection of Indian painting. Her titles and techniques changed but slightly through the years. Transparent watercolor and thin tempera; fragile figures of arresting realism; balanced groupings of darks, whites, and fresh colors make up her inimitable art.

Joe H. Herrera, son of Quah Ah, made an exciting debut in a one-man show at the Museum of New Mexico in 1952 at about the time of his graduation from the University of New Mexico. Paintings in this exhibition in which he introduced a new abstract style in an old technique, were largely improvisations upon petroglyphs and pictographs of the Southwest. Such titles as *Altar, Creation,* and *Pictograph,* Herrera presented in sprayed casein tempera of muted colors. Although the masterful guiding influence of his professor, Raymond Jonson, was clearly evident in the artist's perfection of these works, Herrera himself set a new trend among several Indian painters with his creative projection of ancient elements. Herrera's *Symbols of Fall* won the Twentieth Century Art Club of St. Louis Prize in 1956. Unfortunately for his art, the demands of office in both Pueblo councils and state agencies have claimed most of Herrera's time since, but he is young enough, and his understanding of international implications of American Indian art deep enough, that his exceptional talent may regain right-of-way.

Cochiti themes in both abstract and seminaturalistic styles are pursued by Ku-pe-ru (Theodore Suina) who draws from present-day ceremonials as well as prehistoric motifs on rocks and pottery. His tattered Koshare in off-blacks and grayed whites evoke the ghostly clownish mood of these important religious personages; and the textures of sandstone and tufa which he effects through spray and spatter, impart an appropriate aura of antiquity to Ku-pe-ru's petroglyph-inspired designs. Such paintings are currently winning awards for the artist, who counts the 1947 Grand Prize of the Inter-Tribal Ceremonial among his honors.

Stimone paints in his Cochiti home and occasionally exhibits his pictures in Santa Fe, especially at fiesta time. These works are not exploratory, yet through the years they retain the spontaneous and frank simplicity of the true primitive. Dancers, singers, drummers, farmers, and all the Cochiti characters appear again and again in these pictures with the recurrent newness of the ceremonials and pueblo events in actuality.

Ow-u-Tewa (Manuel Chavez), Cipriana Romero, and Gregory Trujillo are other capable though seldom active painters of Cochiti.

342

Plate XXIX. ANTHONY DA, San Ildefonso Pueblo. *The Lower Valley.* 1959. Casein tempera. Collection of Richard M. Howard.

Plate XXX. STANLEY MITCHELL, Navajo. *Man and Woman on Horseback Ride.* Ca. 1940. Tempera. Philbrook Art Center.

Figure 120. JOE H. HERRERA, Cochiti Pueblo. *Hunter*. 1954. Casein tempera. Margretta S. Dietrich Collection.

Po-Tsunu (Geronima Montoya) of San Juan Pueblo suddenly won for herself high recognition on the Santa Fe art scene in 1959 with her first one-man show at the Museum of New Mexico. Totally unlike the paintings of any other artist, each work in this display proved her a versatile and adroit painter. The astonishing exhibition, from which every picture was sold, occurred more than twenty years beyond the artist's student work, and after a long interim of service as an art teacher in the Santa Fe Indian School. Obviously, Po-Tsunu had been steadily and very privately maturing her own art as time permitted from duties of family and school. Her paintings in tempera, gouache, and dry brush, and her occasional block prints encompass styles from rather representational figures, reminiscent of her early efforts, to expressionistic abstract compositions. The latter update prehistoric symbols from a wide variety of sources which she has searched with selectivity and adapted with ingenuity. Po-Tsunu's inventive use of color in these paintings is equally remarkable, for hues are audaciously or retiringly bright, or are muted to tones of natural earths, or are simply monochrome, as the case may be. In her first actual competition, the Museum of New Mexico in 1961 awarded its highest purchase prize to her meditative *Rain God*. Several prizes have been hers, since.

Poquin Tahn (Asencion Trujillo), until his recent death, was a steadily developing artist. He used tempera paint to indicate different textures despite the essentially flat surfaces in his San Juan scenes. His small classic figures, especially of horses, were seen in both Santa Fe and Tulsa shows, and at the Inter-Tribal Ceremonial where they won an award.

Juan Aquino and Manuel Trujillo, both honorably mentioned in Philbrook Art Center annuals; Robert Aquino, a young prizewinner with his decorative genre; and Joe Ortiz, Ned Montoya, and Tommy Montoya, new entrants in the exhibitions, all are San Juan artists of prospect.

Zia Pueblo, which has produced some excellent painters, is at present represented by only a few, among whom are Rafael Medina, Diego Salas, Waka, and a few lesser-known artists such as Jose Medina. These men all do conservative work in a conventionalized pictorial manner. Rafael Medina paints hunting and various rain dances of primitive feeling with vigorous strokes of dark, rich paint. Again, in lighter vein, he creates lovely shimmering effects of darks and lights on pale grounds. Waka, most experienced of this group, retains much of the free action observed in his former work, but less of the resourceful adaptations from Zia's beautiful pottery—perhaps because he has lived in San Juan Pueblo

344

for years. Hunters, farmers, and dancers continue to be his favorite subjects.

Zia's most distinguished artist, Ma-Pe-Wi, until his disability in a motor accident in 1955, continued to be a prolific painter, one of the finest the modern school has produced. His versatile and perceptive portrayals of all main aspects of pueblo life were on many occasions easily acknowledged first-prize winners in the principal Indian exhibitions. In addition, some of his paintings were chosen by exacting juries for inclusion in shows representing the best of all New Mexico artists. Velino was one of the few Pueblo artists devoting almost exclusive time to painting. The warm realism of his art has changed but little through the years, although the naturalistic aspects have increased in use of perspective, modeling, and other devices somewhat academic in manner. Velino's draftsmanship and brushwork, and his inventive revelation of familiar subjects have advanced toward perfection in their own field. Ma-Pe-Wi's art is internationally honored and is included in nearly every major Indian painting collection. It is still to be hoped that his health can be restored to enable him to extend so important a contribution.

Jose Rey Toledo remains the first-ranking painter of Jemez Pueblo even though employment that has taken him far afield to North Dakota has curtailed his art in recent years. His bright, engaging work, which won prizes in early annual shows, may still be seen now and then in exhibitions of Southwest artists. A deft touch of humor often pervades his lively paintings of less known aspects of Jemez life and ceremony. Toledo is a graduate of the University of New Mexico and a former art teacher at the Santa Fe Indian School.

Emeliano Yepa, another fine artist of Jemez, is no longer living, but a relatively large and promising student group at the Jemez Day School has begun to take over painting in the pueblo. Among these, Alonzo Lucero, Lupita Lucero, Lawrence Tosa, Maxine Gachupin, Paul Gachupin, Mary Coloque, Pete Toya, and Paul Chinana have recently won student prizes for interesting works.

Taos Pueblo with its woodlands and mountain rivers has produced artists with themes quite different from those of the villages below in the Rio Grande Valley. The most successful have been women of whom Pop-Chalee and Eva Mirabal are the most outstanding. Both have pictured the forests, the mountain creatures, and the various events of the remote, northernmost pueblo. Pop-Chalee's art is fanciful and decorative; Eva Mirabal's expresses much more of actuality along with her considerably decorative style. Both women paint mainly in tempera, flatly laid and finely brushed. Although Pop-Chalee rarely enters her work

345

Figure 121. JOSE REY TOLEDO, Jemez Pueblo. *Pine Tree Ceremonial Dance*. 1940.
Tempera. Museum of Art, University of Oklahoma.

in public exhibitions, her paintings have been among those most in demand since she began her career at the Santa Fe Indian School in the mid-1930's. She has had studios alternately in Santa Fe and in Scottsdale, Arizona, during her most productive period, and, at present, she is painting in Long Beach, California. Eva Mirabal works in Taos and occasionally exhibits in the museum shows. She won the Margretta S. Dietrich Award at the Museum of New Mexico, and is represented in permanent collections of the Denver Art Museum and the City Art Museum of St. Louis.

Michael Harvier, with virile and bright primitive works; James Lujan, recognized with an award for his characteristic depiction of Taos ceremony; and Lorenzo Lujan are the names that have intermittently appeared from Taos within the past few years. Gilbert, a younger member of the Lujan family, is a recent winner of a student prize.

Few artists are exploring in paint the powerful and dynamic patterns of Zuñi Pueblo art these days. Theodore Edaakie, who occasionally enters the Inter-Tribal Ceremonial exhibitions to win an award, is the main one who does. His rugged, uncompromising figures deliver much the same impact as those from the brushes of his predecessors of the 1920's. In black, white, malachite green, and touches of orange-red, Edaakie's time-stopping ancestral characters seem to step out of everyone's past.

More pictorial, more influenced, yet full of original insight and design are the paintings of Kai-Sa (Percy Tsisete), Zuñi's most recognized painter. These works, covering a broad field of ceremonial and secular subjects, often appear in group shows and are in principal collections. Kai-Sa can paint with almost photographic realism when he chooses, particularly in some of his studies of animals and ritual paraphernalia; yet, in employing this manner, he seems a stranger to the forthright conventionalization of Zuñi figures in his other paintings. He is a winner of the Denman Prize.

Pete Gasper is outstanding among younger Zuñi painters with his fresh views of tribal mores. He paints with a lightness and delicacy not common in Zuñi painting, although he is an exponent of tradition.

Roger Tsabetsaye, another of the younger artists, presents Zuñi design elements inventively and often as completely abstract compositions. He contrives involved arrangements for Kachina Dancers which result in animated abstract patterns. His fairly realistic birds with complex designs on the bodies are interesting

347

and original. He has recently received prizes in Santa Fe and Scottsdale, and the 1963 first in Southwest division at Philbrook Art Center.

Anthony P. Edaakie is a painter in the old Zuñi tradition whose work is infrequently on view. Zuñi names coming into notice are Robert Toshewana, David Kaskalla, Dixon Shebala, and Edmund Ladd.

Santo Domingo Pueblo painters such as Lorenzo Garcia, Jose J. Garcia, Balardo Nieto, Leo Reano, and C-som-ma-th-ya, who showed such admirable talent in the Studio of the 1930's at the Santa Fe Indian School, have not been heard from, nor have any recognized painters from this pueblo followed them. This apparently has been due to community distrust of the representative arts apart from ceremony. Although such an attitude is understandable in view of the straightforward and largely admirable conservatism of the village, it is none the less unfortunate for the world of art.

One advanced Laguna painter, James Bear, whose artistically resourceful, deeply ethnological works have been known for the past few years to a small number of collectors, seldom exhibits. A group of twenty-five of his 1963 pictures emphasizes ceremonial subjects in pure, flat color with most figures uniformly and broadly outlined, often in white paint on dark or gray papers. The drawing shows marked angularity used to advantage in a somewhat rigid decorative style.

Pueblos largely inactive in adult painting for some years, but now beginning to participate again through the works of creative students, are Tesuque, with Ramon and Tim Vigil, Marco Leno, Lorenzo Pino, Ernest Herrera, and Gerald Panana, all with original and unusual paintings; Picuris, with Jerry Nailor, son of Gerald; Laguna, with Victor Riley, winner of a prize; San Felipe, with Roger Townsend, another winner, and Benny Sandoval, with honors.

Mention should be made of two artists no longer painting in their native Tesuque. Sah-Wa, whose one man show was a principal feature of Marshall Field and Company's store-wide promotion of Southwest Indian arts and adaptations in 1943, took leave of her painting to become a draftsman at Los Alamos early in World War II. On the other hand, Swazo (Patrick Swazo Hinds), who as a young boy was adopted into academic life at the University of California, is today a distinguished and prolific painter quite successfully following two roads at once. His Berkeley studio reveals works in various stages of development of international styles alongside canvases immediately recognizable as authentic Tewa art. The **348** former have won prizes in general West Coast shows while the latter are sought for their original American character. Some works show very capable utilization of the broad cultural advantage of the artist.

Also in the Southwest, the Paiute Tribe now enters the painting field with its promising young artist, Kenneth Thomas, cited with the House of Six Directions Award in 1961 at the Museum of New Mexico.

NAVAJO

Andrew Tsihnahjinnie (Van, Jan, or Andy Tsinajinie) in his thirty-year career has been a paradoxical painter, fluctuating between creations of high artistry and those of chameleon aspect disclosing few of his true abilities. Yet, doubtless no one to date has painted the Navajo as well as he. His ventures into his own world are well worth waiting for. In these, he brings the remote people and private events of the vast Navajo country into hailing distance without divesting them of the old untamed beauty. The races, the hunts, the sings and singers, flocks, shepherds and weavers, dancers with fire or feathers, the gamblers and sorcerers and countless denizens of the Lukachukai, the wide plateau, and the San Juan Valley all are immortalized by him. Often Tsihnahjinnie receives awards in the annual shows although he enters his pictures sporadically.

Ha-So-De, somewhat of an exponent of Tsihnahjinnie in their Santa Fe student days, is painting again. After some severely disorienting war experiences followed by university study and several lines of work, he now devotes part time from state employment to his art. Much of the boldness and directness of his prewar paintings remain, and, though the fresh young spontaniety is gone, Ha-So-De's art now probes more deeply into Navajo mythology and legend. Aspects of these seldom if ever painted are emerging in his recent productions. One of the most gifted of Navajo artists, Ha-So-De has the capacity to yet return as one of the strongest leaders in contemporary Indian art. In 1963, he won a first prize in the Scottsdale National show and a second in the Philbrook Art Center's annual. He also represented the American Indian in the international retrospective exhibition, *The Horse in Art*, at the Fine Arts Gallery of San Diego.

Harrison Begay is perhaps the most popularly known of Southwest Indian painters through his extensive exhibitions, published reproductions, and his own serigraphs. For many years after his Santa Fe Indian School beginnings, Begay experienced a serene and fairly independent development of his fine talent. He was a prolific producer of sensitively drawn and impeccably brushed paintings

349

depicting in a gentle, idealized manner every segment of Navajo life. In recent years his work declined for a time because of illness, but it is on the rise again.

Beatien Yazz (Jimmy Toddy) is nationally known through his illustrations for children's books, but he also has attained recognition as an exhibiting artist through his frequent entrance in Indian annual shows. Much of his work is considerably overlaid by influences from other artists, both Indian and non-Indian, yet, in instances where his individual statement is clear, Yazz proves to be a painter of genuine ability. Such an instance stands out in *Feather Dancers*, winner of a grand prize at the Inter-Tribal Ceremonial, and in his *Nine Nights Ceremony* in the permanent collections of the Philbrook Art Center. In the latter, he evokes the eerie, unearthly atmosphere of a psychological drama dominated by the Navajo Talking God despite the distractions of grotesque trees and posterish mesas (those regrettable intrusions which have frequently marred Navajo painting). So far, Yazz reaches his high mark in his slight and delightful paintings of small furred and feathered animals of the Navajo country as seen in the M. L. Woodard Collection. These subjects he handles with intimate knowing, as if exclusively for himself and close friends and not for the open world.

Yel-Ha-Yah (Charlie Lee) is known mainly for his animal pictures, particularly those of horses. These are more or less representational, the best possessing a passive, decorative quality which shows both delicacy and strength of technique. The artist's special manner of rendering foreground detail of shrubs, grasses, and cacti has differentiated his own work and has added certain regional style elements to Navajo painting.

Robert Chee is an energetic and capable young painter whose talents seem only partially indicated in his many pictures. It would seem that his firm, spontaneous line and expertly laid flat color might well be directed into amplifications of choice aspects of his work such as the incidental abstract elements which at present far outclass his pictorial material. The latter is disorganized and often veers toward caricature.

Bobby Hicks is essentially an abstractionist, although he seldom follows the conventions and figures of the tribal sandpaintings. His own interpretations of various life forms and his experiments with unusual color and mannerisims are intriguing and often admirable. In the present stage of Hicks's art, his idea outranks his technique and indicates a substantial reserve for development. He commendably tackles such subjects as *Evolution of Life*, *Embryology*, and *Spirits of the Universe*.

350

Figure 122. BEATIEN YAZZ, Navajo. *Feather Dancers*. 1954. Tempera. M. L. Woodard Collection.

Stanley Mitchell, a miniaturist and character portrayer of delightful original-ity, has turned trader in Indian art products. His paintings have been missed in the exhibitions since his last appearance at the Philbrook Art Center a few years ago. It is to be hoped that he will soon include his own color-studded stylizations of Navajo life among his regular stocks and in the annual shows.

351

Two Navajo artists who were career painters from their Santa Fe Studio days until their untimely deaths were Gerald Nailor, who died in 1952, and Quincy Tohoma (Tahoma), who died in 1956. Their works are widely known and increasingly sought. Nailor perfected the facile, decorative manner for which he was early noted, but Tohoma's style changed from serenity to one expressive of near violence—from quiet, pastoral scenes and orderly ceremonial patterns to highly agitated portrayals of animals, hunts, and battles that glorified struggle and cruelty. Yet it is the latter work for which he is most recognized, and which extends his natural powers of draftsmanship and imagination. Through his individual studies of foreshortening and anatomy, Tohoma won for his pictures high praise from academically trained artists of note, and the admiring response of the public. Whatever one may think of these later paintings as Indian art, he must recognize the command of techniques and devices of the artist's own making which convey the opposition and impact of brutal contests in all sorts of situations on the hunting ranges of the old days.

Also among Navajo painters are James Wayne Yazzie, a gifted and independent primitive, who exhibits his large arresting native scenes at the Navajo Arts and Crafts Guild building; Stanley Battese, recipient of several prizes for works indicative of worthier accomplishments; Wade To'dachine (Wade Hadley), of high talent and scant production; Stanley K. Bahe, with derivative tendencies curtailing natural ability; Tso Yazzy, newcomer with a Philbrook Art Center prize; and Peter Haskie, Arthur C. Begay, Walter Shirley, and Herbert Tom. Student winners of honors or awards are Lucy Wilson, Bob Martine, Harry Begay, Ernest Franklin, and Raymond Platero; and, those with notable beginnings are Eddie Chester, Thomas Gamble, Betty Nilchee, Lorenzo Platero, Rae Joe, and Henry Walters.

APACHE

Of contemporary Apache artists, Allan Houser is undoubtedly most popular. He has pursued a steady and successful career since his Santa Fe studies, and has been one of the most regular prize winners, mostly in the Philbrook Art Center's annuals. Through adding sculpture of distinction to his accomplishments, he won a Guggenheim Foundation grant, and a citation from the American Society of Medalists. It is not evident that Houser's painting has surpassed the highest at-

352

tainments of his early Santa Fe years, yet should it do so, it would be excellent indeed. Many of the later pictures, done in various media, are illustrative, somewhat in the manner of celebrated earlier painters of the Old West.

Nehakije (Steven Vicenti), until his youthful death in 1949, turned his attention now and then from stock raising and rodeo championships to his fine talents for painting Jicarilla Apache life. His few works, all of beauty and sensitivity, remain the best among the rare paintings from that area.

A younger Vicenti, Carl, appeared in the 1963 Philbrook show to win a prize. Calvin Vigil, also of the Jicarilla, has a special aptitude for painting birds, deer, and other animals in unexpected settings of combined naturalism and decoration. Imaginative and strangely conceived landscapes sometimes surround the quite lifelike figures in these works. Vigil also depicts ceremonial and other scenes in more traditional manner. His paintings are in the collections of the Denver Art Museum and the Philbrook Art Center.

Frank Vigil's hunting scenes and historic Apache subjects are seminaturalistically rendered in a fashion that is old despite the artist's preoccupation with anatomical representation. His palette, which frequently runs to sombre grays producing gaunt and gloomy moods, is perhaps the most arresting feature of his work. Vigil has exhibited but few times lately.

Ignatius Palmer shows his paintings mainly in the tribal arts center near his home in the Mescalero Apache area. Large and impressive figures of Gan Dancers and other ceremonial personages appear in flat, outlined constructions in most of these. Palmer is one of the few Apache artists who have consistently combined painting with duties and distractions of reservation life.

Another exponent of Mescalero Apache mores, Rudolph Treas, is an authoritative painter who imparts convincing realism and action to his subjects. Composition through which he controls and balances lively movement is one of Treas's strong points. He won an award from the School of American Research, Santa Fe.

Richard Caje, a young newcomer, brings a fresh touch of humor and caprice to more familiar Apache scenes. If he draws upon his own aptitudes and dispenses with copied elements, he should make some very good paintings.

Wilson Dewey, one of the most capable Apache artists, Wesley Nash, and Richard Chester have been missing from recent shows, while Gilbert Casen is a first exhibitor of interest.

353

PLAINS

Among artists of the Plains group, Howe, Woodring, West, Davis, and Bosin stand out at present, although more than fifty Plains names have come into notice since the opening of the annual competitions at the Philbrook Art Center in 1946.

Oscar Howe, Sioux, first recipient of the Mary Benjamin Rogers Memorial Award, has many prizes and honors to his credit and is represented nationwide in museum and private collections. He is in the midst of a distinguished career during which he has been an international exhibitor while still in high school, an artist-in-residence and graduate of two universities, a public school director of art, and, at present, a professor of art and member of museum and institute staffs at the State University of South Dakota. Since his formative studies in the Studio at Santa Fe, Howe has intensively pursued his Sioux art researches and evolvements even though he has remained almost the only exponent of tribal painting tradition in his home territory. Only a few times has his work sacrificed its originally Sioux-oriented stylization to more ordinary pictorial representation, and it merits one of the highest places in contemporary Indian art. Through analyzing patterns and constructions of precursory Dakota arts, Howe has proved in his own inventive works how much of the traditional can be projected through modern painting. Even obscure and nearly forgotten ideas and practices, encompassing generations, are brought to view and toward universal appreciation in his finely executed abstract paintings.

Although Carl Woodring, Osage, has been a steady worker and an inventive painter, his art has only within the last few years come into the fore with prizes in both Tulsa and Santa Fe. He has explored diverse styles and thus far appears most adept in abstract approaches to complex themes, minimizing detail but concentrating on pattern and essential idea. For organization, he relies mainly upon juxtaposition of darks and lights, balancing areas of well modulated color. While Woodring's compositions are taking on an appearance which might be superficially construed as completely contemporary, they retain basic pre-modern elements and techniques which authenticate them as Indian.

Walter Richard West (Wah-pah-nah-yah), Cheyenne, in addition to his long service as art director to Indian students at Bacone College, continues a prodigious output of his own paintings. His themes cover a vast range of Cheyenne tribal lore and activities—from sacred rituals to children's games. Revealing lesser influences from his own fine arts education, West's pictures adhere to somewhat representative stylizations in flat, firmly outlined areas of tempera paint. Particularly in

354

Figure 123. WAH-PAH-NAH-YAH, Cheyenne. *Throwing Away a Wife*. Ca. 1950. Tempera and gouache. Southern Plains Indians Museum, Anadarko, Oklahoma.

large groupings, such as in *Dance of the Soldier Societies*, West accurately interprets diverse components of an involved ritual. When he employs his aptitudes for design, color, and character interpretation in these multifigured paintings, the composition becomes absorbing art rather than illustration alone.

355

More recognized for his mural art, Archie Blackowl, Cheyenne, now rarely enters his tempera paintings in museum exhibitions; however, these appear occasionally in Indian arts centers and small galleries. Dancers and ceremonial groups, hunts and animals, at times too heavily depicted, are his usual subjects.

Jesse E. Davis (Asa-Woya), Cheyenne-Comanche, a longtime exhibitor, commands attention with painting that remains native despite academic influence. The latter is not intrusive except in instances of composition that seems too contrived or drawing that appears stilted. In general, his work is fluid, forceful in action, and comprehensive in tribal subject. His selection of line produces slight yet cogent indication of figure structure. The robust reds, greens, and blues which accent his flatly applied palette give a spirited if occasionally exaggerated effect. Carefully designed details such as shields and costume decorations prove the artist's concern for correctness. Warriors, dancers, hunters—all active subjects are his. Davis won the Grand Prize at the Philbrook Art Center in 1957.

Blackbear Bosin, Kiowa-Comanche, through his extensively reproduced *Prairie Fire*, no doubt is one of the most universally known of Indian painters. Although this picture has qualities that excite strong popular admiration, it represents a more literal and exaggerated style than is usually seen in Indian painting. Bosin is an exceptional draftsman, composer, and illustrator, and, in his earlier more naive works, he reveals talents of a perceptive and resourceful artist. Particularly in the collections of the University of Oklahoma, one may see fine arts potentialities in early Bosin paintings evocative of huntsmen and buffalo in the old days. However, the emerging pictorial approach that later was to dominate Bosin's work was evident in his entries in early annual shows at the Philbrooks Art Center where he repeatedly has been an award winner.

Bearer of an honored name among Kiowa artists is Lee Tsa Toke, son of Monroe. He has begun to win recognition as a painter in his own right with several prizes. He largely follows in the fashions of the founding artists of the Kiowa school, although he favors finer detail, greater variation in color, and more involved arrangements than usually observed in works of the forerunners.

Al Momaday is long established as a painter of his native Kiowa themes, although he recently has ventured into the portrayal of scenes from other tribes. To his paintings of the Kiowa, he brings a depth of knowledge and an ease of handling that is missing from his interpretations of other groups. His natural forte at present is in expansively conceived, boldly executed patterns associated with the virile color and strong action of Kiowa ceremony and design. Momaday has for several years given much time to productive guidance of young art stu-

356

dents in the Jemez Pueblo school, yet he has exhibited regularly in the principal Indian shows where he has won a number of prizes, including a recent first at the Philbrook Art Center.

George Keahbone, Kiowa, has been absent for years from the exhibitions, in which he was a first-prize winner, but recently he has returned with paintings showing his still capable, and thoughtfully matured direct presentation of tribal subjects. While he has lived in Taos and Santa Fe, necessarily painting irregularly since his student days, Keahbone nevertheless remains, in his own individual way, completely Kiowa in his art. This, in absentia, belongs to that of the Oklahoma tribe.

Among a relatively large number of other Kiowa painters are Roland White Horse, an early prizewinner who now works privately; David Williams, a recent winner; Dennis Belindo and Moses Turkey, who have received honorable mentions; and Woody Big Bow, with several traditional paintings permanently exhibited in Oklahoma State University.

Albin R. Jake, Pawnee, who died in 1960 at the age of thirty-eight, reflected many aspects of eastern Plains customs and history in his broadly detailed, semi-representational views. Unusual color contrasts, arresting arrangements of lights and darks, and spirited action animate these works. Jake also experimented with perspective in some pictures, and handled it interestingly amid otherwise flat planes. *Bear Dance*, winner of both the grand prize and a regional first prize in the 1956 annual at the Philbrook Art Center, is a good example of his essentially pictorial art.

M. Riding-In (Marlene Supernaw), Pawnee, is one of the few women painters of the Plains tribes. She is most known for her stylized documentaries of seldom depicted Pawnee customs. Her *Morning Star Ceremony* won for her a first prize at the Philbrook Art Center, and *Pawnee Doctor Dance*, honors at the Museum of New Mexico.

Acee Blue Eagle, Pawnee-Creek, one of the best-known artists of Oklahoma, was an active painter from the mid-twenties until his death in 1959. He exhibited extensively and won numerous honors including those from the Ethiopian government, the Indian Hall of Fame, and the Philbrook Art Center's grand prize of 1951. Among purchasers of his works were Eleanor Roosevelt and Alfonso, former King of Spain. At one period he toured internationally, presenting exhibitions of his paintings with lectures, native songs, and dances. He studied and later taught, at Bacone College. He also studied at the University of Oklahoma, and briefly at Oxford University. Blue Eagle's usual painting style was broad

357

and direct and two-dimensional. In instances, it seemed to partake of the poster, and was least successful when it imitated the styles of tribes other than those of his own dual antecedents. However, when interpreting scenes he knew intimately, Blue Eagle produced paintings which were both sensitive in execution and thoughtful in content. He often transmitted through them something of his own simplicity and winsomeness.

Further Plains painters include Calvin Larvie, Sioux, imaginative and promising artist of some seasons ago; Gerald Osborne, Pawnee, an earlier exhibitor receiving an award; Frank Brave, Osage-Cherokee; Jim Redcorn, a recent prizewinner; Paul Pahsetopah, Osage; Victor Pepion Blackfoot, and Ernie Farmer, Bannock-Shoshone, both cited for honors. Leonard Riddles, Comanche, won a Philbrook first prize in 1963.

WOODLAND

Artists from the Woodland tribes are increasingly entering shows along with painters of the Southwest and Plains areas. Cross-influences already are being accelerated by these intertribal art associations. It therefore seems pertinent that notable painters now classified as Woodland should be considered here.

One of the principal Woodland artists is Fred Beaver, Creek-Seminole. He is a prolific painter with a long succession of major prizes to his credit, including the first Waite Phillips Indian Artists Award ever bestowed, 1963, at the Philbrook Art Center. His pictures are adroit, colorful, and decorative in a meaningful manner that commands interest beyond that usually aroused by largely illustrative art. Beaver should write the stories and legends to accompany these excellent depictions of native scenes. With his comprehensive knowledge of the subject, he should be able to offer a well rounded and fascinating view of Southeast Indian life.

Another Creek recipient of years of prizes and honors is Solomon McCombs. The mode of his art, too, is decorative, and it occasionally goes beyond into expressions of marked sensitivity. Directness, simplicity, and a command of color, in both choice and technique, characterize McCombs's authentic observations of tribal subjects in a variety of forms.

Noah Deere, Creek, a painter offering high promise in the first works he exhibited in 1949, has had lengthy intervals between showings because of illness. In his prize pictures at the M. H. deYoung Museum, San Francisco, and the Philbrook Art Center, his bright talents are evident. These works attest to his main-

358

Plate XXXI. Oscar Howe, Sioux. *War Dancer*. 1956. Casein tempera. Collection of the artist.

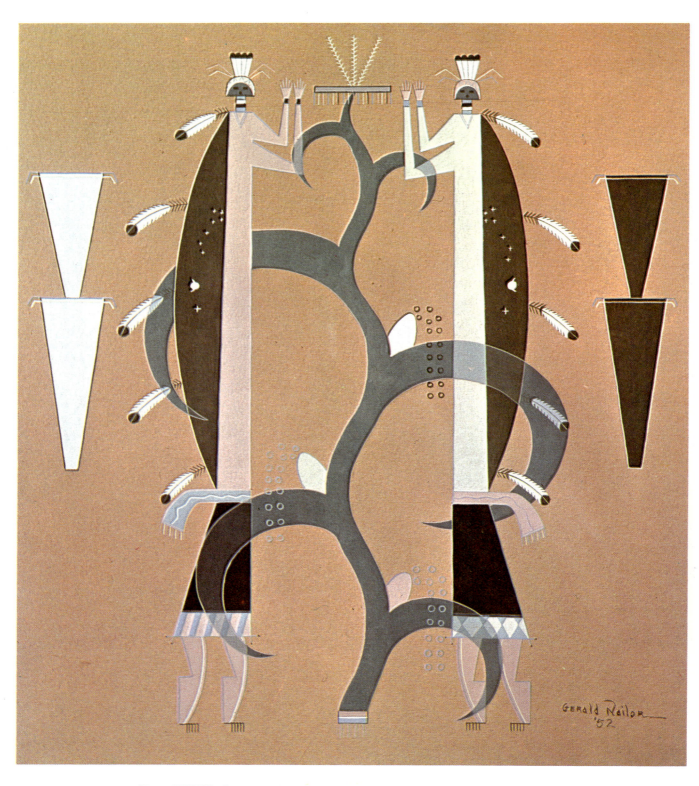

Plate XXXII. GERALD NAILOR, Navajo. *Beganiskidi, Bearer of Seeds, with Corn Design.* 1952. Tempera. Collection of Mrs. Hall Adams.

tenance of individuality amid borrowings and influences, and to a command of all technical abilities necessary to good painting, plus a communicable sensitivity to mood and meaning. Deere interplays transparent and opaque paints to suggest motion or to create atmospheric effects. In his *Creek Ball Game*, transparent washes of ice blue freeze both sky and lake in a winter setting where gray-blue hills loom along the horizon to give cold depth. His figures subtly suggest anatomical structure in their sure, spare outlines, and the essentially schematic faces express character and emotion. The comparatively few prizes thus far awarded Deere are scarcely indicative of his ability.

C. Terry Saul, Choctaw, is one of the most widely recognized Woodland artists with his consistently thoughtful and exploratory works. In a new development wherein he sharply incises lines in dark paint superimposed on a ground of white, he produces selective delineations of dance forms and other tribal figures of delicate beauty. This expressive mode follows upon his predilection for emphasis on facile line and flat color in his works of many years. Always a searcher for uncommon motifs in his tribal sources, Saul has been a frequent recipient of awards for his contributions in Denver, Santa Fe, and Tulsa.

Tom Dorsey (Two Arrows), of the northeastern Onondaga Tribe, does striking paintings which bear the mark of the professional designer. He intelligently combines non-Indian influences with native figures and fashions to produce decorative compositions of imagination and force. His work seems somehow related to the theater and ballet in its dramatic qualities, yet it is certainly Indian drama. He uses the silhouette, the emblazoned border, the spotlight of bright color to point up his themes, and whimsically places small units, or sprays a white spiral, to ornament a setting. Dorsey's works are in New York and Tulsa museums but appear too sparsely in the Southwest shows.

Patrick Desjarlait, Chippewa, exhibited in the first three Philbrook annual shows where his Riveraesque composition, *Wild Rice Harvest*, won first prize in the Woodland division in 1947. In 1963, he returned west to win the Walter Bimson Award, the grand prize, in the Scottsdale National exhibition with a painting as well composed and as exciting in action, but less successful in color and artistic expression. With work clearly showing the stamp of the professional artist, and easily compatible with the main body of contemporary painting, Desjarlait might well interpret native subjects in the general exhibitions where Indian themes are rarely presented with understanding.

Be-Doni-Qut (Jerry Maulson), Chippewa, uses a low-keyed casein palette with spray and stencils to produce misty atmospheres in unusual views of Wood-

359

land personages and animals of legendary and more recent days. His honors-winning student work is surprisingly mature.

Bronson Edwards, Ottawa, has been a faithful participant and sometimes prizewinner in exhibitions since the beginning of the major annual competitions. He paints animals and hunting scenes in an active, illustrative manner.

Cecil Dick, Cherokee, although his art has been glimpsed only occasionally since his student days, is well worth noting for his consistent originality. He has always been an innovator in composition and in color while dramatizing experiences and legends of his tribe. Balance and rhythm control the ostensibly carefree action in his pictures, which are always fascinating. Conjured colors in combinations and application reminiscent of Gauguin produce excitement even in his simplest subjects, such as those from animal fables of the Cherokee.

Joan Hill (Cheas-se-quah), Creek-Cherokee, while a representationalist in an occasionally flamboyant illustrative vein, brings selective line and stylized composition to her pictures. Her academically inclined technical skill renders her paintings less native in superficial aspect, yet does not lessen the artist's ability to project her evident knowledge of important tribal features. Particularly worthy are her depictions of less tried subjects and her feminine interpretations of the ceremonies and works of women.

Also offering a distaff view of the Cherokee Nation, Jimalee Burton (Ho-chee-nee) has exhibited her paintings from Canada to Mexico in both group and one-man shows. The artist's 1961 showing of twenty-four paintings in Sarasota, Florida, proved the value of perseverance and study, for, from her naive entries in the first Philbrook Art Center annuals, she has traveled a long way artistically to merit enthusiastic criticism. In reviewing this exhibition, one critic mentions "old images . . . in newly created interpretations," "dramatic close-ups," and "mood and action which makes earlier illustrative subjects look stilted by comparison."[17] Of her varied themes, Mrs. Burton's explorations of myths and legends seem most successful.

The Cherokee have contributed extensively to the Woodland roster of notable artists. Among them are Alfred Johnson, a winner of first prize for pictorial works; Helen Boswell, recipient of a major award at the M. H. de Young Museum, San Francisco; and Joe Waano-Gano and Barbara Cornine, both honorably mentioned in recent shows.

Additional Woodland names noteworthy for honors and awards are Jimmie Anderson, Bunny Randall, and William Sampson, Jr., Creek; Louis W. Ballard, Quapaw; Woody Crumbo, Potawatomie, mentioned more particularly for his

360

murals; Dwight E. Philip, Choctaw; Charles Pushetonequa and Antoine Warrior, Sauk and Fox; and Louis Mofsie, Winnebago-Hopi, with glowingly painted Woodland-oriented works showing marked aptitude for dynamic design.

Fast-growing participation is coming from the Northwest Coast, including Alaska, where the painters stand artistically apart. A number of tribes, with one or two representatives each, contribute developments from the massive motifs of sea and rain-forest—wooden mask and totem patterns, and deeply involved designs from whales and bears and birds—a continent away from the eastern Woodlands, and yet further from the Southwest and Plains. Among these artists are Ernest Desautel, Colville; Henry D. Gobin and V. Henry Woodworth, Snohomish; Jeri Spencer, Yakima; Victor Ward, Eric Johnson, and Clifford Thomas, Tlingit; and George Clutesi, Seshaht. Exciting prospects lie ahead for these men and others who may join them.

By far the largest contingent from the Northwest is the Eskimo. Fishing and hunting activities and the unique abstract patterns of the Far North motivate the Eskimo painters' art. Transparent and opaque watercolors, ink wash, oils, crayons, and pencils are the media through which the Eskimo artists produce a selective realism which is strikingly regional and completely communicative. For their prizes and honors, these painters are especially noteworthy: Richard Davis Takilnok, winner of two major awards at the M. H. de Young Museum; Wilbur Walluk, Agnes Gough, Kivetoruk Moses, of exceptional ability, Gabriel Monignok, and Jerry Norton. Norton is an extraordinarily perceptive and skilled young artist who catches the crisp and frosty scenes of the Arctic in crystal-clear watercolors for sky, sea, and ice, and warm-toned gouache for hides, furs, and woods. Also appearing with interesting pieces are Florence Nupok, John Elavgak, Jerry Kiakak, and Robert Mayokuk.

There is a future for Indian painting in the art of the world and a peculiar need for the ideology of Indian art in its own land. As America awakes increasingly to her indigenous cultural riches, Indian painting will become more and more understood and appreciated. Its examples will augment permanent collections of art, and its fund of motifs and techniques will enrich the creative activities of artists in the several fields.

There are today, and for many years to come there will be, among the growing Indian populations, artists who possess both the willingness and the capability for contributing toward this important role which the art of the aboriginal peoples has already begun to play in America's art of the future. From the painters, such work as has been presented here is a splendid showing, yet much could be added before the time of the ultimate assimilation which seems inevitable for the American Indian people. It is the painters who are yet near enough to the vast, rich stores of native traditions to understand them who could most effectively and happily develop and project Indian painting in full measure.

This does not mean retardation for the Indian artists, for they are already abreast in the contemporary idiom; in fact Indian painters were "Modernists" in the days of the Awatovi murals and the classic Mimbres and Tusayan ceramics. Modern Indian paintings can continue to spring fresh and vital, entirely individual, from native sources.

The painters who wish to develop such art deserve understanding support from institutions, collectors, and the general public. In addition to such attention as has been given, juries could welcome Indian paintings for consideration in group shows, galleries outside the Indian areas might present Indian painting

362

11. A Future for Indian Painting

where it is little known as modern art, colleges could inaugurate studies in Indian art, and schools might hang paintings by Indians as well as paintings about them. Thereby, the artists would be given to feel that theirs is a significant art which it is very much worth their while to advance, from sources in its own tradition, within and part of the general advancement of America's whole culture.

Much has been said about the achievement of a national art in America, one which becomes free at last from Europe. It even has been suggested that Indian art might be strategic in such an art, as Mexican paintings of the temples and codices became determinant in the modern painting of Mexico. But, in the first place, America is still too young and yet "too many selves to know the one" to have arrived at significant art homogeneity. Perhaps the heterogeneous national character of America is to be reflected in the national art, lending it distinctive features from many arts and various stocks of mankind which merge in a diversified oneness that is characteristically American. In the second place, as compared to the population ratios of Mexico, the Indian populations of the United States constitute a small minority which, although capable of contributing a proportionately great richness to the national art, could not be representative in the measure the native peoples have been in Mexico. Here, rather, the strain of Indian art must somehow enter the flow of the many strains toward a national art expression, not losing its own identity but contributing identifying features to the whole.

Of this contribution, those who have long known of the values of Indian painting have already spoken; among them:

Frederic H. Douglas: ". . . a search for the means of building up a truly American art which stands on its own feet instead of aping the art of other lands **363** without understanding them might well include a study and mastery of the forms of American Indian art."[1]

Alice Corbin Henderson: "[The Indian is] a race whose art is itself the finest possible contribution to our national life."[2]

Edgar L. Hewett: "The best we can do is to save what we can of that priceless heritage [Indian art] and make every effort to comprehend it; then . . . avail ourselves eagerly of this which came from our own soil."[3]

Olive Rush: "We may well envy them their heritage, we may well protect and foster and encourage it, for it is precious to our civilization. We need its virility, its refreshing power."[4]

Herbert J. Spinden: "In a world that grows mechanical he [the Indian artist] seems able to keep contact with illusion. And this is well because nations are made great by illusions which enrich the spirit and establish the interdependence of individuals in a social organism."[5]

Walter Pach: "More than we realize, this soil has affected the character of the American people. . . . The art of the Indians, so eloquent of this land, is American art, and of the most important kind."[6]

In another aspect, the Indian painters have something of timely pertinence to offer American art, and that is a view toward a wider concept of art. The Indian concept of art for life, art for everyone, art not apart in an exotic world might well be considered in America today much more than it is.

The modern American, as much as did his indigenous predecessor, needs art in his everyday life, for he needs art's insights in more fully realizing the peace and order that are in the designs of nature, and in comprehending something of the elements and functions of the gigantic and minute patterns in a universe which is comparatively as strange to him, with all his technology, as it was to the pre-Columbian American. Whereas the main function of art in primitive days was one of helping to keep man from being destroyed by nature, that of art in modern times may well be one concerned in some way with preventing nature, including man himself, from being destroyed by man.

Modern art certainly has the opportunity for as great a purpose as had any art before it, and artists are aware of the challenges of the contemporary world. Some painters are producing groping or chaotic or evasive work in the face of immense overpowering unknowns. Some remain purely decorative in their art while others are reaching toward the nonobjective. A number are seeing through superficial aspects to underlying vital elements and are seeking to clarify and interpret them. Few attempt a completely literal statement about anything, for they realize

364

Figure 124. ALICE SEABIYENTEWA, Hopi. *Abstract Design*. 1961. Polychrome bowl. Museum of Northern Arizona. Cat. No. 2254/E-2220.

that the driving forces of the modern world have advanced beyond the things which are readily seen and understood. The largely representational painting of a past era seems inadequate for today's more complex needs, and much of the modern artist's work is again taking on many characteristics of primitive art. In fact, the modern painter has upon occasion frankly gone to the primordial artist for suggestion, and, in much of his most moving expression, there are indications of the imaginative approach, the meaningful abstraction, the direct, potent style of the true primitive, and a comparably functional quality.

Yet, much of contemporary painting is incomprehensible and unavailable to the average American—that same individual who eagerly accepts the most advanced design in material equipment. Something is wrong in this situation. Perhaps it is due to both the frequent, although usually inadvertent, exclusiveness of the artist and to the inadequate system in which American art exists. The general public regards artists as extraordinary individuals and galleries as occasional places, art itself as unobtainable except in prints and photographs. As for becoming actively engaged in painting, Clyde Kluckhohn has so rightly said, "Americans usually are scared out of being artists."[7]

This sort of situation does not exist in Indian society where everyone participates in art in some measure and painting is strange to no one. In every painting the inner significance is invariably conveyed by the artist to the beholder, for everyone understands and respects the purpose and language of art. Painting is not set aside to be seen only on holidays and special occasions, but is very much integrated with the daily life. It is this concept of art which deserves consideration not only by artists but by everyone who has anything to do with presenting painting to the American public.

Such a concept, which is akin to that of the Indian's in its inclusiveness, is already beginning to function in some localities. There are instances where painting is slowly moving out from the congestion of the art centers to people in other parts of the country, where unknown artists working in the hinterlands are being sought out for representation in certain of the major exhibitions, and where outlying communities are initiating distinguished art activities of their own. With such beginnings, it should be possible for individual participation in painting— both active and appreciative—to be extended through a knowledge of Indian art.

To the Indian himself, the advancing role of his painting in the art of America can mean much. Through it he may not only continue to grow esthetically, but he may at last have an opportunity to make statements of his own about his own culture, even to restore creatively in visual form many of its extinct aspects. Countless volumes have been written about the Indian, yet he has rarely written; his truest record is in his art, particularly his modern painting. Herein the record lives, and is growing, from his point of view. Yet it is far more than a record. Modern Indian painting is a way of sharing beauty and a philosophy of life, as the Indian knows it, in a form available to his fellow men. Through this art, the Indian bridges a cultural gap, for his contemporary painting relates to both the old traditions and the new. It is at once of America's primal heritage and of her most modern expression.

367

Notes

*[Numbers in parentheses refer to the numbered entries
in the list of references that follows these notes.]*

Chapter 1.   THE EARLIEST ART

1. Bryan (63). Griffin (284) p. 368. Howells (341). Johnson (358). Roberts (490, 491, 493).
   Science (513).
2. Roberts (493).
3. Figgins (268). Roberts (486) p. 4; (493) p. 403.
4. Roberts (486).
5. *Ibid.* p. 26.
6. Roberts (488) pp. 25, 26.
7. Roberts (486) pp. 30, 31.
8. Roberts (488) p. 32.
9. Harrington, M. (295) p. 90.
10. *Ibid.* p. 34.
11. *Ibid.* p. 111.
12. Hibben (323, 325).
13. Harrington, M. (296).
14. Strong (554).
15. Cressman (100).
16. Caldwell (71). Haag (289).
17. Newcomb (448) Pl. XI, 20; pp. 67, 71.
18. Ford (273) p. 333. Griffin (284) pp. 323, 355, and Fig. 102.
19. Caldwell (71) p. 6.
20. Harrington, M. (295) p. 182. Romer (495) pp. 80-81.
21. Nelson (446) pp. 498-99.
22. Roberts (493). Science (513). Wormington (600).
23. Wendorf (581).

369

24. Harrington, M. (295) Fig. 76. Steward (548) Pl. 8.
25. Howells (341). Jenness (351). Roberts (493).
26. Dall (107), Gladwin (287). Hrdlicka (342). Linné (389). Nordenskiöld, E. (453).

Chapter 2. *BASIC CONSIDERATIONS*

1. Kroeber (378, 379).
2. Johnson (357). Caldwell (71).
3. Douglass (142). Krieger, A. (376) p. 251. Linton (394) p. 592.
4. Caldwell (71). Krieger, A. (376).
5. Kroeber (378) p. 391.
6. *Ibid.* p. 389.
7. Wissler (595) p. 213.
8. Haeberlin (291).
9. Duran (175). Fewkes (231). Kelemen (363). Mexico (424). Sahagun (504). Valliant (569, 570).
10. Fewkes (251) p. 25.
11. Fewkes (260) p. 275.
12. Setzler (516). Shetrone (517).
13. D'Harnoncourt (109) Pt. 2, p. 18. Holmes (335, 336). Vaillant (568).
14. Ford (273). Phillips (469). Waring (576).
15. Krieger, A. (374).
16. Strong (556) p. 34.
17. Ekholm (179, 180).
18. Caldwell (71).
19. *Ibid.* Krieger, A. (374, 376). Strong (556).
20. Grosse (286).
21. Benavides (40) p. 55.
22. Steward (548) p. 421.
23. Catlin (75) Vol. 2, p. 248.
24. Schoolcraft (512) Vols. 1 and 2.
25. Mallery (405) p. 27.
26. Mallery (403) p. 401.
27. Fewkes (251) p. 15.
28. Bynner (69) p. 65.
29. Chapman (81) p. 120.
30. Chapman (78).
31. Linton (391) p. 17.
32. Krieger, H. (377) p. 521.
33. Boas (47) p. 10. *See also* Lesley (385) p. 12.
34. Klee (441) p. 8.
35. Kubler (381).
36. Austin (27, 29). Boas (48, 49). Fewkes (260). Oakes (457). Pijoan (470).
37. Austin (27, 29). Densmore (115). Henderson (307, 309). Hewett (315, 316, 317).
38. Henderson (309).

39. Bandelier (32) Pt. 1, p. 152.
40. Boas (49) p. 75.
41. Chapman (79) p. 30.
42. Linton (391) p. 24.

Chapter 3. *THE SOUTHWEST*

1. Amsden (14) p. 1. Kroeber (379) p. 33.
2. Amsden (14). Roberts (489).
3. Cressman (100). Ekholm (179). Roberts (491). Setzler (515).
4. Amsden (15) p. 44.
5. Seltzer (514).
6. Roberts (489).
7. *Ibid.*
8. Douglass (142). Hawley (305).
9. Roberts (483).
10. Roberts (489).
11. Kidder (367). Mera (421).
12. Gladwin (278, 279, 280).
13. Gladwin (280) p. 5.
14. Haury (301).
15. Amsden (13). Haury (302).
16. Gladwin (279, 280).
17. Haury (300).
18. Haury (304).
19. Haury (299, 300).
20. Haury (300) p. 128.
21. Kluckhohn (373).
22. Hall (293) p. 100.
23. Harrington, J. (294) p. 529.
24. Dittert (124).
25. Matthews (413) p. 68.
26. Amsden (12). Harrington, J. (294).
27. Harrington, J. (294). Hodge (333) Vol. 1. Swanton (564).
28. Harrington, J. (294) p. 526.
29. *Ibid* p. 506.
30. Benavides (40) p. 44.
31. Hewett (312) p. 16.
32. Zaráte-Salmerón (604) Vol. 12, No. 3, p. 183.
33. Harrington, J. (294) p. 515.
34. Alexander (6). Swanton (564).
35. Matthews (413).
36. Dittert (124). Farmer (221). Keur (365).
37. Hester (311). Hill (329). Kluckhohn (373).
38. Roberts (489).

39. Amsden (12). Hester (311). Keur (353).
40. Sapir (506).
41. Bandelier (32) Pt. 1. Hodge (333) Pt. 1. Wedel (577). Worcester (598).
42. Harrington, J. (294) p. 512.
43. Worcester (598).
44. Hodge (332).
45. Harrington, J. (294). Opler (458).
46. Hodge (333) Pt. 1.
47. Bandelier (32) Pt. 1, p. 178.
48. Kidder (367). Schoolcraft (511).
49. Hodge (333) Pt. 1.
50. *Ibid.*
51. Benavides (40) p. 39.
52. Harrington, J. (294) p. 519. Hodge (332) pp. 442-43.
53. Kidder (367).
54. Fewkes (245) p. 663; (251) p. 18.
55. Fewkes (241, 247, 251, 260).
56. Reed (478) p. 486.
57. Kluckhohn (373).
58. *Ibid.*
59. *Ibid.*
60. Matthews (411) p. 385. Reichard (479) Vol. 1, p. 61. Stevenson (544) p. 335.
61. Harrington, J. (294). Hodge (333) Pt. 1.
62. Abert (1) p. 10.
63. Winship (587) pp. 527-28.
64. Harrington, J. (294).
65. *Ibid.* and Hodge (333) Pt. 1, p. 66.
66. Guernsey (287, 288).
67. Judd (360). Reagan (474).
68. Yeo (603).
69. Kidder (368).
70. Guernsey (287, 288).
71. Amsden (13). Haury (299).
72. Gladwin (278). Haury (302).
73. Douglas (135) p. 11.
74. Kidder (367) p. 111.
75. Amsden (13) p. 44.
76. Haury (299, 300).
77. Fewkes (262).
78. Bradfield (56). Douglas (136) pp. 419-22, Pls. 2E, F, 3A. Fewkes (257, 258, 261, 262). Hurst (343). Jenks (348-350). Kabotie (361). Kelemen (363) Pls. 106, 107. Smithsonian Institution, Miscellaneous Collections (529, 530).
79. Cosgrove (97). Dickey (121). *New Mexico Quarterly* (450).
80. Fewkes (257) p. 24, Fig. 13.
81. Smithsonian Institution, Miscellaneous Collections (530) Fig. 84c.
82. Fewkes (258) p. 542, Fig. 72.
83. Chapman (86) Pt. 2, p. 8. *See also* Jenks (350) p. 137.

84. Kidder (97) p. xx.
85. Hewett (317) p. 353.
86. Fewkes (260).
87. Fewkes (255). Guernsey (287). Kidder (368).
88. Beckwith (36-39). Judd (360). Reagan (474, 476).
89. Beckwith (39).
90. Steward (548, 549).
91. Fewkes (225).
92. Chapman (77).
93. Bandelier (32) Pt. 2.
94. Smith (528) p. 55.
95. Roberts (485) Pls. 13, 14.
96. Martin (406) Pl. 59.
97. Mindeleff, C. (427) p. 181.
98. *El Palacio* (183). Tichy (565) p. 60.
99. Hewett (320, 321).
100. Bandelier (32) Pt. 2, pp. 222.
101. *Ibid.* p. 225.
102. Winship (587).
103. Goddard (281).
104. Villagrá (572) p. 142.
105. *Ibid.* p. 140.
106. Bliss (45).
107. Brew (58, 59, 60).
108. Fewkes (242).
109. Cushing (105) p. 493.
110. Fewkes (242) p. 599.
111. Bolton (51) p. 186.
112. Fewkes (242).
113. Fewkes (254).
114. Fewkes (234).
115. Brew (59).
116. Fewkes (242) p. 594.
117. *Ibid.* p. 631.
118. Brew (60) p. xii.
119. Fewkes (242).
120. Fewkes (234).
121. Fewkes (242).
122. Fewkes (234).
123. Fewkes (229, 234, 242).
124. Fewkes (242) p. 605.
125. Parsons (466) p. 559.
126. Fewkes (242, 254) pp. 582-84; (260).
127. Hough (340) Pl. 89.
128. Brew (59, 60).
129. Smith (528).
130. *Ibid.*

373

131. *Ibid*. Fig. 41c.
132. *Ibid*. Fig. 76a.
133. *Ibid*. Fig. 25.
134. Fewkes (260).
135. Smith (528) Figs. 11, 12.
136. *Ibid*. Figs. 48, 49a, 59.
137. *Ibid*. Pl. D.
138. *Ibid*. Fig. 43a, c.
139. *Ibid*. Fig. 45a.
140. *Ibid*. Fig. 18jj-qq.
141. *Ibid*. Pl. A.
142. *Ibid*. Fig. 48b and text.
143. *Ibid*. Pl. D and Fig. 60.
144. Hibben (326) p. 131 (327-328).
145. Hibben (328) p. 269.
146. Hibben (326).
147. Hibben (327).
148. *Ibid*. p. 180.
149. Hibben (328) pp. 273-74.
150. *Ibid*. cover (color plate).
151. Mindeleff, V. (428) p. 131.
152. Stevenson, M. (547) p. 438.
153. *Ibid*. Pl. 108.
154. Fewkes (265) Pl. III, 5.
155. Fewkes (238).
156. *El Palacio* (182, 191).
157. White (583) Pl. 11a, b.
158. Parsons (467).
159. *Ibid*.
160. Parsons (465).
161. White (583) Pl. 12a, b.
162. Bandelier (32) Pt. 1. Parsons (467). Stephen (540) Pt. 1. Stevenson, M. (547).
163. Fewkes (265) p. 244. Stephen (540) Pt. 1, Fig. 144; Pls. 5-7, 10.
164. Bunzel (64). Fewkes (266). Stevenson, M. (547).
165. Fewkes (233) Pl. 1. Parsons (467). Stephen (540) Pt. 1.
166. Stirling (551).
167. Fewkes (232). Stevenson, M. (546).
168. Stevenson, M. (545) p. 550, Pl. 22.
169. Dorsey, G. (130) Pl. 92. Fewkes (264) Pl. 17; (246) Pl. 46.
170. Voth (573) Pl. 42.
171. Fewkes (263) p. 113, Fig. 3; (265).
172. Fewkes (227) p. 86, (240) p. 133, Fig. 2.
173. Fewkes (267) Pl. 1. (251).
174. Fewkes (227) p. 85.
175. Dorsey, G. (129).
176. Fewkes (252) Pl. 46.
177. *Ibid*. pp. 104-105.

178. Fewkes (242) pp. 612-13.
179. Fewkes (263) (265) pp. 240-41, Pl. 4. Stevenson, M. (546).
180. Fewkes (265) p. 226.
181. Fewkes (263) p. 121.
182. Fewkes (227) p. 33.
183. Voth (573).
184. *Museum of New Mexico Bulletin* (442).
185. Villagrá (572) p. 144.
186. Bolton (51) p. 146.
187. Amsden (12) p. 117.
188. Winship (587) pp. 404. 558.
189. *Ibid.* pp. 561-62.
190. *Ibid.* p. 563.
191. Cushing (106) p. 333.
192. Bandelier (32) Pt. 1, p. 218.
193. Fewkes (260).
194. *Ibid.*
195. Chapman (91).
196. Fewkes (234, 242, 252). Hough (340).
197. Bolton (51) pp. 179, 186, 241-43, 269.
198. Ball (31). Bunzel (64). Chapman (91). Fewkes (227, 256, 266). Hodge (333) Pt. 1. Hough (339, 340). Parsons (467). Roberts (492). Smith (528). Stephen (540) Pt. 1. Stevenson, M. (547). White (583).
199. Dunn (144).
200. Fewkes (227, 265, 266). Stevenson, M. (547).
201. Bunzel (64).
202. Parsons (465).
203. Fewkes (242).
204. Bunzel (64). Stevenson, M. (546).
205. Bunzel (64). White (583).
206. Fewkes (242, 252). Judd (360). Roberts (484, 492).
207. Fewkes (242) Pl. 128.
208. Stevenson, M. (543) Figs. 454-59.
209. Bunzel (64). Stevenson, M. (547).
210. White (583).
211. *Ibid.*
212. Hough (339).
213. Fewkes (266). Hough (399). Parsons (467). Stephen (540). Setvenson, M. (547).
214. Hough (339). Stevenson, M. (547). White (583).
215. Hough (339).
216. *Ibid.*
217. Mindeleff, V. (428).
218. Fewkes (227). Stevenson, M. (547). Parsons (467). White (583).
219. Hough (339, 340).
220. Hough (340).
221. *Ibid.*
222. Fewkes (242).

375

223. Fewkes (227, 242). Stevenson, M. (547). White (583).
224. Austin (27) p. 388.
225. Guernsey (287) Fig. 37b. Kidder (368) pp. 192-199, Fig. 90a, g, j, o.
226. Keur (365) p. 63.
227. Schaafsma (510) Figs. 7-12.
228. Matthews (411).
229. Reichard (479) Vol. 2.
230. Kroeber (378).
231. Alexander (6).
232. Fewkes (234, 238, 242).
233. Haeberlin (291).
234. Stevenson, J. (544).
235. Stevenson, M. (546).
236. Bandelier (32) Pt. 1.
237. Parsons (467).
238. Newcomb (448). Wissler (593).
239. Henderson (309) p. 3.
240. Kluckhohn (373).
241. Reichard (479) Vol. 2.
242. Wyman (602).
243. Matthews (411). Newcomb (448). Reichard (479) Vol. 2.
244. Mera (420).
245. Yeo (603).
246. Roberts (485) Pls. 61-63.
247. Mallery (404) Pl. 2; (405) Fig. 33.
248. Alexander (6). Goodwin (282). Kroeber (378). Opler (458). Parsons (467).
249. Bourke (53). Goodwin (282). Kane (362).
250. Opler (458).
251. Bourke (53).
252. Benavides (40). Winship (587).
253. Bourke (53). Mallery (405) Pl. 33.

Chapter 4. *THE PLAINS*

1. Strong (555). Wedel (578, 579).
2. Strong (554, 555). Wedel (577, 578).
3. Strong (555).
4. Caldwell (71) p. x.
5. Harrington, J. (294). Kidder (367).
6. Bolton (51) p. 230.
7. *Ibid.* p. 227.
8. Winship (587) p. 504.
9. *Ibid.* p. 505.
10. Villagrá (572) p. 157.
11. Winship (587).
12. Strong (554). Wedel (578).

13. *Ibid.*
14. Winship (587) p. 507.
15. Wedel (577).
16. Strong (555) p. 377.
17. Strong (554).
18. Winship (587) p. 504.
19. Wissler (589).
20. Wissler (593).
21. Wedel (577) p. 327.
22. Mooney (432). Schoolcraft (512) Vol. 2. Strong (555). Swanton (560). Wedel (577). Will (584).
23. Strong (554). Swanton (560, 564).
24. Swanton (560).
25. Mooney (403). Wissler (595).
26. Fletcher (271) pp. 36-37, 605. McGee (416) pp. 158-60. Wissler (595) p. 155.
27. Hodge (333) Pt. 1.
28. Bushnell (67).
29. Bushnell (66). Mooney (429). Swanton (557, 559).
30. Swanton (564).
31. Swanton (563).
32. Swanton (561).
33. Bushnell (66).
34. McGee (416). Swanton (557, 558).
35. Swanton (564) p. 389.
36. Griffin (283).
37. Swanton (561) p. 373.
38. Bushnell (67). Mooney (429). Swanton (562).
39. Bushnell (66) p. 16, (68) p. 132.
40. Wedel (580) p. 324-27.
41. Shetrone (517) p. 315. Strong (555) p. 386.
42. Strong (554) p. 290.
43. Shetrone (517).
44. Mooney (429) p. 14.
45. *Ibid.* p. 11.
46. Strong (555).
47. Dorsey, G. (128). Mooney (432) p. 363.
48. Strong (555). Wedel (577).
49. Will (584).
50. Strong (555).
51. Will (584) p. 305.
52. Mooney (432).
53. Mooney (431).
54. Wissler (595).
55. Mooney (431) Pl. 78.
56. *Ibid.*
57. Wissler (593) Chapt. 7.
58. McGee (416) p. 174.

377

59. Maximilian (415) Pt. 1.
60. Eastman (177) p. 7.
61. Kurz (382) p. 142.
62. Grinnell (285).
63. Eastman (177).
64. Kurz (382) p. 351.
65. Fletcher (271).
66. Miximilian (415) Pt. 1, p. 326.
67. Kurz (382) p. 32.
68. Catlin (75) Vol. 1, p. 148.
69. Alexander (6). Dorsey, J. (132). Fletcher (271). Wissler (593).
70. Wissler (593).
71. Alexander (6).
72. *Ibid.* and Fletcher (271).
73. Mooney (431) p. 242.
74. Dorsey, G. (128) pp. 57-59.
75. Dorsey, J. (132).
76. Wissler (593).
77. Mooney (431).
78. Densmore (114).
79. Dorsey, J. (132).
80. Dorsey, G. (128).
81. Dorsey, G. (127).
82. Densmore (114) p. 86.
83. Dorsey, J. (132) p. 451.
84. Wissler (593) p. 121.
85. Dorsey, G. (128) p. 57.
86. Densmore (114).
87. Wissler (593) pp. 129-30.
88. Antiquetes Mexicaines (16). Chavero (93). Duran (175). Kelemen (363). Mexico (424). Museo Nacional de Arqueologia (438). Nuttall (455). Vaillant (569, 570).
89. Lewis (387) Vol. 1, p. 109.
90. *Ibid.* Vol. 3, p. 31.
91. *Ibid.* Vol. 2, p. 346.
92. Eastman (177) p. 32. Wissler (593).
93. Wissler (593) p. 159.
94. Carter (73).
95. Mooney (431) p. 221.
96. Alexander (6).
97. Mooney (430). Wissler (595).
98. Spier (533).
99. Wissler (595) pp. 174-75.
100. Winship (587) p. 558.
101. *Ibid.* p. 560.
102. Burpee (65) p. 366.
103. *Ibid.* p. 332.
104. Lewis (387) Vol. 1, p. 128.

105. *Ibid.* p. 112.
106. *Ibid.* p. 167.
107. *Ibid.* p. 281.
108. Bradbury (55) p. 134.
109. Brackenridge (54) p. 146.
110. James (347) Pt. 2, p. 73.
111. *Ibid.* p. 149.
112. *Ibid.* p. 208.
113. Maximilian (415) Pt. 2, p. 102.
114. *Ibid.* p. 263-64.
115. *Ibid.* p. 287.
116. Bodmer (50).
117. Maximilian (415) Pt. 2, p. 264.
118. *Ibid.* p. 102.
119. *Ibid.* p. 99.
120. *Ibid.* p. 264.
121. Catlin (75) Vol. 1, p. 105.
122. *Ibid.* p. 43.
123. *Ibid.* p. 31.
124. Kurz (382) p. 226.
125. *Ibid,* p. 309.
126. *Ibid.* p. 351.
127. Wissler (593).
128. Catlin (75) Vol. 2, Pl. 312.
129. Ewers (220).
130. Vatter (571).
131. Dorsey, J. (132). Fletcher (271).
132. Mallery (404). Mooney (431).
133. Mallery (404).
134. *Ibid.*
135. Mooney (431).
136. McGee (416) p. 176.
137. Fletcher (271).
138. Mooney (431).
139. Wissler (593).
140. Spier (531).
141. Lowie (400).
142. Wissler (593) p. 135.
143. Fletcher (271) p. 342. Long (347) Pt. 1, pp. 312-13.
144. Fletcher (271) p. 557. Mallery (404) pp. 49-50; (405) p. 219-20. Maximilian (415) Pt. 2,
      p. 278.
145. Lewis (387) Vol. 2, p. 165.
146. Densmore (114) p. 173.
147. *Ibid.* p. 116.
148. Fletcher (271).
149. Lewis (387) Vol. 2, p. 362.
150. Mallery (404) p. 52.

379

151. Fletcher (271) p. 615.
152. Densmore (114) p. 116. Maximilian (415) Pt. 1, p. 99.
153. Mallery (404) p. 50.
154. Fletcher (271) pp. 353-54. Hodge (333) Pt. 2, pp. 185-86.
155. Mallery (404) p. 48.
156. Maximilian (415) Pt. 2.
157. Alexander (10) Vol. 1, p. 9.
158. Mallery (404, 405).
159. *Ibid.*
160. Fletcher (271) p. 611.
161. Jensen (352) p. 85.
162. *Ibid.*
163. Cronau (101, 102).
164. Stirling (550).
165. Blish (43).
166. Alexander (10) Vol. 2.
167. Blish (43) Vol. 1, pp. 10, 11.
168. *Ibid.* Vol. 2, p. 2.

Chapter 5. *THE EARLY MODERN PAINTERS*

1. Abert (1) p. 6.
2. Milwaukee Public Museum (426).
3. Mallery (404) Figs. 124-34.
4. *Ibid.* Fig. 128.
5. Mallery (405) p. 563.
6. *Ibid.* Pls. 39-48.
7. *Ibid.* Pl. 40.
8. *Ibid.* Pl. 48.
9. *Ibid.* p. 738.
10. *Ibid.* Pl. 53.
11. *Ibid.* p. 741.
12. Shufeldt (518) pp. 241-43.
13. *Ibid.* p. 244.
14. *Ibid.* p. 241.
15. Fewkes (251).
16. Sahagun (504).
17. Chavero (93).
18. Fewkes (251) p. 13.
19. *Ibid.* p. 13.
20. *Ibid.* p. 13.
21. *Ibid.* p. 14.
22. *Ibid.* p. 14.
23. *Ibid.* p. 14.
24. *Ibid.* p. 15.

25. *Ibid*. Pl. 25.
26. *Ibid*. Pl. 3.
27. *Ibid*. Pl. 50.
28. *Ibid*. Pl. 53.
29. *Ibid*. Pls. 16, 26, 31, 45.
30. *Ibid*. Pls. 32, 58.
31. *El Palacio* (219).
32. Spinden (534) p. 51.
33. *Ibid*.

Chapter 6. CRESCENCIO AND HIS FOLLOWERS

1. Hewett (313) p. 67.
2. *El Palacio* (197) cover; (181) cover and opp. p. 49.
3. Hewett (319) p. 126.
4. Hewett (313) p. 69.
5. Hewett (319).
6. De Huff, E. (110, 111).
7. *Ibid*. and *El Palacio* (185).
8. Hewett (317) pp. 144-45.
9. Hewett (313) p. 69.
10. Hewett (317) pp. 80-81.
11. *Ibid*. p. 85.
12. Spinden (534) p. 51.
13. Henderson (308).
14. *Ibid*.
15. *Ibid*.
16. *Ibid*.

Chapter 7. THE FOUNDING OF THE KIOWA SCHOOL

1. Jacobson (346) p. 8.
2. *Ibid*. p. 8.
3. *Ibid*.
4. Vaillant (570).
5. Nuttall (455).
6. Denman (113).

Chapter 8. THE SANTA FE MOVEMENT, 1919-1932

1. Austin (27) pp. 382, 385.
2. Blumenschein (46) pp. 178-79.
3. Curtis (103) p. 51.
4. De Huff, E. (111).

5. *El Palacio* (186).
6. *El Palacio* (184, 186).
7. Sterne (542).
8. Sloan (522).
9. Pach (461) pp. 343-44.
10. Pach (460) p. 58.
11. *El Palacio* (187).
12. *El Palacio* (188) p. 183.
13. *El Palacio* (190).
14. Adams (2).
15. Cahill (70) pp. 127, 130.
16. *El Palacio* (195).
17. *El Palacio* (196).
18. Hewett (314).
19. De Huff, J. (112).
20. Indian Arts Fund (344).
21. Henderson (307) p. 91.
22. Henderson (308).
23. *Ibid.*
24. *El Palacio* (201).
25. *El Palacio* (200).
26. *El Palacio* (203).
27. Denver Art Museum (116).
28. *El Palacio* (204) pp. 229-30.
29. *Ibid.* p. 230.
30. *El Palacio* (208).
31. Hogue (334) pp. 214-218.
32. *El Palacio* (206).
33. *El Palacio* (207) p. 310.
34. *El Palacio* (209).
35. *Ibid.*
36. *Brooklyn Museum Quarterly* (61).
37. Spinden (534) p. 49.
38. *Brooklyn Museum Quarterly* (61) p. 55.
39. *El Palacio* (211) p. 158.
40. *El Palacio* (212).
41. *El Palacio* (213) pp. 245-46.
42. Sloan (527).
43. *Ibid.* p. 56.
44. *Review of Reviews* (482) pp. 436, 443.
45. Sloan (527) p. 5.
46. *Art Digest* (18).
47. Sloan (525) p. 167.
48. Sloan (524) p. 243.
49. *New York Times* (451).
50. Oak (456) p. 389.

51. *Ibid.* p. 392-394.
52. Pach (462).
53. Berry (41) p. 152.
54. Spinden (535) p. 4.
55. Spinden (534) p. 49.
56. Spinden (537) p. 12.
57. Jewell (353).
58. Jewell (354).
59. Bauer (34) p. 191.
60. Barnard (33).
61. *Art Digest* (18) p. 32.
62. *Art News* (25).

Chapter 9.   THE SANTA FE MOVEMENT, 1932-1937

1. Meriam (423) p. 648.
2. *Ibid* p. 125.
3. Rush (498) p. 635.
4. Rush (496).
5. *Literary Digest* (396).
6. Austin (30) p. 381.
7. *Ibid.* p. 384.
8. *Art Digest* (19).
9. Rush (496, 501).
10. Rush (498) p. 638.
11. Hewett (317) p. 145.
12. Curtis (103) p. 65. Eastman (177) pp. 155-56.
13. Meriam (422) p. 256.
14. *El Palacio* (194) p. 124.
15. Rush (497).
16. Saenz (503).
17. Rush (500).
18. Addison Gallery (4).
19. Fletcher (271) p. 145.
20. Douglas (137).
21. Devree (119).
22. Nehakije (443).
23. Nehakije (444).
24. Kelemen (363).
25. Fassnacht (222).
26. Cantieni (72).
27. Tschudy (566).
28. Dunn (149).
29. Rush (502).
30. La Farge (383) p. 66.

Chapter 10. RECENT DEVELOPMENTS

1. D' Harnoncourt (108). Douglas (141).
2. Jewell (355).
3. *El Palacio* (202).
4. Frazier (275).
5. Pach (463) Chapt. 5.
6. Finley (270).
7. Portner (473).
8. Berryman (42).
9. Harrison (297).
10. Jewett (356).
11. Dunn (161, 162).
12. United States Information Agency (567).
13. Dunn (172).
14. Dunn (173).
15. Dunn (174).
16. Kabotie (361).
17. Edelson (178).

Chapter 11. A FUTURE FOR INDIAN PAINTING

1. Douglas (138).
2. Henderson (308) p. 19.
3. Hewett (317) p. 27.
4. Rush (501) p. 2.
5. Spinden (537) p. 12.
6. Pach (462).
7. Kluckhohn (372) p. 243.

References

ABBREVIATIONS

AA	American Anthropologist
AAAM	American Anthropological Association, Memoirs
AMAP	American Museum of Natural History, Anthropological Papers
BAEB	U.S. Bureau of American Ethnology, Bulletin
BAER	U.S. Bureau of American Ethnology, Annual Report
EP	El Palacio, Museum of New Mexico
IAIA	Introduction to American Indian Art, Exposition of Indian Tribal Arts, Inc.
IAW	Indians at Work, U.S. Department of the Interior
JAF	Journal of American Folk-Lore
MP	Medallion Papers, Gila Pueblo
NMAR	U.S. National Museum, Annual Report
NYT	New York Times
PMP	Peabody Museum of Archaeology and Ethnology, Harvard University, Papers
SAR	Smithsonian Institution, Annual Report
SMC	Smithsonian Institution, Miscellaneous Collections

REFERENCES

1. Abert, J. W. Journal of Lt. J. W. Abert from Bent's Fort to St. Louis. *U. S. Senate Documents*, 29th Congress, Vol. 8, No. 438, Washington, 1846.,
2. Adair, John. *The Navajo and Pueblo Silversmiths*. Norman: University of Oklahoma Press. 1944.
3. Adams, Corinne D. "Southwestern Art at Salt Lake City." *EP*, Vol. 11, No. 3, 1921, p. 36.

4. Addison Gallery of American Art. *Paintings and Pottery by Students of the Santa Fe Indian School*. Andover, Mass.: Phillips Academy, 1934. [Exhibition catalog.]

Albritton, Claude C. *See* Wendorf.

5. *Albuquerque Journal*. "Indian Artists are Exhibiting in Washington." Nov. 8, 1953, Art Sec.

6. Alexander, Hartley Burr. "North American Mythology." *The Mythology of All Races*. Vol. 10. Boston: Marshall, Jones Co., 1916.

7. ———. "The Art of the American Indian." *Nation*, Vol. 132, No. 3435, 1931, pp. 501-503.

8. ———. *Pueblo Indian Painting*. Nice: C. Szwedzicki, 1932. [Color plates.]

9. ———. "The Bad Heart Buffalo Manuscript." *Theatre Arts*, Vol. 16, No. 1, 1932, pp. 39-41.

10. ———. *Sioux Indian Painting*. 2 vols. Nice: C. Szwedzicki, 1938. [Color plates.]

11. *American Magazine of Art*. "Revival of Indian Art." Vol. 24, No. 5, 1932, p. 376.

12. Amsden, Charles Avery. *Navajo Weaving*. Santa Ana, Calif.: Fine Arts Press, 1934.

13. ———. "An Analysis of Hohokam Pottery Designs." *MP*, No. 23, 1936.

14. ———. *The Ancient Basketmakers*. Southwest Museum Leaflets, No. 11, Los Angeles, 1939.

15. ———. *Prehistoric Southwesterners from Basketmaker to Pueblo*. Los Angeles: Southwest Museum, 1949.

Antevs, Ernst. *See* Sayles (509).

16. *Antiquités Mexicaines*. "Le Manuscript du Cacique." Genève: Henri de Saussure, 1891.

17. *Art Digest*. "Great Tribal Exhibition Will Reveal Indians True Place in Art." Vol. 5, No. 20, 1931, pp. 5-6.

18. ———. "Indian Tribal Arts Exhibition Starts on Long Tour of Nation." Vol. 6, No. 6, 1931, p. 32.

19. ———. "Indian Artists Take Up Mural Painting." Vol. 7, No. 7, 1933, p. 32.

20. ———. "Truly Native." Vol. 10, No. 13, 1936, p. 26.

21. ———. "Amelia Elizabeth White Donates Her Collection of Indian Art to the People." Vol. 12, No. 10, 1938, p. 12.

22. ———. "New York Views Art of the Indian." Vol. 15, No. 10, 1941, pp. 11, 22.

23. Art Institute of Chicago. "Native Indian Art on Exhibition at Chicago Women's Club." *Weekly Newsletter*, Jan. 12, 1935, p. 2.

24. ———. "Paintings by Young Indians on Exhibition." *Weekly Newsletter*, Dec. 7, 1935, p. 2.

25. *Art News*. "Indian Art." Vol. 30, No. 36, 1932, p. 12.

26. ———. "Newark: Paintings by Indians." Vol. 36, No. 17, 1938, p. 20.

27. Austin, Mary. "Indian Arts for Indians." *Survey Graphic*, Vol. 60, No. 7, 1928, pp. 381-88.

28. ———. "Why Americanize the Indian?" *Forum*, Vol. 82, No. 3, 1929, pp. 167-73.

29. ———. "Indian Poetry." *IAIA*. Pt. 2, New York, 1931.

30. ———. "American Indian Murals." *American Magazine of Art*, Vol. 26, No. 8, 1933, pp. 380-84.

31. Ball, Sydney H. "The Mining of Gems and Ornamental Stones by American Indians." *BAEB*, No. 128, 1941.

32. Bandelier, Adolph F. A. "Final Report of Investigations among the Indians of the Southwestern United States 1880-1885." *Archaeological Institute of America, Papers*. American Series 3, Cambridge, Pt. 1, 1890; Pt. 2, 1892.

33. Barnard, Eunice Fuller. "Indian Art Comes into its Own." *NYT*, No. 29, 1931, Sec. 5, pp. 12-13.

34. Bauer, Catherine K. "Indian Tribal Arts." *New Republic*, Vol. 69, No. 891, 1931, pp. 191-92.

35. Baumann, Gustave. *Frijoles Canyon Pictographs*. Foreword by A. V. Kidder. Santa Fe: Writers Editions, Inc., 1939.

36. Beckwith, Frank. "Some Interesting Pictographs in Nine Mile Canyon, Utah." *EP*, Vol. 31, No. 14, 1931, pp. 216-22.

37. ———. "Indian Rock Pictures in Utah." *EP*, Vol. 31, Nos. 22-23, 1931, pp. 361-68.

38. ———. "Serpent Petroglyphs in Nine Mile Canyon." *EP*, Vol. 33, Nos. 15-16, 1932, pp. 147-49.

39. ———. "Ancient Indian Petroglyphs of Utah." *EP*, Vol. 38, Nos. 6-8, 1935, pp. 33-40.

40. Benavides, Fray Alonso de. *Memorial of 1630*. Trans. by Mrs. Edward E. Ayer. Chicago: Privately printed, 1916.

41. Berry, Rose V. S. "American Inter-Tribal Indian Art," *Art and Archaeology*, Vol. 32, Nos. 5-6, 1931, pp. 147 & 159ff.

42. Berryman, Florence S. "News of Artists and Exhibitions." *Star*, Washington, Nov. 8, 1953, p. E-6.

43. Blish, Helen H. *The Amos Bad Heart Buffalo Manuscript*. 3 vols. Typescript in American Museum of Natural History, New York. n.d.

44. ———. "The Drama of the Sioux Sun Dance." *Theatre Arts*, Vol. 17, No. 8, 1933, pp. 629-34.

45. Bliss, Wesley L. "Preservation of the Kuaua Mural Paintings." *American Antiquity*, Vol. 13, No. 3, 1948, pp. 218-23.

46. Blumenschein, E. L., and B. G. Phillips. "Appreciation of Indian Art." *EP*, Vol. 6, No. 12, 1919, pp. 178-79.

47. Boas, Franz. "The Mind of Primitive Man." *JAF*, Vol. 14, No. 52, 1901 pp. 1-11.

387

48. ———. "The Decorative Art of the North American Indians." *Popular Science*, Vol. 63, 1903, pp. 481-98.

49. ———. *Primitive Art*. Serie B: Skrifter 8. Oslo, Instituttet for Sammenlignende Kulturforskning, 1927.

50. Bodmer, Charles. "Atlas." *Early Western Travels*, Vol. 25, Cleveland: A. H. Clark Co., 1906. [Series of paintings illus. Maximilian, Prince of Wied's "Travels in the Interior of N.A., 1832-34."]

51. Bolton, Herbert Eugene. *Spanish Exploration in the Southwest*. New York: Scribners, 1916.

52. Boswell, Peyton. "In Character: A Tribute to Miss Amelia Elizabeth White's Encouragement of Indian Art." *Art Digest*, Vol. 12, No. 10, 1938, p. 3.

53. Bourke, Capt. John G. "Medicine Men of the Apache." *BAER*, No. 9, 1892, pp. 443-603.

54. Brackenridge, H. M. "Journal of a Voyage up the River Missouri, 1811." *Early Western Travels*, Vol. 6, Pt. 1. Ed. by R. G. Thwaites. Cleveland: Arthur H. Clark Co., 1904, pp. 9-166.

55. Bradbury, John. "Travels in the Interior of America, 1809-1811." *Early Western Travels*, Vol. 5, Ed. by R. B. Thwaites. Cleveland: Arthur H. Clark Co., 1904.

56. Bradfield, Wesley. *Cameron Creek Village*. Santa Fe: School of American Research, 1931.

57. Bramlett, William. "Following an Ancient Indian Trail." *IAW*, Vol. 3, No. 15, 1936, pp. 39-44 [illus.].

58. Brew, J. O. "The First Two Seasons at Awatovi." *American Antiquity*, Vol. 3, No. 2, 1937, pp. 122-37.

59. ———. "Preliminary Report of the Peabody Museum Awatovi Expedition of 1939." *Plateau*, Vol. 13, No. 3, 1939.

60. ———. *See* Smith.

61. *Brooklyn Museum Quarterly*. "American Indian Drawings." Vol. 17, No. 2, 1930, pp. 55-56.

62. Brown, Milton. "The Indian Discovered." *Parnassus*, Vol. 13, No. 3, 1941, pp. 123-25.

63. Bryan, Kirk, and Louis L. Ray. "Geologic Antiquity of the Lindenmeier Site." *SMC*, Vol. 99, No. 2, 1940.

64. Bunzel, Ruth L. "Zuni Katcinas." *BAER*, No. 47. 1932, pp. 837-1086.

65. Burpee, Lawrence J. (ed.) *Journals and Letters of Pierre Gaultier de Varennes de La Verendrye and His Sons*. 1733-34, Toronto: The Champlain Society, 1927.

66. Bushnell, David I. "Native Villages and Village Sites East of the Mississippi." *BAEB*, No. 69, 1919.

67. ———. "Villages of the Algonquian, Siouan, and Caddoan Tribes West of the Mississippi." *BAEB*, No. 77, 1922.

68. ———. "Virginia Before Jamestown." *SMC*, Vol. 100, 1940, pp. 125-58.

69. Bynner, Witter. *Indian Earth*. New York: Alfred A. Knopf, 1930.

70. Cahill, E. H. "America Has Its Primitives." *International Studio*, Vol. 75, No. 299, 1922, pp. 80-83.

71. Caldwell, Joseph R. *Trend and Tradition in the Prehistory of the Eastern United States*. AAAM No. 88. Illinois State Museum Scientific Papers, Vol. 10, Springfield, 1958.

Campbell, Joseph. *See* Oakes.

72. Cantieni, Joseph F. Letter to Dorothy Dunn. Berea College, Berea, Kentucky, April 7, 1937.

73. Carter, John G. "The Northern Arapaho Flat Pipe and the Ceremony of Covering the Pipe." *BAEB*, No. 119, 1938, pp. 69-102.

74. Cassidy, Ina Sizer. "Indian Artists." *New Mexico*, Vol. 16, No. 11, 1938, pp. 22ff.

75. Catlin, George. *Illustrations of the Manners, Customs, and Condition of the North American Indians*. Vols. 1 and 2, 8th ed. London: H. G. Bohn, 1851.

76. Cecchi, Emilio. "Disegni Indiani." *Dedalo*, Anno 12, Milano-Roma, 1932 pp. 563-73.

77. Chapman, Kenneth M. "Graphic Arts of the Cave Dwellers." *EP*, Vol. 3, No. 2, 1916, pp. 37-41.

78. ———. "The Evolution of the Bird in Decorative Art." *Art and Archaeology*, Vol. 4, No. 6, 1916, pp. 307-16.

79. ———. "The Cave Pictographs of the Rito de los Frijoles, New Mexico." *EP*, Vol. 4, No. 1, 1917, pp. 29-31.

80. ———. "What the Potsherds Tell." *Art and Archaeology*, Vol. 11, Nos. 1 and 2, 1921, pp. 39-44.

81. ———. "Life Forms in Pueblo Pottery Decoration." *Art and Archaeology*, Vol. 13, No. 3, 1922, pp. 120-22.

82. ———. "The Indian Fair." *Art and Archaeology*, Vol. 18, No. 5-6, 1924, pp. 215-24.

83. ———. "A Feather Symbol of the Ancient Pueblos." *EP*, Vol. 23, No. 21, 1927, pp. 526-40.

84. ———. "Post-Spanish Pueblo Pottery." *Art and Archaeology*, Vol. 23, No. 5, 1927, pp. 207-13.

85. ———. "Bird Forms on Zuni Pottery." *EP*, Vol. 24, No. 2, 1928, pp. 23-25.

86. ———. "Indian Pottery." *IAIA*. Pt. 2. New York, 1931.

87. ———. "America's Most Ancient Art." *School Arts*, Vol. 30, No. 7, 1931, pp. 387-402.

88. ———. "Decorative Arts of the Indians of the Southwest." *Laboratory of Anthropology, General Series*, Bull. No. 1, 2nd rev., Santa Fe, 1934. [82 items, mimeo.]

89. ———. "Ancient Pottery of the Pueblos." *IAW*, Contemporary Arts and Crafts Number. 1936, pp. 24-27.

90. ———. *Pueblo Indian Pottery.* 2 vols. Nice: C. Szwedzicki, 1936, 100 plates.

91. ———. "The Pottery of Santo Domingo Pueblo." *Memoirs of the Laboratory of Anthropology*, Vol. 1, Santa Fe, 1936.

92. ———. "The Cave Pictographs of the Rito de los Frijoles." Appendix 1 to *Pajarito Plateau and its Ancient People.* Albuquerque: University of New Mexico Press, 1938.

93. Chavero, Alfredo (ed.) *Lienzo de Tlaxcalla.* Mexico: Oficina Tipografica de la Secretaria de Fomento, 1892.

Clark, William. *See* Lewis.

94. Collier, John. "Does the Government Welcome the Indian Arts?" *American Magazine of Art*, Vol. 27, No. 9, Pt. 2, 1934, pp. 10-11.

95. Colton, Harold S. *Hopi Kachina Dolls.* rev. ed., Albuquerque: University of New Mexico Press, 1959.

96. *Connoisseur.* "Exposition of Indian Tribal Arts." Vol. 88, No. 361, 1931, pp. 209-10.

97. Cosgrove, H. S. and C. B. *The Swarts Ruin: Report of the Mimbres Valley Expedition, 1924-1927.* PMP, Vol. 15, No. 1. Cambridge, Mass., 1932.

98. Coze, Paul. "L'Art Sauvera-t-il, les Peaux-Rouges?" *A B C Magazine*, Onzieme Année, No. 127, Paris, 1935, pp. 174-77.

99. ———. "Les Indiens Peints par Eux-Mêmes." *L'Illustration*, 94 Année, No. 4861, Paris, 1936.

100. Cressman, L. S. *Archaeological Researches in the Northern Great Basin.* Carnegie Institution of Washington Publications, No. 538, Washington, 1942.

101. Cronau, Rudolf. *Im Wilden Westen:* Eine Künstlerfahrt durch die Prairien und Felsengebirge der Union. Leipzig: Braunschweig, 1890.

102. ———. *Amerika.* 2 vols. Leipzig: Derlag von Ubel und Müller, 1892.

103. Curtis, Natalie. "Our Native Craftsmen." *EP*, Vol. 7, No. 3, 1919, pp. 51-53.

104. ———. "An American Indian Artist." *Outlook*, Vol. 124, No. 1, 1920, pp. 64-66.

105. Cushing, Frank H. "A Study of Pueblo Pottery as Illustrative of Zuni Culture Growth." *BAER*, No. 4, 1886, pp. 467-521.

106. ———. "Outlines of Zuni Creation Myths." *BAER*, No. 13, 1896, pp. 321-447.

107. Dall, W. H. "Masks, Labrets, and Certain Aboriginal Customs." *BAER*, No. 3, 1884, pp. 67-203.

108. D'Harnoncourt, Rene. "Living Arts of the Indians." *American Magazine of Art*, Vol. 34, No. 2, 1941, pp. 72-77.

109. ———. "Indian Art of the Hemisphere." *American Indian*, Vol. 1, No. 2, pt. 1 and No. 3, pt. 2, 1944.
———. *See* Douglas (141).

110. DeHuff, Elizabeth Willis. Letter to Mrs. Charles H. Dietrich. Augusta, Georgia, Sept. 13, 1951.

111. ———. Letter to Dorothy Dunn Kramer. Augusta, Georgia, June 6, 1963.

112. DeHuff, J. D. "How Shall We Educate the Indians?" *EP*, Vol. 13, No. 5, 1922, p. 62.

113. Denman, Leslie Van Ness. *Peyote Ritual*. San Francisco: Privately printed by the Grabhorn Press, 1957. [Paintings and description by Tsa Toke.]

114. Densmore, Frances. "Teton Sioux Music." *BAEB*, No. 61, 1918.

115. ———. *Music of Santo Domingo Pueblo, New Mexico*. Southwest Museum Papers, No. 12, Los Angeles, 1938.

116. Denver Art Museum. *Indian Leaflet Series*. 1930-35, 64 compilations.

117. ———. *Indian Design Series*, Vols. 1, pls. 1-24; 2, pls. 25-130, 1934.

118. ———. *The Native Artist and His World*. 1948. [Exhibition catalog.]

119. Devree, Howard. "American Indians." *NYT*, March 29, 1936, Sec. 9, p. 9.

120. ———. "American Art." Address at Festival of Contemporary Arts, University of Illinois, recorded by Radio Station WILL, Urbana, March 6, 1948.

121. Dickey, Roland. "The Potters of the Mimbres Valley." *New Mexico Quarterly*, Vol. 27, Nos. 1-2, 1957, pp. 36-51 and supp. illus.

122. Dietrich, Margretta S. "Their Culture Survives." *New Mexico*, Vol. 14, No. 2, 1936, pp. 22-23, 45ff.

123. ———. *Modern Masterpieces of American Indian Art*. Santa Fe: Laboratory of Anthropology, n.d. Serigraphs by Louie H. Ewing. [Text for paintings only.]

124. Dittert, Alfred E., Jr., Jim J. Hester, and Frank Eddy. *An Archaeological Survey of the Navajo Reservoir District, Northwestern New Mexico*. Monographs of the School of American Research and the Museum of New Mexico, No. 23, Santa Fe, 1961.

125. Dixon, Roland B. "The Color Symbolism of the Cardinal Points." *JAF* Vol. 12, No. 44, 1899, pp. 10-16.

126. ———. *The Building of Cultures*. New York: Chas. Scribner's Sons, 1928.
———. *See* Swanton (564).

127. Dorsey, George A. *The Arapaho Sun Dance: the Ceremony of the Offerings Lodge*. Field Columbian Museum, Anthropological Series, Vol. 4, No. 75, Chicago. 1903.

128. ———. *The Cheyenne*. Field Columbian Museum, Anthropological Series, Vols. 9 and 10, No. 9, Chicago, 1905.
———. *See* Kroeber (380).

129. Dorsey, George A. and H. R. Voth. *The Oraibi Soyal Ceremony*. Field Columbian Museum, Anthropological Series, Vol. 3, No. 1, Chicago, 1901.

130. ———. *The Mishongnovi Ceremonies of the Snake and Antelope Fraternities*. Field Columbian Museum, Anthropological Series, Vol. 3, No. 3, Chicago, 1902.

131. Dorsey, James Owen. "Omaha Sociology." *BAER* No. 3, 1884, pp. 205-370.

132. ———. "A Study of Siouan Cults." *BAER*, No. 11, 1894, pp. 351-544.

133. ———. "Omaha Dwellings, Furniture, and Implements." *BAER*, No. 13, 1896, pp. 263-88.

134. ———. "Siouan Sociology." *BAER*, No. 15, 1897, pp. 205-44.

135. Douglas, Frederick H. "Indian Isms." *Art Digest*, Vol. 7, No. 19, 1933, p. 11.

136. ———. "Circular Designs in Indian Art." *School Arts*, Vol. 34, No. 7, 1935, pp. 397-400ff.

137. ———. "Denver Art Museum Curator Reviews Indian Exhibit at Museum." *Santa Fe New Mexican*, May 4, 1935, p. 3. [Reprinted in El Palacio, Vol. 38, Nos. 24-26, pp. 129-132.]

138. ———. "Indian Art and American Art." *Western Artist*, Vol. 1, No. 8, 1935, p. 3.

139. ———. "Indian Art as a Basis for American Art." *Bulletin, American Library Association*, Vol. 29, No. 9, 1935, pp. 575-78.

140. ———. "Indian Art in the Southwest." *Design*, Vol. 43, No. 8, 1942, pp. 12-13.

141. ———. and Rene d'Harnoncourt. *Indian Art of the United States*. New York: Museum of Modern Art, 1941.

142. Douglass, A. E. "The Secret of the Southwest Solved by Talkative Tree Rings." *National Geographic*, Vol. 56, No. 6, 1929, pp. 737-70.

143. Dunn, Dorothy. "A Development of the Representation of the Sciences in Abstract Indian Design." *IAW*, Vol. 1, No. 21, 1934, pp. 24-30.

144. ———. *Earth Colors*. U. S. Indian School, Santa Fe, 1934, 6 pp., mimeographed.

145. ———. "Indian Art in the Schools." *IAW*, Vol. 3, No. 1, 1935, pp. 20-21.

146. ———. "Indian Children Carry Forward Old Traditions." *School Arts*, Vol. 34, No. 7, 1935, pp. 426-35.

147. ———. "The Julius Rosenwald Fund Murals." *IAW*, Vol. 3, No. 14, 1936, pp. 26-27 and frontis.

148. ———. "Pueblo Indian Painting." *IAW*, Contemporary Arts and Crafts Number, 1936, pp. 30-31.

149. ———. "Show by Ha-oz-ous, Apache Indian, at Art Museum is Recommended by Reviewer." *Santa Fe New Mexican*, March 18, 1937, p. 2.

150. ———. "Art Work, Santa Fe Indian School, Santa Fe, New Mexico." *Art Education Today*. New York: Columbia University, 1937, pp. 51-53.

151. ———. "Artists of Taos Pueblo." Series in *Taoseno*, Vol. 2, Nos. 19, p. 1; 22, p. 1; 23, p. 4; 24, p. 4; 25, p. 4, Taos, N. M., 1941.

152. ———. "Indian Painting Can Progress." *EP*, Vol. 57, No. 4, 1950, pp. 99-108.

153. ———. "The Development of Modern American Indian Painting in the Southwest and Plains Areas." *EP*, Vol. 58, No. 11, 1951, pp. 331-53. [Summary of paper, AAA Conv., El Paso, 1951.]

154. ———. "Pablita Velarde: Painter of Pueblo life." *EP*, Vol. 59, No. 1, 1952, pp. 335-41.

155. ———. "Nehakije: Apache Artist." *EP*, Vol. 59, No. 3, 1952, pp. 71-76.

156. ———. "The Art of Joe Herrera." *EP*, Vol. 59, No. 12, 1952, pp. 367-73.

157. ———. *Contemporary American Indian Painting*. Washington: National Gallery of Art, 1953. [Exhibition catalog.]

158. ———. "America's First Painters." *National Geographic*, Vol. 107, No. 3, 1955, pp. 349-77. 18 color plates.

159. ———. "Contemporary Indian Painters." *Indians of the Americas*. Washington: National Geographic Society, 1955, pp. 397-408.

160. ———. "Opportunities for the Indian Painter." *Smoke Signals*, No. 14, U. S. Indian Arts and Crafts Board, Washington, Feb., 1955, pp. 1-4.

161. ———. *Pittura Contemporanea degli Indiani d'America*. Catologo della Mostra. Roma: Auspici del' U. S. Information Service, 1955.

162. ———. *Peinture Indienne Americaine Contemporaine*. Bruxelles: Musées Royaux d'Art et Histoire, 1955. [Exhibition catalog.]

163. ———. "Indian Art is Ours." *Ceremonial*, Inter-Tribal Ceremonial Association, Gallup, N. M., Aug. 11-14, 1955, pp. 25-34.

164. ———. "Awa Tsireh: Painter of San Ildefonso." *EP*, Vol. 63, No. 4, 1956, pp. 108-15.

165. ———. *Contemporary Indian Painting*. Santa Fe: Museum of New Mexico, 1957. [Exhibition catalog.]

166. ———. "Oscar Howe: Sioux Artist." *EP*, Vol. 64, Nos. 5-6, 1957, pp. 167-73.

167. ———. "The Art of Pablita Velarde." *EP*, Vol. 64, Nos. 7-8, 1957, pp. 231-32.

168. ———. "Of Time, Quality, and Southwest Indian Painting." *Quarterly Bulletin*, Roswell [N. M.] Museum and Art Center, Vol. 5, No. 4, 1957.

169. ———. "Guidance and Evaluation of the Indian Artist." Paper presented at conference on Indian Art, University of Arizona, Tucson, March 21, 1959.

170. ———. "The Studio of Painting, Santa Fe Indian School." *EP*, Vol. 67, No. 1, 1960, pp. 16-27.

171. ———. *Contemporary Indian Art Annual*. Santa Fe: Museum of New Mexico, 1961. [Exhibition catalog.]

172. ———. *Paintings by American Indians*. William and Leslie Van Ness Denman Collection. San Francisco: California Palace of the Legion of Honor, 1962. [Exhibition catalog.]

173. ———. *Indian Paintings from the Margretta S. Dietrich Collection*. Santa Fe: Museum of New Mexico, 1962. [Exhibition catalog.]

393

174. ———. *Contemporary American Indian Paintings from the Margretta S. Dietrich Collection*. Washington: U. S. Information Agency, 1963. [Exhibition catalog, will be translated into language of each exhibiting country.]

175. Durán, Fray Diego. *Historia de las Indias de Nueva España*. 2 vols. and atlas of facsimiles. Mexico: J. M. Andrade y F. Escalante, 1867 and 1880.

176. Dutton, Bertha P. *New Mexico Indians Pocket Handbook*. Santa Fe: New Mexico Association on Indian Affairs, 1961.
———. *See* Hewett (322).
———. *See* footnote p. 75.

177. Eastman, Charles A. *The Indian Today*. New York: Doubleday & Co., 1915.
Eddy, Frank W. *See* Dittert (124).

178. Edelson, Elihu. "Sarasota Art." *News*, Sarasota, Florida, Oct. 1, 1961, p. 6.

179. Ekholm, Gordon F. "The Archaeology of Northern and Western Mexico." *The Maya and Their Neighbors*, New York: D. Appleton-Century Co., 1940, pp. 320-30.

180. ———. Excavations at Guasave, Sinaloa, Mexico. *AMAP*, Vol. 38, Part 2, 1942.

181. *El Palacio*. Crescencio Martinez. [Photographs of artist.] Vol. 4, No. 1, 1917, cover and opp. p. 49.

182. ———. Jemez Murals. Illus. by A. B. Reagan. Vol. 4, No. 2, 1917, pp. 46, 48, 50, 52, 54, 56.

183. ———. "This Year's Work at Otowi." Vol. 4, No. 4, 1917, p. 4a.

184. ———. "Art of Crescencio Martinez." Vol. 5, No. 4, 1918, p. 59.

185. ———. "Exhibit by Indian Pupils." Vol. 6, No. 9, 1919, pp. 142-43.

186. ———. "More Tewa Paintings." Vol. 6, No. 13, 1919, p. 215.

187. ———. "Exhibit of Indian Paintings." Vol. 8, Nos. 5-6, 1920, p. 125.

188. ———. "Indian Artists Honored." Vol. 8, Nos. 7-8, 1920, pp. 182-83.

189. ———. "Indian Drawings on Exhibit." Vol. 8, Nos. 7-8, 1920, pp. 216-17.

190. ———. "Paintings by Indians." Vol. 10, Nos. 13-14, 1921, p. 23.

191. ———. Jemez Murals. Illus. by A. B. Reagan. Vol. 12, No. 2, 1922, pp. 17, 19, 20-23.

192. ———. "Prizes for Indian Handicraft." Vol. 12, No. 6, 1922, p. 81.

193. ———. "The Independent Show." Vol. 12, No. 8, 1922, p. 109-10.

194. ———. "First Annual Exhibition of Indian Arts." Vol. 12, No. 9, 1922, p. 123-24.

195. ———. "The Southwest Indian Fair." Vol. 13, No. 8, 1922, pp. 93-97.

196. ———. "Indian Shop in New York." [Amelia Elizabeth White's American Indian Gallery.] Vol. 13, No. 12, 1922, p. 160.

197. ———. Crescencio Martinez. [Photograph of the artist.] Vol. 15, No. 7, 1923, cover.

198. ———. Paintings by Velino Shije. Vol. 16, No. 5, 1924, cover, and pp. 70-71.

199. ———. "Mimbres Ruins, Excavated by Bradfield, Give Clues to Ancient Basket Makers." Vol. 16, No. 10, 1924, pp. 153-4.

200. ———. "Awa Tsireh at Chicago." Vol. 19, No. 10, 1925, p. 218.

201. ———. "Elite Expected for Indian Art." Vol. 19, No. 11, 1925, pp. 232-33.

202. ———. "Olive Rush." Vol. 19, No. 11, 1925, pp. 233-34. [Reprint from Chicago Daily News.]

203. ———. "Indian Art Exhibition." Vol. 22, No. 7, 1927, pp. 153-54.

204. ———. "Indian Artists in New York." Vol. 22, No. 11, 1927, pp. 229-30.

205. ———. "The Indian Fair." Vol. 23, No. 13, 1927, pp. 343-46.

206. ———. "Indian Paintings at Roswell." Vol. 24, Nos. 7-8, 1928, pp. 131-32.

207. ———. "Indian Defense Association Exhibit." Vol. 25, No. 19, 1928, pp. 309-10. [Reprint from *San Francisco Chronicle*.]

208. ———. "Anthropological Laboratory at Santa Fe." Vol. 26, No. 1, 1929, pp. 4-6.

209. ———. "Pueblo Art in Spain." Vol. 26, No. 6-7, 1929, pp. 120-21.

210. ———. "Hall of Indian Arts." Vol. 29, No. 14-15, 1930, pp. 260-65.

211. ———. "Oqwa Pi in Milwaukee." Vol. 30, No. 10, 1931, p. 157-59.

212. ———. "Dedication of Laboratory of Anthropology." Vol. 31, No. 9, 1931, pp. 137-44.

213. ———. "Exhibit of Tribal Arts." Vol. 31, No. 15, 1931, pp. 244-46.

214. ———. "Pueblo Art Display." [Wo-Peen]. Vol. 34, Nos. 21-22, 1933, pp. 169-70.

215. ———. "Pueblo Painters." Vol. 35, Nos. 3-4, 1933, pp. 27-28.

216. ———. "Successful Indian School Show." Vol. 40, No. 22-24, 1936, pp. 22-24.

217. ———. "Many Mural Paintings at Awatovi." Vol. 43, No. 7-9, 1938, pp. 52-53.

218. ———. "Annual Indian School Exhibit." Vol. 46, No. 5, 1939, pp. 112-15.

219. ———. "Historic Indian Paintings." Vol. 48, No. 11, 1941, p. 259.

220. Ewers, John Canfield. *Plains Indian Painting*. Palo Alto: Stanford University Press, 1939.

221. Farmer, Malcolm F. "Navajo Archaeology of the Upper Blanco and Largo Canyons, Northern New Mexico." *American Antiquity*, Vol. 8, No. 1, 1942, pp. 65-79.

222. Fassnacht, Annette. "Exhibition Shows How Indian Artist Profits by Contact with Ancient, Modern Art." *Santa Fe New Mexican*, May 9, 1936, p. 3.

223. Fewkes, Jesse Walter. "A Few Summer Ceremonials at Zuni Pueblo." *Journal of American Ethnology and Archaeology*, Vol. 1, Part 1, 1891.

224. ———. "A Suggestion as to the Meaning of the Moki Snake Dance." *JAF*, Vol. 4, No. 13, 1891, pp. 129-38.

225. ———. "A Few Tusayan Pictographs." *AA*, o.s., Vol. 5, No. 1, 1892, pp. 9-26.

226. ———. "The Ceremonial Circuit Among the Village Indians of Northeastern Arizona." JAF, Vol. 5, No. 16, 1892, pp. 33-42.

227. ———. "A Few Summer Ceremonials at the Tusayan Pueblos." *Journal of American Ethnology and Archaeology*, Vol. 2, Part 1, 1892.

228. ———. "A Central American Ceremony Which Suggests the Snake Dance of the Tusayan Villagers." *AA*, o.s., Vol. 6, No. 3, 1893, pp. 285-306.

229. ———. "Awatobi." *AA*, o.s., Vol. 6, No. 4, 1893, pp. 363-75.

230. ———. "The Walpi Flute Observance: A Study of Primitive Dramatization." *JAF*, Vol. 7, No. 27, 1894, pp. 265-87ff.

231. ———. "On Certain Personages Who Appear in a Tusayan Ceremony." *AA*, o.s., Vol. 7, No. 1, 1894, pp. 32-52.

232. ———. "A Comparison of Sia and Tusayan Snake Ceremonials." *AA*, o.s., Vol. 8, No. 2, 1895, pp. 118-41.

233. ———. "The Oraibi Flute Altar." *JAF*, Vol. 8, No. 31, 1895, pp. 265-82.

234. ———. "Preliminary Account of an Expedition to the Cliff Villages of the Red Rock Country, and the Tusayan Ruins of Sikyatki and Awatobi, Arizona in 1895." *SAR, 1895.* 1896, pp. 557-88ff.

235. ———. "The Tusayan Ritual: A Study of the Influence of Environment on Aboriginal Cults." *SAR, 1895.* 1896, pp. 683-700.

236. ———. "The Prehistoric Culture of Tusayan." *AA*, o.s., Vol. 9, No. 5, 1896, pp. 151-73.

237. ———. "The Miconinovi Flute Altars." *JAF*, Vol. 9, No. 35, 1896, pp. 241-55ff.

238. ———. "Tusayan Katcinas," *BAER*, No. 15, 1897, pp. 245-313.

239. ———. "Tusayan Snake Ceremonies." *BAER*, No. 16, 1897, pp. 267-312.

240. ———. "Morphology of Tusayan Altars." *AA*, Vol. 10, No. 5, 1897, pp. 129-45.

241. ———. "The Growth of the Hopi Ritual." *JAF*, Vol. 11, No. 42, 1898, pp. 173-94.

242. ———. "Archaeological Expedition to Arizona in 1895." *BAER*, No. 17, pt. 2, 1898, pp. 519-744.

243-. ———. "Preliminary Account of an Expedition to the Pueblo Ruins near Winslow, Arizona in 1896." *SAR, 1896.* 1898, pp. 517-38.

244. ———. "Hopi Basket Dances." *JAF*, Vol. 12, No. 45, 1899, pp. 81-96.

245. ———. "Tusayan Migration Traditions." *BAER*, No. 19, pt. 1, 1900, pp. 573-633.

246. ———. "Tusayan Flute and Snake Ceremonials." *BAER*, No. 19, pt. 2, 1900, pp. 957-1011.

247. ———. "An Interpretation of Katcina Worship." *JAF*, Vol. 14, No. 53, 1901, pp. 81-94.

248. ———. "The Owakulti Altar at Sichomori Pueblo." *AA*, Vol. 3, No. 2, 1901, pp. 211-26.

249. ———. "The Lesser New-Fire Ceremony at Walpi." *AA*, Vol. 3, No. 3, 1901, pp. 438-53.

250. ———. "Sky-God Personations in Hopi Worship." *JAF*, Vol. 15, No. 56, 1902, pp. 14-32.

251. ———. "Hopi Katcinas, Drawn by Native Artists." *BAER*, No. 21, 1903, pp. 3-126.

252. ———. "Two Summers' Work in Pueblo Ruins." *BAER*, No. 22, pt. 1, 1904, pp. 3-195.

253. ———. "Antiquities of the Mesa Verde National Park: Spruce Tree House." *BAEB*, No. 41, 1909.

254. ———. "The Butterfly in Hopi Myth and Ritual." *AA*, Vol. 12, No. 4, 1910, pp. 576-94.

255. ———. "Preliminary Report on a Visit to the Navajo National Monument, Arizona." *BAEB*, No. 50, 1911.

256. ———. "Antiquities of the Mesa Verde National Park: Cliff Palace." *BAEB* No. 51, 1911.

257. ———. "Archaeology of the Lower Mimbres Valley, N. M." *SMC*, Vol. 63, No. 10, 1914, pp. 1-53.

258. ———. "Animal Figures on Prehistoric Pottery from the Mimbres Valley, N. M." *AA*, Vol. 18, No. 4, 1916, pp. 535-45.

259. ———. "Prehistoric Villages, Castles, and Towers of Southwestern Colorado." *BAEB*, No. 70, 1919.

260. ———. "Designs on Prehistoric Hopi Pottery." *BAER*, No. 33, 1919, pp. 207-84.

261. ———. "Designs on Prehistoric Pottery from the Mimbres Valley, N. M." *SMC*, Vol. 74, No. 6, 1923.

262. ———. "Additional Designs on Prehistoric Mimbres Pottery." *SMC*, Vol. 76, No. 8, 1924.

263. ———, and J. G. Owens. "The Lalakonta: A Tusayan Dance." *AA*, o.s., Vol. 5, No. 2, 1892, pp. 105-29.

264. ———, J. G. Owens, and A. M. Stephen. "The Snake Ceremonials at Walpi." *Journal of American Ethnology and Archaeology*, Vol. 4, 1894, pp. 1-126.

265. ———, and A. M. Stephen. "The Mamzrauti: A Tusayan Ceremony." *AA*, o.s., Vol. 5, No. 3, 1892, pp. 217-45.

266. ———. "The Na-ac-nai-ya: A Tusayan Initiation Ceremony." *JAF*, Vol. 5, No. 18, 1892, pp. 189-221.

267. ———. "The Pa-lu-lu-kon-ti: A Tusayan Ceremony." *JAF*, Vol. 6, No. 23, 1893, pp. 269-84.

268. Figgins, J. D. "The Antiquity of Man in America." *Natural History*, Vol. 27, No. 3, 1927, pp. 229-39.

269. ———. "A Further Contribution to the Antiquity of Man in America." *Proceedings of the Colorado Museum of Natural History*, Vol. 12, No. 2, Denver, 1933.

270. Finley, David E. (Foreword). *Contemporary American Indian Painting.* Washington: National Gallery of Art, 1953. [Exhibition catalog.]

Fishler, Stanley. *See* Newcomb (448).

271. Fletcher, Alice C., and Francis LaFlesche. "The Omaha Tribe." *BAER*, No. 27, 1911, pp. 15-654.

272. Flint, Ralph. "Tribal Arts of the Indian Now on Exhibition." *Art News*, Vol. 30, No. 10, 1931, pp. 5-8.

273. Ford, J. A., and Gordon R. Willey. "An Interpretation of the Prehistory of the Eastern United States." *AA*, Vol. 43, No. 3, pt. 1, 1941, pp. 325-63.

274. Fowke, Gerard. "Archaeological Investigations." *BAEB*, No. 76, 1922.

275. Frazier, Bernard. *Philbrook Art Center.* Tulsa: Philbrook Art Center, n.d.

276. Frederick, M. C. "Some Indian Paintings." *Land of Sunshine*, Vol. 15, No. 4, 1901, pp. 223-27.

277. Gilpin, Laura. *The Pueblos.* New York: Hastings House, 1941.

278. Gladwin, Harold S. "Excavations at Snaketown II: Comparisons and Theories." *MP*, No. 26, 1937.

279. ———. "Excavations at Snaketown III: Revisions." *MP*, No. 30, 1942.

280. ———. et al. "Excavations at Snaketown I: Material Culture." *MP*, No. 25, 1937.

281. Goddard, Pliny Earle. *Indians of the Southwest.* 3rd ed. Handbook Series No. 1. New York: American Museum Natural History, 1934.

282. Goodwin, Grenville. "White Mountain Apache Religion." *AA*, Vol. 40, No. 1, 1938, pp. 24-37.

283. Griffin, James B. "The Archeological Remains of the Chiwere Sioux." *American Antiquity*, Vol. 2, No. 3, 1937, pp. 180-81.

284. ——— ed. *Archeology of the Eastern United States.* Chicago: Univ. of Chicago Press, 1952.

285. Grinnell, George Bird. "Coup and Scalp Among the Plains Indians." *AA*, Vol. 12, No. 2, 1910, pp. 296-310.

286. Grosse, Ernst. *The Beginnings of Art.* New York: D. Appleton Co., 1900.

287. Guernsey, Samuel J. *Explorations in Northeastern Arizona 1920-23.* PMP, Vol. 12, No. 1, Cambridge, 1931.

288. ———, and Alfred Vincent Kidder. *Basket-maker Caves of Northeastern Arizona.* PMP, Vol. 8, No. 2, Cambridge, 1921.

——. *See* Kidder (368).

289. Haag, William G. "Early Horizons in the Southeast." *American Antiquity*, Vol. 7, No. 3, 1942, pp. 209-22.

290. Haddon, Alfred C. *Evolution in Art.* London: Walter Scott Ltd. 1895.

291. Haeberlin, H. K. "The Idea of Fertilization in the Culture of the Pueblo Indians." *AAAM*, Vol. 3, Lancaster, Pa., 1916, pp. 1-55.

292.   ———. "The Northward Spread of Horses Among the Plains Indians." *AA*, Vol. 40, No. 3, 1938, pp. 429-37.

293.   Hall, Edward Twitchell, Jr. "Recent Clues to Athapascan Prehistory in the Southwest." *AA*, Vol. 46, No. 1, 1944, pp. 98-105.

294.   Harrington, John Peabody. "Southern Peripheral Athapaskawan Origins, Divisions, and Migrations." *SMC*, Vol. 100, 1940, pp. 503-32.

295.   Harrington, Mark Raymond. *Gypsum Cave, Nevada*. Southwest Museum, Papers, No. 8, Los Angeles, 1933.

296.   ———. *Ancient Site at Borax Lake, California*. Southwest Museum, Papers, No. 16, Los Angeles, 1948.

297.   Harrison, Gladys. "Comprehensive Exhibit of Indian Art at National Gallery Proves Enjoyable Display." *Times-Herald*, Washington, Nov. 15, 1953, p. M5.

298.   Hartley, Marsden. "The Scientific Esthetic of the Redman." *Art and Archaeology*, Vol. 13, No. 3, 1922. pp. 113-19.

299.   Haury, Emil W. "Some Southwestern Pottery Types." Series 4. *MP*, No. 19, 1936.

300.   ———. "The Mogollon Culture of Southwestern New Mexico." *MP*, No. 20, 1936.

301.   ———. "Stone Palettes and Ornaments." *MP*, No. 25, 1937, pp. 121-34.

302.   ———. "Pottery Types at Snaketown." *MP*, No. 25, 1937, pp. 169-229.

303.   ———. "Figurines and Miscellaneous Clay Objects." *MP*, No. 25, 1937, pp. 233-45.

304.   ———. "A Possible Cochise-Mogollon-Hohokam Sequence: Recent Advances in American Archaeology." *Proceedings of the American Philosophical Society*, Vol. 86, No. 2, Philadelphia, 1943.

305.   Hawley, Florence M. *Significance of the Dated Prehistory of Chetro Ketl*, Chaco Canyon, N. M. Albuquerque: University of New Mexico Press, 1934.

306.   ———. *Field Manual of Prehistoric Southwestern Pottery Types*. University of New Mexico, Anthropological Series, Bulletin 291, Vol. 1, No. 4, Albuquerque, 1936.

307.   Henderson, Alice Corbin. "A Plea for the Study of Indian Culture." *EP*, Vol. 15, No. 6, 1923, pp. 91-92.

308.   ———. "A Boy Painter Among the Pueblo Indians and Unspoiled Native Work." *NYT*, Sept. 6, 1925, sec. 4, pp. 18-19.

309.   ———. "Modern Indian Painting." *IAIA*. Pt. 2. New York, 1931.

310.   ———. "Indian Artists of the Southwest." *American Indian*, Vol. 2, No. 3, 1945, pp. 21-27.

311.   Hester, James J. "An Ethnohistoric Reconstruction of Navajo Culture, 1582-1824." *EP*, Vol. 69, No. 3, 1962, pp. 130-38.
       ———. *See* Dittert (124).

399

312. Hewett, Edgar L. "Antiquities of the Jemez Plateau, N. M." *BAEB*, No. 32, 1906.

313. ———. "Crescencio Martinez-Artist." *EP*, Vol. 5, No. 5, 1918, pp. 67-69.

314. ———. "Art of the Earliest Americans." *EP*, Vol. 13, No. 10, 1922, p. 124.

315. ———. "Native American Artists." *Art and Archaeology*, Vol. 13, No. 3, 1922, pp. 103-12.

316. ———. "Indian Ceremonies." *Art and Archaeology*, Vol. 18, No. 5-6, 1924, pp. 207-14.

317. ———. *Ancient Life in the American Southwest*. Indianapolis: Bobbs-Merrill Co., 1930.

318. ———. "The Frescoes of Kuaua." *EP*, Vol. 45, No. 6-8, 1938, pp. 21-28.

319. ———. *Pajarito Plateau and Its Ancient People*. Albuquerque: University of New Mexico Press, 1938.

320. ———. "Pre-Hispanic Frescoes in the Rio Grande Valley." *Archaeological Institute of America, Papers of the School of American Research*, No. 27. Santa Fe, 1938.

321. ———, and Wayne L. Mauzy. *Landmarks of New Mexico*. Albuquerque: University of New Mexico Press, 1940.

322. ———, and Bertha P. Dutton. *The Pueblo Indian World*. Albuquerque: University of New Mexico Press, 1945.

323. Hibben, Frank C. "Association of Man with Pleistocene Mammals in the Sandia Mountains, New Mexico." *American Antiquity*, Vol. 2, No. 4, 1937, pp. 260-63.

324. ———. "The Gallina Phase." *American Antiquity*, Vol. 4, No. 2, 1938, pp. 131-36.

325. ———. "Evidences of Early Occupation in Sandia Cave, New Mexico, and Other Sites in the Sandia-Manzano Region." *SMC*, Vol. 99, No. 23. 1941.

326. ———. "Wall Paintings at Pottery Mound." *Archaeology*, Vol. 8, No. 2, 1955, p. 131.

327. ———. "Excavations at Pottery Mound." *American Antiquity*, Vol. 21, No. 2, 1955, pp. 179-80.

328. ———. "Prehistoric Paintings at Pottery Mound." *Archaeology*, Vol. 13, No. 4, 1960, pp. 267-74, and cover.

329. Hill, W. W. "Some Navajo Culture Changes During Two Centuries." *SMC*, Vol. 100. 1940, pp. 395-415.

330. Hirn, Yrjö. *The Origins of Art*. New York: Macmillan Co., 1900.

331. Hodge, Frederick Webb. "The Early Navajo and Apache." *AA*, o.s., Vol. 8, No. 3, 1895, pp. 223-40.

332. ———. "Notes." *Land of Sunshine*, Vol. 13, No. 6, 1900, pp. 441-44.

333. ———. (ed.). "Handbook of American Indians North of Mexico." *BAEB*, No. 30, pts. 1 and 2, 1910-11.

334. Hogue, Alexander. "Pueblo Tribes Aesthetic Giants, Indian Art Reveals." [Reprint from Dallas *Times-Herald*.] *EP*, Vol. 24, No. 12, 1928, pp. 214-18.

Holder, Preston. *See* Waring.

335. Holmes, William H. "Art in Shell of the Ancient Americans." *BAEB*, No. 2, 1883, pp. 117-305.

336. ————. "Illustrated Catalogue of a Portion of the Collections Made by the Bureau of Ethnology During the Field Season of 1881." *BAEB*, No. 3, 1884, pp. 427-510.

337. ————. "Pottery of the Ancient Pueblos." *BAER*, No. 4, 1886, pp. 257-360.

338. ————. "Origin of Form and Ornament in Ceramic Art." *BAER*, No. 4, 1886, pp. 437-65.

339. Hough, Walter. "A Collection of Hopi Ceremonial Pigments." *NMAR*, 1900, pt. 2. 1902, pp. 463-71.

340. ————. "Archaeological Field Work in Northeastern Arizona: The Museum-Gates Expedition." *NMAR*, 1901. 1903, pp. 279-358.

341. Howells, W. W. "The Origins of American Indian Race Types." *The Maya and Their Neighbors*. New York: D. Appleton-Century Co., 1940, pp. 3-9.

342. Hrdlicka, Ales. "Melanesians and Australians and the Peopling of America." *SMC*, Vol. 94, No. 11, 1935.

343. Hurst, C. T. "Some Interesting Mimbres Bowls." *EP*, Vol. 40, Nos. 7-9, 1936, pp. 37-41.

344. Indian Arts Fund. "Indian Art, Preservation and Development." *Bulletin*, No. 2, Santa Fe, 1926.

345. *Indians at Work*. "Paintings Done by Students at Santa Fe Indian School Receive Wide Recognition." Vol. 5, No. 1, 1937.

346. Jacobson, Oscar Brousse. *Kiowa Indian Art*. Nice: C. Szwedzicki, 1929. [Color plates.]

347. James, Edwin (compil.). "Account of an Expedition from Pittsburgh to the Rocky Mountains, 1819-20." Pts. 1 and 2 in Vols. 14 and 15. [S. H. Long's Account.] *Early Western Travels*. Ed. by R. G. Thwaites. Cleveland: A. H. Clark Co., 1905.

348. Jenks, Albert Ernest. "The Significance of Mended Bowls in Mimbres Culture." *EP*, Vol. 31, Nos. 10-11, 1930, pp. 153-72.

349. ————. "Architectural Plans of Geometric Art on Mimbres Bowls." *EP*, Vol. 33, No. 3-6, 1932, pp. 21-64.

350. ————. "Geometric Designs on Mimbres Bowls." *Art and Archaeology*, Vol. 33, No. 3, 1932, pp. 137-39.

351. Jenness, Diamond (ed.). *The American Aborigines, Their Origin and Antiquity*. Toronto: University of Toronto Press, 1933.

Jennings, J. D. *See* Setzler (516).

352. Jensen, Mrs. Dana O. "Wo-Haw: Kiowa Warrior." *Bulletin of the Missouri Historical Society,* Vol. 7, No. 1, 1950, St. Louis, pp. 76-88.

353. Jewell, Edward Alden. "Exhibit of Inter-Tribal Arts." *NYT,* Dec. 1, 1931, p. 25.

354. ———. "A Tradition Lives On." *NYT,* Dec. 6, 1931, sec. 9, p. 18.

355. ———. "The Redman's Culture." *NYT,* Jan. 26, 1941, p. X9.

356. Jewett, Eleanor. "Three Art Institute Exhibits of Interest." *Chicago Daily Tribune,* June 5, pt. 1, 1954, p. 20H.

357. Johnson, Frederick (ed.). "Man in Northeastern North America." *Papers of the R. S. Peabody Foundation for Archaeology,* Vol. 3, Phillips Academy, Andover, 1946.

358. ———. et al. "Radiocarbon Dating." *Science,* Vol. 125, No. 3241, 1957, pp. 240-42.

359. Jones, Hester. "Museum of New Mexico's Second National Traveling Exhibition of Indian Painting." *EP,* Vol. 63, No. 1, 1956, pp. 3-5.

360. Judd, Neil M. "Archaeological Observations North of the Rio Colorado." *BAEB,* No. 82, 1926.

361. Kabotie, Fred. *Designs from the Ancient Mimbreños with a Hopi Interpretation.* San Francisco: The Grabhorn Press, 1949.

362. Kane, Henry. "Devil Dance." *EP,* Vol. 42, Nos. 16-18, 1937, pp. 93-94.

363. Kelemen, Pál. *Medieval American Art.* 1-Vol. ed., New York: Macmillan Co. 1956.

364. Kennard, Edward A. *Hopi Kachinas.* New York: J. J. Augustin, 1938.

365. Keur, Dorothy Louise. *Big Bead Mesa, an Archaeological Study of Navaho Acculturation, 1745-1812.* Memoirs of the Society for American Archaeology No. 1, Menasha, Wisc. 1941.

366. Kidder, Alfred Vincent. *Pottery of the Pajarito Plateau and of Some Adjacent Regions in New Mexico. AAAM,* Vol. 2, pt. 6, Lancaster, Pa., 1915.

367. ———. *An Introduction to the Study of Southwestern Archaeology.* Papers of the Southwestern Expedition, No. 1, Phillips Academy. New Haven: Yale University Press, 1924.

368. ———, and S. J. Guernsey. "Archaeological Explorations in Northeastern Arizona." *BAEB,* No. 65, 1919.

    ———. *See* Guernsey (288).

369. Kirchoff, P. "Peintures Rituelles des Indiens au Musée d'Ethnographie." *Beaux Arts,* Paris, April 13, 1934, pp. 1ff.

370. Kissell, Mary Lois. "Indian Weaving." *IAIA.* Pt. 2. New York, 1931.

371. Klah, Hasteen, and Mary C. Wheelwright (recorder). *Navajo Creation Myth: The Story of Emergence.* Navajo Religion Series, Vol. 1, Santa Fe: Museum of Navajo Ceremonial Art, 1942.

372. Kluckhohn, Clyde E. *Mirror for Man.* New York: McGraw-Hill Co., 1949.

373. ———, and Dorothea Leighton. *The Navaho.* Cambridge: Harvard University Press, 1946.

———. *See* Wyman (602).

374. Krieger, Alex D. "An Inquiry into Supposed Mexican Influence on a Prehistoric Cult in the Southern United States." *AA,* Vol. 47, No. 4, 1945, pp. 483-515.

375. ———. *Culture Complexes and Chronology in Northern Texas with Extension of Puebloan Datings to the Mississippi Valley.* Austin: University of Texas Press, 1947.

376. ———. "New World Culture History: Anglo-America." *Anthropology Today.* A. L. Kroeber et al. University of Chicago Press, 1953, pp. 238-64.

———. *See* Wendorf.

377. Krieger, Herbert W. "Aspects of Aboriginal Decorative Art in America." *SAR, 1930.* 1931, pp. 519-56.

378. Kroeber, A. L. *Native Culture of the Southwest.* University of California, Publications in American Anthropology and Ethnology, Vol. 23, No. 9, Berkeley, 1928.

379. ———. *Cultural and Natural Areas of Native North America.* Berkeley: University of California Press, 1939.

380. ———, and George A. Dorsey. *Traditions of the Arapaho.* Field Columbian Museum, Anthropological Series, Vol. 5, No. 81. Chicago, 1903.

381. Kubler, George. *The Shape of Time.* New Haven: Yale University Press, 1962.

382. Kurz, Rudolph Friederich. "Journal of Rudolph Friederich Kurz, 1846-52." Trans. by Myrtis Jarrell. *BAEB,* No. 115, 1937.

383. La Farge, Oliver. *As Long as the Grass Shall Grow.* New York: Longman's Green and Co., 1940.

———. *See* Sloan (527).

La Flesche, Francis. *See* Fletcher.

Leighton, Dorothea. *See* Kluckhohn (373).

384. Leighton, Morris M. "Geological Aspects of the Findings of Primitive Man Near Abilene, Texas." *MP,* No. 24, 1936.

385. Lesley, Parker. "Primitive Art and the Contemporary View." *Primitive Art,* University of Minnesota, 1940, pp. 7-12.

386. Le Viness, W. Thetford. "The Pottery Mound Murals." *New Mexico,* Vol. 37, No. 3, 1959, pp. 22-23ff.

387. Lewis, Meriwether, and William Clark. *Original Journals of the Lewis and Clark Expedition* 1804-1806. 8 vols. Ed. by R. G. Thwaites. New York: Dodd, Mead and Co., 1904.

388. Libreria Anticuaria. *Codex Dresdensis Maya.* Mexico: G. M. Echaniz, 1947.

389. Linné, S. "Archaeological Researches at Teotihuacan, Mexico." *The Ethnological Museum of Sweden Publication,* No. 1, Stockholm, 1934.

403

390. ———. "Mexican Highland Cultures." *The Ethnological Museum of Sweden, Publication* No. 7, Stockholm, 1942.

391. Linton, Ralph. "'Primitive' Art." *American Magazine of Art,* Vol. 26, No. 1, 1933, pp. 17-24.

392. ———. *The Study of Man.* New York: D. Appleton-Century Co., 1936.

393. ———. "Primitive Art." *Kenyon Review,* Vol. 3, Jan. 1941, pp. 34-51.

394. ———. *The Tree of Culture.* New York: Alfred A. Knopf, 1957.

395. *Literary Digest.* "Natural Artists among Indians." Vol. 115, No. 14, 1963, p. 11.

396. ———. "Artists with Never a Thought for Fame." Vol. 116, No. 11, 1933, p. 15.

397. ———. "They Stand out from the Crowd." Vol. 116, No. 12, 1933, p. 9.

398. Lowe, Jeannette W. "Earth Tones in Tempera by Talented Indians." *Art News,* Vol. 38, No. 6, 1939, p. 11.

399. ———. "Lo, the Rich Indian: Art of the American Aboriginals." *Art News,* Vol. 39, No. 18, 1941, pp. 6-8.

400. Lowie, Robert H. "Crow Indian Art." *AMAP,* Vol. 21, pt. 4, 1917.

401. ———. "Studies in Plains Indian Folklore." *University of California, Publications in American Archaeology and Ethnology,* Vol. 40, No. 1, 1942, pp. 1-28.

402. Luxan, Diego Perez de. *Journal of the Expedition into New Mexico Made by Antonio de Espejo, 1582-3.* Trans. by George Peter Hammond and Agapito Rey. Quivira Society: Los Angeles, 1929.

403. Mallery, Garrick. "Sign Language Among North American Indians Compared with That of Other People and Deaf Mutes." *BAER,* No. 1, 1881, pp. 263-552.

404. ———. "Pictographs of the North American Indians: A Preliminary Paper." *BAER,* No. 4, 1886, pp. 3-256.

405. ———. "Picture Writing of the American Indians." *BAER,* No. 10, 1893, pp. 3-807.

406. Martin, Paul S. *Lowry Ruin in Southwestern Colorado.* Field Museum of Natural History, Anthropological Series, Vol. 23, No. 1, Chicago, 1936.

407. ———, and John Rinaldo. *Modified Basket Maker Sites, Ackmen-Lowry Area, Southwestern Colorado.* Field Museum of Natural History, Anthropological Series, Vol. 23, No. 3, Chicago, 1939.

408. Mason, Otis Tufton. "Aboriginal American Basketry." *NMAR,* 1902, pt. 2. 1904, pp. 171-548.

409. *Masterkey.* "Hopi Native Drawings." Vol. 27, No. 1, 1953, pp. 26-27.

410. Matthews, Washington. "Navajo Weavers." *BAER,* No. 3, 1884, pp. 371-91.

411. ———. "The Mountain Chant: A Navajo Ceremony." *BAER,* No. 5, 1887, pp. 379-467.

412. ———. "Songs of Sequence of the Navajos." *JAF,* Vol. 7, No. 26, 1894, pp. 185-94.

413. ———. "Navajo Legends." *Memoirs of the American Folk-Lore Society*, Vol. 5, Boston, 1897.

414. ———. "The Navajo Night Chant." *JAF*, Vol. 14, No. 52, 1901, pp. 12-19.

Mauzy, Wayne L. *See* Hewett (321).

415. Maximilian, Prince of Wied. "Travels in the Interior of North America, 1832-1834." Pts. 1, 2, and 3 in Vols. 22, 23, and 24 of *Early Western Travels, 1748-1846*. Ed. by R. G. Thwaites. Cleveland: A. H. Clark Co., 1906.

416. McGee, W. J. "The Siouan Indians: A Preliminary Sketch." *BAER*, No. 15, 1897, pp. 153-204.

417. Mecham, J. Lloyd. "The Second Spanish Expedition in New Mexico: 1581-1582." *New Mexico Historical Review*, Vol. 1, No. 3, 1926, pp. 265-91.

418. Mera, Harry P. "Ceramic Clues to the Prehistory of North Central New Mexico." *Technical Series of the Laboratory of Anthropology*, No. 8, Santa Fe, 1935.

419. ———. "The Rain Bird: A Study in Pueblo Design." *Memoirs of the Laboratory of Anthropology*, No. 2, Santa Fe, 1938.

420. ———. "Reconnaissance and Excavation in Southeastern New Mexico." *AAAM*, No. 51, Menasha, Wisc., 1938.

421. ———. "Style Trends of Pueblo Pottery." *Memoirs of the Laboratory of Anthropology*, No. 3, Santa Fe, 1939.

422. Meriam, Lewis, "Indian Education Moves Ahead." *Survey Graphic*, Vol. 66, No. 5, 1931, pp. 253-57ff.

423. ———, and associates. *The Problem of Indian Administration*. Institute for Government Research Studies in Administration. Baltimore: Johns Hopkins Press, 1928.

424. Mexico. *Antiquedades Mexicanas*. "Codices Baranda, Colombino, Dehesa, Porfirio Diaz." Mexico: Oficina Tipografica de la Secretaria de Fomento, 1892.

425. Millington, C. Norris. "American Indian Water Colors." *American Magazine of Art*, Vol. 25, No. 2, 1932, pp. 83-92.

426. Milwaukee Public Museum. *Sioux Indian Drawings*. Robert E. Ritzenthaler, text; W. Ben Hunt, color; L. G. Tishler, cover and layout. Milwaukee, 1961. 8 pp., 36 color plates, folio.

427. Mindeleff, Cosmos. "The Cliff-ruins of Canyon de Chelly." *BAER*, No. 16, 1897, pp. 73-198.

428. Mindeleff, Victor. "A Study of Pueblo Architecture: Tusayan and Cibola." *BAER*, No. 8, 1891, pp. 3-228.

429. Mooney, James. "The Siouan Tribes of the East." *BAEB*, No. 22, 1894.

430. ———. "The Ghost-dance Religion and the Sioux Outbreak of 1890." *BAER*, No. 14, pt. 2, 1896, pp. 641-1110.

431. ———. "Calendar History of the Kiowa Indians." *BAER*, No. 17, pt. 1, 1900, pp. 129-445.

432. ———. "The Cheyenne Indians." *AAAM*, Vol. 1, pt. 6, 1905-7, pp. 357-442.

433. Moorehead, Warren K. "The Cahokia Mounds." *University of Illinois, Bulletin Series.* Pt. 1, Urbana 1929.

434. Morang, Alfred. "Annual Indian Art Exhibit. *EP,* Vol. 47, No. 5, 1940, pp. 117-18.

435. Morley, S. G. *The Ancient Maya.* Palo Alto: Stanford University Press, 1946.

436. Morris, Earl H. "Beginnings of Pottery Making in the San Juan Area, Unfired Prototypes and the Wares of the Earliest Ceramic Period." *AMAP,* Vol. 28, pt. 2, 1927.

437. ———. "Notes on Excavations in the Aztec Ruin." *AMAP,* Vol. 26, pt. 5, 1928.

438. Museo Nacional de Arqueologia, Historia y Etnografia de Mexico, Talleres Graficos. *Codice Mendocino.* 1925.

439. Museum of Fine Arts of Houston. "Indian Art of the Southwestern United States." *Bulletin,* Vol. 7, No. 1, 1944, pp. 8-9.

440. Museum of Modern Art. *American Sources of Modern Art.* Introd. by Holger Cahill. New York, 1933.

441. ———. *Paul Klee.* 3rd ed. Statements by the artist and others. Ed. by Margaret Miller. New York, 1945.

442. Museum of New Mexico. "Refugee Pueblo Cache Acquired." *Bulletin,* March 1, Santa Fe, 1963.

443. Nehakije (Steven Vicenti). "Jicarilla Apache Winter." *World Youth,* Jan. 11, Boston, 1936, p. 11.

444. ———. "Apache Water-color Exhibition on at Art Museum by Steven Vicenti." *Santa Fe New Mexican,* Apr. 10, 1936, Sec. 1, p. 3.

445. Nelson, N. C. "Archaeology of the Tano District, New Mexico." *EP,* Vol. 7, Nos. 9-12, 1919, pp. 177-183.

446. ———. "The Antiquity of Man in America in the Light of Anthropology." *SAR, 1935.* 1936, pp. 471-506.

447. Newcomb, Franc J. and Gladys A. Reichard. *Sandpaintings of the Navajo Shooting Chant.* New York: J. J. Augustin, 1937.

448. ———, Stanley Fishler, and Mary C. Wheelwright. *A Study of Navajo Symbolism.* PMP, Vol. 32, No. 3, Cambridge, 1956.

449. New Mexico Association on Indian Affairs. *Indian Art Series* Nos. 1 [Pueblo Indian Paintings] to 13, Santa Fe, 1936.

450. *New Mexico Quarterly.* "Designs from Ancient Mimbres Pottery." Vol. 29, No. 2, 1959, pp. 214-22ff. [More than 40 illustrations from Cosgrove Collection.]

451. *New York Times.* "Native American Art." Dec. 1, 1931, p. C. [Editorial.]

452. ———. "Rivera on the Horizon." Dec. 20, 1931, sec. 8, p. 10 X.

453. Nordenskiöld, Erland, Friherre. *Comparative Ethnographic Studies,* Vol. 9, Göteborg: Elanders Boktryckeri Aktiebolag, 1931.

454. Nordenskiöld, Gustav Erik. *Cliff Dwellers of the Mesa Verde.* New York: Steckert, 1901.

455. Nuttall, Zelia. *Codex Nuttall.* Facsimile of an Ancient Mexican Codex. Cambridge: Peabody Museum of Archaeology and Ethnology, Harvard University, 1902.

456. Oak, Liston M. "A Renaissance of American Indian Art." *International Studio,* Vol. 102, Dec. 1931, pp. 388-401.

457. Oakes, Maud [recorder], and Joseph Campbell. *Where the Two Came to Their Father: A Navajo War Ceremonial Given by Jeff King.* Bollingen Series 1, New York: Pantheon Books, 1943. Color plates.

458. Opler, M. E. "A Summary of Jicarilla Apache Culture." *AA,* Vol. 38, No. 2, 1936, pp. 202-23.

459. ———. "Myths and Tales of the Jicarilla Apache Indians." *Memoirs of the American Folk-Lore Society,* Vol. 31, New York, 1938.

Owens, J. G. *See* Fewkes (263), (264).

460. Pach, Walter. "Art of the American Indian." *Dial,* Vol. 68, No. 1, 1920, pp. 57-65.

461. ———. Notes on the Indian Water-Colours." Dial, Vol. 68, No. 3, 1920, pp. 343-45.

462. ———. "Indian Tribal Arts." *NYT,* Nov. 22, 1931, sec. 8, p. 13.

463. ———. *The Art Museum in America.* New York: Pantheon Books, Inc., 1948.

464. Parsons, Elsie Clews. "Ritual Parallels in Pueblo and Plains Cultures." *AA,* Vol. 31, No. 4, 1929, pp. 642-54.

465. ———. "Isleta, New Mexico." *BAER,* No. 47, 1932, pp. 193-466.

466. ———. "Early Relations between Hopi and Keres." *AA,* Vol. 38, No. 4, 1936, pp. 554-60.

467. ———. *Pueblo Indian Religion.* 2 vols. Chicago: University of Chicago Press, 1939.

468. ———. "A Pre-Spanish Record of Hopi Ceremonials." *AA,* Vol. 42, No. 3, 1940, pp. 541-42.

Phillips, Bert. *See* Blumenschein.

469. Phillips, Phillip. "Middle American Influences on the Archaeology of the Southeastern United States." *The Maya and Their Neighbors.* New York: D. Appleton-Century Co., 1940, pp. 349-67.

470. Pijoan, Jose. *Arte de los Pueblos Aborigenes.* Madrid: Espasa-Calpe, s.a., 1931.

471. Pop-Chalee. "My People's Art." *School Arts.* Vol. 36, No. 3, 1936, pp. 146-47.

472. Porter, James A. "What is American Art?" Letter to *NYT,* Dec. 27, 1931, sec. 8, p. 12X.

473. Portner, Leslie Judd. "Diversity in Three New Shows." *Washington Post,* Nov. 15, 1953, p. 6L.

Ray, Louis L. *See* Bryan (63).

407

474. Reagan, Albert B. "Some Archaeological Notes on Nine Mile Canyon, Utah." *EP*, Vol. 31, No. 4, 1932, pp. 45-71.

475. ———. "Notes on Ashley and Dry Fork Canyons in Northeastern Utah." *EP*, Vol. 31, No. 8, 1932, pp. 122-31.

476. ———. "Some Archaeological Notes on Hill Canyon in Northeastern Utah." *EP*, Vol. 31, No. 15, 1932, pp. 236-42.

477. ———. "Indian Pictures in Ashley and Dry Fork Valleys in Northern Utah." *Art and Archaeology*, Vol. 34, No. 4, 1933, pp. 201-205ff.

478. Reed, Erik K. "Information on the Navaho in 1706." *AA*, Vol. 43, No. 3, pt. 1, 1941, pp. 485-87.

479. Reichard, Gladys A. *Navaho Religion.* 2 vols. Bollingen Series, 18. New York: Pantheon Books, Inc., 1950.
    ———. *See* Newcomb (447).

480. Renaud, E. B. *Pictographs and Petroglyphs of the High Western Plains.* Archaeological Survey Series, Report No. 8, University of Denver, 1936.

481. ———. *Petroglyphs of North Central New Mexico.* Archaelogical Survey Series, Report No. 11, University of Denver, 1938.

482. *Review of Reviews.* "Glimpses of Indian Life at the Omaha Exposition." Vol. 18, No. 4, 1898, pp. 436-43.
    Rinaldo, John. *See* Martin (407).

483. Roberts, Frank H. H., Jr. "Early Pueblo Ruins in the Piedra District of Southwestern Colorado." *BAEB*, No. 96, 1930.

484. ———. "Ruins at Kiatuthlanna, Eastern Arizona." *BAEB*, No. 100, 1931.

485. ———. "The Villages of the Great Kivas on the Zuni Reservation, New Mexico." *BAEB*, No. 111, 1932.

486. ———. "A Folsom Complex: Preliminary Report on Investigations at the Lindenmeier Site in Northern Colorado." *SMC*, Vol. 94, No. 4, 1935.

487. ———. "A Survey of Southwestern Archaeology." *SAR, 1935,* 1936, pp. 507-33.

488. ———. "Additional Information on the Folsom Complex." *SMC*, Vol. 95, No. 10, 1937.

489. ———. "Archaeology of the Southwest." *American Antiquity*, Vol 3, No. 1, 1937, pp. 3-33.

490. ———. "Developments in the Problem of the North American Paleo-Indian." *SMC*, Vol. 100, 1940, pp. 51-116.

491. ———. "The Pre-Pottery Horizon of the Anasazi and Mexico." *The Maya and Their Neighbors.* New York. D. Appleton-Century Co., 1940, pp. 331-40.

492. ———. "Archaeological Remains in the Whitewater District, Eastern Arizona." Pt. 2, Artifacts and Burials. *BAEB*, No. 126, 1940.

493. ———. "The New World Paleo-Indian." *SAR, 1944,* 1945, pp. 403-34.

494. Robinson, Francis W. "A Gift of Water Colors by Pueblo Indians." *Bulletin of the Cincinnati Art Museum*, Vol. 9, No. 1, 1938, pp, 2-13.

495. Romer, Alfred S. "Pleistocene Vertebrates and Their Bearing on the Problem of Human Antiquity in North America." *The American Aborigines, Their Origin and Antiquity*. Chapt. 2, Toronto: University of Toronto Press, 1933.

496. Rush, Olive. "Indian Murals at Santa Fe, New Mexico." *Contemporary Arts*, Nov.-Dec., 1932, p. 8.

497. ———. "Indian Students Show Work." *Santa Fe New Mexican*, May 4, 1933, p. 4.

498. ———. "The Young Indians Work in Old Forms." *Theatre Arts*, Vol. 17, No. 8, 1933, pp. 635-38.

499. ———. "Exhibit of Indian Paintings," *EP*, Vol. 36, Nos. 25-26, 1934, pp. 198-201.

500. ———. "Remarkable Paintings by Indians at Art Museum." *Santa Fe New Mexican*, May 7, 1934, p. 4.

501. ———. "New Mexico Art—Past, Present and Future." Santa Fe, 1934. Typescript.

502. ———. "Annual Indian Art Show." *EP*, Vol. 42, Nos. 19-21, 1937, pp. 105-09.

503. Saenz, Moises. Indian Education. Address to U. S. Indian Service Educators of United Pueblos, Albuquerque, Dec. 1, 1933, 5 pp., mimeographed.

504. Sahagún, Bernardino de. *Florentine Codex: General History of Things of New Spain*. 12 vols. Trans. by Arthur J. O. Anderson and Charles E. Dibble. Santa Fe: School of American Research and the University of Utah, 1950-1961.

505. *Santa Fe New Mexican*. "Big Indian Art Show Opens." Nov. 8, 1953. Sec. A, p. 5.

506. Sapir, Edward. "Internal Linguistic Evidence Suggestive of the Northern Origin of the Navajo." *AA*, Vol. 38, No. 2, 1936, pp. 224-35.

507. Sayce, R. U. *Primitive Arts and Crafts*. London: Cambridge University Press, 1933.

508. Sayles, E. B. "Some Southwestern Pottery Types." *MP*, No. 21, Series 5, 1936.

509. ———, and Ernst Antevs. "The Cochise Culture," *MP*, No. 29, 1941.

510. Schaafsma, Polly. "Rock Art of the Navajo Reservoir." *EP*, Vol. 69, No. 4, 1962, pp. 193-211.

511. Schoolcraft, Henry Rowe. *Oneota or Characteristics of the Red Race of America*. New York: Wiley and Putnam, 1847.

512. ———. *Information Respecting the History, Conditions, and Prospects of the Indian Tribes of the United States*. 6 vols. Philadelphia: Lippincott, Grambo, and Co., 1851-1857.

513. *Science.* "Oldest Traces of Man in the Americas." Vol. 124, No. 3218, 1956, pp. 396-97.

514. Seltzer, Carl C. *Racial Prehistory in the Southwest and the Hawikuh Zunis.* PMP, Vol. 23, No. 1, Cambridge, 1944.

515. Setzler, Frank M. "A Prehistoric Cave Culture in Southwestern Texas." *AA,* Vol. 37, No. 3, 1935, pp. 429-45.

516. ———, and J. D. Jennings. "Peachtree Mound and Village Site, Cherokee County, North Carolina." *BAEB,* No. 131, 1941.

517. Shetrone, Henry Clyde. *The Mound Builders.* New York: D. Appleton and Co., 1931.

518. Shufeldt, R. W. "A Navajo Artist and His Notions of Mechanical Drawing." *SAR, 1886,* pt. 1. 1889, pp. 240-44.

519. Sims, Agnes. "An Artist Analyzes New Mexico's Petroglyphs." *EP,* Vol. 55, No. 10, 1948, pp. 302-09.

520. ———. "Migration Story in Stone." *EP,* Vol. 56, No. 3, 1949, pp. 67-76.

521. ———. *San Cristobal Petroglyphs.* Santa Fe: Southwest Editions, 1950. Prints, folio.

Sitting Bull (artist). *See* Stirling, Matthew W. (550).

522. Sloan, John. "Paintings by Indians in New York." *EP,* Vol. 8, Nos. 3-4, 1920, p. 79.

523. ———. "Indian Exposition." *Art Digest,* Vol. 5, No. 9, 1931, p. 32.

524. ———. "The Indian as Artist." *Survey Graphic,* Vol. 67, No. 5, 1931, p. 243ff.

525. ———. "The American Indian as Artist." *Hobbies,* Vol. 12, No. 8, 1932, pp. 165-70.

526. ———. "Indian Art." *Inter-Tribal Indian Ceremonial, Program,* Gallup, N. M., 1941.

527. ———, and Oliver La Farge. *IAIA.* Pt. 1. New York, 1931.

528. Smith, Watson. *Kiva Mural Decorations at Awatovi and Kawaika-a.* PMP, Vol. 37. (Reports of Awatovi Expedition No. 5), 1952. Serigraphs by Louie Ewing.

529. Smithsonian Institution. "Explorations and Field Work in 1915." *SMC,* Vol. 66, No. 3, 1916, pp. 84-89. Mimbres designs.

530. ———. "Exploration and Field Work in 1921." *SMC,* Vol. 72, No. 15, 1922, pp. 64-74. Mimbres designs drawn by Mrs. George Mullett.

531. Spier, Leslie. "An Analysis of Plains Indian Parfleche Decoration." *University of Washington, Publications in Anthropology,* Vol. 1, No. 3, Seattle, 1925.

532. ———. "Plains Indian Parfleche Designs." *University of Washington, Publications in Anthropology,* Vol 4, No. 3, Seattle, 1931.

533. ———. "The Prophet Dance of the Northwest and Its Derivatives: The Source of the Ghost Dance." *American Anthropological Association, General Series in Anthropology* No. 1, Menasha, Wisc., 1935.

534. Spinden, Herbert Joseph. "Indian Artists of the Southwest." *International Studio*, Vol. 95, No. 393, 1930, pp. 49-51ff.

535. ———. "Fine Art and the First Americans." *IAIA*. Pt. 2. New York, 1931.

536. ———. "Indian Symbolism." *IAIA*. Pt. 2, New York, 1931.

537. ———. "Indian Art on its Merits." *Parnassus*, Vol. 3, No. 7, 1931, pp. 12-13.

538. ———. "Fine Arts of the First Americans." *Scholastic*, Vol. 29, No. 6, 1936, pp. 21-22.

539. Stephen, Alexander MacGregor. "The Navajo." *AA*, o.s., Vol. 6, No. 4, 1893, pp. 345-62.

540. ———. *Hopi Journal*. Ed. by E. C. Parsons. Columbia University, Contributions to Anthropology, Vol. 23, pts. 1 & 2. New York: Columbia University Press, 1936.

541. ———. *Hopi Indians of Arizona*. Southwest Museum Leaflets, No. 14, Los Angeles, 1940.

———. *See* Fewkes (264, 265, 266, 267).

542. Sterne, Mabel Dodge. Letter to Mrs. Wilson, Curator of Art, Museum of New Mexico. April 21, 1920, Taos, New Mexico.

543. Stevenson, James. "Illustrated Catalogue of the Collections Obtained from the Indians of New Mexico, 1879-1880." *BAER*, No. 2, 1883, pp. 307-465.

544. ———. "Ceremonial of Hasjelti Dailjis and Mythical Sandpainting of the Navajo." *BAER*, No. 8, 1891, pp. 229-85.

545. Stevenson, Matilda Coxe. "The Religious Life of the Zuni Child." *BAER*, No. 5, 1887, pp. 533-55.

546. ———. "The Sia." *BAER*, No. 11, 1894, p. 3-157.

547. ———. "The Zuni Indians." *BAER*, No. 23, 1904.

548. Steward, Julian H. "Petroglyphs of the United States." *SAR 1936*. 1937, pp. 405-25.

549. ———. "Archaeological Reconnaissance of Southern Utah." *BAEB*, No. 128, 1941, pp. 275-356.

550. Stirling, Matthew W. "Three Pictographic Autobiographies of Sitting Bull." *SMC*, Vol. 97, No. 5, 1939, 46 plates.

551. ———. "Origin Myth of Acoma and Other Records." *BAEB*, No. 135, 1942.

552. *St. Louis Post-Dispatch*. "St. Louis Art Discovery." Aug. 13, 1950, p. 5. [Ptgs. by Wo-Haw; color photos. by Jack Gould.]

553. Strong, William Duncan. "The Plains Culture Area in the Light of Archaeology." *AA*, Vol. 35, No. 2, 1933, pp. 271-87.

554. ———. "An Introduction to Nebraska Archaeology." *SMC*, Vol. 93, No. 10, 1935.

555. ———. "From History to Prehistory in the Northern Great Plains." *SMC*, Vol. 100, 1940, pp. 353-94.

556. ———. "Cross-Sections of New World Prehistory." *SMC*, Vol. 104, No. 2, 1943.

411

557. Swanton, John R. "Indian Tribes of the Lower Mississippi Valley and Adjacent Coast of the Gulf of Mexico." *BAEB*, No. 43, 1911.

558. ———. "New Light on the History of the Siouan Peoples." *Journal of the Washington Academy of Sciences*, Vol. 13, No. 3, 1923, pp. 33-43.

559. ———. "Aboriginal Culture of the Southeast." *BAER*, No. 42, 1924.

560. ———. "Some Neglected Data Bearing on Cheyenne, Chippewa, and Dakota History." *AA*, Vol. 32, No. 1, 1930, pp. 156-60.

561. ———. "Early History of the Eastern Siouan Tribes." *Essays in Anthropology*, Kroeber Anniversary Volume. Berkeley: University of California Press, 1936, pp. 371-81.

562. ———. "Siouan Tribes and the Ohio Valley." *AA*, Vol. 45, No. 1, 1943, pp. 49-66.

563. ———. "The Indians of the Southeastern United States." *BAEB*, No. 137, 1946.

564. ———, and Roland B. Dixon. "Primitive American History." *AA*, New Series, Vol. 16, No. 3 ,1916, pp. 376-412.

565. Tichy, Marjorie F. "A Painted Ceremonial Room at Otowi." *EP*, Vol. 54, No. 3, 1947, pp. 59-69.

566. Tschudy, Herbert B. Letter to Dorothy Dunn. April 13, 1936, Brooklyn Museum, N. Y.

567. United States Information Agency. *Indianische Tradition*. Eine Austellung der Universität von Oklahoma, 1959 [Catalog, Germanic exhibitions.]

568. Vaillant, George C. *Some Resemblances in the Ceramics of Central and North America*. MP, No. 12, 1932.

569. ———. *Artists and Craftsmen in Ancient Central America*. Guide Leaflet Series, No. 88, New York: American Museum of Natural History, 1935.

570. ——— (ed.). A Sacred Almanac of the Aztecs: *Tonalamatl of the Codex Borbonicus*. New York: American Museum of Natural History, 1940.

571. Vatter, Ernst. "Historienmalerei und Heraldische Bilderchrift der Nordamerikanischen Präriestämme." *Ipek Jahrbuch*, 1927. Leipzig: Klinkhardt und Biermann, 1927, pp. 46-81.

572. Villagrá, Gaspar Peréz de. *History of New Mexico*. Ed. by F. W. Hodge and trans. by Gilberto Espinosa. Los Angeles: Quivira Society, 1933.

573. Voth, H. R. *The Oraibi Powamu Ceremony*. Field Columbian Museum, Anthropological Series, Vol. 3, No. 2, Chicago, 1901.

574. ———. *The Oraibi Summer Snake Ceremony*. Field Columbian Museum, Anthropological Series, Vol. 3, No. 4, Chicago, 1903.

———. *See* Dorsey, George A. (129, 130).

575. Wallace, Henry A. "The Government Welcomes the Arts." *Proceedings of the Twenty-Fifth Annual Convention of the American Federation of Arts*. Washington, May, 1934.

576. Waring, A. J., and Preston Holder. "A Prehistoric Ceremonial Complex in the Southeastern United States." *AA*, Vol. 47, No. 1, 1945, pp. 1-34.

577. Wedel, Waldo Rudolph. "Culture Sequence in the Central Great Plains." *SMC*, Vol. 100, 1940, pp. 291-352.

578. ———. "Prehistory and the Missouri Valley Development Program. Summary Report on the Missouri Basin Archaeological Survey in 1946." *SMC*, Vol. 107, No. 6, 1947.

579. ———. *Prehistoric Man on the Great Plains*. Norman: University of Oklahoma Press, 1961.

580. ——— et al. "Archaeological Researches in the Missouri Basin by the Smithsonian River Basin Surveys and Cooperating Agencies." *American Antiquity*, Vol. 14, No. 4, 1949, pp. 257-66.

581. Wendorf, Fred, Alex D. Krieger, and Claude C. Albritton. *The Midland Discovery*. Description by T. D. Stewart. Austin: University of Texas Press, 1955.

582. Wheelwright, Mary C. (recorder). "Hail Chant and Water Chant." *Navajo Religion Series*. Vol. 2, Santa Fe: Museum of Navajo Ceremonial Art, 1946.
———. *See* Klah.
———. *See* Newcomb (448).

583. White, Leslie A. "The Acoma Indians." *BAER*, No. 47, 1932, pp. 17-192.

584. Will, George F. *Archaeology of the Missouri Valley*, AMAP, Vol. 22, pt. 6, New York, 1924.

Willey, Gordon R. *See* Ford.

585. Willoughby, Charles C. "A Few Ethnological Specimens Collected by Lewis and Clark." *AA*, Vol. 7, No. 4, 1905, pp. 633-41.

586. ———. "Indian Masks." *IAIA*, Pt. 2. New York, 1931.

587. Winship, George Parker. "The Coronado Expedition, 1540-1542." *BAER*, No. 14, pt. 1, 1896, pp. 329-613.

588. Wissler, Clark. *Some Protective Designs of the Dakota*. AMAP, Vol. 1, pt. 1, 1908.

589. ———. "Influence of the Horse in the Development of Plains Culture." *AA*, Vol. 16, No. 1, 1914, pp. 1-25.

590. ———. *Costumes of the Plains Indians*. AMAP, Vol. 17, pt. 2, New York, 1916.

591. ———. *Structural Basis to the Decoration of Costumes among the Plains Indians*. AMAP, Vol. 17, pt. 3, New York, 1916.

592. ———. *The American Indian*. 2nd ed. New York: Oxford University Press, 1922.

593. ———. *North American Indians of the Plains*. Handbook Series, No. 1, New York: American Museum of Natural History, 1934.

594. ———. *Indian Cavalcade*. New York: Sheridan House, 1938.

413

595. ———. *Indians of the United States*. New York: Doubleday, Doran and Co., 1940.

596. Woodruff, K. Brent. "Material Culture of the Teton Dakota." *South Dakota Historical Collections*, Vol. 17, Pierre, 1934, pp. 605-47.

597. Woodward, Arthur. *A Brief History of Navajo Silversmithing*. Museum of Northern Arizona, Bulletin No. 14, Flagstaff, 1938.

598. Worcester, Donald E. "Early Spanish Accounts of the Apache Indians." *AA*, Vol. 43, No. 2, pt. 1, 1941, pp. 308-12.

599. Wormington, H. M. *Prehistoric Indians of the Southwest*. Popular Series, No. 7, Denver: Colorado Museum of Natural History, 1947.

600. ———. *Ancient Man in North America*. 4th ed. Popular Series, No. 4, Denver: Colorado Museum of Natural History, 1957.

601. Wyman, Leland C. (ed.) *Beautyway: A Navaho Ceremonial*. Myth recorded and trans. by Father Berard Haile; sandpaintings rec. by L. Armer, F. Newcomb, M. Oakes. Bollingen Series, 53. New York: Pantheon Books, Inc., 1957.

602. ———, and Clyde Kluckhohn. *Navaho Classification of Their Song Ceremonials*. AAAM No. 50, Menasha, Wisc., 1938.

603. Yeo, Herbert W. Southwest Pictographs. 14 vols. + Unpub. researches deposited in Laboratory of Anthropology, Santa Fe, c. 1956, texts and photos.

604. Zárate-Salmerón, Fray Geronimo. "Relating all the things that have been seen and known in New Mexico, as well by sea as by land, from the year 1538 till that of 1626." Trans. by C. F. Lummis in *Land of Sunshine*, Vols. 11 and 12, 1899-1900.

INTRODUCTORY NOTES

An asterisk preceding a name indicates an artist (painter).

art: refers to American Indian painting, and arts, to the several American Indian arts, unless designated as *general,* or by nation.

artist: refers to Indian painter unless otherwise designated.

artist's name: the most prevalent signature, i.e., the one preferred by the artist at the time of painting, is listed first or only. Secondary listings denote less used signatures or locally known common name.

awards and prizes: due to large number and kind, can be only representatively indicated, as under individual artist reference.

collections and collectors: are listed for reasons most pertinent to the text.

culture: includes basic arts for all groups particularized. For modern tribes, ceremonial, dance, religion, and separate cultural items, particularly those pertaining to art, will be found under those headings.

depiction: key depictions of main aspects of various cultures are listed. No attempt, of course, has been made to include all depictions mentioned in the text.

SFIS: Santa Fe Indian School (United States Indian School, Santa Fe, New Mexico).

Some subjects of a very inclusive nature have only representative references indicating areas in which others may be found.

416

Index

417

418

421

423

425

427

428